THE OXFORD HISTORY OF PI

# The Golden Age of Indian I

Jan Westerhoff unfolds the story of one of the richest episodes in the history of Indian thought, the development of Buddhist philosophy in the first millennium CE. He starts from the composition of the Abhidharma works before the beginning of the Common Era and continues up to the time of Dharmakīrti in the sixth century. This period was characterized by the development of a variety of philosophical schools and approaches that have shaped Buddhist thought up to the present day: the scholasticism of the Abhidharma, the Madhyamaka theory of emptiness, Yogācāra idealism, and the logical and epistemological works of Diṅnāga and Dharmakīrti. The book sets out to describe the historical development of these schools in their intellectual and cultural context, with particular emphasis on three factors that shaped the development of Buddhist philosophical thought: the need to spell out the contents of canonical texts, the discourses of the historical Buddha and the Mahāyāna sūtras; the desire to defend their positions by sophisticated arguments against criticisms from fellow Buddhists and from non-Buddhist thinkers of classical Indian philosophy; and the need to account for insights gained through the application of specific meditative techniques. While the main focus is the period up to the sixth century CE, Westerhoff also discusses some important thinkers who influenced Buddhist thought between this time and the decline of Buddhist scholastic philosophy in India at the beginning of the thirteenth century.

**Jan Westerhoff** was educated at Cambridge and the School of Oriental and African Studies. He has taught Philosophy at the Universities of Oxford and Durham and is presently Professor of Buddhist Philosophy at the University of Oxford, and a Fellow and Tutor in Theology and Religion at Lady Margaret Hall, University of Oxford. His books include *Ontological Categories* (2005), *Nāgārjuna's Madhyamaka* (2009), *Twelve Examples of Illusion* (2010), *The Dispeller of Disputes: Nāgārjuna's Vigrahavyāvartanī* (2010), *A Very Short Introduction to Reality* (2011), and *The Non-Existence of the Real World* (2020) all published by Oxford University Press.

THE OXFORD HISTORY OF PHILOSOPHY

*French Philosophy, 1572–1675*
Desmond M. Clarke

*The Lost Age of Reason: Philosophy in Early Modern India 1450–1700*
Jonardon Ganeri

*American Philosophy before Pragmatism*
Russell B. Goodman

*Thinking the Impossible: French Philosophy since 1960*
Gary Gutting

*British Ethical Theorists from Sidgwick to Ewing*
Thomas Hurka

*British Philosophy in the Seventeenth Century*
Sarah Hutton

*The American Pragmatists*
Cheryl Misak

# The Golden Age of Indian Buddhist Philosophy

Jan Westerhoff

OXFORD
UNIVERSITY PRESS

OXFORD
UNIVERSITY PRESS

Great Clarendon Street, Oxford, OX2 6DP,
United Kingdom

Oxford University Press is a department of the University of Oxford. It furthers the University's objective of excellence in research, scholarship, and education by publishing worldwide. Oxford is a registered trade mark of Oxford University Press in the UK and in certain other countries



First published 2018
First published in paperback 2023



British Library Cataloguing in Publication Data
Data available

Library of Congress Cataloging in Publication Data
Data available

ISBN 978–0–19–873266–2 (Hbk.)
ISBN 978–0–19–887839–1 (Pbk.)

लोकोत्तरे लौकिके च प्रज्ञापारमितेऽमिते ।
दश पारमिताकारे प्रज्ञे देवि नमोऽस्तु ते ॥

In the world and world-transcendent,
Beyond the Wisdom Gone Beyond,
In ten-perfected form resplendent,
Wisdom-goddess, praise to you!

(From a hymn to the Perfection of Wisdom, Pandey 1994: 125)

# Acknowledgements

I would like to express my gratitude to my teachers, colleagues, and friends, from whom I have learned much about the history of Indian Buddhist thought, in particular to David Seyfort Ruegg, Jay Garfield, Mattia Salvini, Dan Arnold, Jonathan Gold, Jonardon Ganeri, Tom Tillemans, Greg Seton, and Parimal Patil. Special thanks are due to the Buddhist Studies Research Seminar at King's College London, where some of the material was presented, and to Mark Siderits, who provided me with detailed comments on the fourth chapter.

Their comments have helped me greatly in improving this book; while I cannot claim that the remaining mistakes are completely original, they are, however, wholly my own work.

Finally, I would like to thank my wife Yuka Kobayashi and our daughter Sophie for their support and patience while I was writing this book.

# Contents

# Analytical Table of Contents

# Diagrams of Schools and Thinkers

The following two diagrams are intended to provide the reader with a synoptic survey of the main schools and thinkers discussed in this book. For the sake of simplicity I have omitted schools and thinkers that only play a subsidiary role in the following pages. Both diagrams take the form of a 'subway map', each line represents a school, and each stop or circle its approximate date of origin. Connections between lines represent linkages between individual schools. Even where there is no explicit 'interchange', spatial proximity indicates conceptual affinity; it is no accident that tantra and tathāgatagarbha run on either side of the Yogācāra line.

The first diagram simply identifies the different lines in terms of the different schools they represent. In the second diagram all the names of schools are omitted for the sake of simplicity; instead, the names of thinkers and of some key texts associated with these schools are superimposed on the respective lines. A section at the right-hand side lists names of the main non-Buddhist thinkers that make an appearance in the following pages.

These diagrams are supposed to supplement the discussion in the following pages, not to replace it. Given the considerable uncertainty about the dates of individual thinkers, about what constitutes a 'school', how these schools are interconnected, and which thinkers are supposed to be associated with which schools the pieces of information provided by the diagrams should be taken as pointers, not as facts. Unfortunately, the history of Indian Buddhist thought is considerably more complicated than what can be summarized in two diagrams. Nevertheless, I hope that the simplified picture they represent will help the reader to navigate the complexities of the development of Buddhist philosophy in India.

The Main Schools of Indian Buddhism

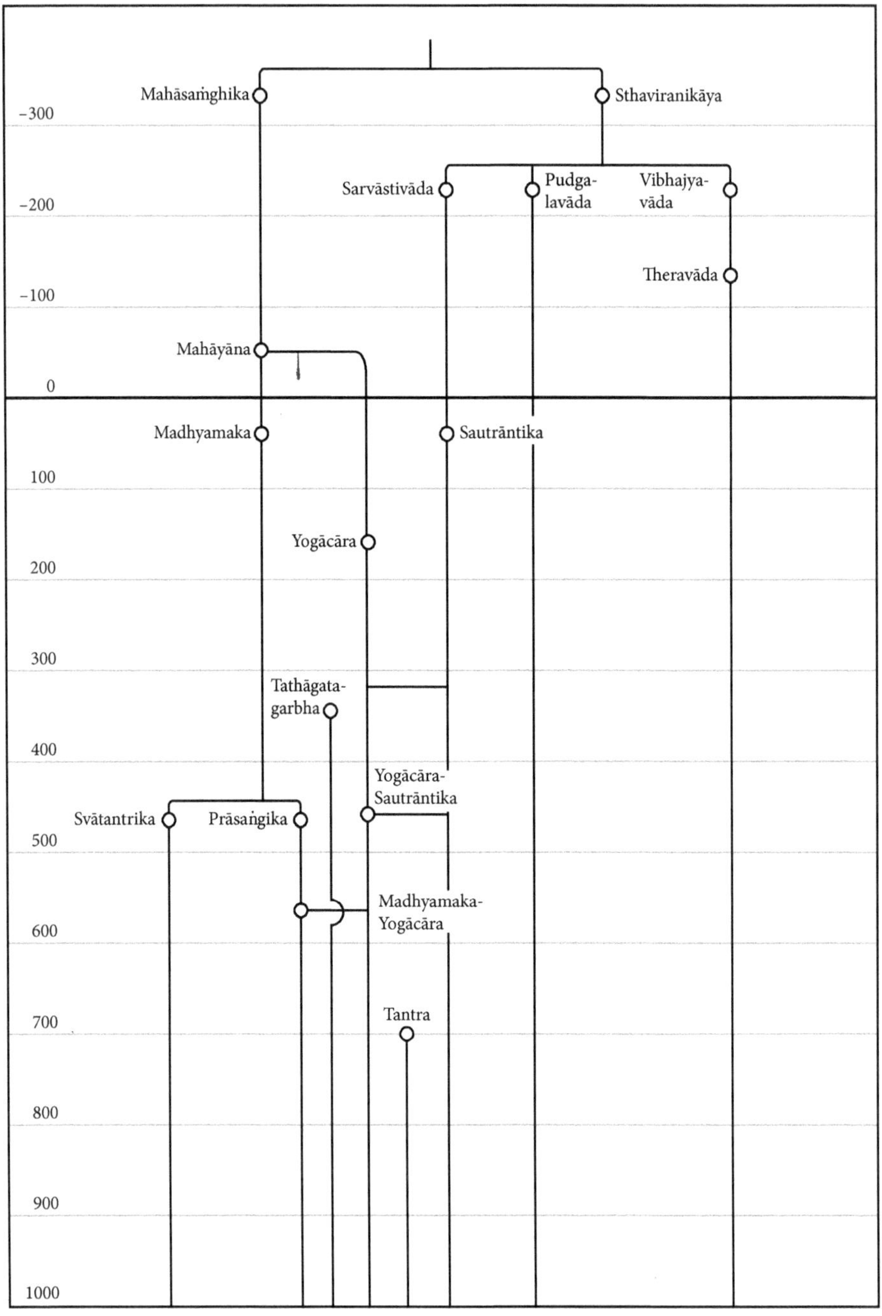


Diagram of philosophical schools

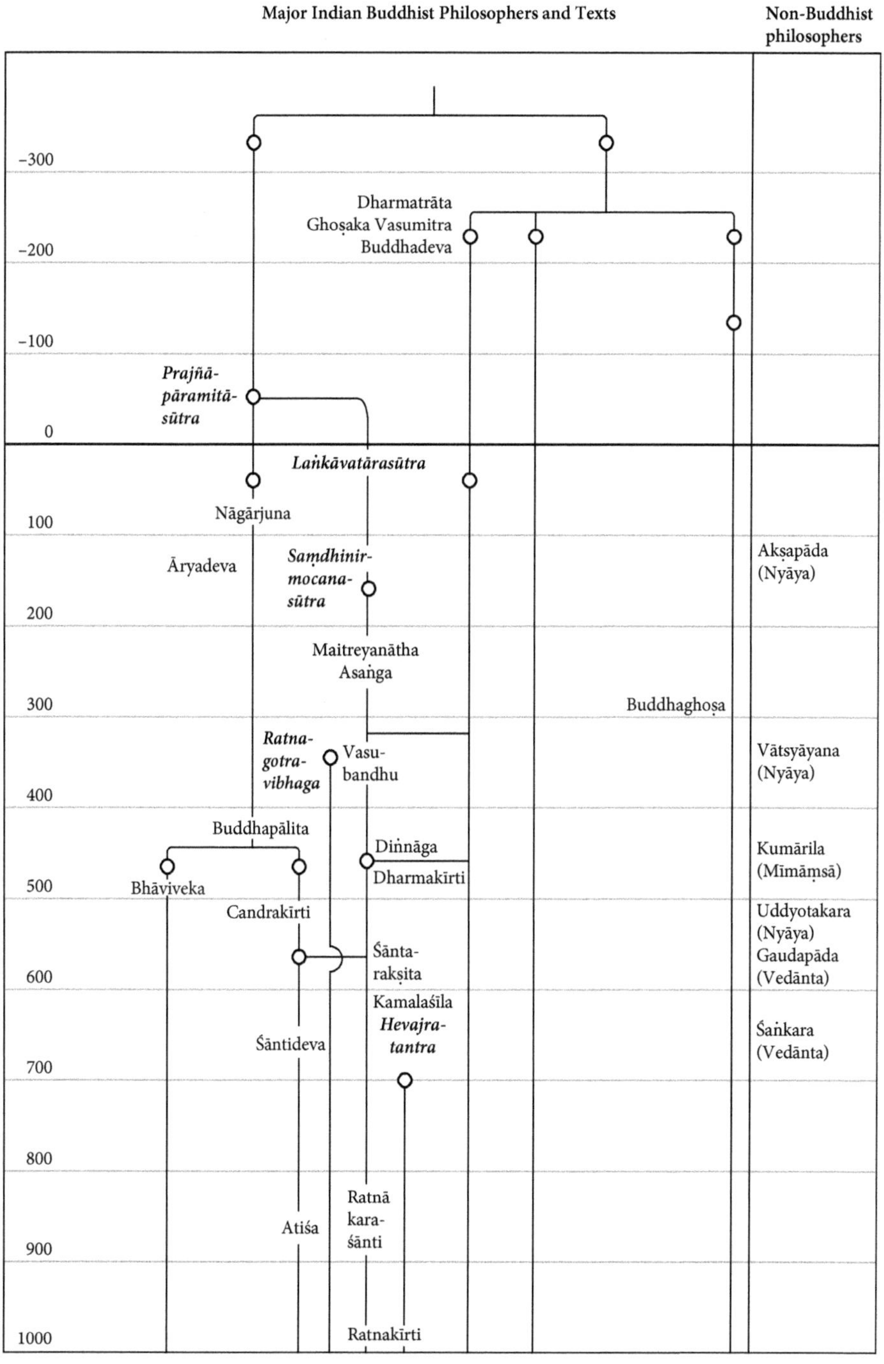

Major Indian Buddhist Philosophers and Texts
Non-Buddhist philosophers
-300
-200
-100
0
100
200
300
400
500
600
700
800
900
1000
Dharmatrāta
Ghoṣaka Vasumitra
Buddhadeva
Prajñā-
pāramitā-
sūtra
Laṅkāvatārasūtra
Nāgārjuna
Āryadeva
Saṃdhinir-
mocana-
sūtra
Maitreyanātha
Asaṅga
Buddhaghoṣa
Ratna-
gotra-
vibhaga
Vasu-
bandhu
Buddhapālita
Diṅnāga
Dharmakīrti
Bhāviveka
Candrakīrti
Śānta-
rakṣita
Kamalaśīla
Hevajra-
tantra
Śāntideva
Ratnā
kara-
śānti
Atiśa
Ratnakīrti
Akṣapāda
(Nyāya)
Vātsyāyana
(Nyāya)
Kumārila
(Mīmāṃsā)
Uddyotakara
(Nyāya)
Gaudapāda
(Vedānta)
Śaṅkara
(Vedānta)

Diagram of thinkers and texts

# Introduction

To the modern historian, Buddhism is a phenomenon which must exasperate him at every point, and we can only say in extenuation that this religion was not founded for the benefit of historians.[1]

## 1. Buddhist Philosophy in India: A Wheel Ever Turning

The wheel: metaphor for the Buddhist doctrine

One of the most famous of all Buddhist metaphors is, without doubt, the description of the Buddha's teaching, the *dharma*, as a wheel. The very first teaching of the Buddha, after all, came to be known as the 'discourse turning the Wheel of the Doctrine' (*dharma-cakra-pravartana-sūtra*). Why precisely the teaching should be compared to a wheel might not be altogether obvious to us, and it was also not obvious to some of the Buddhist scholastics, who discussed the matter in considerable detail. Vasubandhu describes a specific realization of the teaching as the wheel of dharma, namely the so-called 'path of seeing' (*darśana mārga*), the first direct, non-conceptual insight into emptiness.[2] This is considered to be like a wheel because it moves quickly,[3] conveys the meditator to further spiritual realization, and crushes the defilements under it. The Sarvāstivāda master Ghoṣaka considers the noble eightfold path to be a wheel, because some of its parts correspond to the spokes, others to the hub and to the rim.[4] Later Tibetan commentators explain the wheel metaphor by reference to the universal monarch (*cakravartin*), whose attribute is a wheel.[5]

[1] Conze 1980: 15.

[2] *Abhidharmakośa* 6: 54c: *dharmacakraṃ tu dṛṅmārgaḥ*, which the *bhāṣya* explains as *tatsādharmyāddarśanamārgo dharmacakram*, Pradhan 1975: 371: 4–5, Poussin and Pruden 1988–90: 3. 995.

[3] According to Sarvāstivāda theory, the path of seeing lasts only for fifteen moments, being followed in the sixteenth moment by the 'path of meditation' (*bhāvanā mārga*). See Poussin and Pruden 1988–90: 3. 996; Bhikkhu Dhammajoti 2009: 451.

[4] Pradhan 1975: 371: 7–9, Poussin and Pruden 1988–90: 3. 996.

[5] This idea derives probably from the image of the wheels of the monarch's chariot rolling over the territories of his realm. Such a monarch is also said to be born with the mark of the wheel on his hands. See Stutley and Stutley 1977: 58.

As the king's dominion extends from country to country, so the Buddha's teaching extends from master to successive disciples.[6]

Buddhist thought in India: permanence and change

A fairly obvious feature of a wheel is its combination of the static and the dynamic. After a 360-degree revolution a wheel returns to its original position while also having moved to another place. In this respect it resembles the development of Buddhist thought in India. In one sense it stays always the same, to the extent that all of its manifold developments can be traced back to some element of the Buddha's original teaching (though not necessarily a very explicit one); in another sense it is continuously changing, varying the way the Buddhist message is conveyed relative to different audiences and different times. Our discussion in the following pages attempts to be faithful to both aspects, giving an account of the changing manifestations of Buddhist philosophy while also examining the extent to which it is a coherent enterprise drawn from the single source of the Buddha's insight.

## 2. Philosophy as a Game

The game as a heuristic device for understanding philosophy

The development of Buddhist philosophy in India is a complex phenomenon that stretched over more than one millennium and a half, and consists of an intricate web of schools, thinkers, texts, and concepts, all embedded in the wider context of Indian philosophical and cultural history. In order to understand complex phenomena, humans need simple models. One such a model is a game. Philosophy is occasionally compared to a game,[7] and indeed there are a number of parallels between the two: there are players and teams (philosophers and their schools), rules (the canons of argumentation), matches (encounters between thinkers or schools), wins and losses (successful and unsuccessful arguments), and there is development through a series of games. While it is easy to list the ways in which philosophy is *not* like a game (in games it is usually clear who has won, unlike in philosophy; philosophy is about fundamental features of the world, while games are not about anything; and so on), the similarities are sufficiently numerous to employ the example of a game as a heuristic device for explaining the structure of my exposition of Buddhist philosophy in India.

Four factors shaping a game

I am first going to describe a number of factors that shape the dynamics of philosophical developments. We can distinguish four: *arguments*, *texts*, *meditative practices*, and *historical background*. Arguments correspond to the techniques players use in the game, while thinkers may be compared to the players, and their debates to the games played. The influence of meditative techniques may be compared (somewhat crudely) to the inner states of

[6] Cabezón 1994: 37. [7] Huizinga 1949: 146–57.

the players and how these affect their playing techniques, while the historical background functions like the condition of the pitch, the temperature, humidity, and so on.

Narrating the game

Once we have the factors in place, we can begin narrating the game. Our narrative will be largely one of the performance of different teams (philosophical schools), and within this larger frame we will be looking at individual players (particular philosophers), their own accounts of games they played (texts), and at distinctive moves in those games (concepts characteristic of the individual schools).

Sources the narration is based on

Before beginning the actual narrative, it is important to give some consideration to the sources it is going to be based on. The history of a game may be based on recordings or descriptions of famous matches, comparisons of sets of rules, interviews with players, and so on. In the context of a history of Buddhist philosophy our resources are largely[8] text-based. These texts are, on the one hand, foundational texts like the Buddhist *sūtra*s (and, in the context of our present investigation, these are to a large extent Mahāyāna *sūtras*)[9] and, on the other hand, commentarial texts that in some way explicate or expand on the meaning of the foundational texts. These can be direct commentaries, or works that attempt to explicate the meaning of a group of foundational texts in a more summative manner. All of these then can give rise to further comments and explications, forming the basis of an inverted scholastic pyramid of more and more commentarial layers.

Foundational texts and commentaries

Philosophical debates in ancient India

Of course the description of a match is considerably different from the match itself, and if the commentary may correspond to the description of a match, the actual matches correspond to the philosophical debates that took place in ancient India. In this context the comparison with games is quite apt for describing what constituted a kind of ancient Indian intellectual spectator sport. Unfortunately we do not have any transcripts of these debates, but commentarial works are often structured in the debating mode, written as if the explicator was giving his interpretation of the text in front of an audience of heckling interlocutors. The author will present his view of what a specific passage means, and then suggest answers to objections from (real or imagined) opponents trying to undermine his interpretation. Gaining an understanding

[8] I say 'largely' because, unlike other ancient philosophical traditions (such as those of ancient Greece and Rome), the Buddhist philosophical tradition is a living one. The game continues to be played, and while this is helpful for the scholar of Buddhist philosophy in many respects, we must not forget that while present practice can give us some pointers towards what philosophical practice in ancient India was like, it is necessary to keep in mind that about a millennium of intellectual development and conceptual history separates the current philosophical tradition from its ancient Indian ancestor.

[9] As a matter of fact the Buddhist *tantra*s should be included amongst these foundational texts as well. However, the philosophical foundation of Buddhist tantra is not very well researched at present, and our exposition will only make occasional references to tantric texts.

of the debating context helps us to understand what *doing* philosophy in ancient India really amounted to.

Doxographical works

Apart from the foundational texts and their commentaries there is one further set of sources that is useful for our present discussion. These are doxographical works, expositions of a variety of Buddhist or non-Buddhist views that give us an insight into the way the ancient Indians made sense of the diversity of philosophical ideas that surrounded them. These texts did not present a historical narrative, a story of how philosophical views developed successively, but arranged thinkers, texts, and concepts into groups of philosophical schools and usually set out their discussion in opposition to a specific position that was deemed correct and superior to all of these. This could take place by simply pitching the different schools against each other, or by arranging them in a hierarchy, where different schools are taken to approach the one true theory more or less closely. Doxographic presentations provide us with a bird's eye view of matches between different philosophical 'teams', even though we have to take into account that they are always composed with a specific philosophical agenda in mind.

The game's view of the game

After looking at what kind of sources are at our disposal for narrating the game, a final thing to consider is the game's view of the game. When we narrate the history of a complex game with a long history, we do so from our own perspective, and from our own historical position—indeed, how else could we possibly narrate it? Yet the players of the game will have had their own view of the nature of the pursuit they were engaged in, and if their assumptions differed considerably from those we use in narrating the game, it is worthwhile to make them explicit and to determine whether this discrepancy leads to problems for our narrative.

## 3. Factors Determining the Game

Histories of Buddhist philosophy as partial pictures

There are various histories of Buddhist philosophy currently available in Western languages, some of them composed by eminent scholars in the field.[10] What, then, is the purpose of writing yet another one? The most obvious reason is that Buddhist philosophy is a vast topic spanning two-and-a-half millennia and the cause of significant intellectual developments in practically every country in Asia. As such, any monograph of the topic can at best be a partial snapshot, delineating some of the major developments, and barely mentioning or leaving out countless others. Such a snapshot is invariably the result of what appears most salient to its author, and different histories will thereby present different facets of the complex history of Buddhist

[10] See e.g. Conze 1962, Zotz 1996, Guillon 1997.

philosophical thought. This book is no different. What, then, are the key aspects of the history of Buddhist philosophy that this books seeks to describe?

Period covered: Abhidharma up to Dharmakīrti

First of all, I am not attempting to cover the whole development of Buddhist thought from the historical Buddha up to the present through all Buddhist cultures, but focus on a specific, seminal place and period: the golden age of Buddhist philosophy in India, from the composition of the Abhidharma texts (about the beginning of the first millennium CE) up to time of Dharmakīrti (sixth or seventh century CE), with some, albeit limited, consideration of its history between Dharmakīrti and the end of the Buddhist scholastic tradition on the Indian subcontinent at the beginning of the thirteenth century. Within these temporal and spatial parameters, I want to describe how the development of Buddhist philosophy was influenced primarily by three key factors: *arguments*, *texts*, and *meditative practice*.[11] Each of these three factors determined the shape of Buddhist philosophy in important ways.

Social, economic, political factors

We will only occasionally mention the fourth factor mentioned above, historical background. This is not because I believe that considerations of social, economic, and political factors are of no importance for understanding the history of Buddhist philosophy in India. There is no doubt that such factors contributed to shaping the history of Buddhism as a whole,[12] even though the danger that the political flavour of the day may influence or distort the conception of India's intellectual past presented in histories with a strong emphasis on the political dimension is not to be underestimated. Two particularly clear examples are Frauwallner's theories of the Aryan basis of Indian philosophy,[13] and Ruben's history of Indian philosophy along Marxist lines.[14]

In addition, how relevant the social, economic, and political events that might have had an effect on the development of the *Buddhist religion* in general are for explaining the history of *Buddhist philosophy* in particular is frequently difficult to determine. Even for times and places where we have plenty of information about social, political, and economic factors (say, post-Enlightenment Europe), writing the history of philosophical ideas of this period in terms of these factors seems hardly straightforward and possibly of limited importance for illuminating their contents. In the case of ancient India our knowledge of these matters is extremely limited and fragmentary, and while it would be

[11] We can line these up with the three epistemic instruments (*pramāṇa*) distinguished by Buddhist authors such as Vasubandhu (Gold 2015a: 100): inference (*anumāna*), scriptural testimony (*āgama*), and perception (*pratyakṣa*) understood as perception arising as the result of meditative practice (*yogipratyakṣa*). Note that there is no overall consensus within Buddhist thought on the number of the epistemic instruments. Candrakīrti appears to accept the set of four epistemic instruments given by Nyāya, Diṅnāga restricts them to two, perception and inference, while Nāgārjuna seems to reject all of them (at least if understood in a substantialist sense).

[12] See e.g. Ling 1973.

[13] Frauwallner 1939.

[14] Ruben 1954. See Franco 2013: 6–16 for a good discussion of the background of both of Frauwallner's and Ruben's approaches.

foolish to deny that society, economics, and politics did influence the history of philosophy in India to *some* extent, it is hard to establish potential correlations with a high degree of certainty.[15] As any influence they might have had also appears to be less decisive than that of arguments, texts, and meditative practices, we will only mention connections with these historical factors in a few instances.

### a. *Arguments*

Arguments as driving the history of philosophy

When thinking about the history of philosophy we might be forgiven for thinking that it is the arguments that drive its entire development. There are certain answers to certain philosophical questions, and philosophers come up with arguments to back up some of these answers. Whoever has the most successful argument, the story goes, will create the most successful philosophical theory, which then attracts various refutations and counter-arguments, the best of which will then become the most notorious, and so on. This picture is certainly too simplistic to account for the history of any philosophical tradition, but it contains the fundamental insight that arguments and the competition between them is one of the key driving forces of philosophical development. In the context of Indian Buddhist philosophy it is also important not to focus solely on the argumentative exchanges within the Buddhist tradition, but also on the debates Buddhists had with exponents of the different schools of classical Indian philosophy, as there are numerous instances where the expository framework and also the contents of Buddhist philosophy are influenced in important ways by its interaction with non-Buddhist schools.

Development of Buddhist philosophy: three stages

Roger Jackson proposed a three-stage model of the development of Buddhist thought in India.[16] During the first stage (roughly the first three centuries of Buddhism's existence) Buddhism participated in inter-sectarian discussion with various non-Buddhist schools (such as the Jains, Cārvāka, and Ājīvika schools), thereby making its own doctrinal position more precise. This was followed by a second stage (beginning around the time of Aśoka in the third century BCE) during which Buddhists were primarily debating with Buddhists. At this time of mainly intra-sectarian debate the bases of the four Buddhists schools distinguished in traditional doxographies were established; the aim of the game was not so much to establish the truth of Buddhism in the face of its detractors, as to refute interpretations of the Buddha's words that were conceived as erroneous. In the third stage the Buddhists appear to be turning outwards again. Over the centuries Indian philosophical schools had developed a plethora of more advanced philosophical techniques which could be used to

[15] For recent interesting work on potential correlations between ancient Indian philosophy and political factors see Bronkhorst 2011a, Eltschinger 2013, Walser 2015.
[16] Jackson 1993: 99–107.

Debates with non-Buddhist schools

address old disputes once again, but this time from a new perspective.[17] They began to argue with each other in a manner that did not presuppose the validity of any one of their particular worldviews, and tried to base their entire argumentative exchanges on premisses that both opponents could accept, together with a set of shared logical and epistemological assumptions.[18] The influence of non-Buddhist arguments on the development of Buddhist philosophy was obviously most pronounced during stages 1 and 3. Given the focus of this work on the first millennium CE, I will be looking primarily at phase 3 to find out how the interaction with non-Buddhist arguments influenced the development of Buddhist philosophy. After a period of intra-Buddhist debate of considerable complexity, which could, nevertheless, take all of the familiar Buddhist assumptions as agreed upon, Buddhists

> suddenly found themselves defending the existence of past and future lives against Cārvāka materialists, the possibility of liberation against both materialists and Mīmāṃsākas, their denial of universals against the Vaiśeṣikas, their rejection of a creator God against the Naiyāyikas, the theory of momentariness against the Sāṃkhyas and Jainas—and the theory of no-self (*anātman*) against virtually everybody.[19]

This necessity to provide arguments for claims that were previously simply assumed is a clear example of how the dynamics of argument acts as a driving force behind Indian Buddhist philosophy. But arguments are not everything, and especially for forms of philosophy developed against a religious background, sacred texts are another key factor that influences the way their history takes shape.

### b. *Sacred texts*

In an important sense the sacred texts—in this case, the Buddhist canon—provide the goal of philosophical argumentation. The claims made in the canon are the claims which are to be argued for, analyzed, and expanded on in Buddhist philosophical texts. However, that does not mean that the Buddhist philosophical enterprise is simply trying to provide arguments for already established conclusions. First of all, which texts are to be regarded as canonical is far from straightforward, as the multiplicity of Buddhist canons testifies. Secondly, even within the context of a set of texts that are regarded as authoritative, the Buddhist hermeneutic distinction between the interpretable

[17] It is interesting to note that once Indian Buddhism is translated to Tibet we find a resurrection of phase 2, with a nearly exhaustive dominance of intra-sectarian disputes, because there are virtually no proponents of other schools to debate with.

[18] Of course this did not work quite as smoothly as the participants might have hoped. Compare, for example, the Nyāya and Madhyamaka disagreements about the status of rules used in debates discussed in Nāgārjuna's *Vaidalyaprakaraṇa* (Westerhoff 2018).

[19] Jackson 1993: 105.

Interpretable/definite distinction as source of variation in Buddhist philosophy

(*neyārtha*) and the definite (*nītārtha*) texts allows for a surprising amount of variation amongst Buddhist positions. If there are specific utterances of the Buddha that are to be taken literally, and others that require interpretation, variations of which ones are to be put in which category can produce a considerable divergence between different interpretative positions. The foregrounding of specific texts or sets of texts to support particular interpretations of the Buddhist doctrine is therefore to be understood (alongside the dynamics of argumentative exchanges) as a second key factor that shaped the course of Buddhist philosophy in India.

### c. *Meditative practice*

Finally, we have to keep in mind that Buddhist texts are not just meant to be read, but supposed to be practised. In particular, they constitute a set of instructions to bring about a gradual (or perhaps sudden) cognitive shift that is indicative of the mind changing from the unenlightened to the enlightened state. It is sometimes pointed out that the formation of the Buddhist canons was frequently open-ended, insofar as during the development of Buddhism new texts appeared that were later regarded as canonical.[20] This, together with the natural open-endedness of argumentative exchanges, contributed in an important way to the dynamic development of Buddhist thought. But there is yet another source of open-endedness involved. The Buddha (and subsequent Buddhist masters) taught a set of meditative techniques which their disciples were supposed to put into practice in order to develop certain insights into their teaching at the experiential level. These techniques generated a plethora of inner experiential states in the practitioners, and the ensuing phenomenology needed to be conceptualized within a suitable framework, answering such questions as what these states were, how they were related to ordinary experiences, what the reason for their soteriological efficacy was, and so forth. As the set of meditative techniques Buddhist practitioners employed was elaborated and enlarged during the development of Buddhism, the philosophical frameworks employed to account for these kept developing too. As such, a significant part of the development of Buddhist philosophy can be understood as responding to the need to account for a phenomenology of meditative states.

The need to classify meditative experiences

Three factors as gravitational forces

It is usually impossible to draw very precise distinctions between the three factors of arguments, texts, and meditative practice, claiming, for example, that a given position solely arose because it was a response to a specific non-Buddhist argument, or because if featured dominantly in a text that had just become popular, or because it was needed to a account for some particular item

[20] Whether these were in fact authored later, already composed at the Buddha's time and then hidden, or were somehow produced in a realm other than the world we inhabit is a complex question which we need not settle here.

of meditative phenomenology. These factors overlap and influence each other, and it may therefore be best to think of them as three bodies with different strengths of gravitational attraction, and of the trajectory of Buddhist philosophy as corresponding to that of a particle moving between them, approaching closer to one, and thereby being attracted more by it, then moving more into the gravitational field of another, and so on.

Exaptation of philosophical concepts

It is also helpful to think of the relation of these three factors in terms of the evolutionary concept of *exaptation*. Exaptation describes a case where a feature was evolutionarily developed for one purpose (such as the bird's plumage for temperature regulation) but subsequently served another (in this case, flight). In the same way, a specific concept might originate from a particular doctrinal position, argument, or meditative experience, and may later prove useful to elucidate another textual passage, underpin a quite different argument, or help to conceptualize further forms of meditation. It is not implausible to suggest that the concepts that proved to be especially successful in the development of Buddhist philosophy were those that displayed the greatest degree of exaptive functionality, that is, concepts that, though originating from a specific doctrinal, dialectical, or meditative context could be usefully employed in quite different contexts. Understood in this way, it will be easier to see how reference to each of the three factors allows us to get a better grasp of the different twists and turns of the development of Buddhist philosophy in India over the course of time.

## 4. Narrating the Game: How to Structure the Material

Challenges in structuring a history of Indian philosophy

There are various possible ways of structuring a history of philosophy. We can understand it as a succession of thinkers (as is frequently done in histories of Western philosophy), or as a series of philosophical texts, or as a progression of philosophical schools, or as a sequence of philosophical ideas.

Each approach has its drawbacks. When dealing with ancient Indian thinkers it is frequently unclear when they lived, what they wrote, and even in some cases how many of the same name there were in the first place.[21] Focusing exclusively on the texts makes establishing a historical progression not necessarily easier, since dating the texts and establishing their mutual temporal relations is often far from straightforward. The doxographical

[21] Dasgupta (1922: 1.62) notes that 'it is hardly possible to attempt a history of Indian Philosophy in the manner in which the histories of European philosophy have been written.' Dasgupta's methodological reflections are still pertinent, though his view that 'all the independence of their [i.e. the Indian philosophers'] thinking was limited and enchained by the faith of the school to which they were attached' (63) needs to be reconsidered in the light of the contemporary discussion we find e.g. in Ganeri 2011.

approach that divides the history of Buddhist thought by schools, a device favoured by Indian and Tibetan historians, faces the challenge that much of the seemingly clear division between the different schools is an *ex post facto* arrangement, and that the individual thinkers concerned would have been unlikely to ascribe themselves to the specific schools they are supposed to have belonged to quite so readily. We certainly find numerous Indian Buddhist philosophers who cross the supposed doxographical divides. Vasubandhu made key contributions to the Abhidharma and to Yogācāra, Diṅnāga and Dharmakīrti were important Yogācāra thinkers but also form what is usually considered to be a separate logico-epistemological school. Kambala, a lesser-known author from the sixth century, seems to occupy a position straddling Madhyamaka and Yogācāra. Finally, writing a history of Buddhist thought organized solely by concepts, a *Begriffsgeschichte*, would be a fascinating enterprise, but it is an undertaking that presupposes much more philological and philosophical groundwork than is available at present.

A hybrid structure

Being aware of the drawbacks and advantages of each organizational principle, our history opts for a hybrid approach. We will structure the history of Buddhist thought according to the traditional and plausible historical sequence

Four schools

Abhidharma—Madhyamaka—Yogācāra—Diṅnāga and Dharmakīrti, while paying attention to their mutual interrelations,[22] and discuss the difficulties in clearly differentiating between them.[23] No account of Buddhist thought in India would be complete without discussing the manifold philosophical inter-

Buddhist–non-Buddhist debates

actions between the schools of Buddhist thought and non-Buddhist classical Indian philosophy. The amount and scope of their debates is vast, and in the limits of a concise history such as this our approach has to be selective. We will look in more detail at three sets of debates between Buddhist and non-Buddhist schools: between Madhyamaka and Nyāya, between Yogācāra and Vedānta, and between the school of Diṅnāga and Dharmakīrti and Mīmāṃsā.

Key thinkers

Within the general doxographic and historical framework of the four schools we discuss the key thinkers of each school. It is clear, however, that many of these have produced work crossing the doxographical divisions, and that we might sometimes be dealing with two or more historical personalities that have been

Key texts

merged in the traditional view. While looking at individual thinkers it is also necessary to provide accounts of key works, of philosophical treatises (*śāstras*)

[22] We discuss the relation between Madhyamaka and Abhidharma in Chapter 2 (pp. 99–101, 107–15), that between Yogācāra and Abhidharma and Madhyamaka in Chapter 3 (pp. 200–16), and that between the theories of Diṅnāga and Dharmakīrti and those of the other three schools in Chapter 4 (pp. 259–70).

[23] Questions of differentiation become particularly interesting when considering attempts to combine Madhyamaka and Yogācāra approaches (see e.g. the essays by Westerhoff, Shulman, Gold, and Blumenthal in Garfield and Westerhoff 2015) and when investigating the relation of the theories of Diṅnāga and Dharmakīrti with those of the other three schools.

with clearly identified authors, and of important *sūtras* associated with the different philosophical traditions, texts which are supposed to comprise the essence of philosophical views subsequently elaborated in the more technical treatises. Unfortunately the dating, authorship, mutual relationship, and sometimes scope of the individual texts is often far from clear. Finally, we will need to provide substantial discussion of the key concepts indispensable for understanding the philosophical outlook of each school. Our aim is to make the limitations of each organizational principle evident while ensuring that an informative account of the history of Buddhist thought emerges through their joint presence.

Key concepts

## 5. The Sources of the Game

### a. *The bases of Buddhist philosophy*

Early discourses and Mahāyāna *sūtras*

The main source from which all of Buddhist philosophy flows is, unsurprisingly, the teaching of the Buddha. In the context of the history of Indian Buddhism during the first millennium CE, 'the teaching of the Buddha' is not just taken to comprise the discourses of early Buddhism, but also a variety of other texts, such as the Mahāyāna *sūtras*, as well as the *tantras*. All of these are traditionally considered to have been authored by the Buddha in some form or other, whether in his physical form during the present world-age (*kalpa*) as Buddha Śākyamuni during the time of his life in ancient India, or in another manifestation, or in another space and time altogether. These texts became known gradually over time as Buddhism developed in ancient India; the first Mahāyāna *sūtras* appeared around the beginning of the Common Era, and the first Buddhist *tantras* around the third century CE. The Mahāyāna Buddhist tradition does not see the later origin of these texts as detracting from their claim to authenticity. It argues that these teachings were indeed all authored by the Buddha, though not all were made public at the very beginning, as some doctrines would only be beneficial for beings that lived a considerable time after the Buddha's death. As such, the teachings were hidden until a suitable time for their propagation arose.

The 'original teachings' of the Buddha

Some parts of contemporary Buddhist studies are very interested in determining the 'original teachings' of the Buddha,[24] and separating them from the historical overlay that later generations have added as embellishment, distinguishing supposedly earlier hard conceptual substance from later fluffy pious fiction.[25]

[24] Gombrich 2009, Siderits 2010.

[25] This approach finds its counterpart in attempts to extract the 'historical core' of hagiographical accounts, such as the traditional accounts of the Buddha's life or biographies of later Buddhist luminaries. This strikes me as particularly problematic in the Buddhist case; see pp. 24–34 below for further discussion.

This is not an approach the Buddhist tradition itself adopted, and although not every Buddhist thinker would consider every text as genuine, the conception of the later development of Buddhism as an obscuring force that is somehow clouding the original clarity of the Buddha's teachings is not one we find in ancient Indian texts.[26] For the purpose of discussing the history of Buddhist philosophy, attempting to distinguish which philosophical positions form part of the 'original thinking of the Buddha' and which are later scholastic developments that depart from his original message is not very helpful. This distinction is therefore not one we are attempting to draw in the following pages. It is in fact questionable whether this distinction makes sense at all. As will be seen from various examples in our following discussion, the Buddha's teachings contain a variety of conceptual seeds that later germinate in the development of different philosophical traditions, with different traditions placing different emphases on specific concepts.[27] Each tradition creates its own image of 'what the Buddha really taught' by focusing on those concepts that feature prominently in the philosophical approach the tradition under consideration develops. The different emphases of the different traditions were shaped by the intellectual needs and circumstances of the times in which these traditions developed, and given the importance the Buddha accorded to teachings being suitable for the time, place, and audience that receives them, arguing against the authenticity of later teachings because they go beyond the discussions found in the early *sūtras* is hardly satisfactory. This approach overlooks how much the exposition of the *dharma* needs to be shaped by the beliefs and preconceptions of the audience in order to be soteriologically effective.

Different ways of construing 'original teachings'

Frameworks of philosophical activity: debates, commentaries, doxographies

The *sūtras* therefore form the basis on which the activity of *doing philosophy* in the Buddhist context took place. It is worthwhile to spend some time considering the different forms of intellectual presentation that shaped both the outward appearance and the contents of the activity that constituted ancient Indian philosophical works. We will look at three main frameworks in which Indian philosophizing took place: debates, commentaries, and doxographies.

[26] The modern distrust of the scholastic Indian commentarial tradition is not confined to commentaries on the teachings of the historical Buddha. Kalupahana (2008: 517) believes that central subsequent commentators misunderstood the meanings of Nāgārjuna's, Vasubandhu's, and Diṅnāga's works, and that their messages need to be rediscovered by a direct reading of their text unencumbered by the conceptual frameworks of the commentarial tradition.

[27] This fact needs to be taken into account when considering the development of the different schools of Buddhist philosophy, and the association of particular thinkers with specific schools. Each school created its own 'conceptual lineage', rooted in the Buddha's teaching, by tracing its specific ideas backwards through a selection of *sūtras* and commentarial material. We need, therefore, to be aware that the association of specific authors and texts with a given school might be primarily the outcome of such a retrospective process of lineage creation, and that the authors themselves might not have identified themselves with that specific school. While a useful device for classifying Buddhist philosophers in terms of the main ideas they defend, the idea of a determinate association of each one with a specific school is in many cases a doxographical fiction.

To some extent these are all present in the current form of Western philosophy most readers will be familiar with. The questions after a philosophical lecture can often be best described in terms of a debate: they are *objections* put forward by the audience, the speaker responds by a *defence* of his position. Major works in the history of philosophy (such as Kant's first *Critique* or Wittgenstein's *Tractatus*) give rise to works of secondary literature calling itself 'Commentary on…', and histories of philosophy can often be understood as doxographies organized by thinkers who held the respective *doxa*.

In ancient Indian philosophy these forms of presentation are both more elaborate and more influential than their contemporary Western variants, which may sometimes appear somewhat anaemic. In order to understand what ancient Indian philosophers did and how they did it, it is important to have some understanding of the structure of these forms of presentation, and of the purpose they are supposed to serve.

## *b. Debates*

It is hard to overestimate the importance of debates in Indian intellectual life. Public debates constituted the most important and most visible forms of philosophical exchange. They were an intellectual spectator sport, sometimes held in the presence of a ruler,[28] that attracted considerable audiences. The stakes were high: not only could they make or break a scholar's career; they could also have important consequences for their followers. We frequently read about scholars defeated in debates who not only have to adopt their opponent's position, but have to make all their disciples convert as well. Sometimes even more is at stake (though we have to take these accounts perhaps with a pinch of salt): the defeated debater is expected to cut out his tongue or even to kill himself.[29] Xuanzang (玄奘), a Chinese scholar who travelled through India at the beginning of the seventh century, has this to say about Indian debates:

Public debates

> Assemblies for discussion are often held to test the intellectual capacity of the monks, in order to distinguish the superior from the inferior, and to reject the dull and promote the bright. Those who can deliberate on the subtle sayings, and glorify the wonderful theories with refined diction and quick eloquence, may ride richly caparisoned elephants with hosts of attendants preceding and following behind them. But those to whom the theories are taught in vain, or who have been defeated in a debate, explaining few principles in a verbose way, or distorting the teachings with language that is merely pleasant to the ear, are daubed with ocher or chalk in the face, while dust is scattered

[28] For further discussion of the royal patronage of debates see Bronkhorst 2011a: 175–9.

[29] Eckel 2008: 10, 13–14. A variety of historical documents informs us that tortures reportedly inflicted on the loser of debates were equally gruesome and inventive. In addition to the cutting out of tongues and banishment they include the defeated opponent being 'bruised to death in oil-mills of stone' (Verardi 2014: 26), being boiled in oil (211), having their heads cut off with axes, and being thrown into a wooden mortar and ground to powder (209).

over the body, and are expelled into the wilderness, or discarded into ditches. In this way the good and the evil are distinguished, and the wise and the ignorant are disclosed.[30]

Reading accounts such as these, we indeed get the impression that 'debaters were the rock stars and sports heroes of classical India'.[31]

Debate manuals

Around the first century CE the first explicit manuals for conducting debates were composed. Debates were no informal exchange of ideas where two contestants had a discussion until one gave up, but highly formalized affairs with rules about what responses could be made, what reasons could be given, what unfair tricks an opponent might employ, and, most importantly, how to tell when a debater had lost a debate. The *Nyāyasūtra*, a highly influential text on logic and debate composed in its first form during the first century CE, distinguishes three forms of debate: debate proper (*vāda*), which does not have winning as its main objective, but aims at determining the truth about some disputed matter; tricky debate (*jalpa*), where desire for victory is the main goal for both parties; and destructive debate (*vitaṇḍā*), where the aim is only to prove the opponent wrong, without attempting to prove one's own position. Only debates proper end in the determination of a true conclusion; tricky debates and destructive debates are over as soon as the opponent has nothing left to say. It is only the first, debate proper, which is to be regarded as a philosophical tool; the other two are merely degenerated versions that occur when debates are primarily considered as public performances. Yet debate proper is not only a means for a joint inquiry, but also a tool for teaching philosophy. In this form it continues in Tibetan monastic education (drawing directly on Indian models) up to the present day.[32]

Nyāya: three kinds of debate

Influence on philosophical works

Debate and Vasubandhu's *Viṃśikā*

We find that the practice of debate has influenced the structure of Indian philosophical works to a considerable extent. A very clear example of this is Vasubandhu's *Viṃśikā*. It begins by a verse in which Vasubandhu states that all things are only mental in nature. But instead of elaborating this point further and supplying arguments for the position, the text goes immediately into objections the opponent makes against this counterintuitive position; Vasubandhu then develops this point further by responding to these objections. Even though not all Indian philosophical texts of the first millennium CE show their connection with the debating ground so clearly, in virtually all of them, be they independent works or commentaries, we find some space given to an opponent (or a sequence of opponents that will not necessarily agree with one another); the author then uses the opportunity to explain his account further by answering the opponents one by one.

The influence of debates on the development of Indian Buddhist philosophy is a clear example how the first of the three factors distinguished

[30] Li 1996: 58. [31] Eckel 2008:15. [32] Perdue 1992, 2014.

above—arguments—shape its contents. Buddhist philosophical texts from the first millennium CE are not just expositions of the words of the historical Buddha, but are responses to the claims of its philosophical rivals. While their aim is to establish the truth of the Buddha's fundamental insight, they do so in a way that replies to actual or hypothetical criticisms that were brought forward by the proponents of the non-Buddhist schools. Buddhist philosophy would not be what it is today if it had not developed in a complex interplay with opposing positions that defended radically different views of the world.

Texts as responses to philosophical rivals

## *c. Commentaries*

Commentaries form an immensely important part of the philosophical texts of ancient India. The interrelations between Indian philosophical texts can be visualized in the form of a tree, with a small number of 'root texts' at the bottom, and an ever-expanding structure of commentarial stems, branches, and foliage on top. At the bottom of the tree are the *sūtra*s, texts that attempt to exemplify the ideals of exceeding conciseness (*laghutā*), as well as completeness (*kṛtsnatā*) in the treatment of a particular subject matter, though often doing so at the expense of clarity (*vaiśadya*), the third ideal traditionally associated with theoretical texts in ancient India.[33] A *sūtra* presents material in a series of short, often metrically structured sentences, a format that aids memorization of frequently very large conceptual structures. In fact, calling *sūtra*s short is a considerable understatement, and 'even so laconic a document as a telegram would be prolix compared to a sūtra'.[34] What a *sūtra* has gained in compactness and completeness it loses in clarity, and a text in *sūtra* format is decidedly not intended to be understood on its own. We can compare a *sūtra* to a computer file that needs to be decompressed before it can be read, or to bullet-points on a lecture handout. In the latter case the bullet-points are meant to be accompanied by the speaker's oral presentation, and a *sūtra* may be elucidated in the same way by the teacher's verbal explanation, often after the student has committed the text of the *sūtra* itself to memory. The explanatory expansion of the compressed *sūtra* format can also be provided by a written commentary. Within the Indian scholastic context a variety of different types of commentary are distinguished. It is indicative of the often cryptic style employed in the *sūtra* genre that one type of commentary, called *vivṛti*

Characteristics of a *sūtra*

Different types of commentaries

[33] Ganeri 2010: 192–3. The Buddha's discourses, though also called *sūtra*s, do not fall under this notion of what a *sūtra* is.

[34] Maurer 1981: 8–9. A well-known saying states, with reference to authors of grammatical treatises, that if they can save as much as half a syllable in the formulation of their *sūtra*s they rejoice as they would at the birth of a son (*ardha-mātrā-lāghavena putrotsavaṃ manyante vaiyākaraṇāḥ*). Kielhorn, Abhyankar, and Abhyankara 1960–2: 122.

*vivaraṇa*

or *vivaraṇa*, focuses almost exclusively on grammatical issues. Such a commentary would indicate the division of the words of the *sūtra* (word-breaks are not indicated by spaces in Sanskrit written in *devanāgarī* script), explain the meaning of obscure or technical terms by synonyms, analyse grammatical compounds, in particular long nominal compounds beloved by authors of Indian scholastic literature, and explain how the meaning of the *sūtra* is to be construed on the basis of this analysis.[35]

*bhāṣya*

A second kind of commentary, a *bhāṣya*, operates at a somewhat higher level of abstraction. Its purpose is to connect the individual *sūtra*s so that they form a coherent argumentative whole. It does so by imposing an overall structure on the sequence of the *sūtras*. This involves grouping the *sūtra*s into smaller units that belong together, and establishing breaks between the discussions of different topics. On the basis of this division into thematic groups it is then possible to give more specific explanations of the individual *sūtra*s according to the way in which they fit into these groups. In addition, the *bhāṣya* will attempt to structure the *sūtra*s according to a dialectical narrative, specifying some *sūtra*s as the text's own assertions (*siddhānta*), others as objections raised by the opponent (*pūrvapakṣa*) or hypotheses only entertained for the sake of argument. It is evident that there is considerable flexibility in the way a structure may be imposed on a very concise set of *sūtra*s. A text will usually not indicate when the author himself is speaking, stating his own views, and when he is giving voice to his opponent's position, which he does not share. Such identifications will most often be carried out by commentaries, and a difference in opinion about who is speaking in different sections of the text is obviously going to give rise to very different readings of a single text.

It is therefore the very terseness of the root texts, lacking indication of divisions or structuring, or of objection and reply, that makes it possible to structure them in more than one way, making very different commentarial approaches possible.

*vārttika*

It is at this stage that the necessity of a third kind of commentary, a *vārttika*, arises. This is a commentary on a commentary (i.e. a *bhāṣya*) and presupposes the presence of a variety of commentarial approaches to the underlying sets of *sūtra*s. The *vārttika*'s role as a subcommentary is to assess and compare the specific interpretative choices of the different commentaries to each other, and to establish the superiority of the *bhāṣya* it is a subcommentary on over the others.

The hierarchy of commentaries can obviously be extended beyond the level of subcommentaries. The range of commentarial activities all fundamentally

[35] These four, together with the answering of objections that one might raise against the points made in the *sutra*, constitute the five functions usually attributed to 'commenting' (*vyākhyāna*) texts (Tubb and Bose 2007: 3–5). Note that there is nothing in these five functions that entails a restriction to philosophical texts. A commentary on a poetical text, for example, would be expected to provide information on these five topics as well.

concerned with a single text (i.e. the underlying set of *sūtras*) will, one might expect, eventually obtain an equilibrium, a balanced position where the various interpretative possibilities of the text raised so far have been explored, and where some sort of consensus about how to understand it has been reached. Nevertheless, at this stage we may also find authors who are dissatisfied with the conclusions obtained at this stage, who will compose an entirely new commentary on the root text, bypassing the accumulated rhetorical layers and attempting to establish a fundamentally new reading of the text.[36]

*kārikā*

The *sūtra*-commentary style genre appealed to Indian philosophical writers so much that they composed new texts, called *kārikā*s, that were formally very similar to the received *sūtra* texts, and which presented a new, concise, and complete discussion of a philosophical topic. In some cases they would then compose their own commentary on this new *sūtra*, using this opportunity to expand in prose on the points made in the compressed *sūtra* format.

Buddhist commentaries

The framework of root texts and commentaries which is so central to classical Indian philosophy was adopted by Buddhist philosophers as well. The Buddhists did not, of course, have foundational *sūtra*s of the kind that formed the basis of the six orthodox *darśana*s, like Patañjali's *Yogasūtra*, Kaṇāda's *Vaiśeṣikasūtra*, and so on. The foremost textual basis of Buddhism are the Buddha's discourses, also called '*sūtra*' (or *sutta* in Pāli); despite the fact that they are formally very different from the compressed telegraph style of the *sūtra*s of classical Indian philosophy, they became the subject of considerable commentarial activity.[37] More important for the present discussion, however, are the independent, *sūtra*-style works, the Buddhist *kārikā*s that later philosophers composed in order to express in concise form what they took to be the philosophical message of specific *sūtra*s (often Mahāyāna *sūtra*s). These *kārikā*s were frequently supplied with auto-commentaries. We know very little about the way these *kārikā*-commentary compounds were composed. One historical account, however, relates the way that Vasubandhu composed his famous *Abhidharmakośa*,[38] describing how he would lecture during the day, and then sum up the day's teaching in a verse, the sequence of which became the *Abhidharmakośa*. In this case, the detailed oral exposition would have preceded the succinct expression in a series of *sūtra*s, and it is not unlikely to assume that Vasubandhu's auto-commentary on the *sūtra*s expressed the content of the very lectures they are supposed to have summarized.[39]

Buddhist *kārikā*s and their auto-commentaries

[36] In early modern India, for example, new interest arose in composing fresh commentaries on some of the most ancient of all Indian philosophical texts, the *Nyāyasūtra*s and the *Vaiśeṣikasūtra*s (Ganeri 2011).

[37] Ganeri 2011: 113. [38] See below, pp. 155–6.

[39] The matter is slightly complicated by the doctrinal tension between the root text and the commentary (see below, p. 156). Whether Vasubandhu first interpreted the root text in one way in his oral explanation and in another way in his subsequent commentary in the *Abhidharmakośabhāṣya* is

Even though there are accounts where teachers are supposed to have composed a sequence of *sūtra*s directly (this, for example, is the way Śāntideva is said to have first taught the *Bodhicaryāvatāra*),[40] it seems generally plausible to assume that the order in which a text/commentary compound is studied (first *sūtra*, then commentary) is the inverse of the order in which the two were composed.

Commentarial practice and authorial intent

The very conciseness of the *sūtra* style makes raises the probability that different commentators come up with very different interpretations. Jonardon Ganeri discusses a telling example of two different commentaries on two verses from the *Vaiśeṣikasūtra*.[41] The first commentary reads the first verse as expressing the view of a Vedānta opponent, and the second verse as presenting the text's own view, while the second commentary understands the first verse as the *sūtra*'s own view, and the second verse as that of a Buddhist opponent! Such examples of divergence underline the need for *vārttika*-style commentaries that evaluate the different conflicting interpretations and select the best one. Eventually, it would seem at least, that such evaluation leads to an interpretative consensus on how a specific text is to be best understood, a consensus that in the best possible case manages to approach as closely as possible the meaning that the author originally wanted to convey in the text.

Conflicting commentarial interpretations

Sterility and arbitrariness?

Understood in this way, a philosophical tradition that places as much emphasis on the production of commentaries may be considered as instantiating a peculiar combination of sterility and arbitrariness. It is sterile because the primary aim of the philosophical enterprise is not any kind of conceptual discovery or innovation, but to understand and faithfully reproduce the meaning of a set of texts handed down from the past, whether these are the foundational *sūtra*s of the schools of classical Indian philosophy or the Buddha's discourses. It is arbitrary because in the process of doing so it produces a set of very divergent, sometimes contradictory readings of the same texts, a divergence that is caused largely by the opacity of the very texts the tradition tries to elucidate. This opacity makes it impossible to decide which, if any, of the different interpretations suggested expresses the 'true meaning' of the root text, so that we are left with an enterprise that unsuccessfully navigates between what is—in all likelihood—a vast array of different misunderstandings of a text, with little hope of ever finding out what the author really wanted to say.

something we do not know. In any case, apart from being in tension with the historical narrative of the composition of the *Abhidharmakośa*, the idea that all of the verses of the *Abhidharmakośa* were first composed as an independent work would also not cohere well with the fact that some verses do not seem to be comprehensible without the commentary provided by the *Abhidharmakośabhāṣya*.

[40] See Paul Williams's introduction to Crosby and Skilton 1995: ix–x, and above, pp. 271–2.

[41] Ganeri 2011: 111.

Yet it turns out that the picture of the commentarial tradition as a joint enterprise of zeroing in on the authorial intent,[42] convincing as it may initially appear, is quite unable to account for the complexity of the commentarial endeavour in ancient Indian philosophy. A particularly clear example of this is the case of Vasubandhu's *Abhidharmakośa* and its commentary, the *Abhidharmakośabhāṣya*. The root text presents a comprehensive description of Abhidharma metaphysics from the perspective of the Sarvāstivāda school. The *bhāṣya*, on the other hand, is usually taken to be written from the perspective of the rival Sautrāntika school, frequently criticizing the Sarvāstivāda positions set out in the root text.[43] Interestingly enough, another Buddhist philosopher, Saṃghabhadra, then set out to write a separate commentary on Vasubandhu's *Abhidharmakośa*, called *Nyāyānusāra*, correcting the author's mistaken interpretation of his own text by producing a commentary that accords with Sarvāstivāda orthodoxy.[44] In another text, Saṃghbhadra makes the following remarks on the motivation for his commentarial undertaking:

The text's true intent? Example of the *Abhidharmakośa*

> When the *sūtra* master's [i.e. Vasubandhu's] statements conform to reasoned argument and scriptural authority, I will reproduce them as they are and not attempt to refute them.
>
> [However,] if they contradict the basic purport of the Abhidharma or the *sūtras* in any way, I am determined to scrutinize them further and vow to purge them.
>
> In contrast to the *sūtra* master's erroneous explanations, I will present the correct interpretation and will manifest the true and extraordinary meaning of the accepted doctrines of our school.[45]

It is clear that Saṃghabhadra's aim was not to elucidate what Vasubandhu meant when he composed the *Abhidharmakośa*, for he considers Vasubandhu's understanding of his own work as mistaken. His aim is to produce an interpretation that he considers to be in accordance with the Buddha's discourses and the (Sarvastivāda) Abhidharma texts. But if a commentator could not even be expected to try to recover the authorial intent of the author of the text he is commenting upon, what should we think the Indian philosophical commentators were trying to achieve?

Jonardon Ganeri[46] made the suggestion that a commentary's aim is to establish a connection between a contemporary readership and a philosophical text from the past. This suggestion has the advantage that it allows us to gain better insight into the appeal of the commentarial genre for Indian philosophers, and explains why doing philosophy in a commentarial context, as the ancient Indian authors did, can proceed without falling prey to either sterility

Commentary as connecting past and present

[42] For more discussion of the notion of authorial intent with reference to Buddhist philosophical works see Garfield 2015: 322–6.

[43] See below, pp. 155–6, for further discussion.

[44] See Cox 1995: ch. 3. [45] Cox 1995: 55–6. [46] Ganeri 2011: 102.

or arbitrariness. It is a curious fact that many Indian philosophical works that could easily be conceived of as independent treatises were composed in the form of commentaries on earlier works.[47] There is a continuity of form beginning with texts that are inextricably bound up with the root text they are commenting upon (as in the case of commentaries that are primarily concerned with unpacking the grammar of a set of *sūtras*) up to commentaries that use the work commented upon as mere pegs on which to hang an independent argument.[48] Even at the latter end of this continuum the author attempts to explain his own thought through the lens of an ancient text, underlining the continuity of his thought through its connection with earlier works. The attempt here is not simply to give an exposition of the author's thought (as the example of Saṃghabhadra's commentary clearly indicates) but to explain a present philosophical position against a conceptual background inherited from the past. The text commented on is a *tool* of philosophical activity.

Commentarial activity as a creative enterprise

Conceived in this way, we can understand the Indian commentarial activity as a creative enterprise, rather than as an attempt at philosophical archaeology. Because the aim is not simply philosophical paraphrase[49] but reconceptualization of philosophical insights for a contemporary audience, the tradition escapes the sterility of repeating an inherited orthodoxy. And because such reconceptualization entails rethinking a set of philosophical positions in a systematic way, the charge of arbitrariness fails to have any traction, as it is based on the assumption (which we have now seen to be overly simplistic) that the goal of the commentarial enterprise was to rediscover the unique true meaning of the root text.

The importance of commentarial activity in the work of Indian Buddhist philosophers clearly shows the influence of the second of the three main factors mentioned above: sacred texts. Buddhist philosophy is not an intellectual enterprise that is simply driven by the desire to go wherever the argument takes it, but sees as its aim to analyse, explain, and defend the Buddha's message, and to thereby facilitate its goal to reach liberation from cyclic existence.

Buddhist philosophy as a commentary on the *sūtras*

The focus on commentarial activity provides evidence of Buddhist philosophy's linkage to the primary texts of Buddhism, the *sūtras*, those of early Buddhism and the Mahāyāna *sūtras*, as well as later texts by authors other than the historical Buddha Śākyamuni that were accorded similar authoritative status. This focus is less constraining on the development of Buddhist thought as philosophy than one might think. On the one hand it is true that its philosophical conclusions are fixed at the outset in the form of the basic

[47] See Tubb and Bose 2007: 2–3. [48] Ganeri 2011: 111.

[49] There are, of course, commentaries that have a mainly exegetical aim, but the important point to keep in mind is that exegesis is not a universal, and not even a dominant feature of philosophy conducted in the commentarial mode.

Buddhist doctrines. To this extent we would not expect individual philosophers to come up with a wholly original philosophical message. But on the other hand it is also evident that the amount of philosophical concepts even in the earliest Buddhist texts is so rich that different emphases in their explication can lead to very different philosophical accounts. The idea of a commentarial philosophical tradition as essentially sterile thus could not be further from the truth. As each commentarial enterprise interprets the text's message anew for its specific audience, the resulting philosophical explication has the potential to be as original and unique as the audience for which it is intended.

### *d. Doxographies*

Apart from root texts and the scholastic architecture of commentaries built on top of them, another important source for our understanding of ancient Indian philosophical thought are doxographic texts. Such doxographies give an overview of the views of different philosophical schools. Of course, we might say that any philosophical text that considers objections is to some extent doxographic, since it describes positions other than the ones held by the author. Yet what characterizes doxographic texts as a genre is that they do not treat rival views as one-off actual or hypothetical objections to some philosophical position, but associate them with a specific group or school of thinkers. Objections do not come on their own, so to speak, but emerge from a family background of interconnected beliefs that would give rise to precisely the kind of criticism an objector makes. A good example of the difference is provided by the *Kathāvatthu*, an Abhidharma text that consists of objections and replies to various doctrinal positions (see below, pp. 49–53 for further discussion of this text) and its commentary by Buddhaghosa.[50] The objections in the *Kathāvatthu* itself might be little more than a systematic collection of objections made to expositions of the Buddhist teachings. The commentary then identifies the objections as coming from different rival Abhidharma schools, thereby changing the reading of the text from that of an early Abhidharma Q&A to a doxographic text.

List of objections vs. doxographies

In the Indian context philosophical doxographies primarily arose from Madhyamaka Buddhism, from Jainism, and somewhat later, from Vedānta. Why the Buddhists should have been particularly concerned with doxography is an interesting question. Two answers suggest themselves right away. First, the Buddhists, like the Jains, were newcomers to the Indian philosophical scene. As such their systems lacked the foundation in Vedic texts and foundational *sūtra*s that characterized the different branches of classical Indian

Buddhist interest in doxography

[50] This commentary, the *Kathāvatthuppakaraṇa-aṭṭhakathā* (Law 1969), is of particular interest since it connects the different doctrinal positions with specific schools of early Buddhism. For further information on the works and thought of Buddhaghosa see Law 2007, Heim 2014.

philosophy. It was therefore necessary for them to underline the fact that they defended a worked-out philosophical position not shared by any of the other systems. To make a claim for its independent doctrinal status, it was important that Buddhism would not simply be understood as a variation of an extant system of Indian philosophy. Doxographical discussion allowed the Buddhists to describe how their system was unique and how it differed from other philosophical approaches.

Establishing uniqueness

Anti-substantialism

Second, we will see below that some parts of Buddhist philosophy have a strong focus on the refutation of substantialist assumptions (assumptions that phenomena exist with *svabhāva*; see pp. 107–15 for further discussion). Indeed, making such assumptions is then seen as the key source of philosophical error, and as the ultimate cause that traps us in cyclic existence. The doxographical approach presents a natural framework for demonstrating how substantialist assumptions pervade philosophical theorizing, for non-Buddhists as well as for rival Buddhist schools, and how these can be refuted.

Types of doxographies

a. Defender and interlocutors

Indian doxographical works can be divided into three main classes.[51] The first type takes the form of a dialogue between the defender of a position and one or more interlocutors who ask questions, challenging the defender to uphold his position in the light of their criticism. Here the role of the opponent or opponents is clearly subservient to that of the defender; their purpose is to bring out the defender's system in the clearest possible manner.

b. Exposition and refutation

A second type breaks up the discussion, so that the opponent (*pūrvapakṣa*) describes his position in the first section, while the second section describes the view of the proponent (*uttarapakṣa*), refuting the opponent's position. While this second type still describes the different philosophical schools in such a way that one comes out as the single correct one, they present the opponent with an opportunity to describe his own system in a connected manner, rather than in a way that simply provides a set of cues for the proponent's discussion of his position.

c. Non-hierarchical presentation

The third type, finally, simply sets out the teachings of the different schools without defending the superiority of any one of them over the rest.

Example of b: Bhāviveka

A key example of the second type of doxography is Bhāviveka's *Madhyamakahṛdayakārikā*, together with its auto-commentary.[52] After three chapters

[51] Following Qvarnström 1999: 174.

[52] The beginnings of Buddhist doxography may be seen already in texts such as the *Sāmaññaphalasutta* of the Dīghanikāya and the *Apaṇṇakasutta* of the Majjhimanikāya, as well as in the *Brahmajālasutta* and *Sūtrakṛtāṅgasūtra* with their lists of 62 or 363 views (*dṛṣṭi*). Other Indian doxographical works include Āryadeva's **Skhalitapramathanayuktihetusiddhi* (*khrul pa bzlog pa'i rigs pa gtan tshigs grub pa*) and the second chapter of Bhāviveka's *Madhyamakaratnapradīpa*. In his *Pramāṇasamuccaya* Diṅnāga mentions 'investigations' (*parīkṣā*) of the Nyāya, Vaiśeṣika, and Sāṃkhya system he composed (Hattori 1968: 9; Eckel 2008: 20); unfortunately these works appear to be lost. The Indic tradition of doxography was later continued in Tibetan scholasticism, though it was there confined primarily to differentiating various Buddhist schools.

that describe his own philosophical position, Bhāviveka then spends the next six chapters discussing the views of two rival Buddhist schools, the Śrāvakas and the Yogācāras, followed by an account of four non-Buddhist philosophical systems, Sāṃkhya, Vaiśeṣika, Vedānta, and Mīmāṃsā.

Note that the order of presentation in this (and other) Indian doxographical texts is not historical. The authors of doxographical works were not interested in tracing the development of philosophical schools, beginning with the earliest thinkers and discussing how their thoughts were transformed and expanded in later times. Although this work by Bhāviveka is not the clearest example, it shows how doxographies of this type tend to group systems according to a hierarchy of conceptual sophistication, with the 'worst' views (those regarded to be furthest away from the position that the doxography advocates) discussed first. The order of the discussion of the Śrāvaka and the Yogācāra positions is an indication of this. The Madhyamaka point of view sees the former, with its postulation of material substances, to be further removed from the correct position than the Yogācāra idealism, which is then regarded as a stepping-stone to the correct view of the Middle Way. Hence the Abhidharma position is discussed first, followed by Yogācāra. In a similar manner, the *Sarvadarśaṇa-samgraha*,[53] a fourteenth-century doxography by Mādhava written from the Vedānta perspective, begins with a discussion of the materialist Cārvāka system as the least sophisticated philosophical approach, followed by a discussion of the Buddhist position,[54] working its way through different schools of classical Indian philosophy like Vaiśeṣika, Nyāya, Sāṃkhya, and Yoga, to culminate in a description of the Vedānta point of view.

Doxographic hierarchy

The paradigm example of the third type of doxography is the *Ṣaḍḍarśanasamuccaya*, composed by the Jaina monk Haribhadra (*c.*8th century CE). Haribhadra describes six main doctrines, distinguished by their founder or associated deity (*devatā*): the Buddhists, and the doctrines of Nyāya, Sāṃkhya, Vaiśeṣika, Jainism, and Pūrvamīmāṃsā.[55] Unlike examples of the second kind, Haribhadra's doxography does not present the rival views in order to refute them, but describes the six doctrines without arguing for the superiority of any one. This may be seen as a manifestation of the Jaina 'doctrine of manifold aspects' (*anekāntavāda*), resulting in the view that all the different philosophical discussions contain important insights that help us

Example of c: Haribhadra

[53] Cowell and Gough et al. 2006.

[54] Ranking the Buddhist position as the 'second worst theory' might strike us as curious, given frequent perceptions of Buddhism and Vedānta as closely similar or even identical philosophical systems. (See Ingalls 1954; Nakamura 1983: 131–265; Qvarnström 1989: 101–4; 1999: 175–6.) Yet this perception would have provided *additional* motivation for the Vedāntin to stress the doctrinal difference of his teaching from that of the Buddhists, in order to show that his theory was not simply an offshoot of Buddhism, but an independent account in its own right.

[55] For further discussion see Qvarnström 1999.

to approach liberation. Basing a choice of a specific philosophical system simply on its originator is therefore unhelpful. Haribhadra points out that:

> I have no predilection for Mahāvīra, nor do I hate Kapila, etc. What one must do is to embrace one whose words are *reasonable*. He who has no fault at all, he who has all good virtues—to him I pay homage—be it Brahma, Viṣṇu or Maheśvara![56]

Doxography and soteriology

This attitude justifies the composition of doxographies not simply in a negative manner, as a foil to offset and better explain one's own view, but as an integral part of philosophical methodology: if the aim of philosophical investigation is soteriological, and if different systems of thought contain soteriologically efficacious elements, then the study of doxography forms part of the path to liberation.

## 6. The Game's View of the Game

The account of the history of Indian Buddhist philosophy given here is presented from our own twenty-first-century Western perspective. Like any perspective, it does not present a neutral view of phenomena but comes with a set of fixed assumptions. While such assumptions are an inevitable characteristic of any perspective, problems may arise when these assumptions of the narration clash with some of those of the tradition being narrated. This, I want to argue, is the case in the contemporary historiography of Buddhist thought, and this clash presents a problem that is not discussed sufficiently often or with sufficient clarity. While the solution cannot be to throw out the conflicting assumptions that form part of our perspective (since without them it is unlikely to be the perspective it is), it is important to be at least aware of the existence of this clash in order to be able to find a suitable way of working with it.

Conflicting assumptions about the existence of the past

The 'clash' I have been referring to here concerns diverging assumptions about the existence of the past. These are assumptions that indicate where the perspectives of the modern historian of philosophy and those of the ancient philosophers studied conflict at a fundamental level.

Maxim of charity

On the one hand we want to adopt the maxim of charity relative to the ancient Indian sources we are studying. This means that we want to minimize the number of false beliefs we attribute to these materials, when in doubt try to interpret them on the assumption that what they say is justified, and be suspicious of any interpretations that leave the position in question open to simple yet devastating objections. However, when it comes to considering the

[56] *Lokatattvanirṇaya* 1: 38: *pakṣapāto na me vīre na dveṣaḥ kapilādiṣu | yuktimad vacanaṃ yasya tasya kāryaḥ parigrahaḥ || yasya nikhilāś ca doṣa na santi sarve guṇāś ca vidyante | brahma na viṣṇur vā maheṣvaro vā namas tasmai*, Qvarnström 1999: 180, 188.

Buddhists' account of their own history this assumption of charity does not seem to extend very far.

Nāgārjuna's lifespan

Consider two simple examples. First, traditional Indian and Tibetan histories of Buddhism ascribe to Nāgārjuna an extraordinary long lifespan of several centuries. The modern historian is likely to disregard this as a hagiographical falsification with the aim of accounting for the fact that we have various texts from authors called 'Nāgārjuna' that were composed several centuries apart. According to the traditional histories these were all written by the same person, for he lived for a very long period of time. Second, we also find traditional sources claiming that Nāgārjuna taught at Nālandā University, though our best archaeological evidence suggests that Nālandā was only founded several centuries after the most plausible date for Nāgārjuna. Buddhist historians appear to try to construct a fictitious lineage of a 'Nālandā tradition' that associates most of the major Buddhist philosophers of ancient India with a single educational institution.[57] It thus appears that the modern historian of Buddhist philosophy has to be able to cut through the overgrowth of fabricated agenda-driven history expounded in traditional historical accounts in order to get to the real historical facts behind them.

The Nālandā tradition

'the way it really was'

The difficulty with this approach is not simply that it treats traditional Buddhist historians (rather uncharitably) as either fraudulent or gullible, but that its central underlying assumption, the idea of a set of historical events 'as it really was', contradicts some of the basic ideas that feature prominently within the history of Buddhist thought.

Canon formation

We can get a first idea of the problem at issue by considering the history of Buddhist canon formation. Since the early history of Buddhism, Buddhists have wondered which texts should be considered as the Buddha's words (*buddhavacana*) and therefore as immediately authoritative, and which texts should only be considered as authoritative in a more restricted way. From a contemporary perspective of historical realism we might want to say that all or most of the instances of speech uttered by the historical Buddha in the fifty or so years between his enlightenment and his death should be considered as the true and only *buddhavacana*.[58] But as Matthew Kapstein rightly observed:

[57] For a contemporary take on the 'Nālandā tradition' see Geshe Ngawang Samten 2011. Walser 2005: 78 notes that 'Nāgārjuna's associations with Nālandā are confined to Tibetan Buddhist sources that are concerned with placing him in the transmission lineage for the *Guhyasamājatantra*, a text that was important in the curriculum at Nālandā.' The place of Nāgārjuna and other Madhyamaka masters in the 'Noble Lineage' of the transmission of the *Guhyasamājatantra* is in fact a complex issue that raises numerous historiographical and philosophical concerns. We have more to say on this issue in our discussion of Candrakīrti below, on pp. 137–8.

[58] The question how we can know what the Buddha really said is bracketed here. I am concerned with the ontological point of what the Buddha's teaching could be said to be, rather than with the epistemological question of how we can subsequently reconstruct its contents.

there is no evidence to suggest, however, that anyone within the Buddhist tradition ever actually held such a rigid position; the view must be softened in order to admit into the class of *buddhavacana* not the spatiotemporally determinate speech acts of Śākyamuni alone...[59]

And indeed, such a 'softening' is what we find in the Buddhist discussions. In the *Mahāparinibbānasutta* we find the enumeration of a set of four 'great authorities' (*mahāpadeśa*) to be appealed to in the process of determining whether some teaching is really the word of the Buddha.[60] These four authorities are the Buddha, the community of senior monks, a smaller community of elder learned monks, and a single learned monk. If someone claims to have heard a teaching from any of these four, the monastic community should then investigate whether this teaching corresponds to those of the *sūtras* and the *vinaya*, the monastic code for monks and nuns. We also sometimes find an additional criterion of authenticity, namely that the teaching should correspond to the way things are (*dharmatā*).

4 criteria for authenticity

It is clear that agreement with *sūtra*s and *vinaya* is the criterion with the greatest practical role to play. Reference to the four great authorities is primarily an entry criterion for teachings to be evaluated in this way, and judgments about their correspondence to 'the way things are' are hindered by the fact that for Buddhists any comprehensive reference to the way things are needs to be determined by reference to the Buddha's teaching. We therefore see that the key membership criterion for being *buddhavacana* is not the 'hard' criterion of being expressed by a theoretically dateable utterance of the historical Buddha, but the 'softened' one of being a teaching that in a suitable sense 'says the same thing' as the Buddha's other teachings. This turns the question of what texts count as canonical from a historical to a hermeneutic one. Instead of utterance-tokens we are now concerned with what texts (when properly understood) mean the same. And we might have wanted to leave matters at that, combining a strict understanding of the Buddha's word as historical utterances with an extended conception that also includes other teachings from different historical contexts that agree with the message of the former. However, what we find in the Buddhist case is the merging of the hermeneutical *buddhavacana* with the historical *buddhavacana*. A Mahāyāna text, the *Adhyāśayasañcodanasūtra*, points out that 'All which is well-spoken, Maitreya, is spoken by the Buddha.'[61] This conception, which can be found frequently in Mahāyāna texts,[62] is helpfully summarized by Matthew Kapstein:

Historical and hermeneutic understanding of *buddhavacana*

[59] Kapstein 2000: 124. [60] Bikkhu Anālayo 2014: 73.

[61] 'Well-spoken' (*subhāṣita*) refers here to meaningful statements that lead to the removal of defilements and propound the benefits of nirvāṇa.

[62] Bhāviveka (Eckel 2008: 61) even notes that 'everything that is well spoken in the Vedānta is taught by the Buddha' (*vedānte ca hi yat sūktaṃ tat sarvaṃ buddhabhāṣitam*).

Indeed, a realist reading of the relevant texts places in high relief the conclusion that, though it may seem strange to certain modern sensibilities, figured prominently in Mahāyāna attitudes to scripture throughout Central and East Asia right down to the present day: any text meeting the normative doctrinal criteria for *buddhavacana* must be genuine *buddhavacana* taught by the historical Buddha Śākyamuni himself.[63]

Once that move is made, however, contemporary realist understandings of history have already been left far behind. What drives the Buddhist conception of what has happened when the Buddha taught the *dharma* is not what series of dateable events took place, but what must have been taught by him, given that the contents of the *dharma* properly understood were comprehensively presented. Moreover, the realist conceptions of the past that drive our common understanding of history also do not sit well with a variety of philosophical positions we find defended in Buddhism.

Buddhist philosophy and the existence of the past

The first of these ideas is presentism, the view that only the present moment is real, espoused by the Sautrāntika branch of the Abhidharma. If we accept this position, there is obviously no past (or future), and all that history can amount to is a theory based on traces the past left on the present. There can be mutually inconsistent theories that fit all the facts, and there are no facts about the past to validate one of these theories to the exclusion of all the others. According to this view, the past 'as it really was' is a non-existent object.

1. Presentism

Yet even if we accept that past and future do exist, and are distinguished from the present merely by their lacking efficacy, as the Sarvāstivāda Abhidharma did, this would hardly be sufficient to supply us with a series of historical events in their pure form. For what there really is (or was, or will be), according to these Abhidharma theories, is a complex interaction of fundamental, momentary mental and physical entities, the *dharma*s. The world as we experience it, and the world of the past we would be appealing to in the context of confirming historical claims, is only the highest level of a set of conceptual overlays that are superimposed on the underlying reality.

The past as a conceptual superimposition

This brings us to the second idea, more prominently expressed in later Buddhist texts: the view that there is no uniform object of perception for all observers, even in the present. It is vividly and memorably expressed in an episode of Buddhist traditional history, that of the meeting of Asaṅga with the bodhisattva Maitreya. When Maitreya finally appears to Asaṅga after years of propitiation, he tells him that he has in fact always been by his side, but that Asaṅga's perception was too impure to see him. Asaṅga is sceptical, and Maitreya suggests testing his claim by having Asaṅga carry him around town on his back. And indeed, the story continues, what various people saw in place of Maitreya varied with the purity of their perceptual faculties. Nobody saw the

2. Absence of a common perception of the world

[63] Kapstein 2000: 125.

whole Maitreya, most saw nothing at all, some saw Asaṅga carrying an old dog on his shoulders, and only one (a prostitute, according to one rendition of the story) was able to see Maitreya's feet. This story is obviously making a philosophical point, a point that is elsewhere expressed with respect to traditional Buddhist cosmology by the simile of the three cups of liquid. Where human beings see a cup of water, it is argued, beings reborn in the realm of hungry ghosts see a cup of pus, blood, or similarly unclean substances, while beings in the hell realm see a cup of molten metal. The exact philosophical impact of this example has been subject to a considerable amount of debate, but the central point is clear. When considering beings that inhabit some of the realms of cyclic existence (such as ourselves), the reality we experience is at most partly determined by a mind-independent reality, and is heavily influenced by our perceptual and cognitive setup, which is in turn a result of our karma. What this means is that we cannot expect there to be a shared reality at the experiential level even within a given realm, such as the human one, since beings at different levels of realization may have more or less 'purified' perceptual capacities (as is evident from the story of Asaṅga). If the present is therefore considered so highly dependent on intersubjective, but not objective, factors, such as the shared karmic potential of groups of observers, it is not surprising that Buddhist authors adopted similar views about the past. Providing a historical account of some event could not simply consist in a record of 'what really happened' but had to take into account the perceptive capacities of the beings who perceived the event, and presumably also those of the presumed recipients of the account.

Perception depends on karmic conditioning

While the two philosophical positions just described are the subject of considerable internal debate within the Buddhist tradition (the first primarily in the intra-Abhidharmic discussion between Sarvāstivādins and Sautrāntikas, the latter in connection with Yogācāra), and are defended by various arguments, the following two philosophical points, though equally important for developing a nuanced account of the Buddhist conception of history, are of a somewhat different nature. Even though the positions in question are stated quite explicitly, it is difficult to find direct arguments backing them up in traditional Buddhist accounts. The reason for this may be that they appeared sufficiently obvious to Buddhists at the time, or that they directly followed from other equally obvious assumptions (such as those concerning the supernatural powers of enlightened beings). As our aim here is first and foremost to come up with a plausible account of what the Buddhist account of history (and specifically of the history of Buddhism) amounts to, rather than to defend its truth, the question of how the following two positions may be supported by philosophical arguments is not one that we have to settle here.

3. Trans-historical activities

One aspect of traditional Buddhist history that may appear particularly challenging to the contemporary historian is the apparent ease with which the activities of different figures seem to cross several centuries. One explanation that is sometimes offered for this is the extraordinarily long lifespans of some Buddhist teachers, often connected with claims about their mastery of life-extending alchemical practices. Another possible way of accounting for this, and one that is probably even less palatable to modern Buddhist historians than the idea of Ancient Indian elixirs of eternal life, is to argue that enlightened beings can assume immaterial mystical forms which allow them to manifest at times after their disappearance from this world of dust. The Tibetan historian Tāranātha (1575–1634) uses this idea to explain the existence of tantric works probably composed towards the end of the first millennium CE by Madhyamaka masters that lived in the first or second century.[64] He argues that by assuming such forms these masters could actually compose the given treatises at a later time, and then teach them to disciples living at that time, disciples that would not have been born when they disappeared in their physical form. Another example of an account of a historical figure being instructed by an enlightened being without a material body is the case of Asaṅga and the teachings he received from the bodhisattva Maitreya we have discussed before. These cases are of course very difficult to account for if we consider history (and, more specifically, philosophical history) as being composed solely of the interactions of human agents. But as the sources make abundantly clear, this is not the Buddhist understanding of history.

Mystical manifestations of teachers

The history of Buddhist philosophy is intricately connected with the life of Buddhist teachers, that of the Buddha as well as those of the monks, saints, and sages that came after him. Buddhists texts sometimes mention the idea that in the case of these teachers there is no real difference between the facts of their lives (the events that happened to them) and their teaching activity (the propagation of the Buddha's teaching they caused to happen). The contemporary Tibetan Buddhist teacher Dilgo Khyentse Rinpoche says the following about one of the most important Indian Buddhist masters introducing Buddhism to Tibet:

4. History as teaching

Examples from Tibetan authors

> Guru Padmasambhava, the glorious Master of Uddiyana and king of the Dharma, is the single embodiment of the activities of the Victorious Ones throughout the three times. According to the ways in which sentient beings perceive reality, there exists an inconceivable number of life stories of the three mysteries of his body, speech, and mind.[65]

Connecting with the point just made about the absence of a shared perceived world for beings with different karmic potentials, this stresses that the lives of Buddhist masters are conceived not as lived events they undergo, but as

[64] Wedemeyer 2007: 20. Tāranātha refers to these master as assuming the form of a *vidyādhara* (*rig pa 'dzin pa*), 'knowledge-holder' for these purposes.

[65] Foreword by Dilgo Khyentse Rinpoche, Ye shes mtsho rgyal (1993: 1).

teachings they manifest for the sake of instructing other beings. The same point is made by Tāranātha in his biography of the Buddha,[66] when he comments on the difference between the accounts of the Buddha's life found in the early Buddhist scriptures compared to those of the Mahāyāna. David Ruegg summarizes Tāranātha's conclusions as follows:

> [T]he Buddha's action manifested in common for all those living nearby at that time and possessed of the necessary qualifications—including even those who had erroneous views, Tīrthikas, and also animals—relates to the system of the common Yāna, or to the Śrāvaka system. As to the manner in which his activity was manifested to those persons to be trained specifically by the Mahāyāna in particular, this is recounted in the Mahāyāna-Sūtras. Therefore, in general, there are various versions concerning these matters; and there is in particular a great difference with respect to the greater or smaller amount of blessing in each case. Consequently, although the two systems are not substantially contradictory, it is necessary not to mix the two ways of relating the Buddha's life. Of these two systems that Mahāyānist system is much more elaborate, it belongs to the realm of inconceivable wisdom, it is accessible to the best disciples, and it concerns highly secret action. Nevertheless, the events in the Buddha's life as commonly known to all beings, the length of his life, the order of events in it, the places he visited and so forth relate to the common system; but they are not the Mahāyānist system since its scope is inconceivable, for in it it is difficult to determine a matter as having been exactly so and so with regard to place, time, and action.[67]

The key point Tāranātha makes is that the acts of the Buddha as described in the Mahāyāna texts are actions manifested for a specific audience, with specific karmic potentials, while those described in the early Buddhist texts have been manifested for a different group of disciples. This makes it difficult to account for the lives of Buddhist masters against the background of familiar historical realism,[68] as the fifth Dalai Lama pointed out, again with reference to Padmasambhava:

> You make manifest transformations befitting each creature's vision,
> Changing æons into moments, and moments into æons;
> Laughable, then, to calculate the months and years
> As if your life were that of a common pandit or siddha![69]

Accounting for different versions of the same events

The challenge of the Buddhist historiographer is not just to account for various miraculous events in the life-stories of Buddhist masters, but, more specifically,

[66] *bcom ldan 'das thub pa'i dbang po'i mdzad pa mdo tsam brjod pa mthong bas don ldan sogs.*

[67] Ngawang Gelek Demo 1971: 2–3.

[68] Conze (1962: 232) notes that, '[u]nlike official Christianity Buddhism is not a historical religion, and its message is valid independent of the historicity of any event in the life of the "founder", who did not found anything, but merely transmitted a Dharma pre-existing him since eternity'.

[69] In his colophon of the 1755 Beijing edition of the *Padma bka' thang* of O rgyan gling pa; see Kapstein 2015: 12.

to account for different versions of the same set of events. Traditional accounts solve this problem by combining three ideas: that of a view of reality that is crucially influenced by the karmic potential of different beings, that of history as teaching, and that of a succession of graded teachings.[70] A well-known explanatory device to account for teachings of the Buddha that seem to contradict each other is to point out that these were teachings given to different audiences, audiences which consisted of listeners with different potentials for understanding and with different background assumptions.[71] As the Buddha tailored his teaching to the respective audience, so a realized master could tailor the events of his life, which are in fact nothing but teachings as well, to fit the audience experiencing them.

Avoidance of relativism

It is important to note, however, that this departure from a historical realist stance that postulates that there can only have been a single way things happened, which history should set out to record, does not entail that the Buddhist historians embraced a thoroughgoing relativism according to which any account is as good as any other. Tāranātha, for example, notes right at the beginning of his history of Buddhism in India that earlier accounts of the early history of the *dharma* contained numerous faults, and that his work sets out to eliminate the defects of these previous histories.[72] This is, of course, very much in keeping with a general concern in Buddhist thought of trying to ensure that any criticism of ultimate reality (be this a theory of fundamentally real objects, or a view of the existence of an objectively real past) does not affect our ability to make assertions at the conventional level. That the realist account must be rejected does not entail that we cannot make a reasonable choice between various non-realist accounts.

Tension between charity and naturalism

The preceding remarks show that the maxim of charity leaves us in a curious position with respect to the historiography of Buddhist philosophy. The maxim of charity suggests that we should maximize the rationality of the texts in question and proceed from the assumptions that the arguments the authors of the text presented are defensible. In doing so, we will then also reason from the premise that many, or indeed most, of their conclusions were defensible. As I have argued above, some of their central conclusions have important implications for how the

[70] See Westerhoff 2009: 89–90.

[71] In commenting on verse 30 of Nāgārjuna's *Yuktiṣaṣṭikā*, Candrakīrti explains: 'When you introduce beings who are intellectually uneducated to the view of reality—emptiness—they become utterly confused. Consequently, the noble do not teach them emptiness right at first. Those who are seeking truth motivated by their habitual self-preoccupation tend to be attached to things, so first you must teach them that "everything exists", and then correctly describe [for them] the objects of their desire, since they delight in analyzing the natures of those things.' Loizzo 2007: 180–1.

[72] Chimpa and Chattopadhyaya 1970: 5, 350. See also 187–8, where Tāranātha dismisses views of Madhyamaka chronology according to which Buddhapālita was reborn as Candrakīrti, and Bhāviveka was a direct disciple of Nāgārjuna. He says that such views are 'irrational and groundless' and ask 'how can a person with a critical faculty believe all these?'

past in general, and the history of Buddhist philosophy specifically, are to be understood. Yet these consequences stand in direct conflict with the assumptions of twenty-first-century century naturalism that usually operate in the background when writing the history of Buddhist philosophy. At this stage we seem to be faced with two similarly unappealing options. The first is to drop the naturalist assumptions, the second to assume that some of the key premises the Buddhist philosophers argued from are false, and that the conclusions based on these are mistaken. The first appears to deprive us of some crucial conceptual tools we successfully employ for thinking about the world; the second deprives the study of the history of Buddhist thought as it is presented by the scholars of ancient India of much of its systematic value, since significant parts of the conclusions argued for cannot be rationally defended.

Bracketing naturalist assumptions

I suggest addressing this problem not by giving up the maxim of charity, nor by relinquishing the conceptual framework in which we are presently operating (an attempt that is likely to be doomed from the very beginning), but by momentarily bracketing some of the naturalist assumptions we hold. What this means is that when our views of the world conflict with claims that are relevant for developing an account of the history of Buddhism (such as claims about maximal human lifespans, the objective existence of the past, and so on), we temporarily suspend those views in order to find out how far we can go in our analysis without appealing to them.

By doing so, and by taking into account the ideas about historiography developed by Buddhist writers themselves, it becomes apparent that neither disregarding traditional historical records concerning matters such as Nāgārjuna's lifespan or the members of the 'Nālandā tradition' nor considering them as convenient historical fabrications allows us to address the full complexity of the matter.

Soteriological purpose of histories of Buddhism

The purpose of histories of Buddhism as we find them within the Buddhist tradition is neither exclusively nor dominantly to serve as a report of facts about the past; they rather fulfil a soteriological purpose. There are various reasons for this.

A given description of events may be considered as showing how events had appeared to witnesses with sufficiently purified perception. As such, the Buddhist historian would not be greatly worried by our own lack of historical evidence to support such claims; in fact he might argue that even if we (in our present state, with our present karmic propensities) had been there we would not have seen what other observers with less deluded cognitive faculties would have seen. One of the aims of the historical narrative would then be to acquaint the listener with how events appear to purified perception in order to act as an incentive to produce this kind of perception in oneself.

Alternatively, a historical account could be conceived as a manifestation of *upāya*, of skilful means: matters are related in a certain way not because this is the way things happened as observed from an objective stance, but because describing them in this way is conducive to the liberation of those who hear the account.

Taking into account this soteriological dimension of the history of Buddhism has the consequence that we will not simply try to purge traditional Buddhist historical narratives of all elements that appear to contradict the twenty-first-century Western naturalistic view of the world, and then attempt to extract whatever kernels of fact might be present in the remainder. Instead, bracketing some parts of this view allows us to inquire why a historical narrative is presented in the way it is,[73] why one would want to assume that the world appears in this way to one who has undergone an extensive amount of mind-training as described in the Buddhist texts, or why one would consider that composing a narrative in this specific way creates the kind of mental attitude that is conducive to liberation.

If we consider the case of Nāgārjuna again, the idea of the continuity of the 'Nālandā tradition' to which all the major Indian Buddhist philosophers belonged can be understood to signify the unity of the Buddhist philosophical project and the idea that the various systems proposed by these philosophers are all elaborations of the same central message. The elements in Nāgārjuna's biography which relate to his long lifespan have to be understood in the context of tantric techniques which are considered to make such lifespans possible, and which are in turn based on conceptions of the body very different from the ones familiar in contemporary Western anatomy.

It is important not to regard these narratives as simply an attempt at *post facto* lineage-building of later authors, or as advertisements for the efficacy of tantric techniques, but to keep in mind that many Buddhist writers themselves would have believed that the world as described in these narratives appears in this way to some beings with purified perceptions, and that mental qualities conducive to liberation could be produced by following the examples set out in these accounts. It is theoretically unsatisfactory to regard these accounts as later pious fabrications, or as driven by obvious religious or political agendas in a way that obscures what really happened, simply because Buddhist thinkers have significant objections to the assumption that there is such a thing as the past as it really happened. The assumption of the objective existence of the past is not a claim that is open to empirical confirmation, it is a theoretical posit that historians may or may not avail themselves of, and a philosophical thesis that can be supported by arguments or undermined by them. The Buddhist

Existence of the past as a theoretical posit

[73] In the Tibetan perspectives, hagiographies (*rnam thar*) are understood not simply in a descriptive but also in a normative manner: they are handbooks for how the practitioner on the way to liberation should progress along the Buddhist path: 'The *rnam thar* is a personal message of inspiration about how to live that is sent from the founder of the lineage or *brgyud* of practice down through the centuries to each generation of students' (Chodrung-ma Kunga Chodron 2013: 19).

philosophers were convinced that their arguments provide a successful criticism of it. This constitutes a difference between the Buddhist case and many other instances where we might be tempted to 'uncover the facts behind the myth' or the historical basis of a religious narrative. While in these cases the idea of an objective past is usually not questioned, in the Buddhist case it is. For this reason, we risk failing to understand important aspects of the tradition if we simply import the assumption of the objectivity of the past (as intuitive as it may seem to us) with the conviction that this is as self-evident as it is irrefutable.

# 1

# Abhidharma

## 1. Introducing the Abhidharma

'Begin at the beginning,' the King of Hearts famously said to the White Rabbit, 'and go on till you come to the end: then stop.' Our account of Buddhist thought in India will do neither. First, even though Buddhism continued to develop in India up to the destruction of the great monastic universities in the twelfth century, a caesura sufficiently significant to identify it with the end of the Indian Buddhist scholastic tradition,[1] the majority of our account will focus on thinkers before the time of Dharmakīrti (6th–7th century CE), with not much more than a cursory glance at some of the thinkers from the five to six centuries after him. This is not because the period after Dharmakīrti is of less philosophical interest,[2] but due to reasons of space; the last half-millennium of Buddhist thought in India deserves a volume of its own.

Nor will we begin at the very beginning, with the enlightenment of the historical Buddha Śākyamuni, the event that marks the source from which two-and-a-half millennia of Buddhist thinking flow. The Buddha's enlightenment marks the beginning of his life as a teacher, producing the set of discourses or *sūtras* that constitute the first division, or 'basket', of the Buddhist canon. The second basket, the *vinaya*, consists of the rules and regulations for the monastic order that the Buddha founded, together with a detailed description of the specific situation that gave rise to the introduction of each rule.[3] As such, the *vinaya* is a rich mine of historical information about the living conditions of the monastic orders of monks and nuns in particular, and about Indian society at the time of the Buddha more generally.

Abhidharma: the 3rd basket

It is with the third and final basket, the collection of Abhidharma texts, that we begin our account of how Buddhist thought in India developed. The Abhidharma texts are fundamentally an attempt to systematize, and

[1] Even though Buddhism did not subsequently disappear completely from the Indian subcontinent (the Italian missionary Roberto de Nobili, for example, found Buddhists amongst the Tamils at the beginning of the 17th century (Rajamanickam 1972)), Buddhist scholastic philosophy in India did not survive the destruction of the great centres of learning like Nālandā and Vikramaśīla.

[2] Though some Buddhist historians thought so—see Chimpa and Chattopadhyaya 1970: 255–6.

[3] For a good survey of the *vinaya* literature see Prebish 1994.

systematically expand, the Buddha's teachings as they are recorded in his discourses. Taking into account the way the Buddha taught, the need for such systematization is evident. During the fifty years between his enlightenment and his death the Buddha taught a large number of discourses, all of which were tailored to the capacities and background assumptions of their respective audiences. As such they inevitably contained repetitions, topics that were only very sketchily presented in some discourses but in much more detail in others, and points where there seemed to be tensions or contradictions between different discourses. The aim of the Abhidharma was to proceed from the series of audience-relative expositions that constitute the *sūtra*s to a comprehensive and systematic account of the Buddha's teachings. In doing so a process of carefully examining arguments, systematizing doctrinal positions, providing commentaries on obscure passages, and countering hypothetical and actual objections was set in motion that would characterize all of the subsequent Buddhist philosophical activity in India.

Systematizing the *sūtras*

The term 'abhidharma'

Before considering the contents of the Abhidharma texts, let us briefly look at the term '*abhidharma*'. It consists of the prefix *abhi* and the noun *dharma*. Depending on how the prefix is understood, there are two different ways of interpreting the term compounded in this way. *Abhi* can just mean 'about', or 'with regard to', in which case the Abhidharma is the teaching that has the *dharma* (the teaching the Buddha expounded in the *sūtras*) as its object—it is teaching about the *dharma*. Alternatively, *abhi* can have the meaning of 'higher'; in this case the Abhidharma would be a teaching higher or going beyond the *dharma*. One way in which the Abhidharma could go beyond the teaching of the *sūtra*s is in terms of comprehensiveness. In the Pāli commentarial tradition we find the idea that *sūtra*s explain the main concepts of Buddhist thought only in part (*ekadesen' eva*, presumably restricted to that part that was necessary for the audience in the specific situation in which the *sūtra* was taught), while the Abhidharma explains them in full.[4]

Motives for composing the Abhidharma

The Abhidharma texts differ considerably from the other two baskets, the discourses and the monastic rules. Given this difference, we might wonder what motivated the composition of the Abhidharma texts, and how they might have been influenced by these other kinds of texts. We can distinguish at least three possible motivations for the composition of the Abhidharma: to provide an expansion of matrices (*mātṛkā*); to expand texts composed in a question-and-answer format; and to develop a comprehensive ontological theory.

[4] Ronkin 2005: 26. Interestingly we also find a differentiation of the teachings of the *sūtra*s and Abhidharma insofar as the former is sometimes described as merely a 'way of putting things' (*pariyāya-desanā*), while the latter does not require further explication (*nipparyāya-desāna*), an understanding that coheres well with the idea that the Abhidharma framework describes how matters are at the level of ultimate truth.

## *a. Matrices*

The term *mātṛkā* (etymologically related both to the term 'matrix' and the term 'mother') denotes lists of terms and topics found in the *sūtras*. In the beginning these matrices were quite simple, comprising lists such as the four levels of meditative states (*jhāna*), the five aggregates (*skandha*), the six sense bases (*ṣaḍāyatana*), the eighteen elements of cognition (*dhātu*), and so on. Their function as mnemonic devices was obvious. The formation of such lists helped to keep distinct parts of a discourse in memory as a single unity. In their further elaboration these lists became extremely complex and comprehensive, and they are frequently regarded as the nucleus of the Abhidharma,[5] which is in fact sometimes referred to as the *mātṛkāpiṭaka*, the basket of matrices. The Abhidharma could therefore be understood as a project that spells out the matrices already provided in the *sūtras*, in order to produce a comprehensive account of the Buddhist conception of the structure of the world, and the structure of the path in this world that would lead to liberation.

Matrices as mnemonic devices

A further motivation to develop the matrices in the way the Abhidharma did may be found in the meditative practice of early Buddhism. Even though meditation is a private, introspective enterprise, the observations made and the results achieved are supposed to be intersubjectively communicable. The meditator is not shut up in a world of private experience, but can relate the phenomena he encounters with observations made by meditators who have employed the same kinds of techniques before him. In order to do so he needs to be equipped with a map that gives an account of all the mental phenomena he is likely to encounter, the way they are related to each other, and the way they are related to the path of liberation. The elaborate lists of the Abhidharma provide such a map, a map that makes it possible to traverse the world of internal experience without becoming lost in a chaos of incommunicable mental events.[6] At the same time, the existence of such matrices generates a feedback loop between knowledge and awareness: by knowing which mental phenomena to look for, one will distinguish more of them, thus increasing the detail of the matrix, leading to yet finer distinctions, and so on.

Matrices as maps of meditative states

Despite these obvious connections between the matrices and the Abhidharma, it is questionable to what extent the matrices were associated with the Abhidharma alone. The Pāli commentarial tradition, for example, associates them specifically with the *vinaya*.[7] When mentioned in connection with the *vinaya* they also play the role of digests of longer texts; some monk may not be

[5] For a comprehensive list of modern scholars discussing the connection between the Abhidharma and the matrices see Bhikkhu Anālayo 2014: 22, n. 26.

[6] See Ronkin 2005: 29–30 and ch. 4; Gethin 1992: 165.

[7] Bhikkhu Anālayo 2014: 22–4.

able to recite the *vinaya* but still be able to recite its matrix.[8] It is therefore sensible to regard the matrices (and the fondness for lists in Indian philosophy more generally) as first and foremost a characteristic feature of an oral culture.[9] By structuring topics that are discussed in different places and by providing concise versions of longer texts, they facilitated the retention of the material without the need for written versions. Matrices should therefore be considered as a general background of the Abhidharma tradition, rather than the single nucleus that gave rise to it.

Matrices and oral culture

### *b. Question-and-answer format*

A second motivation for the composition of the Abhidharma may be seen in an expansion of texts composed in a catechetical style of questions and answers. Such texts may be considered to have their natural precedent in discussions between Buddhist and non-Buddhist schools.[10] In this case the questions would consist of the opponent's challenges to the Buddhist theory, and the replies would provide the Buddhist response.[11] While this format may have originally been used to provide sample answers to questions a Buddhist monk might actually face when debating with his brahmanical opponents, the framework can easily be expanded beyond this immediate practical use. Question-and-answer formats can also be used to discuss purely hypothetical replies. On the one hand these may be useful for training in debate, but on the other hand such questions would allow the student to develop a deeper understanding of the material independent of the debate context. In this case questions could function as a set of problems or exercises, challenging the student to come to an understanding of a complex body of material by attempting to produce answers of a similar quality as those provided in the text. The Abhidharma texts may therefore have been motivated by the desire to provide a tool for presenting the whole of the Buddhist doctrine in outline form by adopting the framework of earlier texts composed in question-and-answer form. Nevertheless, we should note that, as in the case of the matrices, the question-and-answer format is not a unique characteristic of the Abhidharma literature. Texts dealing with the *vinaya* and with other matters have been composed in this format,[12] and there is no reason why it is in any way specifically connected with the kind of topics the Abhidharma discusses.

Q&A and debate

Q&A as an aid to understanding

[8] But see Ronkin 2005: 27–8 for an alternative interpretation. She argues that the term *mātikā* in this context did not denote a kind of digest, but 'a set of key words' elaborated in the exposition of the teaching.

[9] Bhikkhu Anālayo 2014: 24–5.

[10] Ronkin 2005: 30.

[11] See the *Mahā-/Cūḷavedallasuttas* and the division of the *Vibhaṅgasuttas* of the Majjhimanikāya for examples of early *suttas* incorporating this question-and-answer format.

[12] Bhikkhu Anālayo 2014: 27–8.

### c. *Providing a comprehensive theory*

The final motivating factor to mention is the desire to provide a comprehensive yet concise presentation of the entire extent of the Buddha's teaching. Rather than simply clarifying and expanding on the contents of the *sūtras* through the discussion of matrices and the consideration of actual and possible objections, the Abhidharma strove towards a maximally comprehensive presentation of the entire Buddhist worldview. Some authors have suggested that in doing so the Abhidharma lost sight of its own aim as a soteriological instrument. The doctrine 'seems to have become an end in itself',[13] 'in its final stage, Abhidharma texts became complex philosophical treatises... whose purpose was the analysis and elaboration of doctrinal issues for their own sake'.[14] This perceived opposition of soteriology and philosophy strikes me as somewhat artificial. When philosophical questions are investigated at a sufficient level of depth, often various subsidiary questions have to be addressed first before any progress with the main question can be made. The subsidiary questions may in themselves be quite complicated, and they may presuppose the answer to yet further questions. At this stage it may appear as if the original problem has vanished out of sight, but this is no more the case than, for example, the discussion of fairly technical architectural problems arising during the design of a house would indicate that we are not engaged in building this particular house anymore. The depth of the Abhidharma analyses should be seen as indicative of the depth of conceptual penetration the early Buddhist schools achieved, rather than as a symptom of scholastic decadence that is somehow losing sight of the soteriological dimension of the Buddhist project. This point is underlined by the fact that the early Buddhist thinkers believed they had good reason to suppose that each of the somewhat technical problems that arose in the discussion of the Abhidharma really had a solution. This reason is the supposed omniscience of the Buddha.

Analysis as an end in itself?

Buddhists assume that with his enlightenment the Buddha obtained universal knowledge, not necessarily knowledge of each individual fact, but comprehensive insight into the nature of all things.[15] This kind of omniscience implies

The Buddha's omniscience

[13] Tilakaratne 2000: 12; Bhikkhu Anālayo 2014: 117.

[14] Cox 2004: 4.

[15] There are parts of the Buddhist canon that seem to conflict with this idea, such as the Buddha's claim that those who attribute omniscience to him misrepresent him (Majjhimanikāya 71, Bhikkhu Bodhi 2001: 587–8) or the fact that the Buddha frequently adjusted monastic regulations because earlier versions led to unforeseen problems. Whether this is evidence that the Buddhist tradition changed its view on the matter of omniscience, or whether this can be accounted for by distinguishing between omniscience in terms of knowing all facts necessary for obtaining liberation and omniscience as a form of philosophical super-knowledge, cannot be decided here. It is worth noting, however, that in the *Siṃsāpasutta* (Saṃyutta Nikāya 56:31, Bhikkhu Bodhi 2000, 1857–8) the Buddha points out that the amount of things he has taught relate to those he knows, but has not taught, as the amount of leaves in his hand relates to all the leaves in the grove: 'So too, bhikkhus, the things I have directly known but have not taught you are numerous, while the things that I have taught you are few.'

Abhidharma as representing the Buddha's omniscient mind

having answers to all the questions about the fundamental nature of reality[16] that the Abhidharma is trying to answer, and the Pāli tradition does in fact draw a connection between the Abhidharma and the Buddha's omniscience, pointing out that one who refuses the Abhidharma refuses the Buddha's omniscience, and is therefore a danger for the unity of the monastic community.[17] For this reason it seems plausible to assume that one of the motivations for composing the Abhidharma treatises was to develop a kind of substitute of the Buddha's omniscient knowledge of the nature of existence and the path to liberation. To this extent it is evident how the *abhi* in Abhidharma could refer to a teaching above or beyond the *dharma*. If we assume that the *dharma* taught in the early Buddhist *sūtras* always represented a specific perspective into the Buddha's omniscient mind, determined by the context in which the discourse was taught and by the capacities of the audience, the Abhidharma set out to go beyond or above this and present a comprehensive picture. To the charge that this involved acceding 'to doctrines that may sometimes have imposed more meaning on the earliest Buddhist teaching than it originally had',[18] the Ābhidharmikas would have replied that this complete meaning was always there in the mind of the Buddha, though its presentation in the *sūtras* only lets us see specific parts. For them, the aim of the Abhidharma is not to impose additional meaning, but bring out and systematize meaning that was there all along.

View of the supernatural status of the Buddha & its consequences

It is worthwhile to point out that the belief in the Buddha's omniscience is a manifestation of a more general view of the supernatural status of the Buddha that shaped Buddhist thought in interesting ways. Some Pāli sources hold that the Buddha was already omniscient as a bodhisattva, that is, prior to his enlightenment.[19] According to this view, the Buddha is not just conceptualized as an ordinary person who became extraordinary through his experience of enlightenment, but as somebody who already possessed extraordinary properties for a long time prior to his life as the historical Buddha. Such a view of the Buddha as in many respects superhuman found its expression in the comprehensive exposition of the teaching in the Abhidharma, attempting to encapsulate some of the insights of his omniscient mind, but it also contributed, via the focus on the extraordinary pre-enlightement qualities of the Buddha as a bodhisattva, to the arising of the Mahāyāna with its emphasis on the ideal of a bodhisattva over and above that of an *arhat*, the soteriological aim of early Buddhism. Moreover, the view of the Buddha as a being transcending time and

[16] Later developments in Buddhist philosophy set out to provide arguments why the Buddha's pronouncements on matters that cannot be verified by ordinary human beings (*atyantaparokṣa*) should be considered as authoritative. See below, p. 239.

[17] Bhikkhu Anālayo 2014: 126. [18] Ronkin 2005: 249.

[19] Bhikkhu Anālayo 2014: 121.

space provides the foundation for such later developments as the theory of Buddha-nature, or the quasi-theistic forms of Buddhism we find in some versions of Pure Land doctrines. Whether the origin of the conception of the supernatural Buddha was a response to a kind of emotional need after the historical Buddha's nirvāṇa[20] or whether it arose for other reasons is not a question we can settle here. It is, however, important to note that it is a conception that, even though it would not strike us as particularly philosophical, had an astonishing number of consequences in the later development of Buddhist philosophy.

Motives for composing the Abhidharma & three factors

It is worthwhile to point out how the motivations for the composition of the Abhidharma we have just described line up with the three factors influencing Buddhist philosophy mentioned before. First, the composition of the Abhidharma is influenced by the Buddhist scriptures, and specifically by the desire to spell out the matrices found in the Buddha's discourses. Second, there is an obvious influence of debating and argumentation on the Abhidharma texts. They answer actual and hypothetical objections to the positions defended in the *sūtra*s and attempt to correct mistaken interpretations. Third, important parts of the explication of the matrices and the attempt to provide a comprehensive theory can be seen as providing a 'meditator's roadmap', a description of states and phenomena a meditator is likely to encounter in meditation. The Abhidharma (like all of Buddhist thought) should therefore not be conceived simply as argument-driven philosophy, but as a conceptual enterprise that is to be located within the coordinates of the Buddha's teachings, and takes account of the meditative experiences resulting from techniques that are part of this teaching.

## 2. The Question of Authenticity

Why is the Abhidharma *buddhavacana*?

When considering the Abhidharma treatises, we are immediately confronted with a complex conceptual problem: how to establish the authoritative status of a set of religious texts. To a smaller extent this problem already arises in the case of the *sūtra*s, but there the question is merely whether a given discourse was in fact spoken by the Buddha. In the case of the Abhidharma, the problem is more comprehensive, since it affects the whole of the Abhidharma collection of texts. What is our justification for regarding them as the authentic word of the Buddha (*buddhavacana*), rather than as later fabrications?

[20] Bhikkhu Anālayo (2014: 126) explains it as 'to some degree a response to the emotional need of the disciples at a time when the teacher had passed away', providing 'a sense of assurance direly needed in the struggle to ensure the survival of the fledgling community of Buddhist disciples in their competition with outsiders'.

Amongst the three baskets that make up the Buddhist canon the Abhidharma obviously stands out. The first two baskets provide us with a clear picture of the discourse situation in which they arose, the *sūtra*s as teachings the Buddha gave to a variety of audiences, the *vinaya* as a set of regulations he put into place in order to structure the life of the communities of monks (and later, nuns). The Abhidharma is nothing like this, but consists of a set of fairly technical treatises that give detailed lists and classifications of topics the Buddha taught in the *sūtras*. Different strategies were employed in order to establish the authenticity of the Abhidharma. The Sarvāstivāda school of Abhidharma believed that their Abhidharma texts had authors other than the Buddha, who compiled topics scattered throughout the discourses in more systematic form (though they consider its main text, the *Jñānaprasthāna*, to have at least been authenticated by the Buddha during his lifetime). So even though the Abhidharma could not be considered as *buddhavacana* in the same sense as the *sūtra*s, the Abhidharma texts could be included in the Buddha's word according to the criterion we met earlier: they accord with the teaching of the Buddha, and are therefore to be considered authentic. In addition, all the topics of the Abhidharma have been discussed in the Buddha's own teaching, just not in that order. The *Catuḥpratisaraṇasūtra* gives the following hermeneutic rule: 'One must rely upon the doctrine, not on the person; upon the meaning, not on the sound; upon a discourse that can be taken literally (*nītārtha*), not on one that must be interpreted (*neyārtha*); upon direct cognition (*jñāna*), not on discursive cognition (*vijñāna*).'[21] Considering the doctrine taught in the Abhidharma and its meaning, it has to be regarded as the word of the Buddha, though the person who composed it was not the Buddha and the sounds that first uttered it did not belong to him. A related consideration makes the claim that the Abhidharma is not just a remix of the teachings of the *sūtra*s, but that the original matrices on which the Abhidharma is based were in fact taught by the Buddha, so that the Abhidharma consists merely of an expansion of that teaching.

Strategies for establishing authenticity

The Theravāda tradition is unique insofar as it is the only school that considers the Abhidharma to have originated in a superhuman realm. Their account holds that because the Buddha's mother, Mahāmāyā, died seven days after the birth of the future Buddha, the Buddha had to find a way to express his filial piety by teaching her the *dharma* later in his life. Because of the tremendous store of good karma that caused her to become the mother of a future Buddha in the first place, she was reborn in the heavenly realm of the Thirty-three.[22]

Supernatural origin of the Abhidharma

[21] Bronkhorst 2009: 177.

[22] There is a minor problem with this account, since the Theravāda tradition also holds that the Buddha's mover was reborn in Tuṣita Heaven, not in the Heaven of the Thirty-three. See Bhikkhu Anālayo 2014: 163–4.

The Buddha went to this divine realm during one rains retreat and taught her the Abhidharma there, as a result of which she accomplished the first major step on the way to enlightenment, stream-entry. After he had descended to earth again by means of a jeweled staircase, he then repeated this teaching to Śāriputra, who passed it on to another 500 disciples. This idea of the Abhidharma originating from a superhuman realm interestingly parallels the belief that the Perfection of Wisdom texts were retrieved from the realm of the *nāgas*.[23] As in the case of the *nāga* realm, the Heaven of the Thirty-three also seems to function as a depository in which teachings that are no longer accessible on earth have been preserved.[24]

## 3. The Abhidharma Schools

As a matter of fact there is no such thing as a single Abhidharma; rather there is a multiplicity of Abhidharma traditions. In the centuries after the Buddha's death his followers split up into what is traditionally conceived of as a division into eighteen schools. What motivated this division is still a matter of debate, though it is clear that the grounds for the disagreements between the schools were not just philosophical, but frequently involved different conceptions of the *vinaya*, that is, disagreements about which rules monks should follow. With the split into the eighteen schools came a split into different traditions of transmitting the three baskets of *sūtras*, monastic rules, and Abhidharma. How much the baskets of the different schools differed from each other is difficult to say, as the collections of their canonical texts often do not exist anymore. The canons of two schools are still extant in their entirety, that of the Theravāda, preserved in Pāli, and that of the Sarvāstivāda, preserved in Chinese and Tibetan. The greatest difference between the two canons are their Abhidharma collections, which consist of different texts. While it is likely that there will have been differences between the *sūtras* and *vinaya* of all of the different schools, their respective Abhidharma texts provide us with the clearest insight into the philosophical views peculiar to the different branches of early Buddhism. Unfortunately we can only reconstruct these views in a partial manner for all the schools other than the Theravāda and Sarvāstivāda, relying on quotations and paraphrases of the positions of these schools we find in later texts. In our discussion we will look at five different schools; in addition

The 18 schools

Five Abhidharma schools discussed here

[23] See below, pp. 91–2. In fact it is intriguing to note that all three schools of Buddhist thought, Abhidharma, Madhyamaka, and Yogācāra (whether the school of Diṅnāga and Dharmakīrti should be considered as a school in the same sense is debatable: see below, ch 4, pp. 250–9) are considered by traditional accounts to have a superhuman, magical origin: the Abhidharma in the realm of the Thirty-three, the Madhyamaka (via the Perfection of Wisdom *sūtras*) in the *nāga* realm, and the Yogācāra in the realm of the future Buddha Maitreya.

[24] Bhikkhu Anālayo 2014: 150.

to Theravāda and Sarvāstivāda we will discuss the Mahāsaṃghika, the Pudgalavāda, and the Sautrāntika. The main emphasis will be put on the discussion of the Sarvāstivāda, simply because of the degree to which it influenced the subsequent development of Buddhist philosophical thought in India. The Theravāda (or, to be more precise, the doctrinal predecessor of what we nowadays refer to as the Theravāda) was transmitted to Sri Lanka in the third century BCE. Its importance on the Indian subcontinent began to decline soon afterwards, and from about the second century BCE its literature developed very much in isolation from the philosophical discussion in India, having little influence on the later development of the Indian Abhidharma tradition. There is, however, one text in the Pāli Abhidharma that forms part of the Theravāda canon, the *Kathāvatthu*, that we want to look at in more detail, because it relates discussions of Theravāda's predecessors to other Buddhist schools, and because it constitutes an important record of early Indian Buddhist philosophical debate.

Reasons for the division

The exact chronology of the division of early Indian Buddhism into different schools, the precise nature of the differences, and even how many schools one needs to distinguish in the first place are all questions that have still not been satisfactorily resolved. It is, in fact, unlikely that they are ever going to be, given the fragmentary and often second-hand nature of the information we have on the different Buddhist schools. Fortunately, for our purposes a rough indication of the relationship between the five schools we shall discuss will be sufficient.

Division at the second council

The first important division occurred during the second council, held at Vaiśāli about a century after the Buddha's death. Since the passing away of the historical Buddha a number of such councils (*saṃgīti*, literally 'recitation') had been held, where monks communally recite the three baskets and thereby agree on and determine their contents. The first of these is said to have taken place at Rājagṛha shortly after the Buddha's death. During the second council a split into two schools, Mahāsaṃghika and the Sthaviranikāya occurred. Accounts

Monastic rules

differ on what the cause of the split was. According to one account the reason was a dispute over the status of a set of ten monastic rules (such as whether it was allowed to drink milk after mealtime, or whether monks could accept gold and silver). The monks that did not accept the ten rules were the Mahāsaṃghikas. Their name, the 'great assembly', might have been chosen because they were in fact the majority, or because they considered themselves

Nature of the *arhat*

to be such. According to other accounts, the split did not actually have its origin in differences about monastic discipline, but resulted from a set of five controversial theses about the nature of an *arhat*, held by a Mahāsaṃghika monk named Mahādeva. All of these theses assume that an *arhat*, despite his liberated status, is still subject to certain limitations (such as being subject to doubt, or erotic dreams). The Mahāsaṃghikas are said to have accepted this more restricted conception of the abilities of an *arhat*, while the followers of the Sthaviranikāya did not.[25] The Sthaviranikāya later split into three major further schools: the Sarvāstivāda, the Pudgalavāda (also sometimes referred to as Vātsīputrīya), and a third group called Vibhājyavāda ('the theory of differentiation'). The only school descending from the Sthaviranikāya that is still extant today is the Theravāda ('the theory of the elders'), though its relationship with the Sthaviranikāya is not entirely straightforward. It might have descended from the Vibhājyavāda,[26] though the term Theravāda as the identification of a school of Buddhism was certainly not commonly used before the twentieth century. The Sautrāntika, finally, most likely arose as a development out of the Sarvāstivāda, disagreeing with the latter's focus on Abhidharma treatises and replacing it by a focus on the *sūtras* (hence their name, the 'followers of the *sūtras*').

### *a. Mahāsaṃghika*

The Mahāsaṃghika school is of particular interest for our study of the development of Indian Buddhist thought because it incorporated various ideas that were developed further in Mahāyana schools, in Madhyamaka, and to a lesser extent, in Yogācāra. We are fortunate insofar as part of the Mahāsaṃghika canon has come down to us; its Abhidharma is extant in Chinese translation.[27] Studying the doctrine of the Mahāsaṃghikas underlines that the Mahāyana was not so much a radical break with the traditions of early Buddhism, but the focus on and development of certain ideas that were already present in early Buddhist texts, though occupying a considerably less central status.[28]

There are certain elements in Mahāsaṃghika thought that prefigure the illusionist doctrines we find in later Buddhist material. We have already mentioned the limitations of the abilities of the *arhat* the Mahāsaṃghika accept. The majority of these concern epistemic limitations: an *arhat* may be ignorant of some matter, may be uncertain, or may learn something from another person. This should not be understood simply as a proto-Mahāyāna denigration of an ideal figure of early Buddhism, but needs to be taken into account as having two main consequences. First, it anchors the ideal of *arhat*-ship within the context of the world around us. To be able to claim liberation

Limitations of the *arhat*

Consequences of this idea

[25] An unfavourable interpretation of Mahādeva's theses is that he himself was subject to all the faults mentioned in his five theses, and that he only used them to protect his own claim towards *arhat*ship.

[26] Conze 1962: 32, 119–20.

[27] As the history of Buddhist thought advanced, the Mahāsaṃghika also split into a variety of sub-schools. We can distinguish three main brances, the Lokottaravāda, the Kaukkuṭika (again divided into Bahuśrutīya and Prajñaptivāda), and the Caitya (Conze 1962: 195 distinguishes four subdivisions of these). For the purposes of this chapter we will largely ignore the difference between the various subdivisions of Mahāsaṃghika.

[28] For a clear exposition of key Mahāsaṃghika positions see Bareau 2013: 55–83.

from suffering, it is not necessary to display a variety of magical abilities, such as knowing the names of people before being introduced, never having to ask for the way when travelling, and so forth. Second, it draws a distinction between the figure of the *arhat* and that of the omniscient Buddha.

The omniscient Buddha

Ascribing omniscience to the Buddha happened quite early in the history of Buddhism, and is not confined to the Mahāsaṃghika, but includes the Sthaviranikāya as well.[29] There is considerable unclarity about the range of this omniscience (whether it only covers matters connected with liberation, or everything there is to be known), and about the motivation of this doctrine in the first place. Some authors claim that it is the result of a desire to metaphysically keep up with the Joneses,[30] but we might equally assume that it has its source in the reluctance to claim equality between the attainment of *arhat*ship, considered as a clearly achievable goal, and the attainment of the historical Buddha.[31]

The Buddha as supramundane

Bringing the *arhat* down to earth, so to speak, and emphasizing its difference from the Buddha, in particular by stressing his omniscience, facilitated the elevation of the Buddha from a historical person to a transcendent entity, an omniscient being without imperfections, supramundane and not tainted by worldly impurities. Of course, this position conflicts with what the canonical texts tell us about the Buddha, as they mention various imperfections: the Buddha got sick, went begging for food without receiving anything, changed monastic rules because they had consequences he did not foresee at the time (and thus could not have been able to see into the future), and so on. One way to respond to this was to argue that there is more to the Buddha than meets the eye when the historical figure is considered. The historical Buddha was a mere fiction, an illusory creature projected onto the world in order to teach worldly beings.[32] His material body (*rūpakāya*) is not his real body but a transformation-body (*nirmāṇakāya*), which is shaped in such a way as to facilitate teaching the *dharma*. Like his life, the Buddha's death and passing into nirvāṇa was just a display; the Buddha has not really disappeared, but we can expect that his great compassion will send further emanations in the future to guide sentient beings to enlightenment.[33]

The illusory Buddha

It is likely that the introduction of the idea of the transcendent nature of the Buddha also led to a form of ontological degradation of the manifest world. If the appearance of the Buddha in the world was only supposed to be a manifestation

[29] Warder 2000: 211–12, Bhikkhu Anālayo 2014: 117–27.

[30] Bhikkhu Anālayo 2014: 123–4 notes that omniscience was attributed to Mahāvīra, the founder of Jainism.

[31] Apart from the fact that the Buddha achieved enlightenment unaided, whereas later *arhat*s achieved it through his teaching (Warder 2000: 211).

[32] For the criticism of this view by the Sthaviranikāya see p. 52 below.

[33] Bareau 2013: 60–1, Conze 1962: 197.

of another, distinct reality, and therefore not really what it appeared to be, how much trust would one then be able to place in other worldly phenomena?

In addition, the Mahāsaṃghikas also expanded the range of the notion of emptiness. While the focus of the Sthaviranikāya was the emptiness of persons (*pudgalanairātmya*), which amounts to the fact that the person can be exhaustively reduced to a group of impersonal elements (*dharmas*), the Mahāsaṃghika considered it to cover the emptiness of *dharmas* (*dharmanairātmya*) as well. An analogy from the *Kāśyapaparivarta* illustrates the distinction, comparing the former to the emptiness of holes termites bore into a piece of wood, the latter to the emptiness of empty space.[34] The emptiness of the termite holes is based on the non-emptiness of something else, namely the wood surrounding it, whereas space does not need such surroundings. In the same way, the emptiness of persons is formulated against a background of substantially existent *dharmas*, while the emptiness of phenomena generalizes this notion, including the *dharmas* in the domain of emptiness as well.[35] For the Prajñaptivāda sub-school of the Mahāsaṃghika this means that phenomena such as the five *skandhas*, which together form the basis on which the person is imputed, do not acquire their designation on the basis of yet smaller components, all the way to the fundamental *dharmas*, but in terms of their mutual relationship with one another.[36] Emptiness is not a notion that only applies at the higher levels of the ontological hierarchy, leaving the lower strata untouched, but pervades the entirety of what there is because of the reciprocal dependence of its elements.

Two kinds of emptiness

With their conception of a division between the two truths that relegated even some of chief the objectives of the Buddhist teaching (enlightenment and nirvāṇa) to the level of conventional reality, regarding it as a merely illusory display, and the expansion of the notion of emptiness to cover all *dharmas*, rather than just specifically the notion of a person, the Mahāsaṃghika doctrines, frequently regarded as predecessors to the Mahāyāna, have direct points of conceptual contact with Madhyamaka theories. In fact it may even have been the case that the founder of Madhyamaka, Nāgārjuna, had particularly close contact with the Mahāsaṃghikas; Joseph Walser has recently argued that Nāgārjuna may have lived as a Mahāyāna monk in a Mahāsaṃghika monastery in Andhra Pradesh during some part of his life.[37] Walser further argues

Mahāsaṃghika and Madhyamaka

[34] Conze 1962: 198.

[35] Takakusu (1975: 122–3) lists as one tenet of the Ekavyāvahārikas that all *dharmas* are to be regarded as 'nominal or mere names (*ākhyātimātra* or *nāmamātra*). All elements are simply names and of no reality'.

[36] Walser 2005: 221. See also 222, 230.

[37] Walser 2005: 89. The theoretical differences between the different schools of early Buddhism seem not to have been too divisive in other terms. Lamotte (1988: 519) points out that 'relations were cordial and easy between members of the different sects', and Warder (2000: 208–9) remarks that, 'for all that they denounce each other's propositions in their theoretical works... monks of different schools are found later to live side by side in the same dwellings (*vihāra*) in apparent

that the positions and arguments developed in Nāgārjuna's main work, the *Mūlamadhyamakakārika*, were developed in such a way as to highlight similarities between the Mahāsaṃghika (and Sāṃmitīya) and Mahāyāna positions,[38] emphasizing its difference from Sarvāstivāda by its criticisim of this Abhidharma school, in order to ensure the survival of the new Mahāyāna movement. Interpreting the Madhyamaka ideas as developments of concepts already present in Mahāsaṃghika texts, rather than describing them as new conceptual innovations, would be one way of underlining the authoritativeness of the Madhyamaka views for an audience sceptical towards the Mahāyāna.

Mahāsaṃghika and Yogācāra

In addition to its affinity with later Madhyamaka ideas the Mahāsaṃghika theories also incorporate various conceptual seeds that can be considered to fully flourish in later Yogācāra theories. The Mahāsaṃghikas accept a form of foundational consciousness (*mūlavijñāna*) that persists even through states of deep meditative concentration, a form of consciousness that is originally pure,[39] though in its present state soiled by passions.[40] It is distinct from the individual sense faculties and acts as their basis, as the root of the tree supports its branches.[41] The resemblance with the conception of the *ālayavijñāna* that is going to play a key role in later Yogācāra is hard to overlook.

Foundational consciousness

Luminosity of consciousness

According to the Mahāsaṃghika, consciousness is also naturally luminous (*prabhāsvara*), a conception that has close similarities with reflexivity of consciousness (*svasamvedana*) that the Yogācārins discuss; such natural luminosity making it possible that consciousness does not just apprehend other things, but can also apprehend itself. This idea of the luminosity and intrinsic purity of the mind can in fact be traced back to the Pāli *sūttas*: in the *Aṅguttara-nikāya* the Buddha points out that 'The mind is luminous, O monks, but it is defiled by adventitious defilements.'[42] This is a notion that is destined to have a long history in Buddhist philosophical thought, not just in the works of the Mahāsaṃghikas and Yogācārins, but also later in Buddhist tantra, where this luminosity is itself considered to be the cause of mind.[43]

Buddha-nature

Finally, some of the Mahāsaṃghika ideas appear to come close to a concept of Buddha-nature that is further developed in later Mahāyāna texts. In the

harmony, and wandering monks were not troubled by questions about their affiliation to a school when seeking lodgings among distant communities.'

[38] Walser 2005: 266.

[39] In this *Tarkajvāla* (Eckel 2008: 117, 312) Bhāviveka attributes the view that mind is luminous by nature (*prakṛtiprabhāsvara, rang bzhin gyis 'od gsal ba*) to the Ekavyāvahārikas (a sub-school of the Mahāsaṃghika).

[40] Silburn 1955: 237; Conze 1962: 132; Kimura 1927: 152.

[41] Bareau 2013: 80.

[42] 1.6.1, *pabhassaram idaṃ bhikkhave cittaṃ tañ ca kho āgantukehi upakkilesehi upakkiliṭṭhaṃ*, see Bhikkhu Bodhi 2012: 97, 1597–9.

[43] Āryadeva quotes the *Jñānavajrasamuccayatantra* in his *Caryāmelāpakapradīpa* as saying that consciousness itself that is arisen from luminosity is mind (*citta*) and thought (*manas*) (*yat prabhāsvarodbhavaṃ vijñānaṃ tad eva cittaṃ mana iti | tan-mūlāḥ sarva-dharmāḥ*, Wedemeyer 2007: 401).

*Buddhasvabhāvaśāstra*, a text ascribed to Vasubandhu only preserved in Chinese translation, their views are characterized as follows:

> If we look at the doctrines of the Vibhājyavādins[44] we see that they preach that '*śūnyatā*' is the origin of all human beings—both wise and ignorant. Because, these classes of men all came into being out of the same '*śūnyatā*'. This '*śūnyatā*' is the nature of Buddha (*buddha-svabhāva*), and this *buddha-svabhāva* is the *mahānirvāṇa*.[45]

This passage ascribes to the Mahāsaṃghikas the idea that emptiness (*śūnyatā*) is a universal property of all beings, and that this emptiness, which is the same as liberation, corresponds to an enlightened nature to be found in all beings. From this view it is only a small step to the view that all beings are already identical to a Buddha—not because they have the potential to achieve liberation, but because the Buddha's enlightened mind is already present in them, even though it is currently obscured by ignorance.

It is important to point out that despite all these similarities the Mahāsaṃghika were, of course, no Mahāyānists, and accepted various positions the Mahāyāna does not agree with. What is interesting, however, is how many of the key positions of later Mahāyāna schools are already present in the Mahāsaṃghika theses, underlining the fact that the development of Buddhist philosophy is not characterized by single-handed innovations of autonomous thinkers, but by gradual shifts in emphasis on particular concepts, shifts which, in the fullness of time, can lead to very distinct philosophical positions, but which proceed by never losing sight of anchoring their innovations in the continuity of the Buddhist tradition, thereby attempting to underline their authoritativeness as the genuine word of the Buddha.

Source of innovations in Buddhist philosophy

### *b. Sthaviranikāya: Theravāda*

We mentioned above that the present discussion will not have much to say on the Abhidharma of the Sthaviranikāya as it continued in the Theravāda tradition, mainly because its influence on the subsequent development of Buddhist philosophy in India was very limited when compared to that of other Abhidharma schools. We will, however, make an exception for the last of the seven books of the Theravāda Abhidharma collection, the *Kathāvatthu*.

*Kathāvatthu*

This work on 'Points of Controversy' is traditionally ascribed to Moggaliputtatissa, who is supposed to have composed it at the conclusion of the third council, held in Pāṭaliputra in the third century BCE.[46] The council is said to have been preceded by a purging of the monastic community of corrupted monks by the emperor Aśoka. After this, Moggaliputtatissa convened a smaller group of monks in order to recite (and thereby agree on an authoritative

[44] The Mahāsaṃghikas are meant here—see Kimura 1927: 152.
[45] Kimura 1927: 151.
[46] As accounts of this council only appear in Pāli sources its historicity has been questioned.

version of) the Pāli Tripiṭaka and its commentaries. Subsequently the *Kathāvatthu* was composed as a way of rebutting interpretations of the Buddha's teaching deemed to be incorrect.

The Theravāda tradition sees no difficulty with including this text, which was manifestly composed by an author other than the Buddha, in the Buddhist canon. They hold that the underlying structure of the text was actually composed by the Buddha himself, anticipating the various ways in which his doctrine might be misunderstood.

The text is traditionally divided into twenty-three books, which each treat a variety of controversial points (219 altogether), one at a time, followed by the views of different early Buddhist schools contrasted with those of the Theravāda. Unfortunately our information on which school entertained which position is somewhat sparse; the *Kathāvatthu* does not provide this at all, and its commentary 'lacks either the will, or the power to enlighten us much regarding the schools [it] names'.[47] Two possible reasons for this spring to mind. First, the association of specific views with certain authors or groups would have been familiar to the author of the *Kathāvatthu* and to his intended audience, so that there would be no need to note it specifically. Second, it may be that the *Kathāvatthu* was meant to be understood first and foremost as a systematic work, describing the correct interpretation of the Buddha's teaching, rather than as a doxographical manual.

Refutation of views opposed to Theravāda

In general, the *Kathāvatthu* tries to establish the correctness of the Theravāda response to the various controversial points (*kathā*) raised. It does so either by citing relevant passages from the *sūtra*s that are taken to support their own rather than the opponents' reading, or by drawing out implications of the opponents' position. In this case it will attempt to show that the opponents' position has some implications that the opponents themselves deny. Thus, for example, regarding the claim that the inhabitants of the god-realm, the *deva*s, do not practise the Buddhist path,[48] the Theravādin points out that their opponents (identified by the commentary as Sāṃmitīyas) also deny that the *deva*s have any moral failings. But if such failings (such as lacking faith in the three jewels) are absent, how could their opponents consistently deny that they follow the Buddhist path? We can clearly observe two of the forces that shape Buddhist philosophy at work here: striving for consistency with the Buddha's own assertions, and striving for consistency in one's argumentative position, that is, not admitting contradictory statements.[49]

[47] Aung and Davids 1915. [48] Aung and Davids 1915: 71–6.

[49] The *Kathāvatthu* is an interesting example of the logical techniques Buddhists employed at a relatively early stage of the development of Buddhist philosophy in India. See Aung and Davids 1915: xlviii–li for some further discussion.

However, this description might give the misleading impression that the *Kathāvatthu* is a neat, point-by-point attempt to establish a Theravāda orthodoxy. This does not correspond to several parts of the texts, where the author's own position is not the one where the discussion ends. For example, section XVIII opens with a discussion of the question whether the historical Buddha was really a human being. The commentary informs us that the opponent's position here is that the Buddha never left Tuṣita heaven (the last place where he is traditionally assumed to have taken birth before being reborn as Prince Siddharta). Instead, he produced a magical creation that lived on earth, but this was in fact not an ordinary human being, but rather something like a mirage in human form. In response to this idea the *Kathāvatthu* first lists events from the Buddha's life, and second various canonical statements where the Buddha says that he was dwelling at one particular place, the idea presumably being that these could not be attributed to a phantom. The opponent (identified by the commentary as a Vetulyaka) then responds with a *sūtra* passage describing the Buddha as one who was 'born in the world and grew up in the world, but having overcome the world, he dwells unsullied by the world',[50] pointing out that, as such, the Buddha could not have lived a life of flesh and blood. With this, the discussion of the matter ends. In a work attempting to defend a certain orthodoxy, such a passage would indeed be strange. How could the opponent have the last word, given that this is clearly not a position that the author of the *Kathāvatthu* endorsed? There are at least two different ways to explain this puzzling fact. First, it is highly unlikely that the text as we have it today was from beginning to end composed by Moggaliputtatissa at the time of Aśoka. Several of the schools referred to may have only arisen several hundred years after this date. As such, it is likely that the *Kathāvatthu* might have been the subject of various additions throughout its history (in fact, in a work with relatively unclear organization such as this additions of this kind could be easily made without disturbing the balance of the entire structure). In this case, additional objections made by the opponents might have been added to the relevant sections, but without also composing at the same time a Theravāda response that refutes the new objection. Another possibility[51] is that part of the point of the *Kathāvatthu* was to acquaint the student with a variety of (often inconsistent) ways of answering a particular

A defence of orthodoxy?

Additions to the text

The *Kathāvatthu* as a pedagogical tool

[50] Aung and Davids 1915: 324. The passage is from Saṃyuttanikāya 3.94 (Bhikkhu Bodhi 2000: 950).

[51] Suggested by Cousins 1984: 67, n. 2: 'In spiritual traditions the world over, instructors have frequently employed apparent contradictions as part of their teaching method—perhaps to induce greater awareness in the pupil or to bring about a deeper and wider view of the subject in hand. The Pāli Canon contains many explicit examples of such methods. (Indeed much of the Kathāvatthu makes better sense in these terms than as sectarian controversy.) . . . Any attempt to analyse all such "contradictions" as representing different textual or historical strata is puerile. Such features must have been present from the beginning.'

question or problem in order to deepen the student's understanding. In this case, the fact that the *Kathāvatthu* does not resolve every disputed point by presenting the official party line to be followed would not be a defect arising from the fact that more and more strata were piled on top of each other, but would be indicative of the text's pedagogical approach. Through being confronted with different ways of addressing a question the student is encouraged to bring his own intellectual and meditative resources to bear in order to resolve the matter. Such a process will lead to greater understanding and penetration of the problems than merely accepting the 'model answers' constituting the way they are resolved in an Abhidharma text.

The *Kathāvatthu* as a depository of philosophical concepts

Overall, the main value of the *Kathāvatthu* for the understanding of the development of Buddhist philosophical thought in India is its presentation of a rich variety of different positions *in nuce*, many of which can be seen to germinate into elaborate philosophical theories in later times. One example is

Docetism

the docetic conception of the Buddha already mentioned, the idea that the Buddha was not a real human being but a manifestation projected into the world. It finds a later reflection in the *Saddharmapuṇḍarīkasūtra*,[52] where the Buddha declares that 'the Tathāgata has an endless span of life, he lasts for ever. Although the Tathāgata has not entered nirvāṇa, he makes a display of entering nirvāṇā, for the sake of those who have to be educated'. Section XVIII.2

Illusory teaching

of the *Kathāvatthu* raises the idea that, due to his phantasmagoric nature, the Buddha did not really teach the *dharma*. It is hard not to notice the parallel with Nāgārjuna's point in verse 25:24b of his *Mūlamadhyamakakārikā* that 'no dharma whatsoever was ever taught by the Buddha to anyone'.[53] Section XXII.4 makes the suggestion that an *arhat* may obtain liberation in

Dreams and reality

alternative cognitive states, such as dreams. It is possible to draw an interesting trajectory between this suggestion and the later Yogācāra point that there is no fundamental, ontological difference between waking consciousness and dreaming. Indeed, if the goal of the Buddhist path, liberation, was accessible in the dream state as well as in the waking state, as the opponent in this section believes, there seems to be a good reason to assume that both states do not really differ in their basic nature. Such examples can easily multiplied. Section XXI.6 holds that the Buddhas exist in all directions of space (a position the commentator

tantra

ascribes to the Mahāsanghikas), XXI.4 raises the point that the Buddha and his disciples have supernormal powers (*siddhi*), ideas that become very important in the later development of Buddhist tantra.

When considering the different positions raised in the *Kathāvatthu* there might be a certain tendency to regard the text's own position as defending

[52] *Saddharmapuṇḍarīkasūtra* XV, Conze 1995: 142, Kern 1963: 302.

[53] *na kva cit kasyacit kaścid dharmo buddhena deśitaḥ*. Some scholars consider this to be the final verse of the *Mūlamadhyamkakārikā*, see Siderits and Katsura 2013: 304–5.

Buddhist orthodoxy against a whole variety of fanciful deviations, such as phantom Buddhas, Buddhas that dwell in all places of the universe, magical powers connected with spiritual realization, and so forth. This, I think, is a tendency to be resisted. Even though the *Kathāvatthu*'s position may often appear to be more commonsensical than that of its opponents, we know too little about the history of these positions to be able to decide in all cases which view is prior to which. It is certainly not satisfactory to ascribe greater doctrinal faithfulness to the positions endorsed by the *Kathāvatthu* simply because they appear to cohere more frequently with the common sense of twenty-first-century readers than the opposing views it describes.

Orthodoxy and deviation

### *c. Sthaviranikāya: Pudgalavāda*

In order to achieve a clear understanding of the Pudgalavāda position it is first of all necessary to say something about the no-self theory held by the remainder of the Abhidharmic schools.

The mainstream Abhidharma interpretation of the Buddha's teaching of non-self is a form of reductionism about persons. The person or self is regarded as ultimately non-existent, even though this does not entail that all talk of persons or selves is false or unhelpful. Rather, such talk is a mistaken way of talking about something else, namely the five physico-psychological constituents (*skandha*). These constituents exist at the fundamental level of reality, and the notion of a person or self is falsely superimposed on them. Reductionism about persons is a specific instance of a more general reductionist position concerning wholes that the Abhidharma defends. Complexes or wholes, from medium-sized dry goods to complexes consisting of a few *dharma*s, do not really exist. The only things that do are their underlying parts, the *dharma*s, which constitute the basis of reality. Wholes do not constitute any addition of being, talk of them is simply a convenient shorthand for talking about the parts being arranged in a special way.

Reductionism about the self

Special case of mereological reductionism

The chief reason for denying the existence of wholes is that the most plausible alternative, namely the view that both wholes and parts are fundamentally real, leads to various problems. It seems that they cannot be the very same entity, since the whole is one, and the parts are many, and nothing can be both one and many, nor does it sound plausible to say that they are distinct. We certainly never encounter a whole separately from its parts, and if the whole is just at the very same place where the assembled parts are, it has to take up space. In this case we have a right and a left part of the whole, and now the problem of the part–whole relation looks as if it is repeating itself, in this case with the whole and *its* parts, instead of the original object and its parts. The most plausible way of avoiding these difficulties, the Ābhidharmikas argue, is to reject the existence of wholes and assume that only the parts, the *dharma*s, form part of reality.

Origins of the non-self theory: doctrinal and meditative

Persons are no exception to this general account. As partite objects consisting of a physical component and a succession of mental events that constitutes our mind, they, too, are fictions employed to talk about the interacting complex of physical and psychological components that is us.

The thesis that there is no substantially existent self, no *ātman*, lies at the very heart of the Buddhist philosophical conception of the world and is its central point of disagreement with non-Buddhist schools of Indian thought.[54] It is clearly stated by the Buddha that such a substantial self cannot be found amongst any of the five psycho-physical constituents that make up the person; indeed, the absence of an *ātman* is, together with unsatisfactoriness (*duḥkha*) and impermanence (*anitya*), one of the 'three seals' (*trilakṣaṇa*) that are considered to characterize all of reality. The meditator examines the five constituents one by one in order to realize that there is no self hiding behind them, and this realization has a profound soteriological impact: it will eventually lead to the overcoming of thirst (*tṛṣṇa*) for sensory and mental experiences that is the cause of the origination of suffering.

Non-self theory: argumentative support

In addition to these doctrinal and meditative origins of the non-self theory, the history of Buddhist philosophy also contains detailed arguments to support it. It is sometimes argued that these arguments for the selflessness of the person (*pudgalanairātmya*) develop the non-self theory in a direction quite different from the way it was originally intended. These arguments set out to establish that there is no substantial self, while there are explicit passages in the Buddha's discourses where the Buddha rejects *both* the idea that there is a substantial self and the idea that there is none.[55] Sometimes this argument is based on the assumption that the Buddha's aim in formulating the non-self theory was practical and soteriological, while later Buddhist authors tried to build a metaphysical structure on a teaching that was itself not interested in philosophical theory-building.[56]

Soteriology vs. theory-building?

While the present volume is not trying to establish 'what the Buddha really taught', and while I am sceptical of some of the methodological presuppositions behind such a project in the first place,[57] it is useful to be aware that the later argumentative support of the non-self theory need not be regarded as aiming at something other than a practical and soteriological purpose. Indian Buddhist authors are clear that there is a difference between an intellectual understanding of the non-self theory and its meditative realization. Only the latter brings with it the cessation of thirst and of the origination of suffering. Yet in order to bring about this realization, and to ensure that it is a realization of the right kind of understanding,[58] it is essential to develop a clear and detailed conception of the view under

[54] Bhattacharya 1973.

[55] *Sabbasāvasutta*, Majjhimanikāya I, 2, Bhikkhu Bodhi 2001: 92–3.

[56] Gombrich 2009: 166.

[57] See my remarks in the Introduction, pp. 24–34.

[58] And not, for example, the view that there is an inexpressible self distinct from all objects of our acquaintance. See Oetke 1988: 163–4.

consideration in the first place. To this end, argumentative support of the non-self theory is indispensable. Arguments supporting the absence of a substantial self are therefore not only of relevance for those who want to defend the Buddhist view against its opponents, but are equally important for the non-debating meditator. To this extent the meditative and the argumentative aspect of this fundamental Buddhist concept support one another.

Mutual support of meditation and argument

The personalists

The term *pudgalavāda* ('personalism') refers to a set of schools that developed out of the Sthaviranikāya; they are characterized by accepting the existence of persons (*pudgala*).[59] Their two main schools are the Vātsīputrīyas (named after their founder, Vatsīputra, according to some accounts a disciple of Śāriputra), which arose around 280 BCE, and the Sāṃmitīya (possibly named after their founder, Saṃmata),[60] which appeared later, around 100 BCE.[61] Their belief in the existence of a person seems to be in tension with the Buddha's doctrine of *anātman*, which denies the existence of a self, and their Buddhist opponents indeed thought the Pudgalavādins failed to account for a central teaching of the Buddha. Yet we should not make the mistake of considering them as a minor heretical sect that quite obviously misinterpreted the Buddha's teachings. First, other Buddhist sects did not regard them as non-Buddhists (*tīrthika*); they are counted as one of the eighteen schools of early Buddhism. Second, their opponents must have regarded the Pudgalavādins as sufficiently serious to merit a detailed response. The first section of the *Kathāvatthu* and the final section of Vasubandhu's *Abhidharmakośabhāṣya* contain long and intricately argued refutations of their position.[62] Finally, they appear to have been a very popular branch of early Buddhism. If the reports of Chinese pilgrims in India are to be trusted, they constituted as much as a quarter of all Buddhist monks in seventh-century India.[63]

Their status amongst the other schools

What, precisely, was the position that the Pudgalavādins set out to defend? They regarded themselves as Buddhists (and were so regarded by others), consequently their conception of the *pudgala* is certainly not identical with that of the brahmanical *ātman*. On the other hand they also want to deny that the *pudgala* is nothing but the five physico-psychological components put together, which is the position of their Buddhist opponents. For the Pudgalavādins, 'the person is known in the sense of a real and ultimate fact',[64] it is not simply a conceptual superimposition on something else that is ultimately real. Put in this way, the Pudgalavādins can appeal to the familiar Buddhist *topos* of

The notion of the *pudgala*

[59] For a comprehensive account of this school see Priestley 1999.

[60] Bareau 2013: 153.

[61] Conze 1962: 123.

[62] We do not know, however, whether both texts deal with the same form or stage of development of the Pudgalavāda ideas. While some Pudgalavāda texts have come down to us in Chinese translation, forming a clear understanding of their position from their own perspective is notoriously difficult.

[63] Conze 1962: 123.

[64] *Kathāvatthu* I.1.VIII, Aung and Davids 1915: 51.

the middle way, defending a position that is neither a belief in a permanent soul nor a position that denies the person anything but merely nominal status. (Needless to say, their Buddhist opponents had a different view of what constitutes a middle position and regarded the Pudgalavādins as having strayed too far in the direction of the eternalistic extreme.) What use the Pudgalavādins saw for their notion of a person is fairly clear. It should be what provides the continuity of a single sentient being throughout this life (being equally present in the infant, the adult, and the old man), as well as across different lives (ensuring that the sower of the karmic seeds is the same one that reaps the results). It can equally be appealed to in an explanation of how memory works, and in an explanation of Buddhist soteriology (showing how the one trapped in saṃsāra is the same one that later obtains nirvāṇa).

Its theoretical use

Inexpressibility of the *pudgala*

One thing that makes it difficult to assess the Pudgalavāda position in detail is that they consider the nature of the person to be inexpressible (*avaktavya*). This makes sense on the basis of the Abhidharma metaphysics they espouse: for the Abhidharma the only ultimately real things are the individual *dharma*s. For the Pudgalavāda the person is not identical with any particular *dharma* (such as those that make up the five *skandha*s), nor is it a mere projection onto a group of *dharmas*. Yet at the same time the person is supposed to exist 'in the sense of a real and ultimate fact', though 'not known in the sense of a real and ultimate fact',[65] not known in the way other real and ultimate things are known. If the Ābhidharmika's ontological framework forms the basis of our talk about what there is, ultimately, then the Pudgalavāda position is simply inexpressible, for neither the Abhidharma's candidates for what is real nor its candidates for what is unreal correspond to the Pudgalavādin's understanding of a person. The only things that are ultimately real for the Ābhidharmika are the *dharma*s, and if the person is not a *dharma*, it cannot be ultimately real. Nevertheless, it is hard to see how an entity that is simply inexpressible could account for mental continuity, karmic responsibility, and so on. We seem to be able to express something when we speak about the potential bearers of continuity or responsibility, so are we simply mistaken about this and do not, in fact, manage to express anything at all? It is particularly difficult to explain how this apparently quite obscure position could be dialectically so successful to be able to account for the strong presence of the Pudgalavāda in the Indian Buddhist culture of the time.

The *pudgala* as accounting for the apparent existence of persons

An interesting recent attempt to spell out the Pudgalavāda position in a way that resolves at least some of these worries has been suggested by Carpenter.[66] She tries to argue that at the heart of the debate between the Pudgalavādin and his opponents is the question of how the Buddhist reductionist position can

[65] *Kathāvatthu*, I.1.I, Aung and Davids 1915: 9.

[66] Carpenter 2015.

account for the apparent existence of persons. On the Abhidharma account, all there is at the most fundamental level of reality is a causal network of *dharmas* coming into existence and passing out of existence at high speed. A key challenge for the Abhidharma ontology is getting from this ultimate theory of the world to the manifest image of a world containing persistent, medium-sized dry goods, as well as persons. There obviously needs to be some account of how this vast network of flashing *dharmas* can be decomposed into distinct causal sub-networks that can plausibly be taken to constitute the tables and chairs we are acquainted with on an everyday basis. This is particularly challenging as some of the causal events that occur will connect an object with its later stages, or will be causal events amongst the object's own constituents, while other causal events will connect it with distinct objects. In the case of a person, considered as a stream of physical and mental *dharmas*, causal events can link one mental state (say, a perception of red) with its successor (the perception of red in the next moment), or they can link various physical and mental states in a person (a certain event in my retina causing a mind-moment perceiving red), or they can link different persons (my raising my arm causing a perception in you). If we want to identify persons as causally connected sub-networks, we will need a way of distinguishing the first two cases of causation from the last one, without already presupposing that we have a way of telling persons apart. If we cannot do this, all the persons I causally interact with would have to be regarded as somehow part of me, and this does not correspond to the way the world presents itself to us in the manifest image, as it appears to be divided into separate persons.

Challenge for the Abhidharma's network view

One way of understanding the Pudgalavāda proposal is as suggesting a way of solving this problem. If we cannot provide an adequate account of what a person is in terms of the structure of causal connections as such, we have to postulate that the causal connections that link one person-moment to its successor, and those that link the person-moments amongst each other, are in some way special. The reason why there is an important difference between my physical state causing my mental state and my physical state causing your mental state is because one causal connection is special, and connected to me, while the other operates between you and me, and is not to be distinguished from other kinds of causal interaction. Thus, what the Pudgalavāda wants to say when arguing that the person is ultimately real is that the specific kinds of causal connections that unify a person cannot be reduced to something else; in particular, they are not just normal causal relations arranged in a specific pattern. They exist *sui generis*, as causally related elements that belong together ultimately and thereby ensure that the person has a privileged place in the Pudgalavāda ontology. Note, however, that this is still arguably a non-self theory, a reductionist theory of persons, and an account that is very far removed from the idea of a permanent *ātman* defended in non-Buddhist

*Pudgala* explained as a special causal connection

schools. There is no core to the person in the Pudgalavāda sense, but simply a network of physical and mental *dharmas* that come into existence and go out of existence at a very quick pace, a network on which the mistaken notion of a permanent, unchanging self is imputed. It is, however, a special kind of network, and because of this persons are to be distinguished from other causal networks mistakenly conceived of as individuals (the causal network that constitutes a teacup, say). When considered in this way, it is also clear why the Pudgalavāda account is inexpressible in the familiar framework of Abhidharma ontology. For all this makes allowance for are momentary *dharmas* that exist at the ultimate level, connected with each other in a framework of causal connections. This framework is uniform, however, and none of its parts differ from other parts in terms of the kinds of connections (rather than the patterns of connections) that hold between its members, which is exactly the position the Pudgalavādin wants to defend.

Whether the Pudgalavāda assumption of privileged connections is really necessary in order to provide a reductionist account of persons from an Abhidharma perspective is a complex question, and one that we will not be able to resolve here. It is worthwhile to note, however, that the Pudgalavādin's opponent has a range of conceptual tools available that he can use in order to provide an account of the distinctness of persons amongst each other, and of the distinctness of persons from other things.[67]

An alternative solution

Starting from a single mental event, we can examine its cause and effects, then the causes of the causes and the effects of the effects, moving successively through an entire causal network. Some of the cause–effect chains branching out in different directions will be connected with one another to a greater extent than others (for example, events on my tongue and nose will cause a causal cascade of olfactory and gustatory events, and these will also causally influence one another). When constructing a causal network beginning with a single event there are two maxims for the inclusion of further events we can appeal to. These are to make the network as large as possible by including the greatest number of events, and to make the network maximally connected, to enlarge the amount of connections between the different events included. The two maxims pull in different directions, yet we can argue that a network that balances both in an optimal way (making it any bigger would reduce overall causal connectedness) is a plausible candidate for a person, since what characterizes a person is not just that it is a bunch of mental and physical events that cause each other, but that these are intricately connected amongst themselves. My physical states might cause your mental states, but their causal

Maximally connected causal networks

[67] The ideas outlined in the following are based on Siderits 2003: ch. 3.

connection with my mental states is considerably more complex than their causal connection with yours.

At this stage the Pudgalavādin's opponent still has to answer the claim that even though we might be able to isolate certain sections of the overall causal network that is cyclic existence by purely structural means (as was just argued), it is still unclear why we should put an emphasis on a particular subset of these rather than on any other of the countless types of structurally distinct parts of the network. Would it not be the case that without a pre-existent notion of a person there would be no way for us to zero in on the maximally connected, maximally inclusive networks? Yet the notion of a person is something we want to get out of this construction, not something we want to put in.

Ethical considerations

One possibility in replying to this charge is to refer to ethical considerations. Assuming that the reduction, and indeed elimination, of suffering is an overall goal of the Buddhist path, and moreover a goal that is not identical with any personal goal, and therefore does not in turn presuppose the concept of a person, we could argue that the causal complexes structurally isolated in the manner above are special because they play an instrumental role in trying to bring about this goal. The complexes isolated in this way are able to analyse, control, and revise their own behaviour, and are for this reason better suited for achieving the goal of minimizing suffering than other complexes that lack these features.

Of course there are various ways in which the Pudgalavādin can respond to this,[68] and we do not have the space here to follow the further course this discussion might take. Suffice it to say, however, that the Pudgalavāda theory is capable of quite sophisticated systematic development; and if some arguments like the ones just made were put forward by the ancient Pudgalavāda philosophers it is not too surprising that their school exerted a considerable influence on the intra-Buddhist philosophical discussion of the time.

Substitute selves?

Despite the inherent systematic interest of their position, it is also worthwhile to consider the Pudgalavādins as one of a series of Buddhist teachings that try to (or at least are seen by their opponents as trying to) develop a notion of a self or person that escapes the Buddhist critique.[69] The Yogācāra's concept

Foundational consciousness

[68] One worry the Pudgalavādin might voice is that there is a certain tension between the justification of introducing the notion of a person on consequentialist grounds, as the most suitable causal complex for reducing suffering, and the idea that it is precisely the notion of a person which is responsible for the suffering of cyclic existence in the first place (Carpenter 2015: 38, n. 61). A second question is why, following the reductionist argument, we should assume that the complexes considered as persons (or, more generally those corresponding to living beings) are supposed to have particular ethical impact. Buddhists would want to claim that the karmic consequence of killing an ox are worse than those of destroying an ox made of clay, but what would the reason for this be, given that both are causal complexes that simply differ in their structural features? (See Priestley 1999: 66.)

[69] See Conze 1962: 122, Bhikshu Thích Thiên Châu 1999: 138–41; Collins 1982: 230–44.

of a foundational consciousness has been sometimes charged with reintroducing the notion of a substantial self through the back door, a charge substantiated by the observation that the foundational consciousness, like the Pudgalavādin's concept of a person, was taken to fulfil some of the theoretical functions believers in substantial selves ascribe to such selves: to account for the mental continuity in this life, for continuity across different lives, and for the working of karma. These notions, the proponent of no-self theories will point out, do not only look like crypto-selves, they also function like one. A similar charge has been brought forward against the later theories of Buddha-nature of *tathāgatagarbha*,[70] postulating an enlightened core in every being that is presently obscured by ignorance but is made fully apparent once enlightenment is achieved. Here similarities with a permanent, transcendent *ātman* of the kind non-Buddhist schools postulate may be brought out much more easily.[71] Whether the notions of the *pudgala*, the *ālayavijñāna*, or the *tathāgatagarbha* are in fact inconsistent with the Buddha's teachings, or whether they are legitimate ways of spelling out ideas it already contains, is a question beyond the scope of the present discussion. Nevertheless it is worthwhile to keep in mind that concurrent with the development of no-self theory in the history of Buddhist philosophy there is also an intellectual stream that appears to pull in the other direction, introducing entities that at least *prima facie* look rather self-like.[72]

Buddha-nature

## *d. Sthaviranikāya: Sarvāstivāda*

We have good evidence to believe that the Sarvāstivāda school was established as a distinct school by the middle of the third century BCE, around the time of the reign of Aśoka.[73] It remained the dominant Abhidharma school until about the seventh century CE, when it was eventually replaced in terms of popularity by the Pudgalavāda.[74]

The Sarvāstivāda Abhidharma

*Jñānaprasthāna*

The Sarvāstivāda Abhidharma, like that of the Theravāda, consists of seven distinct texts, although the individual texts are not identical. The most important of these is the *Jñānaprasthāna*, attributed to Kātyāyanīputra and probably composed during the first to third century after the Buddha's death. Its importance is underlined by the fact that the Sarvāstivāda Abhidharma was also referred to as the 'Abhidharma with six feet' (*ṣaṭpādābhidharma*), where

[70] See Chapter 3, pp. 186–93.

[71] A point underlined by the fact that even some Buddhist writers used the term *ātman* when referring to Buddha-nature, though the precise import of this apparent inconsistency between *anātmavāda* and *tathāgatagarbha* merits a more detailed discussion (such as provided by Jones 2014).

[72] See below for the discussion of substantialism in the context of Sarvāstivāda on pp. 65–6.

[73] The tradition itself locates itself a bit later (in the early second century BCE, the first inscriptional evidence is from the first century CE (Bhikkhu Dhammajoti 2009: 55–6)).

[74] Lamotte 1988: 543.

the *Jñānaprasthāna* is considered to be the body, and the remaining six texts are its feet. The text bears its name 'basis of knowledge' because it is considered as the foundation or starting point of the knowledge of the ultimate (*paramārthajñāna*).[75] Its high status is closely connected with the fact that it represents the viewpoint of the Kashmir Sarvāstivāda, which was recognized as the orthodox variety of the Sarvāstivāda school.

*Vibhāṣā*

A second extremely important Sarvāstivāda text is the *Abhidharmamahāvibhāṣa* (or *Vibhāṣā* for short), a gigantic work said to have been compiled by a council of Kashmirian Sarvāstivādin monks during the time of King Kaniṣka.[76] Because the authority of the *Vibhāṣā* was so central for the Kashmirian Sarvāstivādins they were also referred to as Vaibhāṣikas, or 'commentarians'. The *Vibhāṣā* follows the structure of the *Jñānaprasthāna*, for which it acts as a commentary. However, this work is best understood not as a commentary, but as an encyclopedic work comprising a wide range of early Buddhist viewpoints; not simply orthodox Sarvāstivāda tenets but also viewpoints of other Sarvāstivāda teachers, and doctrines of rival Buddhist schools. It frequently lists the positions of the four great Sarvāstivāda masters (Dharmatrāta, Buddhadeva, Ghoṣaka, and Vasumitra),[77] often declaring Vasumitra's position as the best.

*sarvam asti* & arguments for this position

Sarvāstivāda, 'the theory that everything exists', tells us its central assumption already in its name. The Sarvāstivādins accounted for the somewhat unintuitive theory of momentariness, the view that we live in a kind of cinematographic reality in which every *dharma* only flashes up very briefly on the screen of existence, but at such speed that reality appears to be temporally extended, by the arguably even more unintuitive theory that past, present, and future all exist.

1. Testimony

The Sarvāstivādins present a number of arguments in support of the existence of these three times. A first argument is an argument from testimony. As the Buddha has stated that one of the motivations of striving for liberation is the experience of disgust with material things that have now passed away, we must assume that these things exist in some way to explain their causal efficacy in bringing about the present state of disenchantment with material existence.[78] A second consideration is based on the observation that moments of consciousness need to be based on an object they are about. If there were no

2. Consciousness needs a presently existent object

[75] Bhikkhu Dhammajoti 2009: 94–5.

[76] Cox 1995: 33, Bhikkhu Dhammajoti 2009: 103.

[77] The dates of these four great teachers of the Sarvāstivāda are not settled. A range from the 2nd century BCE (for Dharmatrāta) to the 1st and 2nd century CE (for Ghoṣaka) has been suggested (Bhikkhu Dhammajoti 2009: 139–40, n. 28).

[78] 'It is because past matter exists that the learned *śrāvaka* becomes disgusted with regard to past matter', *yasmāt tarhy asty atītaṃ rūpaṃ tasmāc chrutāvān ārya-śrāvako 'tite rūpe 'napekṣo bhavati*, *bhāṣya* on *Abhidharmakośa* 5:25a, Pradhan 1975: 295: 11–12, Poussin and Pruden 1988–90: 3. 806. See also Bhikkhu Dhammajoti 2009: 63.

past entities, thoughts about these entities would be objectless, and therefore could not exist.[79] The thought underlying this argument becomes particularly pressing in the presence of the theory of momentariness. Given such a theory, every mental state is about a past object, since mental processing takes time, and the object observed will have passed out of existence by the time the processing is finished. As such, it would seem impossible to have any contentful thoughts at all.

A specific version of this argument points out that the Buddhists of course want to assume that the mind has various introspective capacities (we can know, for example, when an instance of mental craving has arisen). The Sarvāstivāda also claims that a mental event (*citta*) cannot be simultaneous with another *citta*,[80] and if the craving cannot be simultaneous with the mind knowing it, the craving must be past relative to it, and, if it is correctly known, must exist.

3. Karmic responsibility

A third argument is based on the necessity to account for karmic responsibility. Karmic traces are supposed to give rise to results at a later time. But if an action that I did in a past life can bear fruit now, this seems to suggest that the past act must in some sense still be in existence, otherwise it could not be efficacious now.

4. Three times as mutually interdependent

Finally, past, present, and future are mutually interconnected notions. If past (and future) were deemed to be non-existent, it seems difficult to see how we could still make sense of the existence of the present. If we do not understand the present as wedged in between past and future, how are we to understand it? And if we believe that that the three times depend existentially on one another, how could it be the case that the present exists, while past and future do not?[81] In this case the entire process of dependent arising conceived of as a temporal process cannot be established, with obvious detrimental consequences for the framework of Buddhist thought as a whole.

Possible responses

It is worthwhile to note in passing that the opponent of the Sarvāstivāda would not find it too difficult to come up with a response to these arguments. The argument from testimony can be countered by appealing to the familiar theory of interpretable and definite teachings. The mere fact that the Buddha appealed to the existence of past entities does not imply that Buddhist philosophers need to take these entities ontologically seriously. They may have been only mentioned as a display of skilful means. The consideration that consciousness needs an object hinges on the further assumption that such objects always have to exist. This is precisely denied by the Sautrāntikas, who claim that in special cases conscious states may be directed at non-existent objects.[82]

[79] Or, alternatively, the consciousness would arise by itself, without requiring an object. See Bhikkhu Dhammajoti 2009: 161–2.

[80] Bhikkhu Dhammajoti 2009: 61, 225.

[81] Bhikkhu Dhammajoti 2009: 63.

[82] Bhikkhu Dhammajoti 2009: 63–5; see discussion below on p. 79.

Finally, the notion of karmic responsibility may be accounted for by finding a way of moving the karmic potential into the present moment, as is done, for example, in the theory of karmic seeds. An act done in the past leaves a karmic seed in a moment of the mind-stream which is then 'copied' into its successor moment, until it bears its karmic fruit in the present moment. In addition, the argument of the interdependence of the three times, which the Sarvāstivādin uses as part of a *reductio* of the denial of the existence of any of them, would be embraced by Madhyamaka, at least when considering the intrinsic existence of time.

While there appear to be a number of considerations that can be put in place in order to support the existence of the three times, a major challenge the Sarvāstivādin has to overcome is the necessity of accounting for the fact that past and future entities lack the power of entities that are present. The present glass of water can quench thirst, yet past or future water cannot. The Sarvāstivāda accounts for this by the theory of 'efficacy' (*kāritrā*). Even though past and future objects all exist, only the present objects possess efficacy, and for this reason they are able to perform functions that past and future objects cannot. Sautrāntika opponents were quick to identify problems with this attempt to split existential from causal status. They pointed out that there are numerous examples of things that are perfectly existent yet not efficacious. A person in a dark room has an existent visual capacity, but this capacity is not efficacious, as it does not produce any visual impression.[83] The Sarvāstivāda responds to this by pointing out that there are various things we can mean by efficacy, and as long as some of these obtain, the object can be considered as existent. The person in the dark room cannot see, so their eyes temporarily lack the capacity (*sāmarthya*) to generate visual impressions. Yet their visual system still exists because it is efficacious in bringing about its own successor-moments (*phala-pratigrahaṇa*). Each moment of the visual system produces the next (hence the visual system persists during the period of darkness and we can still see when the light is switched back on), and for this reason each moment is efficacious.[84]

The notion of *karitrā*

Present existence without efficacy?

There must have been considerable internal debate about how the doctrine of the existence of everything is to be understood, for the Sarvāstivāda commentarial literature lists no less than four possible interpretations, each associated with one of the great Sarvāstivāda teachers, and each illustrated by a particular example.[85]

Different interpretations of 'everything exists'

[83] Bhikkhu Dhammajoti 2009: 126.

[84] As Saṃghabhadra points out: 'If a *saṃskṛta dharma* serves as a cause for the projection of its own fruit, it is said to be [exercising its] *kāritra*. If it serves as a condition assisting [in the producing of the fruit of] a different [series], it is said to be [exercising] its efficacy/function' (Bhikkhu Dhammajoti 2009: 130).

[85] Bhikkhu Dhammajoti 2009: 119–20.

1. Dharmatrāta

The first account, due to Dharmatrāta, compares the change of the temporal status of a *dharma* to melting down a golden vessel to produce another golden artifact. This account is described in terms of *bhava-anyathātva*, a 'difference in terms of mode of being'. The underlying substance of the *dharma* (such as the gold) stays the same, while its mode of being in terms of temporal properties changes (as the piece of gold first has the shape of a vessel and then that of a statue, for example). The difficulty with this approach is that we now need to make sense of the change of temporal properties. In this case it looks as if we need to postulate a second-order time, such that relative to it some entity first has the property of pastness and then of presentness. This is unattractive because we now require another, third level notion of time relative to which the second level changes, and so on, all the way up the hierarchy. Alternatively, we need to think of the notion of 'transformation' appealed to here as itself non-temporal. Such notions do exist (consider, for example, the transformation of one mathematical equation into another), though how this would help in explaining the notion of change relative to temporal properties is, unfortunately, far from clear.

2. Ghoṣaka

The second account, due to Ghoṣaka (described as *lakṣaṇa-anyathātva*, 'difference of characteristics'), presents a relational view of temporal properties. He argues that in the same way one man can be simultaneously attached to three women, so one *dharma* can at the same time have the different characteristics (*lakṣaṇa*) of being past, present, and future. In the example of the womanizer the strength of his attachment to the individual women can vary, and by transferring this to the temporal case we can, for example, argue that as a past *dharma* becomes present, its link with the past declines and its link with the present becomes stronger. This view might strike us as problematic if we believe that the three temporal properties are mutually incompatible: nothing that is present can be either past or future, not even to a minute degree. Yet the trichromatic theory of vision tells us that we see all the colours we can distinguish by perceiving a mix of simultaneously seeing red, blue, and green. So why would we not be able to conceive of every temporal predicate as a mixture of being present, past, and future? Conceiving of time in this way would give us a possibility of distinguishing, for example, between the recent past and the remote future, by arguing that the former is a time with strong relations to the past and weaker relations to the present, while the latter has much stronger relations to the future and much weaker relations to the present.

3. Vasumitra

Account number three, associated with Vasumitra (referred to as *avasthā-anyathātva*, 'difference of state'), also explains temporal properties in a relational manner, though by using a model that differs from Ghoṣaka's. In the same way in which the balls in an abacus do not represent different numbers by intrinsic differences, but by being placed in a specific position relative to another, so the difference between temporal properties is just one of state (*avasthā*), and can be accounted for in terms of relations but not in terms of a difference in substance. One way in which we could spell out this account is in terms of the relation of an object to its function. Present fire is present because it is connected to its function and can therefore heat; fire which cannot do so is either past or future. According to this account, present fire is not intrinsically different from past fire (in the same way as the counter for the thousands in the abacus is not a bigger ball than the counter for the hundreds), but the difference between the two is to be accounted for in relational terms.

4. Buddhadeva

The final account, due to Buddhadeva, continues the relational understanding of temporal properties by observing that roles in a family structure are also not monadic but relational. This account is described as *anyathā-anyathātva*, 'difference of difference'. The idea is that as the same person is labelled as a mother relative to one person and as a daughter relative to another, so entities receive their temporal designation relative to other periods of time. In the same way, something may be past relative to the present and future relative to the very remote past.

It is worth noting that, apart from the first (which is also likely to be the earliest), all accounts characterize temporality in relational terms without implying any change of substance. Of these accounts the Sarvāstivādins selected the third account, that of Vasumitra, as the most satisfactory one. It conceives of temporal properties in terms of a specific state (*avasthā*), which in this context is the phenomenon's efficacy (*karitrā*). As a ball of an abacus receives its numerical value according to where it is placed relative to the framework of the abacus, so the event's temporal status depends on its relation to its *karitrā*.

*sarvāstitva* as a form of substantialism

Various Buddhist opponents have criticized the Sarvāstivāda notion of existence of the three times,[86] and it does indeed appear to be a curious interpretation of the doctrine of momentariness. For it now seems that there is some unchanging underlying basis after all (the continuous existence of all phenomena), which is then transformed when it takes on the efficacy of *karitrā* to form present entities. It interesting to note that the Sarvāstivāda notion of trans-temporal existence may be regarded as one of a number of concepts in Buddhist philosophy that appear to go against the non-self, insubstantialist picture usually regarded as a central characteristic of Buddhist thought. The Pudgalavāda's account of a person is obviously another instance that belongs in the same category, as are later notions such as the Yogācāra's foundational consciousness and the theory of Buddha-nature (*tathāgatagarbha*). We would not necessarily want to presuppose that all these 'substantialist' currents are introduced for similar reasons, though there are certain aspects that may still

[86] *bhāṣya* on *Abhidharmakośa* 5: 27, Pradhan 1975: 297–300, Poussin and Pruden 1988–90: 3. 810–16, Dhammajoti 2009: ch. 5, see also Aung and Davids 1915: 242.

be shared amongst them. As noted above, the dynamics of Buddhist philosophy are not simply determined by following wherever the argument leads, but require (like all philosophical endeavours that claim to spell out the details of a certain religious worldview) a connection with the key tenets of fundamental texts. How exactly these texts are to be interpreted, and what qualifies as 'key', are of course matters that are themselves open to debate. Nevertheless, while there are many ways a text can be read, it might not be interpretable in any way whatsoever, and any interpretation of the Buddha's teaching that ascribes belief in a form of *ātman* to him is unlikely to have been accepted by the Buddhist community.[87]

Substantialism as a rhetorical strategy

One way in which the introduction of these 'substantialist' motives could be explained that does not simply understand them as a flirtation with heretical views is as a rhetorical strategy, that is, as an attempt to attract attention to specific philosophical texts. Ostensibly Buddhist texts that appear to contradict core Buddhist tenets are more likely to attract criticism (and hence interest) from fellow Buddhist authors, and if it can be shown that the contradiction is only apparent, so much the better for the chances of the text to be regarded as both innovative and authoritative.[88] A somewhat more benign view (though not necessarily one that excludes the one just mentioned) is to consider the exposition of 'substantialist' views as an attempt at inclusivism. This means that Buddhist doctrines would be presented in the conceptual framework of non-Buddhist points of view in order to make them more widely understood. Closely connected with this idea is that of the graded teaching of the Buddhist doctrines. The Buddha is supposed to have adapted his exposition in relation to the preconceptions of his audience, and later Buddhist thinkers claim to have embraced this technique. As such, the 'substantialist' views could be understood as a form of teaching the Buddhist doctrine that at a later stage has to be supplanted by more adequate expositions that bring out the teaching of emptiness in a comprehensive manner.

Substantialism and inclusivism

Centrality of causation

Causation plays a central role for Sarvāstivāda, in fact the school was also known by the name *hetuvāda*, 'the theory of causes'. The intrinsic nature (*svabhāva*) of the ultimately existent *dharma*s is causally produced,[89] and the ability to be causally efficacious is what the Sarvāstivādins consider to be the mark of existence. Causal efficacy is a notion that is more comprehensive than

[87] Though certain kind of *tathāgatagarbha* texts came quite close to this, even employing the term *ātman* in the exposition of the Buddhist position (Jones 2014). See above, p. 189.

[88] It has been suggested that Madhyamaka authors pursued a similar strategy in their exposition of the theory of emptiness, giving the appearance of embracing a nihilistic (and therefore non-Buddhist) view, without in fact doing so.

[89] Strictly speaking, this only applies to the conditioned *dharma*s, though these constitute the greatest part of the Abhidharma ontology. Though not causally produced, the unconditioned *dharma*s still possess causal power (Bhikkhu Dhammajoti 2009: 164).

*karitrā*, the mark of the present. Past and future entities, though devoid of *karitrā*, still exist because they are causally efficacious in being able to function as objects (*ālambana*) of mental cognitions of past and future.[90] Causation and the ability to produce effects therefore stands at the very centre of the Sarvāstivāda ontology; if we cannot show that something is causally active we cannot show that it exists at all.

Causation and existence

The most controversial notion in this context is the Sarvāstivāda idea of the simultaneity of cause and effect (*sahabhū-hetu*). They argue that in certain cases cause and effect arise at the same time, rather than sequentially. Such cases are the four great elements which mutually produce one another at a single time, or mental events (*citta*) and their accompaniments (*cittānuvarttin*), which arise together at the same moment. This view of causation is hardly intuitive; in most of the cases of causation we observe, the cause happens first and the effect takes place at a later time. The Sarvāstivādins motivate the theory of simultaneous causation with two examples. The first is the example of the fire and its illumination. The fire and the illumination are distinct things, one causing another, but when we bring the existence of the first about the existence of the second is immediately entailed. The second is the example of a bundle of mutually supporting reeds. The cause of each reed staying upright is the other reeds staying upright, but all the reeds stay upright simultaneously, hence the causes and effects all happen at the same time.[91]

Simultaneity of cause and effect

The theory of simultaneous causation plays its greatest part in the Sarvāstivāda epistemology. According to their theory of knowledge the sense organ, the sensory object, and the perception all exist at the same time. As the former two are causes of the latter as an effect, this account presupposes that cause and effect can temporally coincide. This in turn allows the Sarvāstivādins to endorse a realist epistemology. Without the theory of simultaneous causation an epistemology presupposing the theory of momentariness is inevitably pushed in the direction of some form of representationalism. If the perception that is the effect happens in the moment after the cause that consists of the sensory organ and object, the cause will already have passed away when the perception exists. If we want to assume that perceptions have any objects at all, we will have to postulate some kind of *simulacrum* (such as a representation) that can stand in for the object that no longer exists.[92] The Theravāda attempted to solve this difficulty by introducing the idea that mind-moments and matter-moments could run at different speeds (one matter-moment was

Epistemology

Momentariness and representationalism

Variable speed of moments

[90] Bhikkhu Dhammajoti 2009: 72: 'the possibility of a cognition necessarily implies the true ontological status of the object cognized', 147.

[91] The Yogācārins also use the same example to support the simultaneous causal relationship between the foundational consciousness and the defiled *dharmas*. See Bhikkhu Dhammajoti 2009: 160.

[92] See *Abhidhammatthasaṅgaho*, IV. 8, Bhikkhu Dhammajoti 2007a: 174; Kim 1999.

supposed to last sixteen mind-moments). As a short person and a tall person can walk in unison, as long as the short person takes more steps than the tall person during the same amount of time. In the same way, if mind-moments are shorter than matter-moments, a matter-moment could persist during the existence of two or more mind-moments. The difficulty with this approach is that it does not sit well with the Abhidharma arguments that nothing lasts longer than an instant (*kṣaṇa*). Given that these arguments apply to any *kṣaṇa*, it is hard to see how they could support the claim that *kṣaṇa*s of one kind last longer than *kṣaṇa*s of another kind.[93]

Simultaneity and realism

Simultaneity of causation, on the other hand, allows for a realist epistemology, since the object cognized and the thought cognizing it exist at the same time.[94] In his **Abhidharma-nyāyānusāra-śāstra*, Saṃghabhadra argues that this is the only sensible way of understanding how perception works. If the object of perception had already passed away at the time when the perception happens, perception would appear to arise either uncaused or caused purely by itself, since it has no object. Moreover, how could we be in any way more justified in saying that visual perception perceives a visual object rather than a sound, given that both are equally absent when the perception occurs?[95] On the other hand, if the object perceived as present is not actually present but past, what is the basis of determining which past object is perceived here? If the past objects are all equally non-existent, any one seems to be as good as any other in order to function as an object of visual perception.[96]

Sautrāntika criticism of simultaneous causation

Nevertheless, the coherence of the idea that cause and effect can exist at the same time was questioned by different schools of Buddhist thought, first and foremost by the Sautrāntikas.[97] They argued that when two things arise at the same time, as in the case of two horns of an ox, we cannot determine which causes which. Is it the left horn causing the right horn, or the other way round? Moreover, when we consider our everyday experience of causation, involving seeds and sprouts, potters and pots, or fire and ashes, causation seems to be precisely *not* simultaneous; rather, we observe that the cause exists first and the effect only arises some time afterwards.

Sarvāstivāda response

The Sarvāstivādin seems to have a good reply to the first objection, namely that the two horns are not causally related at all, but rather have a common cause, namely the ox. When one horn is broken off the other is not thereby damaged, indicating that neither is cause or effect of

[93] According to Xuanzang, the assumption that only mental phenomena are momentary, while material objects last for a longer time, was also made by the Sāṃmitīyas (Bhikkhu Dhammajoti 2007a: 174).

[94] Bhikkhu Dhammajoti 2009: 243.

[95] Bhikkhu Dhammajoti 2007a: 137, see also 153.

[96] Bhikkhu Dhammajoti 2007a: 140.

[97] For a discussion of the simultaneity of causation in the context of Madhyamaka thought see Westerhoff 2009: 120–1.

the other.[98] Regarding the second point, the Sarvāstivādin can repeat his examples of the light and the bundle of reeds. Even though not all instances of causation involve the simultaneity of cause and effect, some of them do.[99] How successful such examples (and similar ones, like the two ends of a seesaw, or a leaden ball and the depression in a cushion it produces)[100] are is of course debatable. In the case of the light and its illumination, it is important to be clear about whether the term 'light' refers to whatever holds and sustains the flame (such as an oil-lamp, wick, and oil) or to the flame itself. In the context of this debate the latter seems to be intended.[101] But in this case the illumination appears to be just a property, rather than an effect of the light, in the same way as an object's shape is. The appearance of simultaneity seems to be due to a specific way of conceptualization that regards properties as effects. In the case of the bundle of reeds, one might similarly claim that reconceptualizing the situation removes the appearance of simultaneous causation. If we consider the effect to be the fact that all the reeds stand up together, and the cause to be the ground, the surface structure of the individual reeds, and so on, cause and effect would no longer turn out to be simultaneous.

Direct perception and self-cognition

A clear advantage of the Sarvāstivāda theory of simultaneity of perception and percept is that it can account for the 'vividness and immediacy'[102] of the results of the perceptual process. The reason why perception appears to us as direct is because there is a temporally direct (i.e. simultaneous) connection between the external entity perceived and the mental event perceiving it. Representationalist theories of perception face the difficulty that they have to regard the immediacy of perception to be illusory, since there is strictly speaking no 'direct perception'—we are only acquainted with a stand-in for the perceived object, in the Sautrāntika case a present recollection of an object existing earlier. The Sautrāntikas address this challenge by arguing that the act of perception is self-aware.[103] Because at the same time as apprehending a perceptual object our mind also perceives itself, we have the impression of perceptual immediacy, an immediacy that is not the immediacy of immediate contact with the entity

[98] Bhikkhu Dhammajoti 2003: 37.

[99] By arguing in this way the Sarvāstivādin can also escape the Humean point that simultaneous causation implies that everything happens at the same time. If only some causes and effects temporally coincide causal sequences can still be temporally extended.

[100] Westerhoff 2009: 121.

[101] Bhikkhu Dhammajoti 2003: 38–9 quotes Saṃghabhadra's discussion during which the Sarvāstivādin claims that 'it is not perceived that when the lamp first arises, there is the lamp without the light. It has never been observed that a lamp exists without light.' As we frequently encounter unlit oil-lamps we should assume that the lamp's flame is denoted by terms such as *pradīpaḥ*, *agniḥ*, or *mar me ni mun pa* in passages like *Mūlamadhyamakakārikā* 7: 8–12, *Vigrahavyāvartanī* 34–9, and *Vaidalyaprakaraṇa* 6–11.

[102] Bhikkhu Dhammajoti 2007a: 159.

[103] Bhikkhu Dhammajoti 2007a: 159.

perceived but with the perceptual act itself. The Sarvāstivāda, on the other hand, does not accept this Sautrāntika idea of reflexive awareness (*svasaṃvedana*).[104]

The matter of reflexive awareness becomes very important in later Yogācāra discussions. For the Sarvāstivādins, the awareness that something is directly experienced by me (*idaṃ me pratyakṣam iti*) is a clear indication of the existence of external objects. Perception, a key epistemic instrument (*pratyakṣaṃ pramāṇānāṃ gariṣṭham*) establishes the existence of objects causally simultaneous with it.[105] The Yogācārins, like the Sautrāntikas, accept reflexive awareness,[106] and therefore have a response to the objection that our experience appears vivid and direct to us, even though on the Yogācāra account there are not any external objects whatsoever.

*svabhāva*

While there is no enduring person, Buddhists still need to find a way to account for karma. If there is no self that travels from life to life, or even from moment to moment, how can we be assured that positive and negative karmic potential actually attaches to the mental stream in which it originated, rather than to some other one? Different schools of Buddhism tried to account for this problem in different ways. As we have just seen, the Sarvāstivādins came up with an ingenious idea that is reflected in the school's name *sarva-asti-vāda*, the doctrine that everything exists. They claim that *dharma*s do not arise from a non-existent future, become existent, and then, as they become past, vanish into non-existence again. Rather, *dharma*s exist during all three times. In order to accommodate the blatant implausibility of this view (we cannot use yesterday's or tomorrow's fire to cook today's rice) they had to introduce a couple of additional terms. They used the term *svabhāva* to denote a constant essence persisting through the three times which is the basis of differentiating between things. But while past and presence fire would have the same *svabhāva*, only the present fire would also have efficacy (*kāritra*), a property produced by causes and conditions, which ensures that the *dharma* is actually able to carry out a function. This has the curious property that the *dharma*'s *svabhāva* is actually not to be found in the properties we use to perceive it: the brightness, heat, destructive power, and so forth of the fire are something that manifests in the present, but cannot be part of the fire's atemporal essence.

The relation of the two concepts *svabhāva* and *kāritra* is far from straightforward. On the one hand they cannot be the same, since the former exists throughout the three times, whereas the latter exists only in the present. Yet they cannot be completely distinct either, since what makes the fire the fire is the possession of its intrinsic properties like heat, but if these are completely

[104] Bhikkhu Dhammajoti 2007a: 109–10, 141.

[105] Bhikkhu Dhammajoti 2007a: 141. The Sanskrit citations are from Vasubandhu's autocommentary on verses 15 and 16 of his *Vijñāptimātratāsiddhi* (Ruzsa and Szegedi 2015: 150–2).

[106] See above, pp. 184–5.

removed from the *svabhāva* and only associated with the fire's efficacy, it is then unclear what role this 'intrinsic nature' of fire still has to play. Fittingly, we find Abhidharma sources pointing out that one cannot 'say with any certainty that they are the same or different'.[107]

The Abhidharma notion of *dharmas*

The notion of a *dharma* is commonly defined in an etymological fashion, based on the root *dhṛ* (to hold, to bear) as 'something that holds its own characteristic'.[108] This 'own characteristic' (*svalakṣaṇa*) is unique and remains unchangeable throughout the *dharma*'s existence; it is frequently identified with the *dharma*'s *svabhāva*.[109]

1. Mereological independence

Within the Abhidharma texts we find two important criteria for what makes a *dharma* a *dharma*. The first is *mereological independence*. Something that has parts only borrows its nature from these parts, and such a thing is not sufficiently fundamental to count as a *dharma*. Vasubandhu points out that whatever disappears when its parts are separated is no *dharma*. When the pot is broken, we are left only with shards; when the chariot is disassembled, there is no chariot any more, but only wooden parts.[110] Pots and chariots are therefore no *dharmas*.

2. Conceptual independence

The second criterion is a more abstract version of the first. It is not concerned with the physical parts of an object, but with its conceptual parts: this is the criterion of *conceptual independence*. Vasubandhu points out that if a thing disappears when dissolved by the mind it also cannot be regarded as a *dharma*. The example he provides is that of a water atom. Such a partless particle is mereologically simple, and therefore not ruled out by the first criterion. But a water atom has different qualities: shape, colour, stickiness, and so forth. If we break the atom apart mentally, we are left with no water but only with a conglomeration of properties that collectively characterized it. The only entities that qualify for *dharma*hood by this more stringent second criterion appear to be property instances (sometimes referred to as particularized properties or tropes): this blue colour over here (which is not the same as that blue colour over there), this circular shape over here, and so on.[111]

This double understanding of *dharmas* as mereologically and conceptually independent is not restricted to the Sarvāstivāda Abhidharma. In a Theravāda source[112] we learn that a chariot, a house, and a fist are designated in dependence on their parts put together, but also that time and space are similarly

[107] Frauwallner 1995: 199.
[108] *svalakṣaṇa-dhāraṇāt dharmaḥ*, Bhikkhu Dhammajoti 2009: 19.
[109] Bhikkhu Dhammajoti 2009: 19, 123; Williams 1981: 242.
[110] *Abhidharmakośa* 6:4, Poussin and Pruden 1988–90: 3. 910–11.
[111] The *Abhidharmamahāvibhāṣa* notes that 'the entity itself is [its] characteristic, and the characteristic is the entity itself; for it is the case for all *dharmas* that the characteristic cannot be predicated apart from the *dharma* itself' (Bhikkhu Dhammajoti 2009: 19).
[112] Walser 2005: 242–3.

designated in dependence on the revolution of sun and moon. The chariot is mereologically dependent on its parts, but the revolution of sun and moon are no mereological parts of time and space. They are, rather, complex concepts derived from other concepts and, having been broken down into their constituent concepts, disappear, as the chariot does when it is disassembled. Mereological independence is not sufficient for something to qualify as a *dharma*; what keeps complexes of matter from being a *dharma* also keeps complexes of concepts from being one.

*dravya* and *prajñapti*

The notion of a *dharma* (and of its existence by *svabhāva*) is essential for establishing the key Abhidharma distinction between those things that exist substantially (*dravyasat*) and those that exist only as designations (*prajñaptisat*). Yaśomitra's commentary on the *Abhidharmakośa* points out that 'to be existent as an absolute entity is to be existent as an intrinsic characteristic'.[113] These *svalakṣaṇas*, which are the *svabhāvas* of *dharmas*, are simply the particularized properties; the medium-sized dry goods of our everyday acquaintance are superimpositions that the mind makes on the basis of conglomerations of such properties.[114] Some will be regarded as a pot, some as a chariot, and others as a person.

Existential status of *prajñapti*

What exactly the existential status of designated entities amounts to is a topic on which opinions differ in Abhidharma. In the most extreme case designations are regarded as not amounting to anything over and above mere talk, a convenient shorthand without any existential impact. According to this perspective, the distinction between the two truths boils down to the existence of a single truth, since only the entities that are fundamentally real exist at all. When we speak about the two truths we do not have different kinds of entities in mind, but rather mean two different ways of looking at the same entities. The *Abhidharma-mahāvibhāṣa*[115] points out that:

> There is indeed only one truth, the absolute truth.... The two truths are established in terms of difference in perspective, not in terms of real entities: in terms of real entities, there is only one truth, the absolute truth; in terms of difference in perspective, two types [of truth] are established.

This difference in perspective depends on who is looking: ultimate truth is the way enlightened beings (*āryas*) see the world, conventional truth is that which is reflected in way ordinary beings conceive of it.[116]

[113] *paramārthena sat svalakṣaṇa sat ity arthaḥ*, Wogihara 1990: 889; see Bhikkhu Dhammajoti 2009: 19.

[114] For the later development of the notion of *svalakṣaṇa* in the thought of Diṅnāga see pp. 220–1 below.

[115] Bhikkhu Dhammajoti 2009: 66.

[116] Bhikkhu Dhammajoti 2009: 67.

The fifth-century writer Saṅghabhadra, on the other hand, ascribes a limited existential status to designated entities; like substantial entities they play a role in acquiring knowledge about the world. He notes that:

> when the idea is produced with regard to a thing without dependence [on other things] this thing is *dravyasat*. When it is produced with regard to a thing in dependence [on other things], that thing is *prajñaptisat*, for example, a jug or an army.[117]

According to this understanding, substantial objects produce knowledge about themselves in an unmediated fashion. In most cases, however, knowledge is only produced in a mediated fashion: to know the jug we need to be acquainted with the pieces of clay that make up the jug; to know the army we need to know individual soldiers. To know a *dharma*, on the other hand, we do not need to rely on anything else. For Saṅghabhadhra, designated objects are not just bits of language: they also play an important role in how we get to know objects in the world.[118]

### *e. Sthaviranikāya: Sautrāntika*

It is commonly agreed that the Sautrāntikas developed out of the Sarvāstivāda, and this school has acquired considerable subsequent doxographic prominence by being considered (together with the Sarvāstivāda or Vaibhāṣika) as one of the two schools of the 'lower vehicle' in Indo-Tibetan explications of the different schools of Buddhist philosophy. The name of the school tells us that the *sūtra*s were of particular importance for its followers, and Yaśomitra, a commentator on Vasubandhu's *Abhidharmakośabhāṣya*, defines them as those who regard the *sūtra*s, but not the commentaries (*śāstra*s), as authoritative.[119] The second of these epithets tells us more than the first, since all Buddhists can reasonably be expected to regard the Buddha's discourses as authoritative. The term *śāstra* is here to be understood as referring to the Abhidharma treatises, and it is these, therefore, which the Sautrāntikas were considered to reject. For the Sautrāntikas, it is argued, the authority of the Abhidharma was not simply derivative relative to the *sūtra*s, but was no authority at all. This, however, does not yet tell us anything about the positions the Sautrāntikas defended, and in fact, for a school that is by some considered to be the second major division of non-Mahāyāna Buddhism, there is an extremely limited range of information on its views. No Sautrāntika treatises have come down to us,[120] and it does not appear

Emphasis on *sūtra* over *śāstra*

Limited information available

[117] Walser 2005: 212.

[118] The later development of this ontological dualism by Diṅnāga in terms of the notions of *svalakṣaṇa* and *sāmānyalakṣaṇa* is closer to this understanding: both are taken to exist, though only the former is fundamental. See pp. 220–1 below.

[119] *ye sūtraprāmāṇikāḥ na tu śāstraprāmāṇikāḥ*, Swami Dwarikadas Shastri 1970: 15.

[120] Walser 2005: 229. As Bareau (2013: 204) laconically puts it: 'we know nothing of their domain... neither do we know anything of their literature.'

as if there ever was a distinct Sautrāntika ordination lineage.[121] The term 'school' here refers to doctrinal distinctions, not to the fact that the Sautrāntikas would have had their own set of monastic rules differing from those of other schools. Most of our information about their positions is based on Vasubandhu's *Abhidharmakośabhāṣya*, which is supposed comment from a Sautrāntika perspective on a root text that describes Sarvāstivāda doctrines. It is unlikely that Vasubandhu was the first Sautrāntika (though the term is not attested before his usage in the *Abhidharmakośabhāṣya*),[122] yet how these early Sautrāntika views of 'an anti-Abhidharma Hīnayāna tradition with no literary remains'[123] would relate to Vasubandhu's position, and whether it in turn agrees with the positions of Diṅnāga and Dharmakīrti,[124] which have also sometimes been labelled as 'Sautrāntika' positions,[125] is a moot point.

Rejection of Sarvāstivāda view of time

What seems to be relatively clear, however, is that the Sautrāntikas (at least as described by Vasubandhu) disagreed with the eponymous doctrine of the Sarvāstivāda, the idea that things in all three times exist.[126] Some authors argued that the Sautrāntikas do not appear to be 'a group having a defined set of doctrinal positions', apart from the fact that their 'perspective can be characterized only by a rejection of the definitive Sarvāstivāda position that factors *exist* in the three periods of time'.[127] So far it might be most satisfactory to consider the term 'Sautrāntika' to refer to a broader range of positions unified by the fact that they put special emphasis on the *sūtra*s and reject the Sarvāstivāda theory of transtemporal existence.

The Dārṣṭāntikas

The Dārṣṭāntika school, which is described in Abhidharma treatises as disagreeing with the Sarvāstivāda tradition, was closely related to the Sautrāntika, but the exact nature of their relation is not entirely clear. It may be that the Dārṣṭāntikas represent an earlier school and that the Sautrāntikas split off from this,[128] though Yaśomitra claims that the Dārṣṭāntikas are a particular type of Sautrāntikas, not the other way round.[129] Matters are further complicated by the fact that when both schools are referred to the term Dārṣṭāntika frequently

[121] Willemen, Dessein, and Cox 1998: 109.

[122] Gold 2015a: 5, Kritzer 2003a: 210. Kuījī (窺基) mentions three Sautrāntika teachers: Kumārالāta, the founding teacher of the Sautrāntikas who is supposed to have lived about 100 years after the Buddha's death, Śrīlāta, and a third, who is presumably identical with Vasubandhu (Poussin 1928–9: 221–2).

[123] Jackson 1993: 112.

[124] Singh 1984, 1995. Note, however, the very critical considerations raised by Hayes 1986.

[125] Or at least as the strange hybrid of 'Yogācāra-Sautrāntika'. Indian and Tibetan doxography also mentions the categories of Sautrāntika 'following scripture' (*āgamānuyāyī*) and Sautrāntika 'following reasoning' (*yuktyānuyāyī*), the former referring to the kind of Sautrāntika discussed by Vasubandhu, the latter to the systems of Diṅnāga and Dharmakīrti.

[126] Bareau 2013: 206, *bhāṣya* on *Abhidharmakośa* 5: 27, Pradhan 1975: 297–300, Poussin and Pruden 1988–90. 3. 810–16.

[127] Willemen, Dessein, and Cox 1998: 109.

[128] Willemen, Dessein, and Cox 1998: 108.

[129] Cox 1988: 70, n. 4.

appears to have a pejorative ring to it, a connotation not present in the case of the term Sautrāntika.[130] Their name, derived from *dṛṣṭānta* ('example'), may result from the assumption that they 'were known for their active effort in popularizing the Buddha's teachings, employing poetry and possibly other literary devices... and were particularly skilled in utilizing similes and allegories in demonstrating the Buddhist doctrines'.[131]

If, as the Sautrāntikas hold, the Sarvāstivāda account is to be rejected, what then is the status of past and future entities? According to the exposition of Sautrāntika we find in Vasubandhu's *Abhidharmakośabhāṣya*, everything lasts only for a moment. Not only do past and future entities fail to exist in any substantial way,[132] the present also does not possess any temporal thickness; immediately after coming into existence each moment passes out of existence. The theory of momentariness therefore claims that all constituents of the world, all *dharmas*, whether mental or material, only last for an instant (*kṣaṇa*) and cease immediately after arising. Permanence is a mere appearance produced by the fact that very similar moments rapidly arise and cease one after another, succeeding each other in such quick succession that we are ordinarily unable to perceive them as moments, but only see change that is underpinned by objects that endure through time. This peculiar cinematographic conception of reality conceives of the world as a kind of three-dimensional film projection. Individual *dharmas* succeed each other like frames in a movie, and blur into each other because our perception lacks the temporal discrimination necessary to tell them apart.

Momentariness

Cinematographic conception of reality

Vasubandhu's argument for momentariness[133] takes as its first premise the idea that everything is impermanent, a position that is, of course, well supported by the Buddha's theory of the three marks of existence.[134] If everything eventually perishes, what brings this about in each particular case? There may be an external cause operating on each object, moving it from existence to non-existence, or each object may eventually destroy itself without any external

Vasubandhu's argument for momentariness

[130] Willemen, Dessein, and Cox 1998: 109.

[131] Bhikkhu Dhammajoti 2009: 74.

[132] Candrakīrti, commenting on *Mūlamadhyamakakārikā* 22:11 in the *Prasannapadā*, notes that for the Sautrāntika past and future are empty, though other things are not (*tathā sautrāntika mate 'tītā anāgataṃ śūnyam anyad aśūnyam*, Poussin 1913: 444: 15). Their being empty means that they exist only by force of conceptual construction (*prajñapti*), though not in any ultimately real way. When the Sautrāntika denies the existence of past and future he does not deny that we can meaningfully talk about past and future, though he denies that such talk has any ontological import.

[133] See Siderits 2007: 119–23; von Rospatt 1995, section II.II.D (pp. 178–95) for further discussion of the argument for momentariness from the spontaneity of destruction.

[134] That everything is impermanent does, of course, not entail that everything (or indeed anything) is momentary, and von Rospatt (1995: 14) points out that 'there can be no doubt that the theory of momentariness cannot be traced back to the beginnings of Buddhism or even the Buddha himself'. Like many Buddhist concepts, the theory of momentariness is best thought of as a fruit produced from a conceptual seed present in the Buddha's own teaching.

influence. Once its existential power is exhausted it simply vanishes. The first possibility seems to be what accords most closely with the manifest image of the world, where windows are shattered, flowers wither, and humans die, all because of the influence of external causes (the brick, the heat, the tumor in the brain). Yet there are difficulties with conceptualizing these as causing non-existences, unless we assume that non-existences are real objects, first-class ontological citizens of the world, and not merely linguistic hypostatizations, as the Buddhists assume. The second premise of the argument is therefore the claim that particular non-existences are not things that can stand in causal relations.[135] When something causes the non-existence of something else there is no *thing* that is causally brought into existence.

One way of conceiving of this situation is to argue that because absences are just language-based constructions, nothing perishes at all. There is simply a *transformation* of the window into shards, but nothing has ceased to exist. We merely label the transformed object in a new way. Alternatively, even if some $x$ did really go out of existence (rather than being transformed into something else), what the cause has brought about is the total state of affairs that does not include $x$, or alternatively, the last moment in the succession of moments that constitutes $x$.[136] In neither case has a non-existent object played a part in a causal chain.

If we hold on to the assumptions that things really perish, the second possibility, that everything eventually self-destructs without any need for outside influence, is the one to follow. This self-destruction could happen after a period of time, or immediately after the object comes into existence. Again, the first possibility seems more plausible. Here each individual object is treated like an individual clock that keeps on ticking as long as energy is provided by its coiled spring, but once this is exhausted the clock stops. For each thing there is an internal process such that once this has run its course, the thing goes out of existence. But there is a difficulty with trying to apply this horological imagery to the Abhidharma's fundamental *dharmas*. This is the third premise required for the argument, namely that *dharmas* do not change. For their internal change could neither be understood in terms of the interaction of its internal parts (because *dharmas* have no parts), nor could it be conceived of as a successive gaining and losing of properties. For any thing that gains and loses properties must be ontologically complex, consisting at least of one individual and one property, and *dharmas* are not supposed to be objects of this kind. Vasubandhu spells out his argument against change at the fundamental level in the context of his criticism of the Sāṃkhya theory of transformation (*pariṇāma*). The picture under discussion here is one in which

Criticism of Sāṃkhya

[135] Bareau 2013: 208, Kritzer 2003a: 206.

[136] See von Rospatt 1995: 185, and, more generally, section II.D; Gold 2015a: 108–9.

there is a set of unchanging background entities which gain and lose properties, just like a banana loses its green colour and acquires a yellow one. Yet if this background entity is linked by instantiation relations to these properties, the same background entity would first have the property of 'instantiating property *x*' and then the property of 'instantiating a different property *y*', and thus would change. But if the background entity does not change, and is completely untouched by the changing set of properties, it does not seem to play any ontological role at all. For all we know it might as well not be there, and then the question arises what motivation is still left for postulating such a background. It simply does not seem possible to link up unchanging entities with entities that do change.[137]

But in this case, and if *dharma*s cannot change, we have no choice but to pick the other alternative, namely that the destruction is a result of a thing's inner nature, and that this destruction happens immediately once the thing is produced, since there is no ontological space for any mechanism that could be the cause of a delay.

Three kinds of arguments for momentariness

Within the Buddhist philosophical tradition we can distinguish at least three kinds of arguments developed for establishing momentariness. We have just met the first, which we might call the argument from the *spontaneity of destruction*. We will discuss the other two, an argument from the *momentariness of cognition* and an argument from *change*, later on.[138] Forms of all three arguments make their reappearances in different guises at different stages in Buddhist philosophy.[139]

In accordance with the factors influencing the development of Buddhist philosophy in India mentioned above, we can distinguish at least three major reasons responsible for the popularity of the theory of momentariness in Indian Buddhist philosophy, reasons based on argumentative, doctrinal, and meditative considerations. Which of these is the most influential is difficult to determine, though each plays an important role. We have just seen an example of an important argument for momentariness, based on the notion of the spontaneity of destruction. We will now consider the other two factors that contributed to the prominence of the doctrine of momentariness.

Doctrinal reasons for momentariness

Doctrinally, the theory of momentariness is underpinned by the Buddha's teaching of the 'three seals' that characterize all things: that all existence is suffering, without self, and impermanent. Obviously impermanence has a more comprehensive meaning than momentariness; that everything is impermanent

[137] See Gold 2015a: 30–1.

[138] Feldman and Phillips 2011: 17 distinguish four kinds. In our discussion we group what they call arguments from causal efficacy together with arguments from change.

[139] For a comprehensive discussion of the various forms these arguments can take see von Rospatt 1995: 122–95.

is perfectly compatible with the view that objects persist for more than a moment (everything may cease to exist after a minute, say). Yet the theory of momentariness is one legitimate way of spelling out the impermanence of all things.

Meditative factors influencing the theory of momentariness

One of the motivations for spelling it out in precisely this way may well be based on the results of meditative practice. The idea is that specific meditative techniques based on refining the practitioner's capacity for attention (such as the 'foundations of mindfulness', *smṛti-upasthāna*), closely examining the body, sensations, and other mental states involve being mindful of the arising and ceasing of these states, and eventually lead to a realization of their momentariness. In the *Abhidharmakośabhāṣya* Vasubandhu points out that the foundation of mindfulness with respect to the body is realized once one perceives the body as a conglomerate of atoms and a succession of moments.[140]

Soteriological implications of realizing momentariness

The result of this realization is the ability to free oneself from the unwholesome emotional attitudes directed at the material objects, sensations, and mental states that are responsible for our continued existence in saṃsāra. In his commentary on the *Mahāyānasūtrālaṅkāra* Vasubandhu makes this point explicitly: when meditators direct their attention at the arising and ceasing of conditioned phenomena they perceive that they cease during every moment and dissolve into momentary instances. Otherwise they would not feel disenchantment, would not be free from defilements and obtain liberation, like ordinary beings who also experience cessation, as in the case of death (without being thereby freed from defilements).[141] When the momentariness of all *dharmas* is realized at the experiential level, Vasubandhu argues, the basis for developing attachment and aversion towards conglomerates of these *dharmas* ceases, as there is nothing staying around long enough to get attached to it, a consequence that does not follow if we simply realize the impermanence of things at a coarser level (such as the fact that everybody must die). Schmithausen[142] suggests that the consideration of these meditative experiences might have led to understanding the general claim of impermanence we find in the second seal in terms of the more radical idea of universal momentariness. This may be motivated by the attempt to establish an ontological basis for a meditative practices that are considered to be soteriologically efficacious. The thought is that if the fact that the meditator perceives all *dharmas* as split up into rapidly succeeding moments allows him to free himself from defilements, this must be because this realization allows him to see the world as it really is.

[140] *sāmāhitasya kila kāyaṃ paramāṇuśaḥ kṣaṇikataśca paśyataḥ kāyasmṛtyupasthāṇaṃ niṣpannaṃ bhavati*, Pradhan 1975: 341:14–15, Poussin and Pruden 1988–90: 3. 926.

[141] *manaskāreṇa ca yogināṃ | te hi saṃskārāṇām udayavyayau manasikurvantaḥ pratikṣaṇaṃ teṣāṃ nirodhaṃ paśyanti | anyathā hi teṣām api nirvidvirāgavimuktayo na syur yathānyeṣāṃ maraṇakālādiṣu nirodhaṃ paśyantāṃ*, Lévi 1907: 150: 3–5.

[142] Schmithausen 1973: 197.

The realization of momentariness is not a form of therapeutically useful make-belief that alleviates our emotional entanglement with the world, but an understanding of how the world works at a deep level that is usually hidden from ordinary beings.

Belief vs. realization

Precisely because the realization of momentariness is only available to practitioners after long meditative training, Buddhist philosophers have also come up with arguments to convince those without access to such direct experience of the claim that the entire world consists of a sequence of moments. Nevertheless, even if successful, all these arguments can hope to accomplish is establishing that the theory of momentariness is true. They do not generate an insight into it at the experiential level (in the same way in which our belief that a film in a cinema consists of quickly succeeding still frames does not allow us to see the frames), and it is only the insight at the experiential level that is deemed soteriologically efficacious.

Theory of perception

The theory of momentariness has immediate consequences for the Sautrāntika's account of perception. Perception appears to require temporally extended objects, and the argument just given seems to show that there are no such things. Perception takes place in time, and so the earliest a perception of any *dharma* at moment *t* can arise is at the moment after *t*. At the moment after *t*, however, the *dharma* has already passed out of existence. Yet when we perceive something, we presumably perceive something that exists. The Sarvāstivāda solved this issue by their assumption that the past object, though currently not efficacious, still exists. The Sautrāntikas, on the other hand, accepted that we can perceive non-existent objects, such as past or future entities.[143] Their disagreement with Sarvāstivāda lies primarily in their view of whether there needs to exist a separate object-support condition (*ālambana-pratyaya*) for every perception, something the Sarvāstivāda affirms and the Sautrāntika denies. The basic idea behind the Sautrāntika account is that at one mental moment, *t*, an object is grasped, though no knowledge of the object is produced.[144] This moment *t* then causes its successor moment, *t'*, which produces an inferential knowledge of the object that was grasped at *t*.[145] At *t'* the object-support condition no longer exists, and this object-support condition is also not what is causally responsible for *t'*, which is rather brought about by the immediately preceding condition (*samanantara-pratyaya*) *t*.[146] The knowledge of the external object at *t'* appears under an aspect or form (*ākāra*). This aspect can be understood both as a specific *way* of apprehending

Perceiving non-existent objects

The *ākāra* and its functions

[143] The Dārṣṭāntikas also subsume the cognition of illusory objects, such as the circle created by a whirling firebrand, of objects perceived in meditation, dreams, magical creations, and of contradictory objects like the son of a barren woman amongst perceptions based on non-existent objects (Cox 1988: 49).

[144] Bhikkhu Dhammajoti 2007b: 245–72.

[145] Bhikkhu Dhammajoti 2007a: 158–2.

[146] Bhikkhu Dhammajoti 2007b: 248.

an object, and as an *entity* corresponding to the object so apprehended.[147] This *ākāra* fulfils various theoretical functions. One is to tell apart different instances of knowledge,[148] given that they cannot be differentiated by the external objects they are knowledge of, as these objects no longer exist. Since all knowledge-episodes are without object-support condition, their respective *ākāra* allows us to differentiate one from the other. In addition, the *ākāra* can play a role in distinguishing perceptions of non-existent objects that we intuitively consider as veridical (such as that of a momentary phenomenon like a vase, that has already passed out of existence when we acquire knowledge of it) from those that we do not (such as a mirage). In neither case is there an object-support condition, but in the latter case, as there was never an object in the first place, the *ākāra* cannot resemble it, whereas it does so in the former.[149]

Perceiving past and future

When past and future objects are cognized, Vasubandhu argues in the *Abhidharmakośabhāṣya*, even though the object-support (*ālambana*) of their cognition no longer exists (or does not yet exist), a past or future phenomenon 'is in the way in which it is an object', characterized as having existed in the past, or as going to exist in the future.[150] Thus characterized, the cognition resembles the way the objects existed in the past, thereby supporting the accuracy of such perceptions without object-support from equally objectless illusory perceptions.[151] In this way, when we perceive a past object our perception is directed at the recollection of this object as having existed; when we perceive a future object it is the anticipation of it as going to exist. We do not have to assume that the object itself exists at the time of the perception.[152]

Sautrāntika view of nirvāṇa

The ability to perceive non-existent entities is important for Sautrāntika epistemology, not only in order to explain how we can meaningfully refer to past and future, but also to show how we could be in epistemic contact with other absences, such as nirvāṇa. The Sautrāntikas, in disagreement with the Sarvāstivāda and the Sthaviravada, held that nirvāṇa, being a mere absence (*abhāva*), is not a fundamentally existent thing (*dravya*).[153] In this respect nirvāṇa is comparable to space, another absence from resistance (*saprathigadravya*) that

[147] Kellner 2014: 289. [148] Krishnamacharya 1942: 26–7.

[149] '[T]he Sautrāntika notion is that the *ākāra* corresponds exactly to the external object. It allows no possibility of a cognitive error in a genuine *pratyakṣa* experience' (Bhikkhu Dhammajoti 2007b: 254).

[150] *yadā tad ālambanaṃ tathā asti kathaṃ tad ālambanam abhūt bhaviṣyati ceti*, Pradhan 1975: 299:25, Poussin and Pruden 1988–90: 3. 815.

[151] Cox 1988: 66–7. From this perspective the Sarvāstivāda account of the continuing existence of past objects would be problematic, since we might then assume that we experience such objects as presently existent, which we do not.

[152] The Sautrāntika's opponents object at this point by arguing that rather than perception of a non-existent, what we are dealing with here is the misperception of an existent, namely a mental phenomenon, that is mistakenly considered to be something non-mental (Cox 1988: 67). See also Bhikkhu Dhammajoti 2007b: 255.

[153] Bhikkhu Dhammajoti 2007a: 472, 478.

allows things to move, insofar as nirvāṇa denotes freedom from karmic potential to act, and freedom from the necessity of rebirth.[154] The Sautrāntikas refer to the conceptualization of nirvāṇa as the 'blowing out' of a flame, pointing out that as a flame gone out fails have ontological status, so does liberation.[155] This obviously leads to the question how we can have any knowledge of nirvāṇa, especially as it cannot exert any causal influence on our perceptual system, because absences have no causal powers. As such, a theory of perception that can explain epistemic contact with non-existent entities is required for the Sautrāntikas.

Mental continuity and karma

Like all Buddhist schools, the Sautrāntikas needed a way of accounting for karmic continuity. For this they introduce the concept of a 'support' (*āśraya*), which is the series of physical and psychological moments that make up the person.[156] Even though each moment is very short-lived, individual moments can be 'perfumed' (to use the metaphor given) by a trace (*vāsanā*) of the wholesome or unwholesome character of the action. This karmic scent is then passed on to the moment's successor-moment, which passes it on to its successor, until it finally brings about its karmic fruit at a later time,[157] all moments constituting a continuity of 'subtle mind' (*sūkṣmacitta*) that underlies the working of karmic causality.[158] Some of the wholesome seeds in a persons's mind-stream continue to abide and cannot be destroyed; they will, instead, give rise to further wholesome *dharmas*.[159] This idea can be seen as prefiguring a notion that would later become much more prominent in the Mahāyāna, namely the theory of the Buddha-nature, an indestructible, undefiled essence present in each mental stream which, though presently hidden, would be uncovered through progress on the Buddhist path.

Similarities between Sautrāntika and Yogācāra

The positions we have described above seem to bear some considerable similarity with ideas that are later elaborated in greater detail in Yogācāra.[160]

[154] Bareau 2013: 206. See Conze (1962: section III.3.1) for a comparison of the conceptualizations of nirvāṇa and of space in early Buddhism.

[155] Kritzer (2003a: 206) notes the tendency that in Sautrāntika and Dārṣṭāntika '[m]any of the entities that are said by Sarvāstivāda to be real are reduced in status to mere designations (*prajñapti*)'.

[156] Yogācāra writers used the term 'transformation of the substratum' (*āśraya-parāvṛtti*) to describe the process of awakening as the removal of the unwholesome potentials contained in the mental continuum. See p. 188 below.

[157] Conze 1962: 141–3, Bareau 2013: 206.

[158] Bareau 2013: 209; Warder 2000: 400. Warder notes that most schools of Abhidharma assumed the existence of some form of a series of moments of consciousness. Apart from the necessity of explaining karmic connections, another problem Buddhist accounts needed to solve is the continuity of consciousness after periods of deep meditative absorption, and it appears as if the Dārṣṭāntikas appealed to the notion of subtle consciousness in this respect (Kritzer 2003a: 204).

[159] 'Both Sautrāntikas and Yogācārins maintain that some innate wholesome dharmas can never be annihilated; they remain in the form of "seeds" intact in the "continuity", and new wholesome dharmas will arise from them under favourable conditions' (Conze 1962: 133. See also Jaini 1979: 246–7).

[160] See Kritzer 200a3: 207.

The representationalist position resulting from the Sautrāntika theory of momentariness can be naturally extended into an idealist position if we are able to argue (as Yogācārins indeed did later) that our perception of the world can be accounted for *just* in terms of these representations, without postulating a distinct level of represented objects as well. If we can perceive non-existent objects, it is far easier to understand how it can appear to us that we are living in a world of material objects, even though there are no such things. The Sautrāntika conception of mental continuity can be seen as being developed into a theory of foundational consciousness along Yogācāra lines, and the notion of permanent, wholesome factors within mental *continua* has obvious affinities with *tathāgatagarbha* theory.

Yogācāra as continuation of Sautrāntika?

All of this would make it appear as if there is a line of ideas beginning when the Sautrāntika split off from the Sarvāstivāda, a line which is then later taken up by Vasubandhu and used to criticize the Sarvāstivāda position in the *Abhidharmakośabhāṣya*, acts as a seed for various Yogācāra ideas, and is later incorporated into the systems of Diṅnāga and Dharmakīrti, systems which have at least a strong affinity to Yogācāra.

There are, however, good reasons to be sceptical about this supposed germination of Yogācāra from Sautrāntika. The main difficulty is that we do not have a clear conception of the kind of Sautrāntika that is supposed to have preceded Vasubandhu. As Walser[161] points out, they 'left no physical trace of themselves—no inscriptions, no cache of manuscripts, nothing to locate them either geographically or physically'. Most of the information we have about Sautrāntika beliefs stems from Vasubandhu's *Abhidharmakośabhāṣya*. Did he accurately report their positions? Lacking the original documents to compare Vasubandhu's position with, it is impossible to tell. It has been suggested recently that Vasubandhu, rather than endorsing the Sautrāntika position when composing the *Abhidharmakośabhāṣya*, was in fact already a Yogācārin.[162] This argument is based mainly on the fact that a considerable amount of the Sautrāntika positions (or positions very much like them) that Vasubandhu puts forward against the Sarvāstivāda can already be found in the *Yogācārabhūmi*, an earlier Yogācāra treatise. If this argument is accepted, an alternative to the 'germination' model mentioned above suggests itself. If Vasubandhu explains the Sautrāntika position while in fact holding Yogācāra positions, it is likely that he did so with two goals in mind. The first is to show that certain positions that are very much like Yogācāra positions have a strong basis in non-Mahāyāna scriptures. The orthodoxy of these views can then be underlined by their support from the earliest Buddhist sources. Referring to

Sautrāntika as bridging Abhidharma and Mahāyāna

[161] Walser 2005: 229.

[162] Kritzer 1999, 2003b. For some criticism of Kritzer's position see Bhikkhu Dhammajoti 2007b: 2.

this position as Sautrāntika ('followers of the *sūtras*') helps to make this message even more explicit: the views under consideration are not Mahāyāna distortions but are well entrenched even in a non-Mahāyāna context. Second, the Yogācāra views could consequently be regarded as merely spelling out what is already said more or less implicitly in the *sūtra*-based ('Sautrāntika') positions. The Sautrāntika position described by Vasubandhu would therefore have functioned as a philosophical bridge between non-Mahāyāna and Mahāyāna positions, linking back to the authority of the Buddha's discourses (as opposed to the Abhidharmic treatises), and looking towards the Mahāyāna elaboration of the concepts it already contains *in nuce*.

As we have noted above, the development of Buddhist philosophy is not just determined by the desire to develop better arguments than one's opponents, but it is also requires one to make the case that the conclusions argued for agree with what the Buddha actually wanted to say. As such, Vasubandhu's constructing Sautrāntika as a means to support the authority of Yogācāra as a teaching endorsed by the Buddha would appear to be a sensible move to make by a thinker defending a Mahāyāna position against its non-Mahāyāna critics.[163] An immediate consequence of this position is that the similarity of Sautrāntika and Yogācāra positions would lose much of its interest, as it would seem that the former was described precisely in such a way to make it resemble the latter. Moreover, there is very little we can say about Sautrāntika as an Abhidharma school if the main source we have for information on their views has been composed with an agenda in mind that the early Sautrāntikas would not have shared.

[163] The same attempt has been attributed to Nāgārjuna, who has been argued to have developed his Madhyamaka arguments in a way that stress their similarities with one Abhidharmic school over others. Again, the objective would have been to improve the chances of non-mainstream, Mahāyāna views being passed on by pointing out that they move argumentatively in the same direction as mainstream, non-Mahāyāna views. For more details see Chapter 2, section 00.

# 2

# Madhyamaka

## 1. The Rise of the Mahāyāna and Its Relation to Buddhist Philosophy

Mahāyāna: new developments

The most important development in Buddhism during the period we are considering here was the rise of the Mahāyāna. The Mahāyāna movement brought with it an enormous amount of new (or, as the Mahāyāna would put it: previously unknown) *sūtras*, a new spiritual ideal (that of the bodhisattva, considered as a superior aspiration than the quest for *arhat*ship), and, it would appear, exciting new philosophical developments. A key distinction between the Abhidharma on the one hand and Madhyamaka and Yogācāra on the other is that they are commonly associated with different kinds of Buddhism: the last two are philosophical schools of the Mahāyāna, while the Abhidharma philosophy belongs to what is pejoratively called the 'Hīnayāna' ('little vehicle'), and more neutrally, the Śrāvakayāna.

What the Mahāyāna was not

The history of the beginning of the Mahāyāna and the causes that led to its development are still quite unclear.[1] There is some consensus, however, on what the Mahāyāna was not. It was not a lay movement[2] that tried to shift the balance of power away from the monks and nuns, nor a group of *stūpa* worshippers,[3] nor was it the result of a doctrinal schism between different Buddhist schools,[4] along the lines of the split between Roman Catholicism and Protestantism. The majority of the Mahāyāna's early supporters (when it achieved more widespread support towards the middle of the first millennium CE, several centuries after its inception) were monastics.[5] *Stūpa* worship was not confined to the Mahāyāna,[6] and the notion of a split of the monastic community on doctrinal grounds is quite alien to Buddhism; traditionally such splits took place because of a difference about which monastic rules a given community should follow. This is not too surprising, given that a difference about which rules to adopt can be highly disruptive to the functioning of a

[1] For a survey of recent scholarship on the matter see Drewes 2010, 55–65, 66–74.

[2] This position is particularly associated with Przyluski 1934, Lamotte 1954, and Hirakawa 1990.

[3] Hirakawa 1963.

[4] Silk: 2002: 355–405.

[5] Schopen 1997: 31–2.

[6] Sasaki 1999: 191–3; Schopen 2005.

monastic group, while the beliefs of an individual monk about what he is doing when he is practising meditation tend not to be.

Mahāyāna as a textual movement

The difficulty of connecting the early Mahāyāna with any kind of historical or archaeological evidence have led some to argue that it was a purely textual movement, with a focus on the exposition and transmission of the revealed Mahāyāna *sūtras*, without developing alternatives to the social and institutional framework of Buddhism at the time.[7] This accounts well for the profusion of Mahāyāna *sūtras* we see in the development of Indian Buddhism, a profusion based on a kind of continuous revelation of the Buddha's teaching, with the emergence of texts that are regarded as authoritative even though they may not have been taught by the Buddha during his life on earth.[8] The surprising amount of textual documents the Mahāyāna produced may by itself seem to justify a conception of it as a 'cult of the book'[9] (or, more precisely, if less concisely) a collection of different cults of different books.

An alternative vision of the Buddha

Insofar as it is possible to identify unifying conceptual features underlying the vast corpus of Mahāyāna *sūtras*, one prominent feature is a different vision of what the Buddha is. The Buddha is considered as not having completely disappeared after his *parinirvāṇa*, but as in some sense still present and helping beings to achieve enlightenment. This idea of the Buddha as an enlightened being perpetually acting out of his great compassion began to be considered as an ideal to be emulated, and as preferable to that of an *arhat*,[10] and linked up with an interest in the previous existences of the Buddha as a bodhisattva, or Buddha-to-be. The previous lives are recorded in the *jātaka* stories, which describe the future Buddha as helping other beings out of his great compassion, often by giving up his own life. With this came an intention to follow the ideal of the bodhisattva to become, in due course, a compassionate enlightened

[7] Drewes 2007: 101–43.

[8] The way the status of these texts as *buddhavacana* is assured differs. Some of these are said to have been taught by the Buddha during his earthly life, but given to a group of bodhisattvas for safekeeping, who, after a stay in some divine realm, brought the texts back to earth (see Harrison 1990). Sometimes the *sūtra* will present itself has having been taught in such a divine realm in the first instance (see Powers 2004: 106). Sometimes Buddhas will appear to the practitioner during meditative absorption; when emerging from meditation he will then propagate and expound those teachings (Harrison 1978: 43, 52–4).

[9] Schopen 2005.

[10] From a relatively early stage in the development of Buddhism a distinction is drawn between the enlightenment of the Buddha and that of his disciples, the *arhats*. A Buddha is described as having specific powers that an *arhat* lacks, such as omniscience (Weber 1994; Jaini 1992); in addition, the Mahāyāna holds that the achievement of the *arhat* falls short of that of a Buddha insofar as the former has only overcome the afflictive obstructions (*kleśāvaraṇa*) but not the more subtle cognitive obstructions (*jñeyāvaraṇa*) connected with the fundamental misapprehension of the nature of reality. The Mahāyāna did not reject the ideal of the *arhat* but presented itself as a swift path to a loftier goal, Buddhahood, though this path is one that could also be travelled by those pursuing the more limited goal of an *arhat* (see Harrison 1987).

being like the Buddha himself.[11] This changed conception of the Buddha might be considered as a source for the prominence of the bodhisattva ideal in Mahāyāna, the emphasis on the quality of compassion, and also the profusion of Mahāyāna texts. An important difference between Buddhas and *arhats* is that the former were taken to be omniscient, and as Buddhas-to be the bodhisattvas could therefore be expected to require more knowledge than the *arhats*. This additional knowledge was helpfully supplied by the newly emerging *sūtras* specifically aimed at the needs of bodhisattvas.

Connection between Mahāyāna, Madhyamaka, and Yogācāra

However, so far it is not clear what the connection between Mahāyāna and the philosophical developments of Madhyamaka and Yogācāra was. Even though it has been argued by some scholars that the connection is rather tenuous, questioning whether Nāgārjuna was a Mahāyānist at all, and pointing out that the difference between Mahāyāna and 'Hīnayāna' thought cannot have been that great if a school like that of Diṅnāga and Dharmakīrti could actually be described as combining both in a form of 'Yogācāra-Sautrāntika', the historical connection between Mahāyāna and the schools of Madhyamaka and Yogācāra is too obvious to deny. What is worthwhile investigating, though, is whether the connection is more than a historical accident. Was the Mahāyāna simply a religious development that became associated with specific thinkers and their schools, without having much of an influence on their philosophy,[12] or is there a more fundamental connection between Mahāyāna ideas and those later developed in Madhyamaka and Yogācāra texts? Does the Mahāyāna have any specific philosophical ramifications apart from its religious, doctrinal, and soteriological consequences?

Philosophical consequences of the Mahāyāna view

In fact, the changing view of the Buddha in Mahāyāna texts just mentioned is a particular case of a widening of the Buddhist vision of the world we find in these *sūtras*: a more comprehensive soteriological goal, more extensive cosmological accounts, including 'celestial' Buddhas residing in pure lands, a wider corpus of teachings to be considered as the Buddha's word, describing sets of new, powerful practices.

This extended vision incorporated the pre-Mahāyāna view of the Buddhist path; in particular, it subsumed and endorsed the ideas of the *śrāvaka* and the *pratyekabuddha*.[13] Yet in order to present the conceptions that preceded it as

[11] Williams 2009: 20.

[12] Snellgrove (1987: 90) believes there to be no systematic connection between the theory of emptiness, the Mahāyāna bodhisattva ideal and the Mahāyāna emphasis on compassion: 'However, the combination of these two teachings, the Bodhisattva ideal and the emptiness of all concepts, has probably come about in these texts quite fortuitously without any immediate awareness of the effect that so extreme a philosophical view might have upon what is probably the highest of moral aspiration to be found anywhere in this imperfect world.' Bronkhorst (2009: 118) too claims that the main conceptual innovations behind Madhyamaka and Yogācāra 'had nothing to do with its [i.e. Mahāyāna's] main aspirations'.

[13] *Śrāvaka*s and *pratyekabuddha*s are distinguished by the way they reach the goal of *arhat*ship (the *śrāvaka*s by relying on a teacher, the *pratyekabuddha*s without doing so in their final lifetime,

special cases to be included in the wider compass of the Mahāyāna, it was necessary to de-ontologize them. Both the ordinary, unenlightened conception of the world, as well as the theory of *dharma*s that formed part of the Abhidharma and claimed to describe the ultimate truth about how things exist at the ultimate level, had to be considered as lacking fundamental reality, as fundamentally illusory, though of pragmatic and instrumental value, in order to be able to conceive of them not as conflicting with, but as forming a part of the Mahāyāna vision. The development of a more comprehensive view of the Buddhist world could not consider the more restricted and sometimes contradictory pre-Mahāyāna conception as a complete and ultimately true account, but could only incorporate it as true 'in a manner of speaking'. The world as it appears and the world as early Buddhist *dharma* theory analysed it had to be regarded as a mere illusory reality, in order to be regarded as a reality at all.

De-ontologizing of reality

It is this broadly illusionistic view of the world, I would argue, that forms the best point of connection between the Mahāyāna *sūtra*s and the philosophical developments of Madhyamaka and Yogācāra.[14] To be sure, early illusionistic views exist in Buddhism outside of Mahāyāna *sūtras*,[15] and there is much more to the extremely complex philosophical systems of Madhyamaka and Yogācāra than simply the idea that the world is just like a magic show.[16] Yet if we ask ourselves which ideas from the Mahāyāna *sūtra*s these philosophical texts developed, and which they in turn referred to in order to back up their philosophical perspective by texts considered to be the Buddha's words, the illusionistic view of the world occupies a prominent place. In addition to the possible conceptual reason for the arising of this view just mentioned, the illusionistic view may have a foundation in the meditative practices of early Mahāyānists. While the theory that the entire Mahāyāna arose as the reflection of meditative practices of contemplative ascetics is unlikely to be true,[17] we have textual evidence for meditative exercises supposed to bring about the perception of the Buddha as present in this very world. The *Pratyutpanna-buddha-saṃmukhāvasthita-samādhi-sūtra*, a Mahāyāna text from the second century CE or earlier, teaches a form of meditation (*samādhi*) enabling the

Illusionism as constituting a link

Illusionism and meditative practice

instead contemplating the principle of dependent origination). Morevover, *pratyekabuddhas* do not teach other beings about their attainments, whence their name 'individually enlightened ones'.

[14] A very similar point has already been made by Bronkhorst (2009: 122–3).

[15] See e.g. p. 46 above.

[16] It is certainly the case that the bodhisattva ideal, the development of compassion, and so on are not the first things that come to mind when considering what the central new ideas of Madhyamaka and Yogācāra are. The point suggested above, however, is that the illusionistic view of the world, like the ethical views revolving around the bodhisattva ideal, can be understood as resulting from the enlarged vision of what the Buddha is, while also playing a crucial role in the philosophical visions developed by Madhyamaka and Yogācāra.

[17] Drewes 2010: 61–2.

practitioner to stand face-to-face (*saṃmukhāvasthita*) with the present (*pratyutpanna*) Buddha. After completing a set of meditative exercises, the meditating bodhisattva:

> does not see the Tathāgata through obtaining the divine eye; he does not hear the true dharma through obtaining the range of the divine ear; nor does he go to that world-system in an instant through obtaining magical powers—Bhadrapāla, while remaining in this very world-system that bodhisattva sees the Lord, the Tathāgata Amitāyus, and conceiving himself to be in that world-system he also hears the dharma.[18]

Sight of the Buddha in the present world

The text makes clear that the sight of the Buddha in this case is not due to worldly epistemic super-powers such as the 'divine eye' (*divyacakṣuḥ*) allowing one to see things very far away, or through magical travel to a distant world to observe the Buddha there. It then becomes an intriguing question what the nature of these Buddhas—on the one hand present in this world, on the other, disappearing when the practitioner leaves meditative absorption—actually is. The *sūtra* clarifies this as follows:

> Having thought: 'Did these Tathāgatas come from somewhere? Did I go anywhere?' he understands that those Tathāgatas did not come from anywhere. Having comprehended that his own body did not go anywhere either, he thinks: 'These triple worlds are only mind. Why? Because however I mentally construct things, so they appear'.[19]

The world as mentally constructed

The illusionistic position that things are not as they appear (but, in this case, possess a very different, mentally constructed reality) appears to arise here in order to make sense of specific meditative experiences. In order to account for the meditator's experiences of the Buddha as actually present in the world, it is necessary to regard the ordinary perception of the world, post-meditative experience, and even the meditatively trained perception of the world of the Abhidharma practititioner according to which the Buddha is *not* present in this world, as unable to undermine meditative experience, simply because these former two kinds of perception are not grounded in the way the world really is. These ways of viewing the world (which are the ways the world appears to most

[18] *lha'i mig thob pas de bzhin gshegs pa mthong ba yang ma yin | lha'i rna ba'i khams thob pas dam pa'i chos nyan pa yang ma yin | rdzu 'phrul gyi stobs thob pas 'jig rten gyi khams der skad cig tu 'gro ba yang ma yin gyi | bzang skyong | byang chub sems dpa' de 'jig rten gyi khams 'di nyid na gnas bzhin du | bcom ldan 'das de bzhin gshegs pa tshe dpag med de mthong zhing bdag nyid 'jig rten kyi khams de na 'dug ba snyam du shes la | chos kyang nyan to*, Harrison 1978: 43. Note that even though this passage refers the Buddha Amitāyus, a form of the 'celestial' Buddha Amitābha, other passages of the same *sūtra* make it clear that any Buddha can be the object of this type of meditative exercise.

[19] *de 'di snyam du | de bzhin gshegs pa 'di ga zhig nas byon tam || bdag ga zhing tu song tam | snyam pa las des de bzhin gshegs pa de gang nas kyang ma byon par rab tu shes so || bdag gi lus kyang gang du yang ma song bar rab tu 'du shes nas | de 'di snyam du | khams gsum pa 'di dag ni sems tsam mo || de ci'i phyir zhe na | 'di ltar bdag ji lta ji ltar nram par rtog pa de lta de ltar snang ngo*, Harrison 1978: 46.

people most of the time) are grounded in illusion and have no implications for what exists. The illusionistic worldview therefore coheres naturally with the way the world would be conceived by a practitioner of the kind of early Mahāyāna meditative exercises described in this *sūtra*.

Having now considered a possible conceptual connection point between the Mahāyāna and the subsequent developments in Buddhist philosophy in India, we are ready to turn to the first of its two main schools: Madhyamaka.

## 2. The Madhyamaka School

The Madhyamaka school is one of the most puzzling (and most intriguing) branches of Buddhist philosophy. On the basis of a casual acquaintance with Madhyamaka texts it is far from clear what precisely their doctrine amounts to. David Ruegg has put this well by pointing out that it

> has been variously described as nihilism, monism, irrationalism, misology, agnosticism, skepticism, criticism, dialectic, mysticism, acosmism, absolutism, relativism, nominalism, and linguistic analysis with therapeutic value.[20]

Since the day these lines have been written numerous other -isms, such as deconstructivism, dialetheism, and ontological non-foundationalism, have enlarged the menu of interpretative options even further.

Nāgārjuna's life

In fact our puzzlement with Madhyamaka is likely to begin already with the biography of its founder. We know that the school was founded by Nāgārjuna, an Indian monk and philosopher, and one of the two or three greatest thinkers that Indian intellectual history has produced. It is only exaggerating slightly to say that this is already where our certainties end. When it comes to Nāgārjuna we are unclear about when he lived, where in India he spent most of his time, what texts he composed, and even how many Nāgārjunas there were in the first place.

The prophecy

Nāgārjuna's biography is transmitted to us in a variety of accounts that abound with hagiographical detail. But Nāgārjuna has entered the history of Buddhist thought even before we get to these biographies. If we follow traditional Buddhist accounts, the arising of the Madhyamaka school was no historical accident, but a development already predicted by the historical Buddha Śakyamuni. Nāgārjuna (referred to just as Nāga) is mentioned at various places in the Mahāyāna *sūtra*s and *tantra*s.[21] The most famous of these is a prophecy in the *Laṅkāvatārasūtra*.[22] Addressing the bodhisattva Mañjuśrī, the Buddha declares that:

[20] Ruegg 1981: 2. [21] Walser 2005: 66, 71–3.

[22] Though it is not contained in the earliest version of this *sūtra*: see Walser 2005, n. 29, p. 293.

In Vedalī, in the southern part, there will be a monk widely known as Śrīmān, who will be called Nāga. Destroying the positions of existence and non-existence he will teach my vehicle, the unsurpassed Mahāyāna to the world. He will attain the stage called *muditā* ['joyful', the first Bodhisattva ground] and will pass on to the pure realm of Sukhāvatī.[23]

Other scriptures add detail to this, such as that Nāgārjuna is going to be born 400 years after the death of the historical Buddha, or that he will live for 600 years, but what makes this prophecy particularly interesting is that it says Nāgārjuna will achieve the first Bodhisattva ground (*bhūmi*).[24] This achievement requires realization of emptiness. It ensures that Nāgārjuna not only knows what he is talking about, but has realized it directly.

The biography

The majority of details of Nāgārjuna's life are transmitted to us in a variety of colourful accounts from later writers such as Kumārajīva, Bu ston, and Tāranātha, accounts that exhibit surprisingly little agreement with each other. Jan Yün-Hua gives a succinct account of the common themes, and points out that:

he came from a Brahminical family, was well versed in magic power, and had a romantic life when he was young. After renouncing his worldly life and being initiated into the Buddhist Saṅgha, he studied Mahāyāna texts on the Snow Mountain, went to and obtained more important Mahāyāna scriptures from the palace of the Nāgas under the sea, and won the mind and support of the king of Sātavāhana dynasty. These sources also say that he settled in South India until the last days of his life. He had a long life, lasting several hundred years.[25]

Some of these points merit further comment. The 'romantic life' refers to a period in Nāgārjuna's pre-monastic days reported in Kumārajīva's account and connects with a dominant theme in his biographies, his mastery of magical powers. Nāgārjuna and his friends are said to have procured an invisibility potion and used it to enter into the royal harem unawares, to enjoy the company of the royal consorts. The king finds out about this and is not amused. He sets them a trap and observes the footprints the invisible men leave in the sand, then sends in his soldiers to aim their swords at where their heads would be. All are killed save for Nāgārjuna, who stands immediately behind the king, out of reach of the swords. After this brush with death, Nāgārjuna 'conceives a dislike of the idea of desire'[26] and becomes a monk.

Magical elements

The association with magical powers mentioned here plays an important part in Nāgārjuna's biographies. He is, in fact, counted as one of the famous set

[23] *dakṣiṇāpathavedalyāṃ bhikṣuḥ śrīmān mahāyaśāḥ/*
*nāgāhvayaḥ sa nāmnā tu sadasatpakṣadārakaḥ//*
*prakāśya loke madyānaṃ mahāyānamanuttaram/*
*āsādya bhūmiṃ muditāṃ yāsyate 'sau sukhāvatīm//*
10:165–6, Vaidya 1963: 118, Suzuki 1932: 239–40.

[24] See also MacDonald 2015: 11–12, nn. 34–5.

[25] Yün-Hua 1970: 140–1.

[26] Walleser 1990: 28.

of eighty-four *siddhas*, Indian tantric masters renowned both for their spiritual accomplishments and for their displays of magical powers. Magical elements feature already at the very beginning of his life. Initially his life is predicted to be very short; his parents therefore send him to study at the famous monastery of Nālandā at the age of 7. There the abbot, Rāhulabhadra, is supposed to have taught him to prolong his life by means of the recitation of mantras. Nāgārjuna becomes highly proficient at tantric practice, achieving, amongst other things, the elixir of long life.[27] According to Bu ston, Nāgārjuna managed to extend his life for 600 years. Even after this period he did not die a natural death, but allowed the son of a king to behead him—the king's and Nāgārjuna's lifespan having somehow become linked through their respective longevity practices, the prince was understandably concerned that he should never succeed his father on the throne.

Some biographies describe Nāgārjuna as finding an elixir to make gold, a feat he used in order provide food for the monastic community during a famine. According to other accounts, Nāgārjuna is carried through a river by a cowherd. He creates an illusion of crocodiles that seem to attack them, and when the cowherd has carried him across the river unperturbed, he grants him a boon. The cowherd wants to be a king, and so Nāgārjuna turns him into one, creating elephants, armies, and all kinds of other kingly possessions to go with it. The king, called Śālābhanda, later becomes his disciple, and Nāgārjuna composes the *Ratnāvalī* for him.[28]

*Nāgas* and the Perfection of Wisdom

The second important recurring motive in Nāgārjuna's life-stories mentioned above is already evident in his name: his association with the *nāgas*. His name is a compound of two nouns, *nāga* and *arjuna*. The *nāgas* are mythological snake-like creatures[29] who live in palatial aquatic abodes, in an underwater city called Bhogavatī (*longs spyod can*), under the earth or in mountain caves. *Nāgas* are often depicted as beings that are half-snake, half-man, with a human torso and a lower body in the form of a coiled snake, and are renowned for their great beauty. They are guardians of tremendous wealth (they are sometimes said to have a jewel embedded in their heads), wise, and powerful.

*Arjuna*, Bu ston informs us, refers to someone 'who has procured worldly power'. According Kumārajīva's account, however, the term is a name of a kind of a tree, Nāgārjuna's mother having given birth to him under a tree.[30] According to a third account, the second half of Nāgārjuna's name refers to

27 Walleser 1990: 9. 28 Dowman 1985: 115.

29 A group of tribes from eastern Assam is also collectively referred to as *nāgas*.

30 Walleser 1990: 30. As was Buddha Śākyamuni. The similarity of this 'second Buddha' to the historical one is frequently stressed in traditional accounts. According to Tāranātha, his body is adorned with the 32 auspicious signs that characterized the Buddha's physical body (Lama Chimpa 1970: 110–11). Nāgārjuna is also one of the few figures in Tibetan iconography (together with

the Pāṇḍava brother from the *Mahābhārata* known for his skills in archery,[31] since Nāgārjuna is able to spread the Mahāyāna as securely as Arjuna shoots his arrows.[32]

Be this as it may, Nāgārjuna's association with *nāgas* is of central importance in the story of his life. His biographies speak of two ladies from the retinue of the king of the *nāgas* listening to his teaching, filling the place with the scent of sandalwood.[33] Nāgārjuna then travels to the palace of the *nāga* king under the sea, a place overflowing with a variety of gems and jewels. Amongst these valued possesions of the *nāgas*, the most important one is a rare treasure of Buddhist scriptures, the Perfection of Wisdom (*prajñāpāramitā*) *sūtras*. These are said to have been entrusted by the historical Buddha to the *nāgas* for safekeeping. Their content is supposed to be so subtle that it may be easily misunderstood. For this reason these scriptures must wait for their right interpreter who can correctly explain their meaning. This interpreter is, of course, Nāgārjuna, who brings the scriptures back to the human realm.

The Perfection of Wisdom *sūtras*

The Perfection of Wisdom *sūtras* are a family of highly influential Buddhist texts of varying lengths. Their length is usually indicated in their titles, so we have texts like the Perfection of Wisdom in 8,000 verses, the Perfection of Wisdom in 25,000 verses or even the Perfection of Wisdom in 100,000 verses. These kinds of titles might give rise to two misunderstandings. First, we might think the texts are in verse, even though they are generally in prose. Nevertheless, their length is measured by how many units of thirty-two syllables (verses, or *ślokas*) they contain. The Perfection of Wisdom in 8,000 verses, for example, is about 110,000 words long in English translation—about the length of the book you are reading just now. The second mistaken impression we might have is that the version in 100,000 verses, for example, contains four times as much information as the 25,000-verse version, because it is four times as long. In fact the longer versions of these *sūtras* differ from the shorter ones not so much by including more information, but by spelling out lists in full that are only given in part in the shorter versions.[34] The Perfection of Wisdom in 100,000 verses spells out the claim that '*x* is emptiness, and emptiness itself is *x*' by going through a long list of about 200 items one by one. The shorter versions provide abbreviated forms of these lists, and sometimes only mention their first and last elements.

Different lengths of these texts

Asaṅga, dGa' rab rdo rje, and Guru shakya seng ge, a manifestation of Padmasambhava) who is depicted with the Buddha's protuberance (*uṣṇīṣa*) on the top of his head.

[31] MacDonald 2015: 2. 7, n. 13. [32] Tsonawa 1985: 4. [33] Walleser 1990: 10.

[34] Despite being very critical of Abhidharma ideas, the Perfection of Wisdom texts share its fondness of lists (*mātṛkā*). For the understanding of later developments of the Perfection of Wisdom literature it is worth keeping in mind that *mātṛkā* both means 'mother' and can also, according to Monier-Williams, denote 'an epithet of certain diagrams written in characters to which magical power is ascribed' (Conze 1978: 5–6).

As their name makes clear, the Perfection of Wisdom texts are *sūtras*; they begin with the customary words 'Thus I have heard', and purport to give an account of discourses of the historical Buddha held in front of his disciples (such as Śāriputra) and an assembly of bodhisattvas. They describe the practices a bodhisattva should follow in order to achieve enlightenment. A key element of these practices is the development of the six perfections, generosity (*dhāna*), moral virtue (*śīla*), patience, (*kṣānti*), effort (*vīrya*), meditation (*dhyāna*), and wisdom (*prajñā*). Special prominence is given to the final perfection, the perfection of wisdom; it is sometimes considered to include all the other perfections within it.

Contents of the Perfection of Wisdom texts

Practices of a bodhisattva

The conceptual core of this final perfection is the realization of emptiness, the understanding of the insubstantiality of all phenomena. Despite the fact that the notion of emptiness is the dominant theme of the Perfection of Wisdom texts, they do not present a great number of arguments for the claim that everything is indeed empty, nor do they discuss potential objections. It was Nāgārjuna's aim to provide a set of arguments in support of the claims of the Perfection of Wisdom *sūtras*, to explicate their contents, and to demonstrate their philosophical feasibility.

Emptiness

The composition (or at least the scripturalization) of the Perfection of Wisdom texts is characterized by a process of textual expansion followed by textual abbreviation. We can divide the development of the Prajñāpāramitā texts into four broad sections: the early phase, the phase of expansion, the phase of contraction (each lasting about two centuries), and a final, tantric phase.[35] The earliest phase (about 100 BCE to 100 CE) sees the appearance of the earliest layer of the Prajñāpāramitā texts, a section of the Perfection of Wisdom in 8,000 verses (*Aṣṭasahāsrikaprajñāpāramitā*), which may go back as far as 100 BCE,[36] though the process of composition of the text is likely to have extended over two centuries. This would date the writing down of the first Mahāyāna texts to the same time as (or possibly earlier than) the scripturalization of the Pāli canon.[37]

Development of the Perfection of Wisdom literature

1. The early phase

During the second phase (100 CE to 300 CE) the Perfection of Wisdom texts expanded, resulting in such works as the Perfection of Wisdom in 18,000, 25,000, or 100,000[38] verses (there are even references to a version 125,000 verses

2. The phase of expansion

[35] This division follows Conze 1978: 1–16.

[36] Conze 1994. Even though there are no extant manuscripts of the Prajñāpāramitā texts dating back as far as this, a recently discovered manuscript of the Perfection of Wisdom in 8,000 verses written on birch-bark in the Gāndhārī language can be dated to about 47–147 CE (Falk and Karashima 2011–12; Karashima 2012–13). This manuscript itself appears to be a copy of an earlier text, lending additional plausibility to Conze's assumption that the early Perfection of Wisdom texts pre-date the beginning of the Common Era.

[37] According to traditional accounts, the Pāli canon was scripturalized during the reign of the Sri Lankan king Vaṭṭagāmaṇī between 32 and 35 BCE (Gómez 2002: 59).

[38] This latter version was given to the *nāgas* for safekeeping, even though this is merely an abbreviated version when compared to versions kept—according to Bu ston—in other realms:

in length)—all substantially the same text, but differing in the extent to which repetitive lists are spelt out. During the same period commentarial works on the Perfection of Wisdom texts started to be composed, most importantly a gigantic commentary on the Perfection of Wisdom in 25,000 verses, the *Mahāprajñāpāramitā-upadeśa-śāstra* (大智度論), ascribed to Nāgārjuna, which was translated into Chinese by Kumārajīva. The Sanskrit original, now lost, is supposed to have been even longer (100,000 verses); Kumārajīva only translated the first chapter in full, and provided abstracts of the remaining eighty-nine.

3. The phase of contraction

In the third phase (300–500 CE) the expansive tendency of the Perfection of Wisdom literature is reversed. It is understandable that at this stage of its development the Perfection of Wisdom literature became very hard to read: the texts are difficult in themselves, and the enormous number of repetitions made it difficult to keep the main points in focus. If we are to believe the famous commentator Haribhadra, even scholars of the calibre of Asaṅga had difficulties dealing with them, finding that they 'could no longer ascertain its meaning, because of the great number of repetitions, their inability to distinguish the different words and arguments, and its profundity'.[39] It is therefore hardly surprising that various shorter versions made their appearance during this phase. Two of these are amongst the most famous Buddhist texts: one is the so-called 'Heart Sūtra' (*Prajñāpāramitāhṛdayasūtra*), a work that occupies an important role in virtually all Mahāyāna traditions, the other the 'Diamond Sūtra' (*Vajracchedikāprajñāpāramitāsūtra*). Both of these texts are quite short (the English translation of the former fits easily on one or two pages), but the abbreviation of the Prajñāpāramitā texts was taken to its extreme in the shortest of all versions, the Perfection of Wisdom in One Letter (*Ekākṣarāprajñāpāramitāsūtra*). Subtracting the usual preamble and conclusion it just consists of the letter A. This might appear a little bit less peculiar if we take into account that the sound A is not only the first sound of the Sanskrit syllabary, but can also be prefixed to nouns and adjectives to form their negations. Given the emphasis of the Perfection of Wisdom texts on negating various categories assumed by the Abhidharma, the idea of encapsulating the essence of the Perfection of Wisdom in the word 'not' is not entirely far-fetched.

Significance of the texts for all Mahāyāna schools

Even though the Perfection of Wisdom texts have a special affinity with Madhyamaka, they are certainly not of exclusive interest to proponents of the Middle Way. Prajñāpāramitā texts continued to appear from about 100 BCE through the entire history of Indian Buddhism up to its demise in the twelfth

a 10,000,000-verse version in the realm of the king of the gods, and 1,000,000,000-verse version in the realm of the king of the *gandharvas* (Conze 1978: 18, n. 1).

[39] Conze 1955: 13.

century, and have been studied, summarized, and commented upon by a variety of authors from different Indian Mahāyāna schools. The most famous of these is the *Abhisamayālaṃkāra* traditionally ascribed to Maitreyanātha, Asaṅga's teacher. It is a 273-verse table of contents of the Perfection of Wisdom in 25,000 verses which has dominated the understanding of the text in India and Tibet. Hybrid versions that inserted the divisions of the *Abhisamayālaṃkāra* into the Prajñāpāramitā text itself appeared around the fifth and sixth centuries.

The *Prajñāpāramitāsūtra*s form a thread that can be traced through the entire development of Buddhist philosophy in India (and beyond). It is no over-generalization to say that every Mahāyāna school of Buddhism in India has in some way sought to explicate the Perfection of Wisdom texts, attempting to show how their specific philosophical positions provide the best explanation of the theory of emptiness that these texts set out. All the great Yogācāra masters have composed commentaries on Perfection of Wisdom texts; apart from Maitreyanātha's *Abhisamayālaṃkāra*, Asaṅga wrote a commentary on the Diamond Sūtra (*Vajracchedikaprajñāpāramitāsūtra*), Vasubandhu (at least according to the Tibetan tradition) composed a commentary on the Perfection of Wisdom in 100,000 verses, and Diṅnāga wrote a summary of the principal topics discussed in the Perfection of Wisdom in 8,000 verses, the *Prajñāpāramitāpiṇḍārthasaṃgraha*. Unlike other Mahāyāna *sūtra*s that rose to prominence only within specific philosophical schools, the Perfection of Wisdom texts are of universal significance for the interpretation of any post-Abhidharma school of Buddhist thought in India.

4. The tantric phase

In the last phase of the development of the Perfection of Wisdom texts (600 CE–1200 CE) various works clearly inspired by tantric modes of thought appeared. In these we find the attempt to reduce the essence of the Perfection of Wisdom to a single *mantra* or spell. Such as attempt can already be found in the Heart Sūtra, which encapsulates the text in the *mantra* of the Perfection of Wisdom (*gate gate pāragate pārasaṃgate bodhi svāhā*). In some of these texts we also find the Perfection of Wisdom personified, accompanied by specific rituals for worshipping her. She is depicted in female form, usually with four arms, the inner ones placed in the gesture of teaching the dharma, the outer ones holding a book (the text of the Perfection of Wisdom itself) and a rosary (for the repetition of her *mantra*).

Multiple Nāgārjunas?

After these brief remarks on the nature of the Perfection of Wisdom *sūtras* we can now return to Nāgārjuna's biography. We may wonder whether its different elements do not pull in different directions. On the one hand there is the alchemist and magician, on the other the monk and philosopher who composes treatises to defend the Mahāyāna position. Modern Buddhologists have been wondering this too, and have suggested that we may be dealing with distinct persons living at different times who have all been labelled with the same name.[40]

Nāgārjuna the philosopher

At least three Nāgārjunas have been distinguished in the literature. The first, and the Nāgārjuna most frequently referred to, is the philosopher who lived during the first and second centuries CE. He is also frequently connected with the famous Buddhist university of Nālandā, though this association faces certain difficulties.[41] We do not have evidence for Nālandā as a major monastic establishment before the year 425 CE, a considerable time after the period during which Nāgārjuna is supposed to have lived. Moreover, neither of the Chinese pilgrims Xuanzang (玄奘), nor Yijing (義淨), both of whom spent some time at Nālandā, refer to Nāgārjuna as a famous *alumnus*.[42]

Other Nāgārjunas

The second Nāgārjuna sometimes discussed is a tantric master who probably lived around 400 CE,[43] and the third is an alchemist, probably to be dated around the seventh century.[44] (We also occasionally find references to a fourth Nāgārjuna, an author of medical works.)[45]

This division also leads to a breaking up of the set of over a hundred works attributed to Nāgārjuna: all the philosophical works are considered to be composed by the first Nāgārjuna, while the tantric and alchemical works are taken to have been composed by the later ones. Traditional Buddhist narratives see no particular difficulty in accounting for the fact that different parts of this considerable number of works are likely to have been composed over the span of several centuries, since they argue that Nāgārjuna's alchemistical experiments allowed him to extend his lifespan up to 600 years.

Advantages of the 'multiple Nāgārjunas' account

There are certain advantages to this theory of multiple Nāgārjunas, the chief one being that we can account for most of the motives in the various accounts of Nāgārjuna's life without appealing to anything that would contradict the standard twenty-first-century naturalistic worldview. However, we should note the difficulties we see in traditional accounts of Nāgārjuna's life (the reference to magical abilities, the long lifespan, the diversity of his literary output, the confusion of times and spaces associated with his life) are very much the product of a specific perspective chosen for looking at these accounts.

[40] At this point it is important to distinguish two claims. One is uncontroversial, namely that over the course of Indian history many authors have answered to the name 'Nāgārjuna'. This does not mean that they were all operating under the pseudonym of the Madhyamaka master, or that their works claimed to be authored by him (see Walser 2005: 69). The other, more controversial claim states that the different facets we find attributed *to the Madhyamaka author* in traditional biographies (the philosophical, alchemical, medical, and tantric aspects) have to be understood as applying to different persons, not just to one.

[41] Note, however, the interesting connection with the *nāgas*: both the Buddhist universities Nālandā and Takṣaśīla are supposedly named after *nāgas*, the former after Nanda, the second after Takṣaka. Walker 1968: 2. 107.

[42] Walser 2005: 78.

[43] Lindtner 1982: 11, n. 12.

[44] Walser 2005: 69, 75–9, Eliade 1969: 415–16.

[45] Winternitz 1968: 3. 547, 552–3.

As we have seen in the prophecy from the *Laṅkāvatārasūtra* cited above, Nāgārjuna is considered to have obtained the first bodhisattva ground. As the bodhisattva ascends the different grounds or levels of spiritual accomplishment, he acquires, in addition to the direct realization of emptiness that characterizes reaching the first bodhisattva ground, different sets of abilities. For the first ground these include the ability to live for 100 aeons, magically generate 100 versions of his body, and to teach 100 kinds of teaching.[46] On the basis of this assumption it becomes clear that the traditional biographies of Nāgārjuna, including their descriptions of his various magical powers, being able control his lifespan or the place of his birth, being able to work miracles and so forth, are exactly the kinds of account one would expect.[47] The fantastic, confused, or miraculous appearance of Nāgārjuna's traditional biography only arises if we consider him to have been an ordinary human being, and assume that there is an objective set of truths out there about what happened during the life of that human being. As we noted before, the difficulty with this approach is that it does not cohere with several of the central claims of Buddhist philosophy. We can, I argue, achieve a more nuanced understanding of the complexities of the history of Buddhist thought by provisionally bracketing our contradicting assumptions, rather than attempting to 'straighten out' traditional accounts on the basis of contemporary historiography.

Coherence of the traditional claims made about Nāgārjuna's life

The number of works attributed to Nāgārjuna is large (more than 100 according to the Tibetan canon), but not all of them play the same important role. They include not only the highly theoretical works Nāgārjuna is famous for, but also contain some extremely practical texts: the *Dhūpayogaratnamālā* preserved in the Tibetan canon, for example, contains a recipe for making incense ascribed to Nāgārjuna.[48]

Nāgārjunas's works is with Homer

His single most important work is the Fundamental Verses on the Middle Way (*Mūlamadhyamakakārikā*), a set of 450 verses which is considered as intrinsically linked with Nāgārjuna as the *Iliad* is with Homer: what we speak about when refer to them are the authors of these respective texts.

The central works of Nāgārjuna can be divided into three broad categories: technical philosophical writings, letters, and hymns. The technical philosophical

[46] The higher bodhisattva grounds are characterized by an increase of these numbers. There is nothing in the basis of the realization that differentiates the grounds from each other. See MacDonald 2015: 2. 356.

[47] Yün-hua 1970: 151–2.

[48] McHugh 2012: 267, n. 6, Laufer 1896. If we are to believe Yijing, Nāgārjuna also provided advice on dental hygiene. According to him, the Indian monks he encountered used to chew 'the rough root of the Northern Burrweed... It hardens the teeth, scents the mouth, helps to digest food or relieves heart-burning... This is the means of securing a long life adopted by Bodhisattva Nāgārjuna' (Yün-hua 1970: 28). See also Takakusu 1896: 34–5.

Philosophical works: the *yukti*-corpus

works include six major texts,[49] sometimes referred to as the *yukti*-corpus, or the 'six texts on reasoning' (*rigs pa'i tshogs drug*), and comprise, in addition to the *Mūlamadhyamakakārikā*, two shorter works on the notion of emptiness, the Sixty Verses on Reasoning (*Yuktiṣāṣṭikā*) and the Seventy Stanzas on Emptiness (*Śūnyatāsaptati*), the Dispeller of Disputes (*Vigrahyavyāvartanī*), a discussion of more complex issues raised by the theory of emptiness in question-and-answer format, and the *Vaidalyaprakaraṇa*, a criticism of the sixteen 'categories' concerned with logic and debate discussed by the non-Buddhist Nyāya school. A sixth text, the **Vyavyhārasiddhi*, seems to be no longer extant, apart from a few verses quoted by later authors.[50]

Letters

Nāgārjuna also composed two letters of advice to a king that contain some metaphysical discussion but are primarily concerned with ethical matters. These are the Jewelled Garland (*Ratnāvalī*) and the Friendly Letter (*Suhṛllehka*). These letters also offer a possibility of locating Nāgārjuna somewhat more firmly in space and time. The texts themselves do not give the name of the kings they were addressed to, though their Tibetan and Chinese translations provide us with the names bDe spyod ('good conduct') and Chantaka. Even though records of kings with these names have not come down to us, there is some possibility that the terms do not refer to individual kings, but to the Sātavāhana dynasty or one of its major sites.[51] The Sātavāhana empire was based around Amaravati in today's Andhra Pradesh, and lasted for four and a half centuries, from about 230 BCE to 220 CE. Based on a verse from the *Ratnāvali*, where Nāgārjuna mentions an image of the Buddha seated on a lotus,[52] and the fact that images such as this were available only during the late part of the Sātavāhana dynasty in the Eastern Deccan, Joseph Walser has argued that Nāgārjuna composed the text during the reign of King Yajña Śrī Sātakarṇi (about 175 to 204 CE).[53] The uncertainties inherent in such reasoning are apparent; nevertheless, it is valuable as constituting the best attempt so far at linking up Nāgārjuna's philosophical activity with some dateable events in Indian history.

Nāgārjuna and the Sātavāhana dynasty

Hymns

Nāgārjuna's hymns, finally, are a group of short texts on the Buddha and his transcendent nature, interesting for their positive characterization of ultimate reality. In the *Niraupamyastava*, for example, we find characterizations of the 'Dharma-body' (*dharmamayakāya*) as blissful (*śiva*), stable (*dhruva*), and

[49] In addition, a set of shorter, but nevertheless interesting works are frequently ascribed to Nāgārjuna. See Ruegg 1981a: 26–30 for a concise discussion.

[50] Lindtner 1982: 94–9.

[51] Walser 2005: 63–5. See also Ruegg 1981a: 26–7, n. 59.

[52] 'Please construct from all precious substances images of the Buddha with fine proportions, well designed and sitting on lotuses, adorned with all precious substances', *rin chen kun las bgyis pa yi | sang rgyas sku gzugs dbyibs mdzes shing | legs par bris pa padma la | bzugs pa dag kyang bgyid do stsol*, Walser 2005: 80, Hahn 1982a: 78, Hopkins 1998: 124–5.

[53] Walser 2005: 61, 86.

permanent (*nitya*). There at least appears to be a certain tension between such characterizations and Nāgārjuna's conception of ultimate reality as empty, yet they also provide an interesting link of Nāgārjuna's thought with the theory of Buddha-nature (*tathāgatagarbha*) expounded by some Mahāyāna *sūtras*. What the precise relation between the notion of universal emptiness described by the *Prajñāpāramitāsūtras* and the notion of Buddha-nature found mainly in *sūtras* ascribed to the 'third turning of the wheel of doctrine' (see below, p. 186) amounts to is a question that has occupied the hermeneutical abilities of Buddhist commentators ever since. The main interpretative choice to be made is whether these notions are, despite their seeming tension, somehow compatible with each other and therefore to be assigned to the same level of truth, or whether they are inconsistent, so that one of the two has to be assigned to the category of provisional teachings (*neyārtha*) while only the other can be held as expressing the Buddha's definite position (*nītārtha*).[54]

## 3. The Teachings of the Perfection of Wisdom

A good way of approaching Nāgārjuna's Madhyamaka teachings is by looking at certain prominent topics within the Perfection of Wisdom literature and considering how they were philosophically developed in his works. The scope of the Prajñāpāramitā literature is vast, and its teachings are complex. Nevertheless, there are certain recurrent themes one can identify. Particular important amongst them are:

1. a criticism of the Abhidharma project;
2. the doctrine of illusionism;
3. an explicit acceptance of contradictions.

### *a. Criticism of the Abhidharma project*

The characters that speak in the Perfection of Wisdom *sūtras* are the historical Buddha Śākyamuni, as well as usually various bodhisattvas, and the Buddha's disciple Śāriputra. This 'general of the doctrine' (*dhammasenāpati*) is characterized in these texts as a 'representative of an inferior kind of knowledge',[55] and this signifies the attitude towards earlier schools of Buddhism, and towards the Abhidharma in particular. The Perfection of Wisdom texts frequently criticize the ideals of realized practitioners of earlier Buddhism, the *arhat*s and the *pratyekabuddhas*, and focus instead on the ideal of a

Criticism of the soteriological ideals of early Buddhism

[54] See Ruegg 2010: 176, n. 32. For some discussion of the later Tibetan debate around this question see Brunnhölzl 2007: 43–55.

[55] Conze 1978: 6.

Bodhisattva. Here is how the Perfection of Wisdom in 8,000 verses[56] characterizes their difference:

> A Bodhisattva should not train in the same way in which persons belonging to the vehicle of the *arhat*s and Pratyekabuddas are trained. How then are the *arhat*s and Pratyekabuddhas trained? They make up their minds that 'one single self we shall tame, one single self we shall pacify, one single self we shall lead to final nirvana'.... A Bodhisattva should certainly not in such a way train himself. On the contrary, he should train himself thus: 'My own self I will place into Suchness, and, so that all the world might be helped, I will also place all beings into Suchness, and I will lead to nirvana the whole immeasurable world of beings'.

What is criticized here is not the validity of the realization of the *arhat*s and *pratyekabuddhas*, but their limited scope. The Perfection of Wisdom in 25,000 verses compares the *arhat*s and *pratyekabuddhas* to glow-worms, and the bodhisattvas to the sun.[57] Both have kindled the flame of enlightenment, but the formers' light only illuminates their own immediate surroundings, whereas that of the latter can potentially light up the whole world.

Criticism of the metaphysical assumptions of early Buddhism

The Prajñāpāramitā texts also set out to reject the metaphysical doctrines of the Abhidharma, in particular its conception of fundamentally existent *dharma*s. A concise example is provided by the Heart Sūtra, which explains matters as follows:

> O Śāriputra, any son or daughter of noble family who wishes to practice the conduct within the profound Perfection of Wisdom, should observe in this way:
>
> He properly sees the five aggregates, and sees them as empty of intrinsic nature (*svabhāva*)...
>
> Therefore, Śāriputra, in emptiness there is no matter, no feeling, no notion, no formations, no consciousness;
>
> no eye, no ear, no nose, no tongue, no body, no mind, no form, no sound, no smell, no flavour, nothing to be touched, no *dharmas*;
>
> there is no eye-sphere up to no mind-sphere, no sphere of *dharma*s, no sphere of mental consciousness,
>
> no knowledge, no ignorance, no destruction, up to no destruction of old age and death
>
> no suffering, no arising, no cessation, no path,
>
> no cognition, no attainment, and no non-attainment either.

This passage is a negation of all the categories that form the heart of the Abhidharma's ontological enterprise. The bodhisattva Avalokiteśvara, speaking through the inspiration of the Buddha, goes through the core categories of the Abhidharma system, beginning with the key dichotomy between *nāma* and

[56] Conze 1994: 163. [57] Conze 1955: 33.

*rūpa* as represented by the five *skandhas*,[58] through the twelve *āyatanas*, the twelve *dhātus*, the twelve links of dependent origination, up to the four noble truths and even enlightenment itself, and states that none of them exist in emptiness.

Rejection of Abhidharma's ontological foundations

It is hard to overestimate how radical this step was. The theory of *dharmas* was the standard Buddhist account of how reality was constituted at the fundamental level, a theory that accounted both for what there is at the rock bottom, and what kind of phenomenology is based on this. If all this is rejected, the audience of the Prajñāpāramitā texts (who we have to imagine as well trained in the theories of the Abhidharma) might well have wondered what, if anything, was left.

## b. The doctrine of illusionism

What seems to be left is a world that is not quite what it seems, a mere ephemeral creation similar to an illusion. In the Perfection of Wisdom in 8000 verses the gods question Subhūti, one of the disciples of the historical Buddha:

> THE GODS: Beings are like a magical illusion, are they not just an illusion?
>
> SUBHŪTI: Like a magical illusion are those beings, like a dream. For magical illusions and beings are not two different things, nor are dreams and beings. All *dharmas* also are like a magical illusion, like a dream. The various classes of Saints,—from Streamwinner to Buddhahood—also are like a magical illusion, like a dream.
>
> THE GODS: A fully enlightened Buddha, also, you say, is like a magical illusion, is like a dream? Buddhahood also, you say, is like a magical illusion, is like a dream?
>
> SUBHŪTI: Even Nirvāṇa, I say, is like a magical illusion, is like a dream. How much more so anything else!
>
> THE GODS: Even Nirvāṇa, holy Subhūti, you say is like an illusion, is like a dream?
>
> SUBHŪTI: Even if perchance there would be anything more distinguished, of that too I would say that it is like an illusion, like a dream. For illusion and Nirvāṇa are not two different things, nor are dreams and Nirvāṇa.[59]

[58] In tracing the ancestry of the illusionism of the Prajñāpāramitā texts to the pre-Mahāyāna level it is interesting to note that in the Saṃyuttanikāya (22: 95(3), Bhikkhu Bodhi 2000: 951–2) the Buddha elucidated the five *skandhas* by five illusionistic similes, comparing matter to a lump of foam, feeling to a water bubble, perception to a mirage, volitional formations to the trunk of a banana tree, and consciousness to a magical illusion. See also Bhikkhu Ñāṇananda 1974: 5–7. Verses 12–13 of the *Bodhicittavivaraṇa* ascribed to Nāgārjuna cite this comparison, see Lindtner 1982: 188–9, 259–60.

[59] Conze 1994: 98–9.

Comprehensive illusionism applicable to all entities

The illusionism propounded by the Perfection of Wisdom *sūtras* is comprehensive. We are here not faced with a view of the world that relegates our everyday surroundings to the status of mere appearance in order to underline the truly real status of some religiously transcendent world. Rather, the entire round of existence including all beings, all *dharmas*, various degrees of realized practitioners, the Buddha, and even nirvāṇa are considered illusory in nature. Even the process of leading beings to liberation is compared to a magician dissolving a previously created illusion. Just as we would not want to say that the magician made an elephant vanish, because there was no elephant present in the first place, in the same way, the Perfection of Wisdom texts argue, there are no beings that are led to liberation.[60]

Illusionism and meditative experience

This illusionistic doctrine runs through the entire corpus of the Perfection of Wisdom literature, but, rather surprisingly for such an unintuitive position, the texts do not in fact offer any arguments for *why* we should believe everything is illusory in the first place. Some scholars have suggested that the origin of this illusionistic doctrine is not the conclusion of a set of philosophical arguments, but a reflection of a particular mental state experienced in meditative absorption.[61] The texts would then reflect the particular way the world appears to the meditator, thereby also acting as a guide by providing a description of the kind of state the associated practices are supposed to lead to. Sometimes the 'attainment of cessation' (*nirodhasamāpatti*) is mentioned in this context, an advanced meditative state in which all sensory perceptions and all mental activity are supposed to cease.[62] Whether the world appears in any way to a meditator in this state where all mental activity has been suspended, and whether it could thus appear as a wholly illusory entity, is difficult to say. However, even if the illusionistic experience is not specifically connected with the 'attainment of cessation', the idea that at the core of the description of the world from the perspective of the Perfection of Wisdom texts lies a set of meditative experiences opens up fruitful ways of understanding the origin and the aim of the Prajñāpāramitā.

Ontologizing meditative phenomenology

One way of understanding the illusionism of the Perfection of Wisdom texts (as well as other instances where meditative practices appear to be a factor in shaping Buddhist philosophy) is as an ontologizing of meditative phenomenology. Because the world appears to the meditator in a specific way, and because meditative cognition is regarded as a particularly reliable route to knowledge, the world must also exist in the way in which the meditator experiences it. There is certainly some truth to this idea, but especially in the Madhyamaka context it is important to understand it in a sufficiently nuanced way. The idea seems to be that because of the intrinsic epistemic superiority of

[60] Conze 1994: 90. [61] Schmithausen 1973: 181.
[62] Poussin 1937: 191; Frauwallner 1956: 353–4; Staal 1975: 88.

meditative experience, and because of the soteriological efficacy of the corresponding meditative states which play a key part in progressing on the path to enlightenment, the meditator's phenomenological claims should also be regarded as authoritative ontological claims. Yet the Mādhyamika would disagree with the some key premises of this argument. For them there are no epistemic instruments that by their very nature lead to knowledge of ultimate reality, and it is furthermore mistaken to believe that the efficacy of a theory (including its soteriological efficacy) must rest on the ultimate truth of that theory. As an insubstantial (*niḥsvabhāva*) chariot can fulfil its function of carrying wood, so an empty theory, a theory not grounded in ultimate reality, can lead to liberation. Instead of arguing that the salvific efficacy of specific meditative states and experiences shows that they correspond to the way the world works at the most fundamental level, their very efficacy is sufficient to argue why they, rather than other non-standard phenomenological states,[63] should be cultivated, independent of any claims to ultimate truth. We should therefore be aware that the 'ontologization' of meditative phenomenology happens in Buddhist thought, and that it can explain a great deal about the development of Indian Buddhist philosophy, but that the Buddhist philosophers themselves (certainly the Mādhyamikas amongst them) finally move beyond it when spelling out the theory of the emptiness of emptiness.

Meditative phenomenology need not be grounded in ultimate reality

It is also worthwhile to note the somewhat different role that the Buddhist illusionistic worldview plays in the development of different Buddhist schools. We find early forms of this idea already in some of the canonical *sūtras*, when the Buddha says that 'sensual pleasures are impermanent, hollow, false, deceptive; they are illusory, the prattle of fools'.[64] The immediate aim of these teachings, that compare phenomena to foam,[65] bubbles, mirages, the coreless trunk of a banana tree, and so on is to enable the practitioner to rid himself of attachment and aversion towards these insubstantial things. The Perfection of Wisdom texts added another turn of the screw by extending the illusionistic doctrine from the five psycho-physical constituents (*skandhas*) to nirvāṇa and even to the Buddha himself. The reason for the popularity of this comprehensive illusionism in the development of the Mahāyāna is not difficult to determine. One of its implications is the insubstantiality of the soteriological goal of the non-Mahāyāna Buddhist schools; another is the fundamental equivalence of cyclic existence and liberation. Both of these entail that for a practitioner

Illusionism and the development of different Buddhist schools

[63] For an interesting comparison between the states created by the meditative practitioners and by schizophrenics see Beyer 1988: 84: 'The yogin consciously bases his magical power upon his understanding and hence upon his control of himself and his reality; the schizophrenic's power is based not on control but on chaos.'

[64] *Āneñjasappāyasutta*, Majjhimanikāya 106: *annicā bhikkhave kāmā tucchā musā mosadhammā māyākatam etaṃ bhikkhave bālalāpanam*, Bhikkhu Bodhi 2001: 869.

[65] *Phenasutta*, Saṃyuttanikāya 22:95, Bhikkhu Bodhi 2000: 951–5.

who has gained insight into the illusory nature of reality, the idea of leaving saṃsāra in order to obtain nirvāṇa must appear absurd. This view provides strong support for the ideal of the bodhisattva, a practitioner who, out of compassion for all beings, remains within cyclic existence until he has succeeded in liberating all of them as well. If there is no distinction between saṃsāra and nirvāṇa at the ultimate level, there is nothing the bodhisattva needs to escape from in order to obtain liberation. He can remain in saṃsāra in order to help sentient beings, increasing his insight by means of great compassion, and finally, once all beings have been liberated, can make the cognitive shift that transforms saṃsāra into nirvāṇa and the bodhisattva into a Buddha.

Illusionism and the bodhisattva ideal

At this stage we might wonder about the consistency of the Prajñāpāramitā's worldview. On the one hand it rejects all the Abhidharma categories, and seems to come close to the view that there is nothing at all; on the other hand it does speak about bodhisattvas, about illusory appearances, Buddhas, and nirvāṇa, all of which it appears to take to exist in some way. How can these positions go together?

Consistency of the Prajñāpāramitā's position

### c. *An explicit acceptance of contradictions*

Contradictions (or, at least apparent contradictions) abound in the Perfection of Wisdom literature. How does the Perfection of Wisdom procure all-knowledge? We learn that, 'In so far as it does not procure, to that extent it procures.'[66] How do *dharmas* exist? 'As they do not exist, so they exist.'[67] What does the profundity of the Perfection of Wisdom consist in? 'It cannot be developed by anything, nor by anyone, nor is there anything to be developed. For in perfect wisdom nothing at all has been brought to perfection.'[68]

Edward Conze, one of the most important Western scholars of the Prajñāpāramitā texts, sums up this perplexing situation in a concise manner:

> The thousands of lines of the Prajñāpāramitā can be summed up in the following two sentences: 1. One should become a Bodhisattva... 2. There is no such thing as a Bodhisattva, or as all-knowledge, or as 'being', or as the perfection of wisdom, or as attainment. To accept both these contradictory facts is to be perfect.[69]

It is important to be aware that there is a sense in which the claim that 'there is no such thing as a Bodhisattva' is uncontroversially accepted by early Buddhism, namely the idea that each person (including a bodhisattva) is only a superimposition on a shifting coalition of psycho-physical aggregates, the *skandhas*. But the Perfection of Wisdom texts go further than this. As we saw above, their aim is the rejection of *dharmas*, not just the rejection of higher-level appearances based on *dharmas*. We frequently find the phrase 'bodhisattva or

Non-existence of bodhisattvas

[66] Conze 1994: 136.
[67] Conze 1994: 87.
[68] Conze 1994: 191.
[69] Conze: 1978: 7–8.

bodhisattva-dharma' (*bodhisattvaṃ vā bodhisattvadharmaṃ vā*) as something to be negated, that is, not just the bodhisattva, in the sense of a person existing by *svabhāva*, but also the set of *dharmas* identified in the Abhidharma that can be collectively designated as a bodhisattva are rejected.[70]

Developing arguments for Prajñāpāramitā positions

It is therefore evident that the Perfection of Wisdom texts left Buddhist philosophers with a formidable task: first, to determine what precisely they are saying, and second, to come up with a justification for why what they are saying is true, that is, a justification that does not simply rely on their authority as *buddhavacana*. Would it be possible to come up with arguments in support of the Prajñāpāramitā's startling statements?

Was Nāgārjuna a Mahāyānist?

The first Buddhist philosopher to develop the philosophical position of the Perfection of Wisdom texts in a systematic manner, developing arguments for their conclusions and considering replies to actual and potential objections, was Nāgārjuna. Before we can consider how the three themes just discussed feature in his texts, however, we must first consider a curious historical fact. If Nāgārjuna's role is really to be understood as that of the recoverer (literally or metaphorically) and explicator of the Perfection of Wisdom texts, we would expect him to say so quite explicitly, and to quote the Prajñāpāramitā texts (and Mahāyāna texts in general) frequently in his works. In fact this is not the case at all. Of course matters depend to some extent here on what we consider Nāgārjuna's authentic works to be. If we assume that the *Mahāprajñāpāramitā-upadeśa-śāstra* (大智度論) was written by Nāgārjuna, his association with the Perfection of Wisdom tradition is fairly obvious, and even other texts for which the attribution to Nāgārjuna seems more plausible contain a certain amount of Mahāyāna references. The *Suhṛllekha*, for example, encourages the king it addresses to emulate the Bodhisattva Avalokiteśvara and the transcendental Buddha Amitābha; the fourth chapter of the *Ratnāvalī* explicitly praises the virtues of the Great Vehicle. Nevertheless, this picture is slightly different if we concentrate on the other five works of the *yukti*-corpus, specifically on the *Mūlamadhyamakakārikā*. The only *sūtra* Nāgārjuna refers to by name here is the *Kātyāyanāvavāda* (the Sanskrit parallel to the *Kaccānagotta-sutta*);[71] in addition a variety of other *sūtras* from the Tripiṭaka are quoted, but without explicitly giving their source.[72] Based on this, some twentieth-century Buddhologists have argued that Nāgārjuna's association with the Mahāyāna that forms part of traditional Buddhist history should be questioned.[73] Far from being an explicator of the Prajñāpāramitā texts, or a

[70] On this point see Schmithausen 1977: 45.

[71] In *Mūlamadhyamakakārikā* 15:7. Saṃyutta Nikāya 12.15 (Bikkhu Bodhi 2000: 544).

[72] Warder 1973: 79–81.

[73] See Warder 1973, Kalupahana 1991: 5–8. Ruegg 1981a: 6–7, Lindtner 1982: 21, n. 67, and Bronkhorst 2009: 136 remain unconvinced.

Mahāyāna proselytizer more generally, Nāgārjuna's aim in the *Mūlamadhyamakakārikā*, it is argued, was merely to refute the excesses of scholastic overlay that the Abhidharma works had deposited on the structure of early Buddhism. Their philosophical positions, such as the view of the continuous existence of entities in the past, present, and future, or the notion of *svabhāva* (a term that is not mentioned in the *sūtras* of the Tripiṭaka), are something Nāgārjuna argues against, in order to recover the pure and unfalsified teaching of the historical Buddha.

Both the idea of the rediscovery of historically unpolluted Buddhism,[74] as well as the characterization of Nāgārjuna (and of the Buddha) as 'empiricist philosophers'[75] owe more to modern intellectual concerns than the originators of these 'back to the basics' calls might have thought. Nevertheless, there are certain aspects of this view that seem plausible. From the evidence available in Nāgārjuna's works it is clear that he did not consider himself as an innovator or defender of the 'new' Mahāyāna creed against the benighted Abhidharma heretics.[76] What Nāgārjuna set out to do in the *Mūlamadhyamakakārikā* and his other works is to explicate what he considered the true meaning of the Buddha's words. He saw this meaning as expressed both in the Perfection of Wisdom texts and in the *sūtras* of the Tripiṭaka, and Nāgārjuna was striving to explain the unified philosophical vision of these texts, to supply arguments that are not present or not explicit in these texts, and to defend them against variant interpretations he regards as erroneous, such as those found in the Abhidharma. Still, we might ask ourselves, why does he then not explicitly quote Abhidharma and Prajñāpāramitā texts side by side? Why do all the quotations in the *Mūlamadhyamakakārikā* come from texts of early Buddhism?

Nāgārjuna did not see himself as a philosophical innovator

Salutary verses of the *Mūlamadhyamakakārikā*

First, a fact that earlier authors overlooked, even though it had already been pointed out by Conze[77] some time ago, is that the salutary verses (*nāmaskāra*) in praise of the Buddha by which Nāgārjuna begins his *Mūlamadhyamakakārikā* are clearly derived from a passage in the Perfection of Wisdom in 25,000 verses. Interestingly, though, this citation consists largely of phrases that occur individually in the early Buddhist *sūtras*, though not in the form in which they

[74] Schayer 1931: ix rightly criticizes this 'protestant' conception of Buddhism: 'Daß die Pāli-Philologie so auffallend wenig zur Aufhellung der philosophischen Grundlagen des Hīnayāna beigetragen hat, damit hat es seine eigene Bewandnis. Die falsche Suggestion, daß in der Geschichte einer Religion nur das Ursprüngliche echt, alles Jüngere dagegen mehr oder weniger eine "Entartung" sei, hat von Anfang an den Gang der Studien, ihre Richtung und ihre Methode beeinflußt.'

[75] Warder 1973: 85, 87.

[76] The concept of a Mahāyāna group identity that could have formed the basis of such a self-identification took a long time to develop. The earliest use of the term 'Mahāyāna' is only found in Indian inscriptions dating from several centuries after the appearance of the first Mahāyāna texts. Williams (2009: 28) notes that for 'a monk in the first or second century CE the Mahāyāna as a visible institution was scarcely evident'.

[77] Conze 1975: 595, n. 11.

are put together here.[78] The *nāmaskāra* thereby fulfils a curious double function: on the one hand putting a section of a Prajñāpāramitā text at the very beginning of this key treatise conveys a clear signal about the intellectual lineage in which Nāgārjuna wants to position his work. On the other hand, nothing forces this reading. All the terms Nāgārjuna uses here can be found in the *sūtras* of the Tripiṭaka. The reason for this, and for the prevalence of non-Mahāyāna citations in the *Mūlamadhyamakakārikā*, as well as for the absence of explicit reference to Mahāyāna texts, Walser has argued[79] lies in the specific historical situation the Mahāyāna movement found itself in during Nāgārjuna's times. As a minority school, it was trying to promote the acceptance of its interpretation to a majority of Ābhidharmikas. It would obviously have been of very little use to try to do this by reference to Mahāyāna *sūtras*; even though these explicitly endorsed the superiority of the Mahāyāna interpretation, they were not accepted as authoritative by the Ābhidharmikas. Nāgārjuna's strategy, therefore, was to argue for Mahāyāna conclusions by restricting himself to explicit references to texts that both the Ābhidharmikas and the Mahāyānists would consider as authoritative. We see here a milder form of the problem Buddhists later faced when debating with non-Buddhist opponents. Obviously such debates could not make any reference to scriptural authority, since the two parties did not acknowledge each other's canon. But in the Buddhist case there was such a shared canon, and Nāgārjuna set out to demonstrate that the Tripiṭaka texts that the Ābhidharmikas regarded as authoritative could be given a Mahāyāna reading. This procedure might remind us of the cuckoo and her eggs, but there is no reason to believe that matters appeared in this way to a thinker like Nāgārjuna. His aim was to bring out what he considered to be the authentic meaning of the Buddha's teachings, and to do so in a manner that would convince the largest possible number of his co-religionists.

## 4. Key Themes of Nāgārjuna's Thought

After this brief discussion of the nature of Nāgārjuna's relation with the Abhidharma, let us now get back to the question how the key themes of the Perfection of Wisdom literature that we identified above get taken up in Nāgārjuna's works.

### *a. Nāgārjuna and the criticism of the Abhidharma project*

There are two obvious areas of the Abhidharma project that Nāgārjuna criticizes: their idea of the goal of the Buddhist path as obtaining the stage of a *śrāvaka* or *pratyekabuddha*, which he replaces by the ideal of the bodhisattva, and the Abhidharma metaphysics of *dharmas* as ultimately real entities. In the

[78] Walser 2005: 170–83. [79] Walser 2005: ch. 5.

advice to a king Nāgārjuna gives in the *Ratnāvalī* he is very explicit in pointing out that the Mahāyāna (and the bodhisattva ideal it teaches) constitutes a set of teachings of the Buddha for beings with higher spiritual capacities than those for whom the *sūtra*s of the Tripiṭaka are intended:

Just as a master of grammar teaches even the alphabet to disciples,
Even so the Buddha teaches his doctrine to those to be tamed as it is accessible to them.
He taught his doctrine to some so that they turn away from evil deeds,
To others so that they could accomplish meritorious deeds, to others [a teaching] based on duality.
To some others [he taught a doctrine] beyond duality, deep, terrifying those who are afraid [of such teachings];
The heart of compassion and emptiness, the means of obtaining enlightenment.
Therefore the wise ones must destroy any feeling of aversion towards the Mahāyāna
And generate special faith in order to attain to complete enlightenment.[80]

Nāgārjuna's endorsement of the Abhidharma

This idea of a progression of doctrines (a common *topos* in Indian philosophy and doxography) suggests that the idea frequently found in the secondary literature, that Nāgārjuna's aim was 'to refute the Abhidharma', needs to be seen in a more nuanced manner. In another passage in the *Ratnāvalī* Nāgārjuna advises the king to 'definitely realize with vigour' a list of fifty-seven ethical faults in order to avoid them.[81] This list most plausibly derived from an Abhidharma text.[82] A list of seven kinds of pride given in the same work[83] also derives from Abhidharma sources, and is later included in Vasubandhu's *Abhidharmakośabhāṣya*.[84] Nāgārjuna's attitude is therefore very far from a wholesale rejection of the teachings of the Abhidharma; in this context he explicitly recommends the close study of one of its topical lists (*mātṛkā*). In fact there would have been no reason for rejecting Abhidharma doctrines *tout court*. They are, after all, an attempt to systematize, explicate, and develop the teachings contained in the Buddha's *sūtra*s of early Buddhism, and the fact

[80] *yathaiva vaiyākaraṇo mātṛkām api pāṭhayet |*
*buddho 'vadat tathā dharmaṃ vineyānāṃ yathākṣamaṃ ||*
*keṣāṃcid avadad dharmaṃ pāpebhyo vinivṛttaye |*
*keṣāṃcit puṇyasiddhyarthaṃ keṣāṃcid dvayaniḥśritam ||*
*dvayāniśritam ekeṣāṃ gāmbhīraṃ bhīrubhīṣaṇaṃ |*
*śūnyatākaruṇāgarbham ekeṣāṃ bodhisādhanam||*
*iti sadbhir mahāyāne kartavyaḥ pratighakṣayaḥ |*
*prasādaś cādhikaḥ kāryaḥ samyaksaṃbodhisiddhaye ||*
Ratnāvalī 4: 94–7, Hahn 1982a: 128–31, Hopkins 1998: 147, verses 394–7.

[81] Hopkins 1998: 149. [82] Walser 2005: 226–7.

[83] *Ratnāvalī* 5: 7–12, Hahn 1982a: 134–7, Hopkins 1998: 150–1, verses 407–12.

[84] *bhāṣya* on *Abhidharmakośa* 5.10 (Pradhan 1975: 284–5, Poussin and Pruden 1988–90: 3. 784–5).

that Nāgārjuna considered some of these explications (even very central ones) as mistaken does not mean that he would have rejected them all. Even though it is difficult to be definite about this, there may have been a political (or, to use a favourite Mahāyāna term, 'skilful' (*upāya*)) dimension to Nāgārjuna's acceptance or endorsements of certain Abhidharma positions. We know that the different pre-Mahāyāna schools of Indian Buddhism had distinct but conceptually overlapping Abhidharma texts, even though only two, the Sarvāstivāda and the Theravāda, have come down to us in their entirety. It is not entirely implausible to assume that some of the Abhidharma positions Nāgārjuna takes on board were those defended by the Abhidharma of the monastery in which he was staying. Like the references to Tripiṭaka *sutras*, the references to this canon would have allowed Nāgārjuna to underline the legitimacy of the Mahāyāna outlook in the eyes of his non-Mahāyānist fellow monks.[85]

Emptiness of persons and *dharmas*

The key metaphysical notion of the Abhidharma that Nāgārjuna attacks is that of *svabhāva* or intrinsic nature. His theory of emptiness means simply that all things are empty of intrinsic nature. In early Buddhist teaching the doctrine of emptiness was primarily spelt out as the selflessness of persons (*pudgala-nairātmya*), arguing that there is no permanent, self-sufficient personality core that notions like 'I', 'me', or 'mine' picked out. With Madhyamaka the domain of emptiness expanded so that it covered all non-persons as well; in addition to the selflessness of persons, it gave a prominent position to the selflessness of all *dharmas* (*dharmanairātmya*). The idea of the emptiness of *dharmas* is not entirely straightforward. Whereas persons might be considered to possess a substantial soul or *ātman*, other things do not do so in any obvious sense. For this reason we need a more general notion of what all empty things, persons and non-persons, are empty of, and this is the notion of *svabhāva*. Nāgārjuna characterizes *svabhāva* by two important properties: it is not adventitious (*akṛtrimaḥ*) and not dependent on something else (*nirapekṣaḥ paratra*).[86] If we recall the notion of *svabhāva* we find in the Abhidharma,[87] we remember that an object has some property as its *svabhāva* if this property does not depend on other things, apart from the thing that brought the object into existence in the first place. Thus a chariot is no chariot by *svabhāva* because it borrows its nature from its simultaneously existent components. The great elements (*mahābhūta*) like water, fire, and so on do not derive their nature from anything else. They have their nature by *svabhāva*, yet the Abhidharma has no difficulties with accepting that they are causally produced. But we just saw Nāgārjuna say that dependent things cannot exist by *svabhāva*, and a causally produced *dharma* is of course dependent on the causes and conditions

*svabhāva*

*svabhāva* and causation

[85] On this see further Walser 2005: 225–63. He rightly points out that 'Nāgārjuna's arguments should be examined in terms of the alliances they forge instead of merely whom they attack' (226).
[86] *Mūlamadhyamakakārikā* 15:2. [87] See pp. 70–1 above.

that brought it into existence. It seems as if the Abhidharma and Nāgārjuna meant quite different things when they spoke of *svabhāva*, and if that is the case we might wonder whether Nāgārjuna's rejection of *svabhāva*, setting out to explicate its rejection in the Perfection of Wisdom texts, is really a rejection of the *svabhāva* the Ābhidharmikas had in mind, or whether it is the rejection of something else.

The reason why Nāgārjuna regards being causally produced as incompatible with having *svabhāva*, while the Ābhidharmikas did not see a conflict between these, lies in their different concepts of causation. In order to see why this is the case we need to look more closely at Nāgārjuna's causal argument against *svabhāva*.

The causal argument against *svabhāva*

Nāgārjuna's argument is based on some important assumptions about time. The first is *presentism*. This is the idea that only the present moment, and neither the past nor the future, exists. The second is *momentariness*, the view that nothing has any temporal 'thickness', that all things, once arisen, last only for a moment and disappear immediately afterwards. Causal processes happen in a sequence: first there is a cause (say, a spark), and at a later time the effect arises (the explosion).[88] But this entails that the causal relation is always missing one related object. When the cause exists the effect does not yet exist, and when the effect exists the cause has already passed out of existence. Since the joint premises of presentism and momentariness have squeezed the whole of reality into the present moment, and since the causal relation requires at least two successive moments, one *relatum* of this relation will always fail to exist. It seems as if this shows that causation does not exist, since there cannot be two-place relations without two *relata*. Yet the world appears to us as causal through and through, and the Mādhyamika has to find a way to account for this. He does so by suggesting that even though the effect cannot exist at the same time as the cause, the idea of the effect can. When the cause exists, the effect is supplied by anticipation (when the spark flashes, we expect the explosion); when the effect has arisen, the cause is supplied by memory (we remember the spark when the explosion happens). What this means is that the causal relation inevitably contains one *relatum* that is a conceptual construct, and if this is the case, causation cannot be an objective relation that obtains in a mind-independent manner. Moreover, causally produced things have the property of being causally produced essentially, they would not be what they are without being so produced. If the teacup in front of me had not come into being from a set of causes and conditions it would not be that cup. But this means that the essence of such things involves conceptual construction, and

Causation essentially involves conceptualization

[88] It is occasionally suggested that cause and effect are sometimes simultaneous, e.g. when Jill's going down on the seesaw causes Jack's going up. However, such cases give rise to various complexities we do not have the space to go into in the present discussion.

anything that does so cannot exist by *svabhāva*, since it entails that the object is not what it is all by itself, but in dependence on other things, such as conceptualizing minds. For this reason all causally produced things must be empty.

Abhidharma and Madhyamaka views of *svabhāva* and causation

It is now easier for us to understand why Nāgārjuna considered having a cause as incompatible with having *svabhāva*, while the Ābhidharmikas saw no incompatibility. We recall that for the Sarvāstivādin, the property of having *svabhāva* applies to *dharmas* atemporally. Whether a *dharma* presently exists, has existed or is yet to be, its *svabhāva* is there; the only thing that changes is the *dharma*'s efficacy. But in this case causal production or destruction does not affect the existential status of *svabhāva*, and as such there seems to be little motivation for thinking that such causal relations detract from its self-sufficiency or 'own-being'. Of course, as we have seen, not all schools of Abhidharma accepted this curious idea of continuous existence. The Sautrāntikas considered *dharmas* as momentary phenomena, with no persistent *svabhāva* in the background. Rather, they suggest that as soon as a *dharma* passes out of existence, it causes its similarly momentary successor-*dharma*. Instead of a fire-*dharma* with a continuous *svabhāva* that gains its efficacy only in the present moment, we have a string of fire-*dharmas*, each causing the next.

The Abhidharma's criteria for being a *dharma* (and hence for having *svabhāva*) were formulated in terms of analysis at one point in time. If something does not disappear once it has been taken apart, either physically or conceptually, it is a *dharma*. The fact that a particular fire-*dharma* is caused does not conflict with the fact that as long as it exists in cannot be broken down into more basic constituents in either of these two ways. It is also worthwhile to remember that the reason for denying objects with parts a *svabhāva* is that they are taken to borrow their nature from objects that do not have that nature. A chariot thus borrows its nature from the axle, wheel, and so forth, none of which is itself a chariot. We would not even be able to say that a momentary fire-*dharma* borrows its nature from its cause in this way, for the reason that its cause is a fire-*dharma* too. The fire-*dharma* does not seem to depend on anything that is not a fire-*dharma*. But once we replace the Abhidharma conception of causation with the one we find in Madhyamaka, entities that were formerly regarded as unproblematically possessing *svabhāva* suddenly do not do so any longer. Being causally produced now incorporates an element of conceptual construction, since, the Mādhyamika argues, without the mind's handiwork there would be no causal relation in the first place. The Sautrāntika's momentary *dharmas* are caused by their very nature, and if we properly understand what that means we realize that upon taking their nature apart there is, after all, an element there that, when taken away, will make the *dharma* disappear. If the fire-*dharma* is not causally produced, and thus ultimately dependent on our conceptualization, there would be no fire-*dharma*. The Ābhidharmika and the Mādhyamika do not operate with different conceptions of *svabhāva* and are therefore not talking past each other. They do, however, have different concepts of causation, and this has repercussions on their views of the kinds of things to be considered as having *svabhāva* in the first place.

The mereological argument against *svabhāva*

The second main argument against *svabhāva* Nāgārjuna discusses is not based on the notion of causation, but on the problem of identity or difference of wholes and parts. The argumentative structure will be familiar to us from Abhidharma arguments setting out to show that wholes cannot be ultimately real objects (*dravya*) but must be conceptually constructed (*prajñapti*).[89] Their reason was that if wholes were ultimately real they should stand in a clearly defined relation to their parts. But it turns out that both the assumption that the whole is identical with the parts and the assumption that it is a separate entity distinct from them leads to problems. From this the Ābhidharmikas infer that wholes are no entities in their own right, that they do not exist in the same sense as the parts, but are merely conceptual superimpositions on the parts.

Nāgārjuna now continues this argument on the level of the *dharma*s, that is, he applies it to the entities that came out as ultimately real according to the mereological argument of the Ābhidharmikas. Of course he cannot do so with reference to the first criterion for being a *dharma* (mereological simplicity), as the *dharma*s have no parts. Instead, he focuses on the second, the idea that ultimately real objects must also be simple not just in terms of material decomposition, but also when it comes to conceptual decomposition.

Are *dharmas* the same as their conceptual parts or different?

The question Nāgārjuna is now asking is whether a *dharma* as a conceptual whole is identical with or distinct from its parts. If we consider one of the 'four great elements' (*mahābhūta*), such as the water-element, as a *dharma*, we will naturally want to characterize it as an individual (the *dharma*) that has a number of properties (wetness, stickiness, and so on). Is the *dharma* distinct from its properties, or are they one and the same thing? Suppose they are distinct. In this case we have an individual on the one hand, and various properties attached to it. What is the nature of the individual? If it really is distinct from all its properties, it is just what is left when all its properties have been abstracted away—what in common philosophical terminology is called a *bare particular*. Is this bare particular what it is by its intrinsic nature, that is, by *svabhāva*? If it is, a water-*dharma* would come with two *svabhāva*s or natures, that of being a bare particular and that which is the specific characteristic or *svalakṣaṇa* of water, namely being wet. But nothing can have two natures, since a thing's nature makes it what it is in contrast with other things. So it would be safer to say that a bare particular is not what it is by its own nature.

[89] See above, pp. 71–2.

This, however, just means that it borrows its nature from something else, and, far from having reached ontological rock-bottom with this peculiar idea of an object with no qualities, we now have to continue our analysis. Being a bare particular would in turn be a property of something else, an even barer particular to which this property attached in the same way as the property of being wet attached to the original bare particular. At this stage we can of course repeat the whole argument, and the unappealing prospect of an infinitely descending sequence of barer and barer particulars opens up.

*dharmas* as property-particulars

These kinds of problems might suggest that we took a wrong turn earlier on. We should have rather said that the *dharma*, the whole, is not distinct from its properties, the parts. Of course the literal identity of the two is hard to make sense of, as the *dharma* is one, but its properties are many, and nothing can be both one and many. But we could still spell out this idea by arguing that the entire concept of an individual as a metaphysical condensation nucleus to which properties attach is superfluous in the first place. Instead, we could say that the water-element is not a *dharma* itself, but that it is simply a collection of coexisting property particulars, sometimes referred to as tropes.[90] These property-particulars would then be the real *dharmas*. The water-element is just a conceptual construction; while there is a wetness-trope and a stickiness-trope and so on, which congregate, the *dharma* as an individual is simply superimposed on these in the same way the chariot is superimposed on its parts.

How are property-particulars told apart?

Nāgārjuna now raises the question of what makes all these different particularized properties distinct. On the face of it, the answer seems to be obvious: a particularized property is particularized because it is the appearance of a property at a specific space-time location. What distinguishes two wetness-tropes is that one is wetness here now, and the other wetness there then. But the matter is not a simple as it looks, for if particularized properties are really the only fundamental category we assume (and this is the case with the Abhidharma's *dharmas*) then they should account for all properties, including spatial and temporal properties. That means that 'being at a certain place' and 'being at a certain time' are both tropes as well. They then lose their status as privileged individuators of other tropes.

One way of fixing this problem is as follows. We do not really need special properties in order to individuate one trope from the next. In fact, we do not even need to know which trope is which in order to tell one from the other. Tropes do not exist in a lonely state, but in complexes with other tropes. We can then simply individuate each trope by determining which other tropes it

[90] See above, p. 71.

co-occurs with in a complex we conventionally label as an 'invididual'. This will be different for every trope.

Despite its elegance, this procedure has a crucial weakness. Tropes are no longer individuated according to inner own nature or properties, but with reference to other tropes they co-occur with. This means that each trope depends for being the kind of thing it is on other tropes; it is only through the existence of tropes other than the wetness-trope that not all wetness-tropes coalesce. If this is the case, tropes can no longer be considered as possessors of *svabhāva*.

It thus appears that all ways of spelling out the relations of the parts of *dharmas* to the whole either lead to problematic conclusions or to positions that cannot ascribe *svabhāva* to them.

The argument from change

The last of Nāgārjuna's arguments against *svabhāva* I want to consider takes as its starting point the observation that things around us change. The world we observe is not static but characterized by things continuously changing their properties, coming into existence, and going out of existence. Nāgārjuna sees a conflict between this fact and the potential existence of *svabhāva*. He points out that:

> there is the lack of *svabhāva* of things due to the observation of change.... If *svabhāva* was found, what would change? Neither the change of a thing itself nor of something different is suitable: as a young man does not grow old, so an old man does not grow old either.[91]

Change as arising and ceasing

Let us consider the problem at the level of tropes. If water is hot now, and cold later, what could account for this change? One suggestion might be that the heat-tropes that inhere in this conglomeration of tropes that is the hot water turn into something else. This seems impossible, given that these tropes have heat as their nature. If this is the core of what they are, how could they ever turn into anything else? (This is the point of Nāgārjuna's remark that an (intrinsically) young man could not grow old.) What would rather happen is that the heat-tropes go out of existence, and other, different tropes arise in their stead. This leaves open the problem of what causes these other tropes to arise. Obviously not tropes of the same kind (else there would be no change), nor does it seem satisfactory to assume that they have arisen without a cause. Yet it seems that one of these two possibilities has to obtain if there is to be change at all. If all the tropes only give rise to further tropes just like them, everything will always be the same: a man who is already old will not change into an old man.

[91] *Mūlamadhyamakakārikā* 13: 3a, 4b–5
*bhāvānāṃ niḥsvabhāvatvam anyathābhāvadarśanāt* | [. . .]
*kasya syād anyathābhāvaḥ svabhāvo yadi vidyate* ||
*tasyaiva nānyathābhāvo nāpy anyasyaiva yujyate* |
*yuvā na jīryate yasmād yasmāj jīrṇo na jīryate* ||

A final possibility one might consider is that the tropes are actually permanent, do not come into existence or go out of existence, and that change is just to be explained by a local rearrangement of these tropes. When hot water cools down the heat-tropes neither change nor pass out of existence, they will just go somewhere else. The difficulty with this suggestion is that it does not explain why the permanent tropes arrange themselves in ever-changing combinations. It cannot be anything going on inside them, like the arising and ceasing of some repulsive force, since in this case the tropes would precisely not be permanent, but would be changing. Yet it is this notion of change that we want to explain in the first place, and a theory that involves entities existing by *svabhāva* seems to face considerable challenges in doing so.

Change as recombination

We have thus seen that Nāgārjuna underpins the Prajñāpāramitā's criticism of the ontological part of the Abhidharma project, and of the central notion of *dharma*s that exist by *svabhāva* that this involves, with a variety of arguments involving such different concepts as causation, parthood, or change. These are certainly not all the arguments against *svabhāva* we find in Nāgārjuna's texts, nor are they all we find in the Madhyamaka literature that follow him. But they constitute a representative sample of argumentative approaches to backing up a set of claims made in the Perfection of Wisdom *sūtra*s that also have considerable systematic potential as philosophical arguments in their own rights.

Argumentative support for the claims of the Perfection of Wisdom texts

### b. *Illusionism in Nāgārjuna's thought*

We noted above that the Perfection of Wisdom texts expound a thoroughgoing illusionistic theory; for more-or-less any concept that forms part of the Buddhist path we can find a section of a Prajñāpāramitā text that says that this concept is not real. However, the theory expounded there is not one that defends a kind of appearance/reality distinction such as we can find, for example, in Vedānta. Its aim is not to show that the world we find around us is all empty and hence illusory, while that there is another world separate from this one that is the only real one. The Abhidharma account, on the other hand, can be interpreted as endorsing this appearance/reality distinction: composite objects are the appearance, but the only real things are the individual *dharmas*.

Not a view of 'appearance vs. reality'

Nāgārjuna employ's the Perfection of Wisdom's illusionistic metaphors frequently in his own works. At the conclusion of chapter 17 of the *Mūlamadhyamakakārikā* he notes that:

> 31. Just as the Teacher by his supernatural power fabricates a magical being that in turn fabricates yet another magical being,
>
> 32. so with regard to the agent, which has the form of a magical being, and the action that is done by it, it is like the case where a second magical being is fabricated by a magical being.

> 33. Defilements, actions, and bodies, agents, and fruits, are similar to the city of the gandharvas; they are like a mirage, a dream.[92]

The example of one of the Buddha's miraculous performances, in which he produced a phantom magician who then produced another phantom in turn, illustrates the claim that action is not fundamentally real, nor is the agent who brings it about. Things that lack *svabhāva* can be brought about by other things that lack *svabhāva*, and this point can be generalized: unlike in an appearance/reality scenario where appearances are finally grounded in something substantial, in this case it is insubstantial entities all the way down. The *dharmas* that serve as the basis of partite entities are not any more real than the partite entities themselves. It is perhaps not too surprising that both non-Buddhist and Buddhist critics quickly accused Madhyamaka of nihilism because of arguments such as these.[93] Asaṅga, for example, accuses the Mādhyamikas of misunderstanding the meaning of the Mahāyāna *sūtras*. He claims in the *Bodhisattvabhūmi* that:

The charge of ontological nihilism

> Hence, some who have heard the *sūtras* connected with the Mahāyāna, which are difficult to understand, and associated with profound emptiness, manifest an indirect meaning, do not know the meaning of the description of reality as it really is. Inaccurately, they have views without cogency obtained through mere inference (*tarka*) and say: 'All this is in reality just a designation. Who sees matters in this way sees them correctly.' For those, the designation does not exist in any way, because of the non-existence of a given thing (*vastumātra*) that is the basis of designation. But how will reality be mere designation? In this manner both reality and designation are rejected. Because of the rejection of designation and reality they are to be known as the most extreme kind of nihilist (*pradhāna nāstika*).[94]

Yet the Mādhyamikas take great care to distance themselves from the nihilist position. As their name, 'followers of the middle way', indicates they emphasize the fact that they reject both the extreme of nihilism as well as the extreme of

[92] *yathā nirmitakaṃ śāstā nirmimītārddhisaṃpadā | nirmito nirmimītānyaṃ sa ca nirmitakaḥ punaḥ || tathā nirmitakākāraḥ kartā yat karma tatkṛtam | tadyathā nirmitenānyo nirmito nirmitas tathā || kleśāḥ karmāṇi dehāś ca kartāraś ca phalāni ca | gandharvanagarākārā marīcisvapnasaṃnibhāḥ ||* Siderits and Katsura 2013: 191. The 'city of the gandharvas' is a popular Indian example of an unreal appearance: a city seen in the sky that is not really there.

[93] For further discussion of this point see Westerhoff 2016a.

[94] *ato ya ekatyā durvijñeyān sūtrāntānmahāyānapratisaṃyuktāṃ gambhīrāṃ śūnyatāpratisaṃyuktānābhiprāyikārthanirūpitāṃ śrutvā yathābhūtaṃ bhāṣitasyārthamavijñāyāyoniśo vikalpyāyogavihitena tarkamātrakeṇa ivaṃ dṛṣṭayo bhavanty evaṃ vādinaḥ | prajñaptimātram eva sarvam etat tattvam | yaś ca ivaṃ paśyati sa samyak paśyatīti | teṣāṃ prajñaptyadhiṣṭhānasya vastumātrasyābhāvātsaiva prajñaptiḥ sarveṇa sarvaṃ na bhavati | kutaḥ punaḥ prajñaptimātraṃ tattvaṃ bhaviṣyatīti | tad anena paryāyeṇa tais tattvam api prajñaptir api tad ubhayam apy apavāditaṃ bhavati | prajñaptitattvāpavādāc ca pradhāno nāstiko veditavyaḥ*, Wogihara 1930–6: 1. 46. See Willis 1979: 161, Engle 2016: 81–2.

postulating substantially existent entities. Nāgārjuna stresses the fact that even though things like chariots and pots are neither fundamentally real nor based on something fundamentally real, they can still perform various functions such as carrying wood or water. As a monetary economy does not need anything intrinsically valuable to serve as a guarantor of the value of currencies, but can function by relying on the beliefs and expectations of the participants in its economic exchanges, so things do not need to be grounded in something existing by *svabhāva* to do what they are supposed to do. As long as sufficiently many people participate in a process of joint designation the entities thus designated will continue to exist. This point about the functional efficacy of everyday entities is particularly important for the Mādhyamika, since a charge he sees himself confronted with frequently is that of *moral* nihilism. If, as the opponent claims, the Mādhyamika rejects the existence of all things, he will also reject the existence of karmic potentials. But if this is rejected it seems as if a main incentive for moral behaviour for ordinary people is gone. How can those not yet convinced of the virtues of altruism be held in check without arguing that their non-virtuous actions will, via their karmic fruits, undermine their own selfish desires? Add to this the fact that the Perfection of Wisdom texts the Madhyamaka is based on do not exempt bodhisattvas, the Buddha, and liberation from its all-encompassing view of emptiness, and we may be forgiven for asking to what extent we are still dealing with a form of Buddhism here. It is therefore essential that the Mādhyamika distinguishes existence without *svabhāva* (the way all things exist) from non-existence (as, for example, flowers in the sky and sons of barren women are non-existent), and underlines that the emptiness characterized by absence of *svabhāva* does not entail emptiness of functional efficacy. The fact that things are insubstantial does not mean that they cannot interact with one another, and for this reason cyclic existence, the Buddhist path, and its goal, liberation, have a firm place in the Madhyamaka worldview.

*svabhāva* is not required for functionality

The charge of moral nihilism

### *c. Contradictions and Nāgārjuna's thought*

A casual reading of Nāgārjuna works is likely to give the reader the impression that contradictory statements form an essential part of his philosophy. He frequently employs of a specific form of argument, the tetralemma or *catuṣkoṭi*, which lists four apparently exclusive and jointly exhaustive possibilities, all of which are then rejected. Consider the following example from the *Mūlamadhyamakakārikā*:

Explaining the tetralemma

> 'It is empty' is not to be said, nor 'It is non-empty,' nor that it is both, nor that it is neither; it is said only for the sake of instruction.[95]

[95] 22:11 *śūnyam iti na vaktavyam aśūnyam iti vā bhavet | ubhayaṃ nobhayaṃ ceti prajñaptyarthaṃ tu kathyate*, Siderits and Katsura 2013: 247.

When we reject the view that things are empty, does that not mean that we say that they are non-empty? Denying both seems to be contradictory. But even if we have managed to do so, Nāgārjuna then points out that the denial of both is to be rejected as well. How are we supposed to make sense of passages such as these? Moreover, contradictions do not seem to be limited to tetralemma-style arguments. At the end of the twenty-fifth chapter of the *Mūlamadhyamaka-kārikā* Nāgārjuna points out that: 'This halting of cognizing everything, the halting of hypostatizing, is blissful. No *dharma* whatever was ever taught by the Buddha to anyone.'[96] After spending twenty-five densely argued chapters to explain the teachings of the Buddha (whom Nāgārjuna praises as the 'best of teachers' at the beginning of the work), we now learn that the Buddha never taught anything. We seem to find ourselves in the territory of the Perfection of Wisdom texts again, where one sentence asserts something which the next one then goes on to deny.

Non-classical logic

Some modern interpreters have tried to address the puzzling occurrence of contradictions in Nāgārjuna's arguments by suggesting that he may have adopted a non-classical logic that tolerates contradictions.[97] While these interpretations do not lack a certain technical ingenuity, they appear to be more of a further development of certain Madhyamaka ideas than an attempt at a rational reconstruction of what Nāgārjuna might have had in mind when he composed these verses. Neither in Nāgārjuna's own writings nor in those of his Indian commentators do we find clear evidence that they were trying to develop a non-classical logic, nor that he challenged the principle of the excluded contradiction as a logical law.[98] To this extent we need to understand the contradictions proclaimed by the Perfection of Wisdom texts that the Mādhyamikas set out to explicate as merely apparent, but not as actual contradictions.

The theory of the two truths

There is, however, another hermeneutic device to help us understand what is going on with these apparently contradictory statements that has a clearly attested historical status. This is the theory of the two truths. This doctrine occurs in some form or other in most systems of Buddhist philosophy, though the Mādhyamikas are probably those that made the greatest use of it. It claims that we have to distinguish two different kinds of truth (or two different kinds of reality—the Sanskrit term *satya* can refer to either), a conventional truth of everyday reality (*saṃvṛtisatya*) and an ultimate truth (*paramārthasatya*). Note that we are dealing here with two kinds of truth, not with a truth and a falsity.

[96] 25:24 *sarvopalambhopaśamaḥ prapañcopaśamaḥ śivaḥ |*
*na kva cit kasyacit kaścid dharmo buddhena deśitaḥ*, Siderits and Katsura 2013: 304.

[97] See Priest and Garfield 2002, Garfield and Priest 2009, Priest and Routley 1989. See also Tillemans (2009) for a discussion of dialetheism in view of the fact that 'contradictions were anathema... for later Mādhyamikas' (96).

[98] Ruegg 1969: 384.

Both conventional and ultimate truth have their uses, though they differ in soteriological efficacy. Conventional truth allows us to achieve innerworldly aims (build an aeroplane, calculate the value of $\pi$), while ultimate truth is what we have to realize in order become liberated from saṃsāra; it describes the ultimate nature of reality.[99]

We can then use this distinction to dispel the appearance of paradox in instances of the tetralemma such as the one given above, by arguing that not all its negations relate to the same truth. Rather, when properly understood, what the passage from Nāgārjuna says is that we should not assert that things are *conventionally* empty, since our daily interaction with them relies on the mistaken assumption that they exist with *svabhāva*. Nor should we say that they are *ultimately* non-empty, since when we apply Madhyamaka reasoning to them, reasoning which is designed to uncover ultimate truths about them, we do not find that their existence with *svabhāva* can be supported. If we do not assert these two, we obviously do not assert them both. What about rejecting them both? We cannot do so if we assume that this rejection then gets at the ultimate truth of what reality is. When Nāgārjuna says that these assertions about emptiness are made 'only for the sake of instruction', he rejects the notion that they are in the business of telling us anything about what the world is like at the most fundamental level. The Madhyamaka only asserts them in order to refute specific misunderstandings his opponent may have.

Similarly, we can agree that *ultimately* 'no *dharma* whatever was ever taught by the Buddha to anyone', because at the level of ultimate truth there is no Buddha, no *dharma*, and nobody listening to it. These are all only superimpositions valid on the conventional level, and for this reason it is *conventionally* false to say that the Buddha did not teach.

The interpolation procedure

The distinction between the two truths therefore provides us with an effective means to make sense of the seemingly contradictory statements we find in Nāgārjuna's writings, and also in the Perfection of Wisdom literature. The drawback with this interpretation is that we have to presuppose that the *sūtras* and commentaries in question are incomplete; whenever they say 'there is no *x*' what they really mean is that there is no *x* at the level of ultimate reality, even though we are still allowed to speak about *x* at the level of conventional reality. There is certainly justification for this view, and the later Tibetan scholar Tsong kha pa (1357–1419), who put great emphasis on this 'interpolation procedure', provides a passage of from the *Laṅkāvatārasūtra* to support it.[100] The Buddha points out to the bodhisattva Mahāmati:

[99] Whether these two characterizations of ultimate truth coincide is a complex question in the interpretation of Madhyamaka. See Siderits 2007: 200–4 for some discussion.

[100] Tsong kha pa 2002: 3: 188, see also 215–23.

'Mahāmati, thinking that they are not produced intrinsically, I said that all phenomena are not produced.'[101]

Ultimately real simulacra

The difficulty that arises when this procedure is applied too widely is that the negations we find in the Prajñāpāramitā literature or in Madhyamaka works can easily look as if they only concerned a kind of scholastic epiphenomenon, and not any kind of entity we are familiar with from everyday experience. When the Heart Sūtra says that there is no matter, it means *ultimately real* matter; when the Perfection of Wisdom in 8,000 verses says that a bodhisattva cannot be found, it means an *ultimately real* bodhisattva; and when Nāgārjuna says in the *Vigrahavyāvartanī* that he has no thesis, he means an *ultimately real* thesis. We might then ask ourselves first of all what these strange ultimately real simulacra amount to (just what is the difference between holding an ultimately real thesis and just holding a thesis?) or why it would matter that there are no such things (if there is no ultimately real matter, can mere matter not equally give rise to the kind of attachment the Buddhist path tries to show us to transcend)?[102]

If concerns such as these are raised the method of interpolation has probably been over-applied, not only dissolving seeming contradictions but domesticating various Madhyamaka denials by restricting them to the realm of the ultimate. But this in itself is, of course, no criticism of the distinction between the two truths as a key hermeneutic principle for understanding Nāgārjuna's writings, as well as the Perfection of Wisdom texts they set out to explicate.

## 5. The Commentators

After considering some of the origins of Madhyamaka in the Prajñāpāramitā literature and tracing the continuity of a set of its key themes in Nāgārjuna's works, we want to look at what happened to Indian Madhyamaka in the roughly one thousand years between the composition of the *Mūlamadhyamakakārikā* and the eventual disappearance of scholastic Buddhism in India. This development has produced a vast body of literature of dazzling philosophical complexity, and attempting to do justice to it in a part of a chapter might easily seem like a foolish undertaking. What we can do, however, is point out some conceptual cross-sections, like a trench cut through a field of archaeological excavation, in the hope that at least parts of the major sights come into view. One such possible cross-section is the sequence of commentaries on the school's foundational text, the *Mūlamadhyamakakārikā*. In true Indian scholastic fashion, variant interpretations and divergent conceptions of how

[101] *svabhāvānutpattiṃ saṃdhāya mahāmate mayā sarvadharmā anutpannā ity uktāḥ*, quoted in Candrakīrti's *Prasannapadā*, Poussin 1913: 504: 5–6.

[102] For a modern Tibetan criticism of this 'interpolation procedure' see Lopez 2006: 58–60.

Madhyamaka was to be understood were most frequently made in the form of commentaries that aimed to clarify what Nāgārjuna meant when composing his major work.

Commentaries on the *Mūlamadhyamakakārikā*

Commensurate with its importance, the *Mūlamadhyamakakārikā* is a work that has been frequently commented on in ancient India. Of the commentaries we know of, only a single one, Candrakīrti's *Prasannapadā*, is preserved in its Sanskrit original. An early commentary, the *Akutobhayā* (sometimes considered to be an auto-commentary by Nāgārjuna), Buddhapālita's commentary, and Bhāviveka's *Prajñāpradīpa* are still extant in Tibetan, and further commentaries by Piṅgala and Sthiramati are preserved in Chinese translations. Four further commentaries, by Devaśarman, Guṇaśrī, Guṇamati (Sthiramati's teacher), and Rāhulabhadra are, apart from some occasional quotations, lost.[103] It is particularly interesting to note that Yogācāra masters such as Guṇamati and Sthiramati composed commentaries on the *Mūlamadhyamakakārikā*. This indicates that Nāgārjuna's main work was not primarily conceived of as a treatise with a specific sectarian orientation, but as a fundamental Mahāyāna text with relevance for thinkers with different basic orientations.

In our present discussion we will focus on 'the great triumvirate of Madhyamaka commentators',[104] three scholars who are particularly important for understanding the different kinds of interpretations Madhyamaka thought attracted during its development in India: Buddhapālita, Bhāvikeka, and Candrakīrti.

## a. *Buddhapālita*

The *Akutobhayā*

In order to discuss Buddhapālita and his commentary it is necessary to first go back to a somewhat enigmatic earlier text, the *Akutobhayā*. This is an influential work belonging to the earliest stratum of Madhyamaka after Nāgārjuna. The other prominent works from this period are those of Āryadeva, who is believed to have been Nāgārjuna's direct disciple, but did not compose any commentaries on his master's work. Already in fourth-century India there is a tradition considering the *Akutobhayā* as going back to Nāgārjuna himself, a tradition that would explain the high regard in which this text was held.[105] The relationship between this text and Buddhapālita's own commentary (which, unlike the later commentaries, has no specific title—it is simply called the

Its relation with Buddhapālita's commentary

[103] In addition there is also a partial Chinese version of a commentary ascribed to Asaṅga.

[104] Huntington 1986: 17.

[105] The ascription of the *Akutobhayā* to Nāgārjuna has been repeatedly questioned, mainly because it quotes a stanza from Āryadeva. It is not clear, however, how conclusive this point is. First, the text of the *Akutobhayā* appears to have been somewhat fluid in the way it has been transmitted, so we cannot rule out that this quotation is a later interpolation. In addition it is not unthinkable that Nāgārjuna may have cited a work of one of his disciples, especially as we have renditions of the text in which Āryadeva is not referred to by the term *ācārya* ('master'), but by the more modest *bhadanta* ('venerable', a term used to address Buddhist monks).

*Buddhapālitavṛtti*, 'Buddhapālita's commentary') is interesting. On the one hand the *Akutobhayā* is only half the length of Buddhapālita's commentary, and often only provides a straightforward paraphrase of Nāgārjuna's arguments, while Buddhapālita often expands on the arguments and offers a greater amount of analysis. On the other hand Buddhapālita borrows extremely liberally from the *Akutobhayā*; in fact the final five chapters of both commentaries are virtually identical. On the whole, about a third Buddhapālita's commentary comes straight from the *Akutobhayā*. What is peculiar about this is not so much the extent of the borrowing but the fact that Buddhapālita nowhere points out that he is citing large passages from an earlier commentary on Nāgārjuna's *Mūlamadhyamakakārikā*. Huntington[106] has made the intriguing suggestion that the reason for this was that the *Akutobhayā* was not considered to be a work properly separate from Nāgārjuna's root text, but a set of explanatory notes transmitted in a somewhat fluid form together with that text, notes that may go back to oral explanations of the root verses by Nāgārjuna himself. If this was the case, it would not be so surprising that Buddhapālita does not acknowledge a previous commentator he is citing, since he is simply selecting from an elucidatory tradition considered to have co-originated with the root text itself.

This textual history is interesting because it shows that with Buddhapālita's commentary we can to a certain extent reach back to a relatively early stratum of commentaries on Nāgārjuna's root text. Biographical information on Buddhapālita is scarce. We can approximately date him to *c*.470–540, and like many great Indian philosophers he seems to have been born in South India. The Tibetan tradition regards him as a direct disciple of Nāgārjuna, a claim that requires us either to accept an extraordinarily long lifespan for Nāgārjuna, or a fairly wide understanding of what 'discipleship' is taken to amount to. Tāranātha, for example, explicitly raises the possibility of Nāgārjuna taking up a *vidyādhara* ('knowledge-holder') form to teach disciples after having quit his earthly body.[107] In this way they would still be considered direct disciples of Nāgārjuna, even though they did not meet in human form.

Buddhapālita's life

The only extant work of Buddhapālita's is his commentary on Nāgārjuna's *Mūlamadhyamakakārikā*; the Tibetan tradition also considers him as the author of various other commentaries on the *sūtra*s and *tantra*s, but none of these appear to have come down to us.[108]

Buddhapālita's commentary

In his commentary Buddhapālita analyses and expands on Nāgārjuna's arguments, and he does so exclusively in terms of *prasaṅga* methodology,

[106] Huntingdon 1986: 149.

[107] *rig pa 'dzin pa'i lus nyid kyis* [. . .] *skal ldan rnams la bstan ba yang yin srid de*, Wedemeyer 2007: 20.

[108] Tsonawa 1985: 14.

that is, demonstrating how Nāgārjuna's arguments identify contradictions in the opponent's own assumptions. At the time of Buddhapālita we have already reached a stage where marked differences in interpretation arise—Bhāviveka, who would severely criticize Buddhapālita's expository methodology, can be dated to about 500–570. But as we know that the textual relation between the *Akutobhayā* and Buddhapālita's commentary is quite close, and since the former did not spell out the arguments of Nāgārjuna in anything but *prasaṅga* terms, we may feel more justified to understand Buddhapālita not just as an individual commentator but as representative of a tradition of understanding Madhyamaka arguments that considerably preceded him.[109]

## *b. Bhāviveka*

Bhāviveka, another master of likely South Indian descent, most probably overlapped with Buddhapālita at the beginning of the sixth century, though we have no information on whether they ever met.[110] Unlike in the case of Buddhapālita, who left us only one text, various of Bhāviveka's works have been preserved.

The *Prajñāpradīpa*

Of primary interest for us is his 'Lamp of Wisdom' (*Prajñāpradīpa*), a very detailed commentary on the *Mūlamadhyamakakārikā*, and one that seems to have attracted considerable attention in the Indian philosophical world. At least two sub-commentaries were written on it, Avalokitavrata's massive work (the longest single work in the Tibetan collection of commentarial works, the *bsTan gyur*), and one by Guṇadatta, which is no longer extant.

Bhāviveka's commentary is best known for its criticism of Buddhapālita's commentary, and for its introduction of new argumentative tools for the exposition of Madhyamaka. In explaining Nāgārjuna's arguments, Buddhapālita presents the reader with *prasaṅga* arguments, arguments that start by provisionally adopting some of the opponent's theses, in order to show that a contradiction can be derived from them. Note that this differs in at least one important respect from a *reductio ad absurdum* argument. In the case of a *reductio* we begin with a hypothetical premise (e.g. that there are only finitely many prime numbers) and derive a contradiction from this. As a result, we can

[109] This is not necessarily to be understood as an argument for the greater philosophical accuracy of Buddhapālita's interpretation over later ones. That a specific commentarial tradition is earlier does not necessarily mean that it more accurately expresses the author's intent, or has a greater claim to systematic validity. But it is important to be aware of the histories of these different interpretative approaches in order to provide a nuanced picture of their later interaction.

[110] We have not much biographical information on Bhāviveka, but one noteworthy fact about his afterlife is that the Tibetan tradition considered him to have been later reborn as the Panchen Lama (the lineage of the Panchen Lamas contains various Indian sages before the first Panchen Lama (1385–1438)). Bhāviveka is also sometimes referred to as 'Bhāvaviveka' or 'Bhavya'. The choice 'Bhāviveka' seems to be supported by the majority of evidence currently available, though the matter has not been settled definitely. See Ames 2009.

*prasaṅga* methodology

then not only reject the original statement but also take the *negation* of the hypothetical assumption (there are infinitely many prime numbers) as established. A *prasaṅga* argument takes the first step, but not the second: the contradiction-generating hypothesis must obviously be rejected, but the argument does not commit us to adopt its negation instead.

Supplementing destructive by constructive reasoning

Bhāviveka argues that we should not just explain Nāgārjuna's arguments by showing how they allow us to derive contradictions from the opponent's assertions. In addition to this destructive enterprise, which can be best conceived of as clearing the ground by removing erroneous views, the Mādhyamika also needs to construct a set of positions of his own, and should provide complete syllogistic proofs of these. The contrast between their different ideas of how Nāgārjuna's thought should be explained can already be seen from their remarks on the very first verse of the *Mūlamadhyamakakārikā*, where Nāgārjuna says that:

> Not from themselves, not from another, not from both, nor from no cause,
> do any originated entities ever exist anywhere.[111]

An example: absence of self-causation

In commenting on Nāgārjuna's rejection of the first kind of origination, origination from itself,[112] Buddhapālita points out that:

> To begin with, entities do not originate from their own selves, because their origination would be pointless and because there would be no end to origination. For there is no purpose in the origination again of entities that exist by their own selves. If they do originate again even though they exist, never would they not be originating. That, too, is not accepted.[113]

Absurd consequences of self-causation

We can clearly see here how Buddhapālita backs up Nāgārjuna's claim (who, in this verse, has not provided us with any reason why entities do not originate from themselves) by providing an argument in support. The argument is a *prasaṅga*: it draws out two contradictory consequences from two slightly different conceptions of self-causation. First, causation is a process by which an existent cause brings about a not-yet-existent effect. If, as self-causation presupposes, cause and effect are the same thing, the effect is already there when the cause is, so that no causal relation would in fact have to take place. Secondly, the opponent might think that things are actually more short-lived than they appear: they pass out of existence frequently, but are immediately replaced by near-identical copies caused by the thing that existed in the

[111] *na svato nāpi parato na dvābhyāṃ nāpy ahetutaḥ | utpannā jātu vidyante bhāvāḥ kvacana kecana*, Siderits and Katsura 2013: 18.

[112] It is likely that one of the positions Nāgārjuna had in mind here is that of the pre-existence of the effect in the cause (*satkāryavāda*) defended by Sāṃkhya. For further discussion of self-causation see Westerhoff 2009: 99–104.

[113] Ames 2003: 46.

previous moment. If this thing is the *only* cause of the copy that is produced in the next moment, this scenario could plausibly be described as one of self-causation. The difficulty in this case is that it is hard to explain how anything could ever go out of existence. If all that is needed as a cause is the previously existent thing, everything should be permanent, since the conditions for self-copying always obtain.

Given that neither of these scenarios accurately describes how causation occurs to us (effects follow their causes, and we regularly see things passing out of existence), Buddhapālita can argue that these absurd consequences allow us to reject the idea of self-causation.

Here is Bhāviveka's response to Buddhapālita's exposition:

> That is not right, because no reason and example are given, and because faults stated by the opponent are not answered. Because it is a *prasaṅga* argument, a property to be proved and a property which proves that are opposite in meaning become manifest by reversing the original meaning: Entities originate from another, because origination has a result and because origination has an end.[114]

Three-membered syllogisms

Bhāviveka manages here to condense a number of points into a few words, and it is worthwhile to unpack them carefully. First of all, he points out that reason and example are missing from Buddhapālita's exposition. Bhāviveka thinks that Nāgārjuna's arguments should be presented in a commentary in the form of three-membered syllogisms, which would include reason and example.[115] Such a syllogism would include:

1. a thesis (*pratijñā*) which ascribes the inferred property (*sādhya-dharma*) to the subject of the argument (*pakṣa*);
2. a reason (*hetu*) which ascribes the inferring property (*sādhana-dharma*) to the subject of the argument (*pakṣa*); and
3. an example (*dṛṣṭānta*) of something that has both the inferred and the inferring property.

The syllogism that Bhāviveka supplies[116] in support of Nāgārjuna's claim that entities do not originate from themselves is the following:

A syllogism establishing absence of self-causation

1. Thesis: The six sense-organs [the subject] do not originate from themselves [the inferred property];
2. Reason: because the sense-organs exist [the inferring property];
3. like consciousness.

[114] Ames 2003: 46–7.

[115] This form of the syllogism was introduced by Diṅnāga (*c.*400–80) and constitutes a streamlined form of the five-membered syllogism familiar from Nyāya.

[116] Ames 2003: 50.

Bhāviveka only presents us with a particular instance of a general thesis (Nāgārjuna is not specifically talking about the sense-organs), but he clearly presupposes that a similar syllogism can be produced for any potential candidate for self-production. The sense-organs do not cause themselves because they already exist, and anything that presently exists no longer requires causal production. With the example Bhāviveka mentions, consciousness (*caitanya*), he makes a reference to the Sāṃkhya *satkāryavāda* theory of the pre-existence of the effect in the cause. The Sāṃkhya consider *caitanya* to be another name of *puruṣa*, a pure consciousness that is eternal, non-arising, and therefore also not self-arising.[117] However, one need not follow Sāṃkhya in order to accept this example. Mādhyamikas also accept the existence of consciousness at the conventional level, and things that are already there do not need to be produced.

When Bhāviveka speaks about 'reversing the original meaning' he has in mind a reader of Buddhapālita's commentary who, having been convinced by the *prasaṅga* argument that self-causation has the contradictory consequence of producing something that is already there and continuing to produce it perpetually, might then infer that for this reason objects must be caused by what is different from them, as we experience causation to produce what is not there, and not doing so incessantly. In other words, the reader would have misunderstood the *prasaṅga* argument as a *reductio*, where the rejection of one alternative entails the adoption of the other. Bhāviveka believes that this is a danger connected with employing the *prasaṅga* methodology. As it does not endorse any positive thesis, people might mistakenly adopt the negation of a rejected option, even though it is fundamentally as deficient as the original position.

Misunderstanding *prasaṅga* as *reductio*

Two kinds of negation

He underlines this point by referring to the difference between two kinds of negation, implicative (*paryudāsa*) and non-implicative negation (*prasajya-pratiṣedha*). Originally a grammatical distinction, it was first given a substantial philosophical role by Bhāviveka. An implicative negation automatically endorses one of the remaining alternatives, as when saying that a man is a non-Brahmin we assert that he is a member of one of the other castes. On the other hand, we can also formulate matters slightly differently by saying that a man is not a Brahmin, and mean by this that he does not belong to any of the other castes either (because the system of castes is not applicable to him, or because he lives at a time when there are no castes, and so on). The exact way in which implicative and non-implicative negation are expressed grammatically does not matter; what is important is that we mean different things by them. Now Bhāviveka argues that when Nāgārjuna negates a proposition, such as

117 Ames 2003: 51.

that things are self-caused, he does so in a non-implicative manner, without committing himself to any of the other ways in which a thing could be causally produced. From a Madhyamaka perspective this makes sense, since non-implicative negations are usually employed when we want to reject a presupposition made *both* by a statement and its negation. When we deny that the number three is red, we do not want to say that it has another colour instead (that is, negate it in an implicative manner), but deny that numbers could have any colour at all. In the same way, the different alternatives rejected in Madhyamaka arguments have the shared property of presupposing the existence of objects with *svabhāva* in some form, and if we negate them individually by non-implicative negation that is motivated by our rejection of this underlying assumption.

Nāgārjuna as employing non-implicative negations

Bhāviveka's insistence on spelling out Madhyamaka arguments in the form of syllogisms seems to conflict somewhat with the fact that Nāgārjuna himself did not provide these in the *Mūlamadhyamakakārikā*. If they are so important, why were they not provided by the Master himself? Bhāviveka's explanation is that Nāgārjuna, as the author of a root text (*sūtrakāra*), obviously wants to condense a considerable amount of complex material into the shortest possible form. This is fine for those students who have the mental capacity to understand the text in this form, but for all the others more extensive forms of explanation have to be provided. It is the task of the commentator to draw out the reasoning implicit in the root text and to unwrap it as much as possible in order to make it comprehensible to its audience. Explaining arguments by rendering them explicitly in syllogistic structure makes their underlying machinery visible and thereby generates maximal perspicuity. This is the reason, Bhāviveka claims, why the commenators of Nāgārjuna should explain his arguments in this way, even though he did not do so himself.[118]

Absence of syllogisms in the *Mūlamadhyamakakārikā*

Bhāviveka's explication of Madhyamaka arguments in terms of syllogisms implies the ascription of a thesis (or a multitude of theses) to Nāgārjuna, since it is such theses that syllogisms set out to establish. For Bhāviveka, this has the immediate advantage of preventing the danger of a student getting lost amongst the profusion of *prasaṅga* arguments, where seemingly every proposition is negated. The student may then endorse the wrong kind of positive thesis, namely one that is simply the opposite of a negated thesis and that is rejected as well (as in the case of someone who thought that Nāgārjuna's denial of self-origination implied origination from other things). Of course,

Madhyamaka arguments and philosophical theses

Preventing the wrong positive thesis

[118] Candrakīrti later replies that Nāgārjuna, when writing his auto-commentary to the *Vigrahavyāvartanī*, did not spell out his arguments in syllogistic form, so why should we expect later commentators like Buddhapālita to do so? (Ruegg: 2002: 42–3). Bhāviveka might respond by pointing out that such syllogistic elaborations are specifically for the benefit of later students who can no longer understand the original meaning in its full complexity, so that there is no reason to suppose that the Master himself would have composed a commentary in this way.

Bhāviveka has to defend himself against the charge that such an attempt, helpful as it may seem, goes against certain key assertions of Nāgārjuna's, who seems to reject that he holds a philosophical thesis quite explicitly. One of the most famous passages in this respect is verse 29 of the *Vigrahavyāvartanī*, where Nāgārjuna asserts that:

> If I had any thesis, that fault would apply to me. But I do not have any thesis, so there is indeed no fault for me.[119]

*svabhāva*-free theses

Quotations such as these can easily be multiplied.[120] What Bhāviveka needs to argue (and there is a certain leeway for doing so) is that the type of 'thesis' (*pratijñā*) Nāgārjuna rejects here is a specific kind of thesis (one, we would think, existing in terms of *svabhāva*, and thereby based on an objective, mind-independent world–language link),[121] and that the theses ascribed to Nāgārjuna in his explicative syllogisms are of an altogether harmless, *svabhāva*-free kind that is not affected by Madhyamaka criticism. Still, do the theses Bhāviveka ascribes to Nāgārjuna not concern the ultimate, and does Nāgārjuna not hold that the ultimate is beyond concepts?

Different kinds of conventional truth

Bhāviveka points out that while it is indeed true that there is a sense in which the ultimate truth is free from conceptualization (*niṣprapañca*) and hence is inexpressible and cannot be captured by any thesis, there is also another sense, which he calls 'purified worldly knowledge'(*śuddha-laukika-jñāna*), which is accessible to concepts.[122] Bhāviveka therefore takes the position that not all mundane knowledge is equally bad, and that below the level of enlightened beings, who can access the ultimate truth in a non-conceptual sense, there is also room for improved worldly cognitions, cognitions that are philosophically more sophisticated than those of the common cowherd, while at the same time still firmly located in the realm of the conceptual.

Theses and debates

Apart for seeing them as ensuring that Nāgārjuna's message would not be misunderstood because of its largely negative methodology, Bhāviveka had at least two other reasons to stress the ascription of specific theses to Nāgārjuna's Madhyamaka enterprise. The first has to do specifically with debate. We will remember that debates were of tremendous importance in ancient India for the promotion of ideas, for the prestige of individual scholars and scholarly communities, and for the patronage and its benefits that came with this prestige. In order to ensure the intellectual standing of Buddhism and the worldly endowments of its institutions, it was essential for Buddhist scholars to participate in debates, and one of Bhāviveka's aims in his works is to facilitate

[119] *yadi kācana pratijñā tatra syān na me tat eṣa me bhaved doṣaḥ | nāsti ca mama pratijñā tasmān naivāsti me doṣaḥ*; Westerhoff 2010: 63, Williams-Wyant 2017.

[120] Huntington 2003: 71–4.

[121] For more on this idea see Westerhoff 2009: 17–18, 194–8; 2010: 63–5.

[122] See Eckel 2008: 50, 210–11.

such debate for the Mādhyamikas.[123] Unfortunately, Madhyamaka looks like a philosophical school that does not seem to sit well with debating conventions. If the Mādhyamika wants to enter into a debate with non-Buddhist parties he would have to play by the rules. And the rules of debate, such as those found in the *Nyāyasūtra*, specify that opponent and proponent must have a thesis they each want to defend. Mere intellectual sniping is not allowed; the Naiyāyikas specify a particular violation of debate rules called *vitaṇḍā* in the case of a debater who only wants to refute his opponent, without having a position he himself defends.

The Madhyamaka thesis about the nature of reality

Bhāviveka is clear in pointing out that the Madhyamaka does not commit the *vitaṇḍā*-fault. In fact, according to him, Nāgārjuna himself came up with a thesis about the nature of reality he sets out to establish in verse 18:9 of the *Mūlamadhyamakakārikā*, where he says:

> Not to be obtained by means of another, pacified, free from hypostatization, without conceptualization, not having many separate meanings—that is the nature of reality.[124]

Of course, it is evident that all the terms Nāgārjuna uses in this verse are negative. However, we have something here that is presented in the form of a thesis 'to encourage those who are just beginning'.[125] Even though reality is ultimately beyond words, such negative characterizations can provide the basis of an eventual non-conceptual realization of the nature of reality.[126] From his commentary on this passage we can see clearly how Bhāviveka tries to bring together the need for a thesis to be defended on the one hand, and the Madhyamaka reluctance to make any pronouncements on the ultimate nature of reality on the other. Elsewhere, Bhāviveka is more explicit, formulating the basic thesis of Madhyamaka himself: all things are empty of intrinsic nature (*svabhāva*), and that is their nature.[127]

By establishing that Madhyamaka has a thesis to defend, Bhāviveka could ensure that the thought of Nāgārjuna was able contend in the intellectual arena of ancient Indian debate, demanding responses and setting out to refute contending positions. Ascribing a thesis to Madhyamaka thus appeared not just to have benefits for the Buddhist account seen from the inside (ensuring that amongst all the negations the wrong affirmative statement was not embraced by mistake), but also from the outside perspective, making sure

[123] See Bouthillette 2017.

[124] *aparapratyayaṃ śāntaṃ prapañcair aprapañcitam | nirvikalpam anānārtham etat tattvasya lakṣaṇam*, Siderits and Katsura 2013: 202.

[125] *skye bo las dang po dag yang dag par dbugs dbyung ba'i phyir*, D 3853, dbu ma, tsha 190a2; Eckel 2008: 52.

[126] Eckel 2008: 52.

[127] *kho bo cag gi phyogs la ni ngo bo nyid stong pa nyid yin te | chos rnams kyi ngo bo nyid de yin*, Eckel 2008: 52–3, Ames 2003: 46.

that Madhyamaka philosophy could effectively debate with its Buddhist and non-Buddhist opponents.

Theses and doxography

The final reason for Bhāviveka's concern to elucidate the Madhyamaka thesis is connected with this interest in doxography. His *Madhyamakahṛdayakārikā* and auto-commentary constitute the first surviving example of the doxographical genre in which separate philosophical schools are discussed in individual chapters. In this work Bhāviveka deals with two Buddhist and four non-Buddhist schools, the Śrāvakas and Yogācāras, as well as with Sāṃkhya, Vaiśeṣika, Vedānta, and Mīmāṃsā. The chapters begin with the opponent stating his position, followed by Bhāvavikeka's reply. This structure makes a detailed discussion of rival positions possible, and presents them with the opportunity to describe their positions in a connected way, rather than using the opposing viewpoints as a mine from which objections are drawn more or less at random in order to explain certain aspects of the main theory being discussed. In also allows one to show how Buddhist thought relates to various non-Buddhist schools, achieving a greater integration of the Buddhist debate within the larger intellectual context of the time. Furthermore, one key aim of such doxographic treatises was to establish a doxographic hierarchy,[128] that is, to set out different schools in ascending order of truth. This idea mirrors the early Buddhist distinction between *sūtra*s with interpretable meaning (*neyārtha*) and those that did not need to be interpreted but could be taken literally (*nīthārtha*). Applied to doxographies, this distinction entails that different doctrines are not described as a set of varying wrong views that differ from the one correct view the author wants to defend; instead they are arranged in a hierarchy with the view to be defended at the top. The remaining doctrines can then be arranged in a sequence of positions that succeed in approaching the final view more and more closely. It is then natural to assume that if Madhyamaka is to be included in these doxographies it is essential that it is described as having a set of views to defend, and if a Madhyamaka author wants to structure a doxography such that Madhyamaka comes out at the top, all other positions have to be described as more or less accurate approximations of this final view.

If we look at Bhāviveka's spelling out of Nāgārjuna's arguments in terms of syllogisms, and the specification of Madhyamaka theses this implies, he seems to follow a very sensible expository strategy. He worries that a purely negative, *prasaṅga*-style exposition of Nāgārjuna that, 'based on what their opponents

[128] See Ames 2003: 75. The construction of such hierarchies is very widespread in Indian philosophical texts. Already in the *Chāndogya Upaniṣad* we find the sage Prajāpati instructing Indra about the nature of the real self by guiding him through a series of gradually more sophisticated views (8: 7–15, Radhakrishnan 1969: 501–12, Olivelle 1996: 171–6). It is interesting to note that Prajāpati does not simply tell Indra that all the lower views are deficient, but lets him work out the limitations of each view for himself before introducing a more sophisticated one.

accept, evokes a consequence that is unacceptable to their opponents',[129] might be misunderstood by generating unwarranted affirmative statements. He is also concerned that Madhyamaka should find its rightful place in Indian intellectual life. To this end it was necessary to present Madhyamaka positions in a way that could be defended in debates and included in doxographical hierarchies. Why, then, would these apparently harmless and reasonable expository points generate such forceful criticisms by later Mādhyamika authors, and why does the Buddhist tradition consider Bhāviveka's works to mark the beginning of a key division of Madhyamaka into two incompatible subschools, the Svātantrika and Prāsaṅgika? Before addressing this question we need to consider the other central figure in this dispute: Candrakīrti.

### c. *Candrakīrti*

Legends about Candrakīrti: their philosophical significance

Candrakīrti lived during the first half of the seventh century; as with most Indian thinkers, very little is known about his life. According to Tibetan accounts he was born in southern Indian and was a monk at Nālandā.[130] Like Nāgārjuna, Tibetan sources describe him as either very long lived or as having obtained a form of immortality.[131] Traditional accounts mention his magical abilities, which include milking a picture of a cow drawn on a wall in order to supply the monks of Nālandā with milk and butter, and animating a stone lion to frighten away a hostile army threatening the monastery, which promptly flees in terror.[132] There is a clear philosophical significance to these stories that make their connection with a Madhyamaka master particularly apt. The theory of emptiness entails that things exist without an intrinsic nature or substantial core (*svabhāva*), but that this does not keep them from fulfilling their function at a conventional level. In fact this is precisely the point Nāgārjuna's opponent raises at the beginning of the *Vigrahavyāvartanī*, and Nāgārjuna responds by saying that empty things can still fulfil their functions, an empty chariot can carry wood, an empty blanket can warm, and so on.[133] These stories about Candrakīrti underline the efficacious power of the merely conventional by ascribing additional powers to things that are nothing more than representations. A painted cow cannot give milk, and a stone lion cannot roar, but the story that they can (or the illusory appearance produced by Candrakīrti that they can, depending on how we interpret the story), when

[129] This is Jayānanda's definition (Cabezón 2003: 310).

[130] Once again contemporary Buddhist scholarship distinguishes various authors that were called Candrakīrti. Of particular importance is a commentator on the *Guhyasamājatantra*, sometimes referred to as Candrakīrti II or the 'tantric Candrakīrti'.

[131] Chimpa and Chattopadhyaya 1970: 199. In contradiction to contemporary accounts Candrakīrti is also sometimes described as having lived during the later part of Nāgārjuna's life (Tsonawa 1985: 16.). This is of course less strange than it sounds if one accepts the extraordinary long lifespan traditionally attributed to Nāgārjuna.

[132] Tsonawa 1985: 17–18.

[133] 22, Yonezawa 2008: 218: 8–11; Westerhoff 2010: 27.

read in a Madhyamaka context, stresses that all causal efficacy there is ever going to be flows from the merely conventional.

Candrakīrti's works

Candrakīrti's key works are, first, a comprehensive commentary on Nāgārjuna's *Mūlamadhyamakakārikā*, the 'Clear Words' (*Prasannapadā*), and second, a major independent work in verse together with an auto-commentary, called 'Introduction to Madhyamaka' (*Madhyamakāvatāra*). This latter text subsequently became extremely influential in Tibet. Rather than Nāgārjuna's own foundational work, Tibetan scholars regarded the 'Introduction to Madhyamaka' as the seminal text for the study of Madhyamaka. Scholars from all schools of Tibetan Buddhism wrote commentaries on this text, and it was included as one of the five 'key texts' into the curriculum of the dGe lugs pa school.

His status in Tibet

Given his exalted status in the Tibetan intellectual world, we might think that Candrakīrti's thought was also very influential in India. Surprisingly, this is far from the case. Even though Candrakīrti's works were preserved (and in fact his *Prasannapadā* is the only one of all the commentaries on Nāgārjuna's main work that is still extant in Sanskrit), Candrakīrti's place in the Indian intellectual landscape was—to put it mildly—inconspicuous during several centuries after he composed his works. We know of only one commentator on Candrakīrti's works, Jayānanda, who lived during the twelfth century and wrote a commentary on his *Madhyamakāvatāra*. What is even more surprising is that Candrakīrti did not leave more of a mark in interactions with views he criticized. Given his sustained criticism of Bhāviveka's commentary on Nāgārjuna, we might expect that Avalokitavrata (about 700 CE), the author of the massive subcommentary on Bhāviveka's commentary, would devote a significant amount of space to defend the text he is commenting upon against Candrakīrti's attacks. In fact all Avalokitavrata does is mention Candrakīrti as one of the eight authors who wrote commentaries on Nāgārjuna's *Mūlamadhyamakakārikā*, without discussing Candrakīrti's sustained criticism. While this fact does not allow us to infer too much about Avalokitravrata's own view of Candrakīrti's arguments (he might have thought that they were so deficient as to be unworthy of response, or so devastating that he did not know what to say), it does provide good evidence that Avalokitavrata thought that it was possible to write a commentary on Bhāviveka's exposition of Nāgārjuna without giving an account of Candrakīrti's criticism, and nobody would think he was leaving out anything obvious or declining to discuss trenchant criticism.

His status in India

Even highly influential later Madhyamaka authors, such as Śāntarakṣita (8th century) and Kamalaśīla (*c*.740–95), whose views do not at all cohere well with Candrakīrti, fail respond to his arguments or even mention him. This neglect of Candrakīrti's writings continued with the early transmission of Indian Buddhism to Tibet, from its first introduction up to about 1000 CE. While practically all of the key Indian Madhyamaka writers were translated into Tibetan, Candrakīrti's main texts were not translated until the eleventh century.[134]

Candrakīrti strongly disagreed with Bhāviveka's exposition of Nāgārjuna's arguments and tried to defend Buddhapālita's interpretative stance against Bhāviveka's exposition. His main point is the observation that, due to the curious nature of Madhyamaka thought, apparently procedural or exegetical matters, such as what format to present them in (in terms of *prasaṅga*-arguments or as syllogisms), could in fact not be confined to the merely formal, but have direct implications for the status of conventional reality. We can clearly see this in connection with Bhāviveka's emphasis on spelling out Madhyamaka arguments in terms of syllogisms. Such syllogisms bring with them a thesis that the syllogism is an argument for, a thesis that the Mādhyamika holds independent (*svatantra*) of whatever their opponent accepts. As we have noted before, there seems to be a strong current in Nāgārjuna's works to reject the acceptance of exactly such theses. We are no longer concerned here with the purely topic-neutral question of the best framework for explaining Madhyamaka teachings, because certain frameworks bring assumptions with them that have relevance at the level of the contents of the theory.[135]

Connection between argumentative procedure and philosophical content

That syllogisms bring theses with them is not the only reason Candrakīrti distrusts them as expository devices for Madhyamaka. If we accept a syllogism we also have to be acquainted with its different parts, the subject, the inferred property, and so on, as well as with the various formal properties their relations must exemplify for the syllogism to be valid. According to the traditional Indian conception, all such knowledge is based on epistemic instruments (*pramāṇa*), such as perception or inference. Yet early Madhyamaka is very critical of these epistemological notions; Nāgārjuna discusses them at length in the *Vigrahavyāvartanī*, and Candrakīrti spells out his reasons for rejecting them in a variety of places in his works. In the *Madhyamakāvatāra* he points out that:

Syllogisms and epistemic instruments

> If ordinary cognitions were epistemic instruments (*pramāṇa*), then mundane cognitions would see reality as it is. Then what necessity would there be for those other noble beings? What purpose would the noble path serve?[136]

[134] Two exceptions are his commentaries on Nāgārjuna's *Yuktiṣaṣṭikā* and *Śūnyatāsaptati*, presumably because they were the only Indian commentaries on these texts. See Vose 2009: 19–20.

[135] The closest example of this difficulty in the contemporary context may be the question of the kinds of proof that an intuitionist mathematician can appeal to. Because the intuitionist does not assume that all mathematical facts are eternally settled in some Platonic realm, he cannot, for example, prove a statement by use of a *reductio*. Such proofs presuppose that since either A or not A obtains, showing that A leads to a contradiction allows us to prove not A. But this presupposition is something that the intuitionist cannot accept. The introduction of some supposedly topic-neutral machinery in terms of allowed proof techniques has thus been shown to reintroduce substantial philosophical assumptions through the back door.

[136] 6:30, *lokaḥ pramāṇaṃ yadi tattvadarśī syāl loka evety aparaiḥ kim āryaiḥ | kim āryamārgeṇa bhavec ca kāryam mūḍhaḥ pramāṇaṃ na hi nāma yuktaḥ*, Li 2015.

Yet it is a common *topos* of Buddhist thought, going back to the very beginning of Buddhism, that the naive, unreflected, untrained cognition of the world get its nature thoroughly wrong. This is the reason why we need 'noble beings' such as the Buddha with sufficiently purified cognitions to show us a path we can follow so that we ourselves can see reality as it is. Ordinary cognition is so shot through with mistaken superimpositions resulting from ignorance that we cannot rely on it to give us a dependable account of conventional truth. Candrakīrti fears that Bhāviveka's appeal to syllogisms will bring in its wake the traditional Indian epistemological picture of things that are by their inner nature instruments we can use to obtain knowledge of the world (*pramāṇas*), and others that by their nature are mind-independent objects this knowledge is knowledge of (*prameya*). This picture cannot be accepted by the Mādhyamika.[137]

Madhyamaka and debate

Candrakīrti also sees problems with Bhāviveka's emphasis on the importance of Madhyamaka entering into a debate with rival systems. First, he holds that Nāgārjuna did not teach the arguments in his various works 'out of fondness for debate',[138] that is, to defeat the opponent's position and to establish his own view. In his *Madhyamakāvatāra* he makes it quite clear that attachment to one's own view is something to be given up:

> Attachment to one's own view, and likewise anger at the view of others, are mere conceptions.
> Therefore, those who eliminate attachment and anger and analyse correctly swiftly attain liberation.[139]

Yet it seems as if engagement in debate in this way brings about precisely the kind of attachment to one's own position that the Mādhyamika wants to avoid.

*svabhāva* at the level of conventional reality?

Second, debates must obviously begin from a common ground; assumptions that are not common ground cannot be expected to have any probative force for both parties (a Buddhist and a Naiyāyika will not, for example, regard each other's foundational *sūtras* as authoritative). But since the Buddhist's opponent will conceptualize certain parts of the world as existing by *svabhāva*, the Buddhist will have to accept these claims at least at the level of conventional reality. This, Candrakīrti argues, reduces Madhyamaka to a kind of crypto-realism.

[137] Both Nāgārjuna and Candrakīrti do, however, set out to develop a conception of epistemic instruments and objects that does not appeal to intrinsic natures. They argue that even though we can profitably employ both these concepts, it is essential that we realize that they mutually depend on each other for their existence: there cannot be epistemic instruments without objects they cognize, nor can there be epistemic objects without instruments. For further discussion see Westerhoff 2010, Siderits 2011a.

[138] *Madhyamakāvatāra* 6: 118, *na vādalobhād vihito vicāras tattvam tu śāstre kathitaṃ vimuktyai*, Li 2015, Huntington 2003: 77.

[139] *Madhyamakāvatāra* 6:119, *svadṛṣṭirāgo 'pi hi kalpanaiva tathānyadṛṣṭāv api yaś ca roṣaḥ | vidhūya rāgaṃ pratighaṃ ca tasmād vicārayan kṣipram upaiti muktim*, Li 2015.

We are no longer dealing with a system that rejects entities existing by *svabhāva*, but rather with one that sides with the Mādhyamika's opponent in accepting such entities, the only difference being that he follower of Bhāviveka will relegate the existence of *svabhāva* to the conventional, not the ultimate level. The denial of intrinsic natures characteristic of Madhyamaka seems to be no longer on the table, instead the argument now appears to be about what kind of reality should be assigned to them.[140] Candrakīrti believes that something has gone radically wrong here. First of all, Nāgārjuna spends a considerable amount of time in his foundational work to demonstrate the contradictory nature of entities existing by *svabhāva*. How could we then believe that the Buddhist should incorporate them into their own theory of what reality is like at the level of everyday interaction? Secondly, we might well wonder whether the conventionally real intrinsic natures we have now introduced will not be able to function as objects of clinging just as well as the previous ultimately existent ones. If the key quality that keeps us locked in cyclic existence is grasping, why does it matter whether we develop unwholesome emotional attitudes towards our existent self, a self that exists with *svabhāva* conventionally (or other conventionally existent objects)? The overall result seems to be the same. We now see that what originally looked like a methodological disagreement about how to spell out Nāgārjuna's arguments has at this stage been transformed into an ontological debate about what kind of things exist (this dimension of the dispute between Candrakīrti and Bhāviveka was later stressed by the fifteenth-century Tibetan scholar Tsong kha pa).

Ontological disagreement between Candrakīrti and Bhāviveka

A final point of Bhāviveka's exposition that might create problems for the Mādhyamika is his fondness for doxography. If we arrange various systems of thought in a doxographic map, and additionally consider this to be hierarchically organized, with the systems discussed earlier being regarded as less accurate than the later ones, we have to assume that there are different ways of organizing conventional reality. Obviously none of the systems discussed (apart from possibly the final one, Madhyamaka) is able to provide us with an account of ultimate reality, so what they must do is provide us with gradually better accounts of the conventional reality, that is, the world we all live in. But Candrakīrti makes it clear that he does not accept such a stratification of the conventional that is based on its philosophical analysis. According to him, conventional truth is to be identified with 'what even people like cowherds and women recognize' (*gopālāṅganājanaprasiddha*), that is, with a view of the world that treats the regularities of the conventional world at face-value, without trying to come up with a series of theories of what is going on at the underlying metaphysical level.

No stratification of conventional reality

[140] See Tillemans 2003: 108.

Candrakīrti is therefore convinced that Bhāviveka's commentarial technique is not just to be assessed as an expository device one may or may not find useful, but that it brings with it a host of philosophical assumptions that a Mādhyamika should be wary of accepting. It comes with the idea that Nāgārjuna held particular theses he sets out to establish (rather than just refuting those who, according to the Mādhyamika view, see the world incorrectly), that there are reliable epistemic instruments, that entities with intrinsic nature (*svabhāva*) exist at the level of conventional reality, and that a philosophical analysis of the conventional can supply us with better and better (though no best) theories of the nuts and bolts that underlie the working of the world. As we have just seen, Candrakīrti believes that all of these contradict key Madhyamaka ideas and is for this reason highly critical of Bhāviveka's interpretation.

The Prāsaṅgika–Svātantrika distinction

The later Buddhist tradition saw Candrakīrti's criticism of Bhāvikeka as the decisive point where the Madhyamaka tradition broke up into two distinct sub-schools: the Prāsaṅgika-Madhyamaka, who follow Candrakīrti and his defence of Buddhapālita against Bhāviveka, restrict themselves to *prasaṅga* arguments and do not endorse any of the consequences that Bhāviveka's style of exposition brings with it; and the Svātantrikas, who follow Bhāviveka, and accept theses, epistemic instruments, and *svabhāva* at the conventional level, defending the utility of the philosophical analysis of the conventional. Understood in this way, the split into two sub-schools is certainly a doxographic fiction. Even though Bhāviveka was highly critical of Buddhapālita, his commentator Avalokitavrata does not appear to draw a distinction between the understanding of the two truths the two authors held.[141] If Bhāviveka had perceived a great rift between his interpretation of Nāgārjuna and that of Buddhapālita, it is certainly peculiar that he mentions them all in the same breath. More straightforwardly, even the terms Prāsaṅgika and Svātantrika were not used by Indian Mādhyamikas to describe their own positions, but are retranslations from terms later Tibetan doxographers used in order to provide a systematic description of the different views Madhyamaka authors held. Apart from matters of terminology, it is also highly doubtful that Candrakīrti would have considered himself to be defending one sub-school of Madhyamaka, while his opponent Bhāviveka defended another one. Even though Candrakīrti does not refer to Bhāviveka by name, it is clear that he refers to him when saying:

The distinction as a doxographic fiction

> Even though a logician may take the side of the Madhyamaka school out of a desire to parade the extent of his own dialectical skill, it is evident that the presentation of *svatantra* reasoning becomes, for him, an enormous reservoir where faults pile up one after another.[142]

[141] Lopez 1987: 57–8. [142] Huntington 2003: 82.

For Candrakīrti, Bhāviveka is not a Mādhyamika at all, but a logician (*tārkika*) who only takes the side of Madhyamaka in order to show off his argumentative abilities. From Candrakīrti's perspective we do not have two possible interpretation of Madhyamaka, including one that countenances syllogisms and conventionally real intrinsic natures, but only one. According to him, Bhāviveka's system is not a form of Madhyamaka, but is simply wrong.

Candrakīrti's rise from obscurity

It is difficult to determine how Candrakīrti rose from a relatively obscure Indian philosopher to becoming a highly influential thinker and chief expositor of Madhyamaka. One intriguing suggestion[143] is that Candrakīrti's sudden prominence is intimately connected with the growing popularity of tantric scriptures. We find the triad of Madhyamaka authors Nāgārjuna, his direct disciple Āryadeva, and Candrakīrti repeated later in Indian Buddhism as a triad of tantric authors bearing the same names, living somewhere between 850 and 1000. They are key figures in the so-called Noble Lineage (*'phags lugs*) of transmission of a central tantric work, the *Guhyasamājatantra*. The relationship between these two triads is complex. Traditional accounts believe these to be the same authors, while modern Buddhologists often consider such identification as either the result of fraud (later tantric authors claiming their works were penned by the Madhyamaka luminaries) or confusion (even though the later authors did not claim to be identical with the earlier ones, the tradition has mixed them up because they share the same name). Neither of these claims is particularly helpful in trying to understand what is going on between these two triads, considering the traditional accounts as rather more gullible than they really are. Traditional Buddhist historians like Tāranātha are very explicit in asserting that the tantric works of these authors were not spread when Nāgārjuna and Āryadeva 'were actually residing in this world',[144] and that some of their works were not even composed then.[145] Yet they are also, as Tāranātha stresses, 'uncontroversially composed by the father [Nāgārjuna] and son [Āryadeva]'.[146] To reconcile these claims we have to make assumptions that contemporary Buddhist studies are reluctant to accept, such as extraordinarily long lifespans of the Madhyamaka masters, or assume that the tantric works were written in the second century but then hidden and only circulated towards the end of the first millennium, or that they were composed or taught by the Madhyamaka masters at that later time in some form other than their earthly body.

Candrakīrti and tantra

Tantric works by Mādhyamikas

[143] Raised by Kevin Vose (2009: 27–36).

[144] *'phags pa yab sras 'dzam bu gling du dngos su bzhugs pa'i dus*, Wedemeyer 2007: 18–19.

[145] *mdzad* [. . .] *ma yin te*, Wedemeyer 2007: 19.

[146] *yab sras de rnams kyi mdzad par rtsod pa med la*, Wedemeyer 2007: 20.

Madhyamaka and tantra

Our knowledge of the connection between Madhyamaka as a philosophical school and tantra is very limited, and much more work is necessary to obtain a clear picture of the relation between the two systems of thought.[147] There are, however, some noteworthy facts we can point out. One is that certain conceptual distinctions in tantra were explained according to distinctions in Madhyamaka, sometimes even mirroring the phrasing of Madhyamaka texts.[148] Others are specific claims made in Madhyamaka works (especially by Candrakīrti) that seem to cohere well with specific tantric claims, such as the denial of established epistemic instruments, or a conception of ultimate reality that is not within the purview of human cognitive activities.[149] There are also examples of tantric writers critical of Yogācāra background assumptions,[150] a position that again resonates with Candrakīrti's criticism of the Yogācāra school. Vose[151] suggests that the rise in popularity of Candrakīrti's philosophy is a result of an increased popularity of the Noble Lineage. This would mean that the increased interest in the *Guhyasamājatantra* and its commentaries towards the end of the first millennium led to an increased interest in the other, non-tantric works of Candrakīrti, since the Buddhist tradition draws no boundaries between the Madhyamaka Candrakīrti and the tantric Candrakīrti.

A backwards reflection of popularity?

This may be in part a backwards reflection of popularity, where the later works of an author lead to an increased appreciation of the earlier ones, and in part a result of the fact that there is some systematic affinity between some of the positions the Madhyamaka works defend and interpretations of the tantric texts the Noble Lineage set out to propagate. This suggestion is somewhat speculative and needs to be investigated in much more detail. Yet if further research supports this idea, it would supply us with a good example of the complexity of interactions of texts, authors, schools, and styles of thinking that characterize Indian philosophy, and of the necessity to keep these various interacting factors in mind in order to achieve a nuanced understanding of the way Buddhist philosophy developed in ancient India.

With the works of Candrakīrti our account has reached the middle of the seventh century. Buddhist philosophy (and with it Madhyamaka philosophy) had about another 500 years of activity to look forward to before the decline of Indian Buddhist scholastic tradition at the beginning of the thirteenth century. What characterized this subsequent phase of Madhyamaka thought?

[147] It is usually assumed that the more natural philosophical background for tantra is Yogācāra; we will discuss this point further in Chapter 3.

[148] An example is the adaptation of Nāgārjuna's verse on the two truths in 24:8 of the *Mūlamadhyamakakārikā* by the *Guhyasamājottaratantra*, noted by Isaacson (Wedemeyer 2007: 40, n. 83).

[149] Vose 2009: 28–9. [150] Vose 2009: 33–4. [151] Vose 2009: 31.

## 6. The Great Synthesizers: Śāntarakṣita and Kamalaśīla

Two key thinkers in the further development of Madhyamaka were Śāntarakṣita (725–88) and his disciple Kamalaśīla (*c.*740–95). Their importance has a systematic and a historical dimension. They produced an interesting synthesis of Madhyamaka and Yogācāra, and were two of the Indian teachers playing a crucial role in the transmission of Indian Buddhism (and of Madhyamaka thought more specifically) to Tibet in the eighth century. Thanks to this transmission, even after its decline in the country of its origin Buddhist philosophy of clearly Indian appearance would continue to develop in Tibet up to the present day.

Śāntarakṣita's main works

Śāntarakṣita's philosophical importance is most clearly demonstrated by two of his works, the *Madhyamakālaṃkāra* and the *Tattvasaṃgraha*. The first is a major source for an attempt to bring together the distinct philosophical schools of Mahāyana thought, Madhyamaka and Yogācāra. We will have more to say on this project in the following chapter.[152] The second is a long work of over 3,000 verses, which is preserved in its original Sanskrit together with Kamalaśīla's commentary. The *Tattvasaṃgraha* is of particular interest as a doxographical work. It discusses a wide range of philosophical concepts, such as primordial matter (*prakṛti*), the creator god (*īśvara*), words and their referents (*śabdārtha*), perception (*pratyakṣa*), inference (*anumāna*), the existence of past, present, and future (*traikālya*), and the authoritativeness of scripture (*śruti*), and gives specific attention to the views of different philosophical schools on these concepts. There are, for example, detailed discussions of the account of the self (*ātman*) from the perspective of Sāṃkhya, Nyāya, Vaiśeṣika, Mīmāmsā, Advaita Vedānta, and Jainism. The *Tattvasaṃgraha* is a polemical work to the extent that it endeavours to show the mistakes inherent in all these non-Buddhist views (and some Buddhist ones, such as those of the Vātsīputrīyas) in order to demonstrate the truth of Śāntarakṣita's Buddhist position. Yet independent of its success in this respect, it offers us a fascinating inside view of the state of philosophical debate in eighth-century India, a time that may be considered (both in terms of the variety of theoretical options explored, and in terms of their depth of conceptual penetration) as the peak of its development. Śāntarakṣita's encyclopedic work demonstrates the extent to which Buddhist thought during this period was not an intellectually insulated enterprise, but interacted argumentatively with all the main philosophical currents of the time.

The *Tattvasaṃgraha*

[152] See below pp. 205–12.

Śāntarakṣita and the transmission of Buddhism to Tibet

Śāntarakṣita was also a philosopher with considerable historical significance. Khri srong lde btsan, the second of the 'three great *dharma* kings' (*chos rgyal*), invited him to Tibet, where he became the first abott (*upādhyāya*) of the newly founded monastery of bSam yas, the first Tibetan monastic centre from which the establishment of Tibetan Buddhism began. The details of the transmission of Indian Buddhism from Nālandā monastery to the remote ranges of the Himalayan plateau lie beyond the scope of this history, but it is important just to recall at this point to what extent our knowledge of Indian Buddhist philosophy is indebted to the wholesale adoption of Indian Buddhist intellectual culture by the Tibetans, thereby preserving an immense amount of philosophical works long after their disappearance in their country of origin.

Kamalaśīla and the council of bSam yas

Śāntarakṣita's disciple Kamalaśīla played an equally important historical role, primarily by determining the direction the development of Buddhism took in Tibet. He is traditionally believed to have played a decisive role at the council of bSam yas, which took place around 797 CE. There Kamalaśīla is supposed to have defended the Indian model of a gradual approach to enlightenment, which saw enlightenment as the culmination of a process of purification based on ethical behaviour (*śīla*), meditation (*samādhi*), and insight (*prajñā*), against that of the Chinese model of sudden enlightenment defended by his opponent Heshang Moheyan (a Chinese rendering of 'Mahāyāna').

Gradual vs. sudden conceptions of enlightenment

Heshang Moheyan's account saw the mind as intrinsically pure, and so all that was required for achieving enlightenment was a direct, non-conceptual insight into its nature. According to the Tibetan sources, the king judged Kamalaśīla to be the winner of the debate and declared his exposition of Madhyamaka as the official philosophical approach to be followed. Kamalaśīla is said to have been assassinated soon afterwards by jealous members of the defeated Chinese party.

Unclarities about the council of bSam yas

Most of the claims made about the council of bSam yas are contestable and remain contested: whether there really was a face-to-face debate, or merely a succession of texts written in response to the opponents' views; whether there was a clear outcome of the debate; the precise nature of Heshang Moheyan's views;[153] and even the very historicity of the Chinese monk himself.

Some facts, however, are uncontroversial. First, after this debate Tibet would import all of its Buddhism from India (which, unlike China, was not a military rival at the time), and Chinese Buddhism would not exert any noticeable influence on the further development of Buddhism in Tibet. Second, there is no doubt about Kamalaśīla's view of enlightenment as a result obtained after following a stepwise procedure of training.

Kamalaśīla's *Bhāvanākrama*

One of his most important works, a text in three parts called *Bhāvanākrama* ('Stages of Meditation') describes how

[153] For a detailed account see van Schaik 2015.

the progression of the path to Buddhahood proceeds in stages that build on one another, such as the kinds of insight resulting from a succession of study, reflection, and meditation (*śrūtamayī-prajñā*, *cintamayī-prajñā*, and *bhāvanāmayī-prajñā*), different successive forms of meditative concentration (*samādhi*), calm abiding (*śamatha*) and insight (*vipaśyana*) meditation, a sequence of meditative objects (*ālambanavastu*), and so on.

The parts of the *Bhāvanākrama* partly overlap and repeat discussions of topics. This suggests that they may have not been supposed to form part of one single treatise, but that they were related writings dealing with a common topic composed on separate occasions. It is not implausible to suggest that they might have formed part of the debate at the council of bSam yas, which may have been conducted by the exchange of texts, or may have at least involved such an exchange of texts. In the third part of the *Bhāvanākrama* Kamalaśīla presents an explicit refutation of the view of:

Criticism of the absence of mental activity

> those who think that beings, under the influence of virtuous and non-virtuous acts, born from mental conceptions, wander in cyclic existence after enjoying heaven etc. as the result of their actions, but those who do not think of anything or do not do anything hope to be liberated from cyclic existence without needing to think anything or do any virtuous actions, believing that conduct such as giving has been taught only for ignorant fools. In this way the entire Mahāyāna becomes negated.[154]

Absence of mental activity (*amanasikāra*) is, according to Kamalaśīla, not sufficient for achieving liberation. To escape saṃsāra it is not enough to put oneself into a quietistic state in which conceptual thought no longer arises, but both skilful means (*upāya*) (crucially involving the practice of moral perfections such as generosity) and insight (*prajñā*) need to be cultivated in order to achieve enlightenment.

Whether the approach of Heshang Moheyan was simply to 'switch off your mind', as the above passage suggests, may reasonably be doubted.[155] Even though in later Tibetan scholastic literature the antinomian view of Heshang became a prime exemplar of a position beyond the pale, it is important to note that some of Heshang's position were not suggested for the first time in the history of Buddhist thought, and that as Kamalaśīla could quote numerous *sūtra* passages in his refutation, so could Heshang in support of his own position. Once again, a more nuanced view of the matter than simply asking 'who has got it right' can be achieved by asking ourselves what the different terms and concepts

[154] *yastu manyate cittavikalpasamutthāpitaśubhāśubhakarmavaśena sattvāḥ svargādikarma phalamanubhavantaḥ saṃsāre saṃsaranti | ye punarna kiñciccintayanti nāpi kiñcit karma kurvanti te parimucyante saṃsārāt | tasmānna kiñciccintayitavyam | nāpi dānādikuśalacaryā kartavyā | kevalaṃ mūrkhajanamadhikṛtya dānādikuśalacaryā nirdiṣṭeti | tena sakalamahāyānaṃ pratikṣiptaṃ bhavet*, Namdol 1984: 232.

[155] van Schaik 2015: 133.

already present in the Buddhist teachings were that could be used as a basis to develop such different views as the positions of Kamalaśīla and Heshang.

Later development of Madhyamaka

We do not have the space here to describe further details of the last phase of the development of Madhyamaka in India, or of its relation to the development of tantrism for which it, together with Yogācāra, provided the conceptual basis.[156] Let me mention two related points, however. First, the Yogācāra-Madhyamka synthesis developed by Śāntarakṣita and Kamalaśīla does not constitute the conceptual endpoint of Indian Madhyamaka. Later, the tide began to turn again in favour of 'pure Madhyamaka', and when Dīpaṃkaraśrījñāna (982–1054), better known as Atiśa, added a list giving the lineage of Madhyamaka teachers in the auto-commentary to his best-known work, the *Bodhipathapradīpa*, neither Śāntarakṣita, nor Kamalaśīla, nor any other defenders of the synthetic approach are included.[157] And despite the initial introduction of their system into Tibet, the approach to Madhyamaka taken there was not the Yogācāra-Madhyamaka synthesis of Śāntarakṣita and Kamalaśīla, but from the twelfth century onwards the interpretation of Madhyamaka proposed by Candrakīrti, which is very critical of the Yogācāra approach, became the dominant reading.

Waning of the synthetic approach

Madhyamaka beyond India

The second point to note is that by the beginning of the second millennium Madhyamaka is no longer an exclusively Indian enterprise. One way of making this point is by considering that at this time important Madhyamaka works were composed at places quite far away from the Indian subcontinent. One of Atiśa's teachers, Dharmakīrti (not to be confused with the Dharmakīrti of the logico-epistemological school discussed in Chapter 4), composed his major work, a commentary on the *Abhisamayālaṃkāra*, in Suvarṇadvīpa (modern-day Sumatra or Java), and Jayānanda, a scholar from Kashmir active between 1050 and 1100, authored the only Indian commentary still extant on Candrakīrti's *Madhyamakāvatāra* close to Wutai shan, in China's Shanxi province.[158] In the nine centuries since its beginning in India, Madhyamaka thought developed into a philosophical school that was studied and developed in Central, East, and South-East Asia.

## 7. Madhyamaka and Nyāya

We will have an opportunity to look in greater detail at the relation between Madhyamaka and the other schools of Mahāyāna thought in the following

[156] See Ruegg 1981a: 104–8 for some remarks.

[157] Sherburne 2000: 237–41. Śantarakṣita is cited only once in the text (235, see also 272, n. 24).

[158] Ruegg 1981a: 109–10, 113–14. A significant portion of the *Mahāprajñāpāramitopadeśa* (see p. 94) might also be of Central Asian or Serindian origin (Ruegg 1981a: 32–3).

chapters;[159] I would like to conclude this chapter by considering the relationship between Madhyamaka and the non-Buddhist school of Nyāya. The fundamental text of the Nyāya system are the *Nyāyasūtras*, said to have been compiled by Akṣapāda Gautama in the second century CE. Nyāya and Madhyamaka thus seem to have appeared in close historical proximity, and the two schools have debated with each other from the very beginning of their existence. Two of Nāgārjuna's shorter works discuss Nyāya arguments at great length. In the *Vigrahavyāvartanī* a Naiyāyika, together with an Ābhidharmika, are the main interlocutors;[160] the *Vaidalyaprakaraṇa* is explicitly formulated as a refutation of the sixteen Nyāya categories.[161] An extensive commentary on the *Nyāyasūtras*, the *Nyāyasūtrabhāṣya*, was composed in the fourth century by Vātsyāyana and later became the target of Diṅnāga's attacks; in the seventh century Uddyotakara came to defend Nyāya against Buddhist criticism in another elaborate commentary, the *Nyāyavārttika*.

Nāgārjuna and Nyāya

We are here most interested in the early Buddhist interaction with Nyāya. When Nāgārjuna criticized the Nyāya system he interacted with a very early form of it, a system which cannot be uncritically equated with the one that has come down to us in the *Nyāyasūtras* as we know it today and is expounded in its main commentaries.[162] It is likely that various of the objections the Naiyāyika's opponent raises in these texts, and which are then subsequently provided with a Nyāya reponse, have their source in Madhyamaka.[163] The two systems shaped one another, and their texts exhibit traces of their mutual influence.

Mutual influence of the two systems

Nāgārjuna engages mostly with the epistemological and logical parts of the Nyāya system. His criticism of these Nyāya positions is particularly interesting, since these are not just topics on which Nyāya happens to have views that differ from the Buddhist ones, but because they concern subject matters of sufficient generality to be of relevance to all philosophical discussion, Buddhist or not. It is important to be aware that Nyāya was not just one philosophical system among many, one of the six *darśanas* of classical Indian philosophy, but in its later development, particularly in a form that came to be known as Navya-Nyāya ('new Nyāya')[164] extended its influence far into other fields, beyond what we might identify as the philosophical claims of the Nyāya(-Vaiśeṣika) system. Navya-Nyāya created a technical philosophical language that was not

Pervasive influence of the Nyāya system

[159] We consider the relationship with Yogācāra in section 5 of Chapter 3, and discuss the relationship of Madhyamaka with the schools of Diṅāga and Dharmakīrti in section 7 of Chapter 4.

[160] Westerhoff 2010, Meuthrath 1999. [161] Westerhoff 2018.

[162] It is generally assumed that the first and fifth chapters or *adhyāyas* constitute the oldest part of the text (Meuthrath 1996: x). Some form of the material covered in these chapters is most likely what Nāgārjuna was familiar with and directed his criticism against.

[163] Oberhammer 1963–4: 68, 70; Bronkhorst 1985.

[164] Udayana (*c.*1050) and Gaṅgeśa (*c.*1200) are generally regarded as the founders of the Navya-Nyāya tradition.

just employed in the context of the discussion of the Nyāya itself, but also in the discussion and development of other philosophical schools, such as Advaita Vedānta, Sāṃkhya, and Mīmāṃsā, as well as in non-philosophical contexts such as grammar, poetics, and law.[165]

Of course Navya-Nyāya is removed from Nāgārjuna by a distance of nearly a thousand years. Nevertheless, his engagement with the early Nyāya system in the *Vigrahavyāvartanī* and the *Vaidalyaprakaraṇa* shows that the dispute is not simply about which of two philosophical systems should be regarded as superior, but also about the right methodological framework in which to pursue philosophy.

Criticism of Nyāya logic and epistemology

Yet if Nāgārjuna criticizes not only some of the Nyāya positions, but also the logical and epistemological techniques it recommends for use in philosophical debates, this raises two immediate questions. First, why do the Mādhyamikas not consider it possible to adopt the fairly sophisticated logical and epistemological frameworks Nyāya describes, even if they disagree with the content of some of their assertions? And second, what do they propose to put in their place?

Negation

One clear example where some of the Nyāya logical machinery gets in the way of Madhyamaka arguments is provided by their understanding of negation. Nāgārjuna has the Nyāya opponent object to the Mādhyamika that: 'to the extent to which the negation "there is no pot in the house" is precisely a negation of an existent, your negation is a negation of an existing substance.'[166] The issue here is that, according to the Nyāya understanding, absences can only ever be local absences. If we negate the existence of the pot in the house, we are committed to the existence of pots elsewhere (in the garden, say, or in the potter's workshop), for if the negated thing was not anywhere, how would we even know what we talk about when we negate it? How could we have ever had any epistemic contact with it?

Problems with negating *svabhāva*

Yet this way of viewing negations leads to problems if we apply it to the Madhyamaka understanding of emptiness, which is simply the negation of intrincally real entities (*svabhāva*) anywhere. The Madhyamaka could not even state his theory in a framework in which the assertion of the emptiness of a chariot (that is, the assertion of the absence of *svabhāva* in it) entailed the presence of *svabhāva* elsewhere.

Nyāya syllogisms

A related worry arises when trying to express Madhyamaka inferences in the Nyāya framework of the five-membered syllogism.[167] Such a syllogism needs to incorporate two types of examples, a concordant example (*sādharmya*) and a

[165] Bhattacharya 2001: 102; Ganeri 2008: 109–24.

[166] 11: *sata eva pratiṣedho nāsti ghaṭo geha ity ayaṃ yasmāt | dṛṣṭaḥ pratiṣedho yaṃ sataḥ svabhāvasya te tasmāt*, see Westerhoff 2010: 109–10.

[167] Compare *Vaidalyaprakaraṇa* 28–9, Westerhoff 2018.

discordant (*vaidharmya*) one. If we consider the stock example of such a syllogism, 'there is fire on the hill because there is smoke there' (as whenever there is smoke, there is fire), a concordant example is 'as in the kitchen', while a discordant one is 'as in a lake'. The concordant example is a case where the property to be established (fire) and the mark helping in establishing it (smoke) are co-instantiated in one object, while the discordant example is an object that instantiates neither.[168] This seemingly unproblematic demand for concordant and discordant examples faces difficulties if we try to formulate a common Madhyamaka inference such as 'all things are empty because they are produced dependent on causes and conditions'. As emptiness is considered by the Mādhyamika to be a universal property of all things, any object could be introduced as a concordant example, though he would not be able to provide a discordant example, as there are no things that are not empty.[169]

No discordant example for emptiness

This issue is of considerable importance for Mādhyamikas (and for Buddhists more generally), since the reference to entities that *seem* to exist (composite wholes, persons, entities existing with *svabhāva*) but in fact do not is an integral part of the Buddhist theory of the world. Composite wholes and so forth are conceptual imputations on other entities (some of which are ultimately real for the Ābhidharmika but not the Mādhyamika) that have no more reality than horns of rabbits or sons of barren women: they are mere words (or mere concepts), but without anything behind them that they refer to. Yet the Naiyāyika finds it very difficult to find a place for such objects in his semantics, epistemology, or ontology.[170]

Reference to non-existent objects

It is therefore apparent that the Naiyāyika's logical machinery[171] cannot simply be used as a philosophical framework for formulating the Madhyamaka theory. What, however, should an alternative framework be? If the Mādhyamika wants to compete with the schools of classical Indian philosophy in debate, he cannot simply reject all of the logical and epistemological standards according to which such a debate is conducted. One cannot take part in playing the game without accepting the rules.

168 The counterexample of the lake may have been picked because a lake might sometimes *look* as if there was smoke present in it (when there is mist rising from the lake), though when properly examined we realize that there is neither smoke nor fire.

169 Matilal 1970, 83–110.

170 Matilal (1970: 91) notes that the Naiyāyika 'wants to exclude from logical discourses any sentence which will ascribe some property (positive or negative) to a fictitious entity. Vācaspati remarks that we can neither affirm nor deny anything of the fictitious entity, the rabbit's horn.' As a consequence, Nyāya 'does not admit that a *totally* ficititious entity can be the "object" of any cognitive state, even of an error.... [C]orresponding to each fundamental element of thought or cognitive state there is a fundamental element of reality. The so-called fiction is always constructed out of real elements' (95).

171 The same, Nāgārjuna sets out to argue, is true of the Nyāya epistemology.

Use of logic without accepting its ontological implications

This, the Mādhyamika would agree, is true, but there is also no need to accept them as something more than rules. Rather than rejecting the opponent's logical and epistemological standards altogether, the Mādhyamika wants to accept them in a form that is compatible with emptiness. One way of doing so is exemplified in the *prasaṅga* methodology. If the Mādhyamika does not endeavour to establish any position, but only tries to reduce the opponent's *svabhāva*-involving position to absurdity, all he needs to do is demonstrate this according to the logical standards the opponent takes to be required for the demonstration of absurdity; there is no need for the Mādhyamika himself to adopt these standards. Similary, the Mādhyamikas accept epistemological standards from their opponents, as long as they are sufficiently modified to exclude appeal to *svabhāva*.[172] In this way, dialectical exchange can take place, but in a way that does not already presuppose metaphysical assumptions that are in fact being debated.

[172] I argue in Westerhoff 2018 that Nāgārjuna's main aim in *Vaidalyaprakaraṇa* is to develop a desubstantialized account of the Nyāya categories, that is, an understanding of them that retains much of their methodological usefulness but dispenses with the idea that any of them exist with *svabhāva*.

# 3

# Yogācāra

## 1. Five Stages of Yogācāra's Development

Yogācāra, the second major school of Mahāyāna philosophy, is, together with Madhyamaka, one of India's most successful intellectual exports. While Madhyamaka took hold and flourished in Tibet, Yogācāra became a dominant influence on East Asian thought, continuing its philosophical development in China and Japan after the decline of Buddhist culture in India.

For expository purposes we can divide the development of Yogācāra thought into five successive stages. The first includes the arising of the earliest Yogācāra ideas in Mahāyāna *sūtras* that became crucial texts for the later development of this school. The next four stages comprise the works of specific Yogācāra authors. As Madhyamaka is considered to spring from the thought of one particular author, Nāgārjuna, so Yogācāra can be connected with two Buddhist masters who are usually considered as its founders, the brothers Asaṅga (stage 3) and Vasubandhu (stage 4). But in the same way that Madhyamaka is traditionally considered to hail from a supernatural realm, through the Perfection of Wisdom *sūtras* that have been passed on to Nāgārjuna by the *nāgas*, so Asaṅga is considered to have received his instructions directly from the bodhisattva (and future Buddha) Maitreya, who is also considered to have authored key Yogācāra texts on his own (stage 2). The final, fifth stage encompasses the development of Yogācāra in India after Asaṅga and Vasubandhu, first and foremost in the works of Diṅnāga and Dharmakīrti, two scholars commonly regarded as the founders of the 'logico-epistemological' school. In the following chapter we will deal with their contributions to logic and the theory of knowledge in detail; in this chapter we will focus on their specific contributions to Yogācāra.

In the following discussion we will first provide an overview of the main Indian Yogācāra philosophers in their historical sequence (section 1). We will then have a closer look in section 2 at key Yogācara concepts that characterize the specific philosophical outlook of this school. On the basis of this discussion we can then pay more attention to the specific argumentative, textual, and meditative factors that shaped the Yogācāra viewpoint (section 3). The final two sections consider the relation of Yogācāra to the other main schools of Buddhist philosophy and to the non-Buddhist school of Vedānta.

## a. *Stage 1: The early Yogācāra* sūtras

We have seen in the previous chapter that the first Madhyamaka themes did not just make their appearance in the works of Nāgārjuna, but were already present in certain Mahāyāna *sūtras*, the Perfection of Wisdom texts. In the same way we find two *sūtras* in particular that contain key Yogācāra ideas, and that pre-date later systematic developments of this school in the works of later Yogācāra philosophers. The first of these, the *Laṅkāvatārasūtra*,[1] in fact shows interesting connections with the *Prajñāpāramitāsūtras* in terms of its narrative framing. The title of the text refers to the 'appearance' (*avatāra*) of the Buddha on the island of Laṅkā (present-day Sri Lanka), having just returned from a week of teaching the *nāga* king Sagara in his palace. In Laṅkā he then teaches the discourse that is the *Laṅkāvatārasūtra* to King Rāvaṇa. Rāvaṇa is the king of *yakṣas*, a race of spirits inhabiting various places in nature, in particular trees. They have a close connection with the island of Laṅka, and their ten-headed, twenty-armed king Rāvaṇa is well known in Indian literature as the villain responsible for the abduction of Sītā described in the *Rāmāyaṇa*.

*Laṅkāvatārasūtra*

Date of the *Laṅkāvatārasūtra*

It is most likely that the *sūtra* first appeared in India around 350 CE,[2] though its first versions may be considerably older. Lindtner has argued that the earliest versions of this text were in fact available at the times of Nāgārjuna and Āryadeva and influenced their writing.[3] Not only can we find various parallels between the *Laṅkāvatārasūtra* and Nāgārjuna's key works, there is also a short work of just over fifty verses, called *Bhāvanākrama*, ascribed in the colophon to Nāgārjuna, which is fundamentally an extract of verses from the *Laṅkāvatārasūtra*. In fact the *Laṅkāvatārasūtra* must consider itself as pre-dating Nāgārjuna, since his birth is prophesied in a later part of the *sūtra*.[4]

Introducing key Yogācāra concepts

The main part of the *Laṅkāvatārasūtra* is set up as a dialogue between the Buddha and the bodhisattva Mahāmati. Its contents are very diverse, and its structure far from transparent. There is a chapter on the benefits of vegetarianism, one in which the Buddha imparts several magical formulae to Mahāmati, and a final chapter consisting entirely of more than 800 verses; about a quarter of these already occur in other parts of the text. The *sūtra* covers a wide range of material, and it is no exaggeration to say that it refers to nearly all of the central doctrinal concepts of the Māhāyana. Of primary interest in the present context are the key Yogācāra ideas it introduces, the notion of mere mind, that of the eight kinds of consciousness, and in particular that of a foundational consciousness, which we will discuss in greater detail below. It would be unrealistic to expect of a *sūtra* a detailed systematic development of

[1] For a translation from the Sanskrit see Suzuki 1932; a good recent translation from the Chinese is in Red Pine 2012.

[2] Red Pine 2012: 2. [3] Lindtner 1992. [4] See above, pp. 89–90.

these ideas, and this is in fact not the point of the text. It puts particular emphasis on the direct realization of these concepts, as becomes apparent at the very beginning of the *sūtra*, when the Buddha says:

> Also by earlier *tathāgatas*, *arhats* and fully enlightened Buddhas this *dharma* was taught in this city of Laṅkā on Malaya peak, the supreme knowledge (*āryajñāna*) realized by each for himself[5] which is beyond the argumentative views of the philosophers, the *śrāvakas* and the *pratyekabuddhas*.[6]

A key aim of the *sūtra* is to give a description of this 'inner realization' and indicate what path needs to be taken to generate it at the experiential level. The systematic development of arguments for the theoretical vision this realization expresses is a task for later Yogācāra thinkers.

Despite its discussion of some of the most important Yogācāra concepts, the *Laṅkāvatārasūtra* is not actually quoted by the earliest systematic Yogācāra authors, Asaṅga and Vasubandhu, unlike the second *sūtra* we want to consider here, the *Saṃdhinirmocanasūtra*. This text, which probably appeared in the third century CE (its first Chinese translation was made around 440) is one of the main texts subsequent Yogācāra authors refer to. It discusses a variety of Yogācāra notions, the foundational consciousness, the three natures, and most famously, the three turnings of the wheel of the doctrine. We recall that the opening of the *Laṅkāvatārasūtra* connects that text with the Buddha's teaching to the *nāgas* and hence the Perfection of Wisdom literature, suggesting that teaching of the *Laṅkāvatārasūtra* succeeds, and perhaps supercedes, this earlier doctrine. The opening of the *Saṃdhinirmocanasūtra* is similary interesting for understanding the philosophical direction of the text. We learn that when the Buddha was teaching this text he 'was dwelling in an immeasurable palace arrayed with the supreme brilliance of the seven precious substances, emanating great rays of light that suffused innumerable universes'. This palace was 'limitless in reach, an unimpeded mandala, a sphere of activity completely transcending the three worldly realms, arisen from the root of supreme virtue that transcends the world'.[7] Unlike the early *sūtras*, the *Prajñāpāramitāsūtras*, and the *Laṅkāvatārasūtra*, which are reported as having been taught at identifiable places on earth, this *sūtra* is taught at a place beyond this world. The commentaries on the *sūtra* inform us that the 'supreme virtue' that generated the palace is non-conceptual wisdom, and that it, and all its decorations, are merely mental creations emanated by the Buddha.[8] The idea of magically

*Saṃdhinirmocanasūtra*

The opening of the text

Magic and illusion

[5] On the term (*sva*)*pratyātmāryajñāna* see Suzuki 1930: 421–3.

[6] *pūrvakair api tathāgatair arhadbhiḥ samyaksaṃbuddhair asmiṃllaṅkāpurīmalayaśikhare svapratyātmāryajñānatarkadṛṣṭitīrthyaśrāvakapratyekabuddhāryaviṣaye tadbhāvito dharmo deśitaḥ*, Vaidya 1963: 1, Suzuki 1932: 3–4. The Sanskrit text is problematic, see Suzuki's note on this passage. See also the passage from the *Laṅkāvatārasūtra* cited above on p. 198.

[7] Powers 1995: 5.

[8] Powers 1995: 313, n. 3.

created surroundings is taken up again in the first chapter of the *sūtra*, when it points out that the perception of ordinary beings is in important ways similar to watching a magic show:

For example, a skilled magician or his skillful student, located at a crossing of four great roads, having gathered grasses, leaves, twigs, pebbles, and stones, displays various aspects of magical activities, such as: a herd of elephants, cavalry, chariots, and infantry; collections of gems, pearls, *vaidurya*, conch-shells, crystal and coral; collections of wealth, grain, treasuries and granaries.

Ordinary observers are taken in by this display, others (corresponding to realized Buddhist practitioners) are not so easily deceived:

Having thought: These deceive the eye, they do not emphatically apprehend or manifestly conceive in accordance with how they see and hear, and thereupon they do not subsequently impute conventional designations: This is true, the other is false.

Yet the nature and purpose of these illusionistic examples is importantly different from the ones we find in the *Prajñāpāramita* texts. Rather than suggesting an infinite hierarchy of illusions built on illusions, these examples indicate that the magic show that is the ordinary perception of the world is grounded in the mental. As commentators on the *sūtra* explain, the magician is the underlying mental reality who takes mental items (the sticks and stones of the example) and gives them the appearance of material objects (gems, pearls, and elephants).[9] The framing of the *sūtra*, locating it in a virtually existent palace, underlines the fact that the Buddha's teachings do not constitute an exception to the overall claim of the text that everything is mind-made. Like all other things, they may appear external yet they are in fact of the same nature as the mind.

Mental nature of the world and of the Buddha's teachings

While these *sūtras* introduce key Yogācāra concepts and often illustrate them by intriguing examples, the systematic development of Yogācāra thought happens at a later stage. Therefore, having looked at the prehistory of Yogācāra in some early Mahāyāna *sūtras*, let us now consider the succession of brilliant thinkers who developed the full complexity of the Yogācāra system.

### *b. Stages 2 and 3: Maitreya and Asaṅga*

We can approximately date Asaṅga somewhere between the years 350 and 450 CE.[10] His mother, Prasannaśīlā, is said to have given birth to three brothers from two different fathers. Asaṅga, the eldest, was fathered by a *kṣatriya*, a member of the warrior caste, while the two later brothers, Vasubandhu and

[9] Powers 2004: 45.

[10] Some date ranges for Asaṅga suggested by scholars are 375–430, 290–360, and 365–440 CE (Willis 1979: 49–50). For a survey of the main current debates concerning the figure of Asaṅga see Sakuma 2013.

Viriñcivatsa, had a Brahmin for a father. Unlike many Buddhist masters, these philosophical brothers did not come from southern India but from what is now Pakistan. All three brothers eventually became monks; according to Paramārtha's biography they all belonged to the Sarvāstivāda tradition. There is, however, some evidence that Asaṅga instead belonged to a different Abhidharma school, called the Mahīśāsakas.[11] Members of this school were known for their 'talent for penetrating the subtlety of absorptive meditation'.[12] At this stage we have already encountered two biographical facts that are indicative of prominent features of the Yogācāra system we will come back to later. The first is the intimate connection between Yogācāra and meditative practice. The second is the much closer conceptual connection between Abhidharma and Yogācāra than between Abhidharma and Madhyamaka, where the former mainly functions as an interpretative background against which the latter's arguments are to be interpreted. Unlike Nāgārjuna, whose Mahāyāna associations are evident throughout his works,[13] the founding masters of Yogācāra began their philosophical careers in a non-Mahāyāna context.

Asaṅga and his brothers

Yogācāra and Abhidharma

From the quotations in Asaṅga's own works we can infer that he must have been a devoted and capable student, with a comprehensive knowledge not only of the early Buddhist *sūtras* but also of key early Mahāyāna texts and their associated commentaries. The texts he found particularly challenging to master were the Perfection of Wisdom texts, and he realized that he was in need of conceptual clarification from an authoritative source. According to Tāranātha, he received a tantric initiation from his teacher and began the practice of the bodhisattva Maitreya. This is the beginning of a frequently described episode in Asaṅga's life, an episode that combines biography, religious instruction, and the illustration of philosophical ideas in an interesting way. The eighth-century commentator Haribhadra summarizes it briefly by noting that:

Asaṅga and the Perfection of Wisdom

> though noble Asaṅga understood all the meanings of the words [of the Buddha in general] and had gained realization, he was still not [able to] determine the meaning of the *Prajñāpāramitā* [*sūtras*] because of their profundity, their numerous repetitions, and his not recognizing the precise significance of individual phrases in the nonrepetitious parts [of these *sūtras*]. He became depressed about this, upon which the Bhagavān Maitreya expounded the *Prajñāpāramitā* sūtras... for his sake. After the noble Master Asaṅga had heard these [texts], he as well as Vasubandhu and further [masters] explained them [to others].[14]

Asaṅga's difficulty in grasping the Perfection of Wisdom texts must have completely disappeared as a result of this enlightened instruction, as he

[11] Though this view is criticized in Kritzer 1999: 7–13.
[12] Bareau 2013: 242.
[13] Though see pp. 105–6 above.
[14] Brunnhölzl 2010: 47.

would later compose a—still extant—commentary on the Diamond Sūtra (*Vajracchedikaprajñāpāramitāsūtra*).

Asaṅga's propitiation of Maitreya

Asaṅga propitiated Maitreya for twelve years in all, but at first without any success. The traditional accounts relate that whenever Asaṅga became despondent during his long period of practice he encountered various symbolic situations which convinced him to continue with his efforts. In one somewhat comical episode Asaṅga comes across a man rubbing an iron bar with a cotton cloth, telling Asaṅga that he is in the process of making a needle. He then goes on to show him a set of needles he has already made in this manner, which convinces Asaṅga that, given so much devotion can be shown to accomplish a merely mundane task, his spiritual efforts deserve greater efforts than he has shown so far. After twelve years, Asaṅga encounters a dying dog by the side of the road, its open sores infested with maggots. Asaṅga is overcome with great compassion, not just for the dog but also for the maggots. He resolves to take the maggots out of the dog's wounds and to transfer them to a piece of flesh he cuts from his own thigh. As he bends down to transfer the maggots with his own tongue the dog disappears, and Maitreya stands in front of him. Asaṅga immediately starts to complain to Maitreya that he has been practicing diligently for a long time, and still he was nowhere to be seen. Maitreya responds by saying that:

> Though the king of the gods sends down rain, a bad seed is unable to grow.
> Though the Buddhas may appear, he who is unworthy cannot partake of the bliss.[15]

Maitreya points out that he was always there when Asaṅga was practising, but his deluded mind made it impossible to see him. The two of them set out immediately to demonstrate this. Asaṅga takes Maitreya on his shoulders and carries him through town. Maitreya is completely invisible to most people, though some (with lighter karmic obscurations) are able to see him in some distorted form: some are only able to see Maitreya in the form of a dog on Asaṅga's shoulders, some only see his feet, and so on. Maitreya then tells Asaṅga to hold on to a corner of his robe, and together they ascend to Tuṣita heaven, Maitreya's own celestial realm. According to traditional accounts, he spends between six months and fifty years in Tuṣita, listening to Maitreya's teaching of the Mahāyāna. In particular, Maitreya teaches five texts to him, a highly important set of Yogācāra texts known as the 'five treatises of Maitreya', which includes the *Abhisamayālaṃkāra*, a versified summary of the *Prajñāpāramitāsūtras*, meant specifically to dispel Asaṅga's doubts concerning the Perfection of Wisdom texts.

Maitreya's five treatises

There are at least three noteworthy points about this account. The first is the fact that what causes Asaṅga to directly see Maitreya is an act of great

[15] Willis 1979: 8.

Connection of wisdom and compassion

Role of karma in perception

compassion that has on the face of it very little to do with the practices he has been carrying out for twelve years before this. Illustrating the central Buddhist idea of the inseparability of wisdom and compassion, this event underlines the importance of compassion for bringing about the kind of crucial shift in perspective that is essential for progress on the meditative path. Secondly, the account of some townspeople only being able to see Maitreya in distorted forms is a good example of the Yogācāra idea of the constitutive role our karmic potential plays in the perception of the world. Vasubandhu later relies on this idea at an important point in his argument in the *Viṃśikā*, when he argues that the realms experienced by the beings reborn in hell are not real, but are a collective result of their shared karmic potentialities.

The nature of Maitreya

The final intriguing aspect of this story is of course Asaṅga's encounter with Maitreya and his subsequent visit to heavenly realms.

Maitreya as a 'real person'

Various modern scholars have argued that Maitreya should in fact be considered as a human teacher of Asaṅga, rather than as a transcendent, enlightened being.[16] The reasons given for this claim vary. What is sometimes meant by saying that Maitreya was a 'real person' is that the works ascribed to him were not simply written by Asaṅga. When Asaṅga transmitted Maitreya's works, or composed works under his guidance, the line of argument goes, he was not just writing under a pseudonym, but there was actually a second author involved.[17] This reason finds support in the colophons to Maitreya's works, which clearly state Maitreya, not Asaṅga, as their author. Moreover—and this brings us to the second reason—this author is there sometimes referred to as Maitreyanātha. Tucci[18] believed that this name could not possibly refer to the bodhisattva Maitreya, but was rather the name of a human who worships or is under the protection of the lord (*nātha*) Maitreya. How decisive these points are is not entirely clear. The nominal compound 'Maitreyanātha' can be understood in two different ways. One is Tucci's 'who has Maitreya as a lord', in which case it would clearly refer to a human, or it could mean 'the Lord Maitreya', in which case it would refer to the future Buddha himself.[19]

A main reason behind the interest in the question whether Maitreya was a bodhisattva or a mere mortal is, of course, the issue of dating his works. If these were not composed by Asaṅga himself but by his human teacher, they would have been composed some time before Asaṅga, and so we would have a better idea of how to date these earliest Yogācāra works relative to Asaṅga.

[16] Ui 1929; Tucci 1930.

[17] Ui (1929: 100) notes that '[i]f he [Maitreya] has so many works to his credit, there can be no doubt whatsoever as to his historical existence.'

[18] Tucci 1930: 8.

[19] In fact there are other examples where reference to the '*Bhagavat* Maitreya' is made, a term which in Buddhist contexts only denotes a Buddha.

Questionable assumptions

Yet the whole problem of the historicity of Maitreya seems to rest on some questionable assumptions. First of all, arguing that the *bodhisattva* Maitreya is the Maitreya we are talking about does, of course, not entail that no second author was involved and the works in question were all composed by Asaṅga himself. It is only if we assume that bodhisattvas without physical bodies cannot author texts that we might feel ourselves pushed to the theory that Asaṅga composed all these texts under a pseudonym. This is an assumption we would at least want to present an argument for, since it is completely at odds with some of the key assumptions behind the traditional understanding of Buddhist history discussed above.

But even if we accept the claim that a disembodied bodhisattva could not have composed the works in question, it is still not entirely clear what the claim that Maitreya was a 'real person' would actually amount to. If the issue is just whether Asaṅga's teacher taught him in a physical body, there seems to be no great difficulty in accounting for this from the traditional perspective. According to the doctrine of the 'three bodies' (*trikāya*), enlightened beings can manifest in the world in a wholly physical form (*nirmāṇakāya*). So Maitreyanātha could both have lived at a precisely dateable historical time and have been the emanation of a wholly enlightened being without a physical body.

Concerning Asaṅga's trip to Tuṣita heaven, it is important to keep in mind the extent to which visits to celestial realms can be understood as reports of meditative experiences. Xuanzang writes about Asaṅga going to Tuṣita heaven at night, and explaining the treatises he received there by day to the monks of his monastery.[20] One way of reading this is that the visits to Tuṣita and the instructions received from Maitreya in this way took place either during Asaṅga's nightly meditative experiences, or formed part Asaṅga's dreams.

Asaṅga's own works

In addition to the five treatises of Maitreya which Asaṅga took down from Tuṣita and transmitted to his disciples, he also composed his own works. His *magnum opus* is the voluminous *Yogācārabhūmiśāstra*, the 'Treatise on the Stages of Yogācāra'. It contains a variety of material; its most famous section, the *Bodhisattvabhūmi*, provides an extremely detailed discussion of the stages of the bodhisattva path. The text is also important because it introduces and discusses a variety of key terms of Yogācāra philosophy, such as the eight kinds of minds, the foundational consciousness, and the three natures.

### c. *Stage 4: Vasubandhu*

The third member in this triad of early Yogācāra masters besides Asaṅga and his teacher Maitreya is Asaṅga's brother Vasubandhu. While in the case of Maitreya contemporary Buddhologists wonder whether he existed at all

[20] Beal 1884: 226.

(at least whether he existed as an actual human being), for Vasubandhu the question is not whether there was anyone of that name, but how many there were in the first place.

Diversity of his works

In order to see the motivation for the entire discussion about the existence of multiple Vasubandhus it is necessary to appreciate how diverse Vasubandhu's textual output actually was. One of his traditional epithets is 'Master of 1,000 teachings' (千部論師); he is considered to have composed 500 Hīnayāna and 500 Mahāyāna works. Even though these numbers are most likely to be understood in a symbolic fashion, the works that have come down to us as authored by Vasubandhu cover an impressive spectrum of different aspects of the Buddhist philosophical landscape. As a matter of fact, with the exception of Madhyamaka, Vasubandhu wrote seminal treatises on all of the different branches of Buddhist philosophy in existence at his time: on the two Abhidharmic schools of Vaibhāṣika and Sautrāntika, as well as on Yogācāra.[21]

Vasubandhu's life

Vasubandhu was born as Asaṅga's younger half-brother in Puruṣapura (present-day Peshawar), in the kingdom of Gāndhāra;[22] he shared his Brāhmaṇa father with the youngest of the three of his mother's sons, Viriñci-vatsa. Unlike Asaṅga, Vasubandhu was ordained as a monk in the Sarvāstivāda school. In order to study their doctrines in greater detail he moved to Kashmir, at that time the centre of Sarvāstivāda learning. He probably stayed there for four years.[23] After his return to Puruṣapura he embarked on the enormous project of composing a detailed exposition of the entire Sarvāstivāda system. According to Paramārtha's account, Vasubandhu lived there unattached to any particular Buddhist order and supported himself by lecturing on Sarvāstivāda. At the end of each day he would compose a verse that would form a summary of that day's teaching. This, the colourful account of this episode continues, he would then engrave on a copper plate, hang it around the neck of a drunken elephant, and challenge anyone to refute it. That this literally took place might not be very likely, but the symbolic contents of the story are clear. In the same way in which an elephant, drunk after eating fermenting fruit, indiscriminately crushing everything in its way, can only be controlled by an enormous degree of power and strength, so the would-be opponents of Vasubandhu would have to employ the entirety of their intellectual resources in order find fault with his

Composition of the *Abhidharmakośa*

[21] This claim has to be taken with a small grain of salt, though. As Gold (2015: 4) notes 'our best recent evidence is telling us that "Sautrāntika" is not definitely attested as a doctrinal school before Vasubandhu, and "Yogācāra" definitely postdated him. When Vasubandhu uses the term "Yogācāra" he is generally referring to practitioners of meditational exercises, not to a specific philosophical school' (Gold 2015a: 10).

[22] 'Determining the date of Vasubandhu (or Vasubandhus?) is one of the thorniest issues in the history of Indian Buddhism' (Deleanu 2006: 1. 186). A good overview of the problems associated with dating Vasubandhu is given in Deleanu 2006: 1. 186–94. He suggests placing Vasubandhu between the years 350 and 430 CE.

[23] From about 342 to 346, according to Anacker (2002: 16).

exposition. The engraving onto plates of copper also echoes the fourth Buddhist council in Kashmir, where the words of the Buddha were fixed for posterity in the very same way. This daily exercise, we are supposed to assume, continued for nearly two years, and the over 600 verses Vasubandhu composed in this way formed his most famous work, the *Abhidharmakośa*, the 'Treasury of Abhidharma'. We learn that Vasubandhu then sent this text, together with the enormous sum of fifty pounds of gold, to his old teachers in Kashmir. They sent the sum straight back, and added another fifty pounds, asking Vasubandhu to also compose a commentary to what they perceived as a brilliant defence of Sarvāstivāda doctrines, though one that is expressed in an often very terse and condensed way. The result of this request is the *Abhidharmakośabhāṣya*, particularly noteworthy for what it does not do. Far from a detailed exposition of Sarvāstivāda orthodoxy, the commentary is frequently very critical of the Sarvāstivāda ideas developed in the root text. It is common practice for commentators to raise a variety of criticisms associated with different rival schools in exploring the ramifications of a specific verse of a root text. But in these cases the position of the root text always comes out as the victorious one in the end.[24] Not so in the case of the *Abhidharmakośabhāṣya*. There the Sautrāntika position, not that of the Sarvāstivāda, is the one that Vasubandhu frequently seems to go for.[25] The reasons for this discrepancy between the apparent doxographic affiliations of two parts of the same text are not entirely transparent. Did Vasubandhu change his mind about some of the philosophical beliefs that he set out in the *Abhidharmakośa*? Or was he always critical of the Sarvāstivāda system and is only coming out into the open with this work? In any case, when he sent them the *Abhidharmakośabhāṣya* his former teachers were not amused, and we find clear examples of their very critical attitude in later Sarvāstivāda texts.[26]

Its *bhāṣya*

Vasubandhu and the Mahāyāna

Up this point Vasubandhu's stance towards the Mahāyāna, and particularly towards the works of his half-brother Asaṅga, had been hardly complimentary. Bu ston tell us that he remarked about Asaṅga's prolific output: 'Alas, for twelve years Asaṅga practiced meditation in the forest without success and has written a philosophical system only an elephant can carry.'[27] This changes after Asaṅga sends two of his disciples to recite two Mahāyāna *sūtra*s to Vasubandhu. He quickly becomes convinced of the merit of these texts and, feeling great shame about his previous criticism of the Mahāyāna, looks for a razor to cut out his tongue. We are reminded here of the severe punishment the loser of

[24] For a possible exception see the earlier discussion of the *Kathāvatthu*, pp. 49–53.

[25] As always, we have to treat these doxographic terms with some caution. 'Sautrāntika' is certainly the label Vasubandhu employs for the position he himself favours (Gold 2015a: 25). How this usage relates to that of other writers, and whether all these uses speak about a single system of tenets, is far less clear.

[26] Anacker 2002: 17–18.

[27] Bu ston 2013: 242.

Indian philosophical debates was supposed to undergo in some cases. But in the same way in which a magnanimous opponent usually keeps the worst outcome from happening, Asaṅga's students quickly suggest that seeing his half-brother and learning more about the Mahāyāna from him might be a wiser course. Vasubandhu does so, and Bu ston's account of their interaction provides us with an interesting commentary on the interplay between arguments and meditative practice in shaping Buddhist philosophy. In their discussion Vasubandhu proved to be the quicker thinker than Asaṅga, but even though his older brother was slower, the replies he did produce in the end were often of higher quality. Asaṅga explained this fact to Vasubandhu by pointing out that Vasubandhu has been a scholar during his last 500 lifetimes, so constructing arguments came naturally for him. This was not the case for Asaṅga, who, whenever he got stuck with a philosophical problem, had to consult with the bodhisattva Maitreya who provided him with the answer. While Asaṅga was lacking lifetimes of philosophical training, Vasubandhu was lacking the necessary meditative ability that would have allowed him to purify the obscurations of this mind sufficiently to consult with enlightened beings directly. We can see here how historians of Buddhist philosophy saw its development as being shaped by two distinct routes, one coming from the dynamics of argumentative exchanges, one coming from insights gained during meditative realization, here personified by the two brothers. In this account we also get a clear sense that the latter is regarded as ultimately more authoritative: Vasubandhu carries out special practices to be able to see Maitreya himself as well, while we do not read about Asaṅga training to improve his argumentative skills.

The philosopher vs. the meditator

After his instruction by Asaṅga, Vasubandhu immersed himself in Mahāyāna scriptures. Tāranātha reports that he read through the whole of the Perfection of Wisdom in 100,000 verses in an uninterrupted session of fifteen days and nights, which he spent (for reasons not entirely clear) immersed in a tub of sesame-oil. In his later life as well he would read the Perfection of Wisdom in 8,000 verses as a daily exercise.[28] The output of Mahāyāna works by this 'Master of a thousand teachings' was prolific, including commentaries on the two *sūtra*s recited by the students of Asaṅga that triggered his adoption of the Mahāyāna stance (the *Daśabhūmikasūtra* and the *Akṣayamatinirdeśasūtra*), commentaries on some of the five works of Maitreya, on the *Vajracchedikā-prajñāpāramitāsūtra*, as well has his most famous later works, the 'Twenty Verses' (*Viṃśikā*), 'Thirty Verses' (*Triṃśikā*), and the 'Instruction on the Three Natures' (*Trisvabhāvanirdeśa*). The traditional biographies report that he died in his eightieth year.

Vasubandhu's Mahāyāna works

[28] Lama Chimpa 1970: 171.

Multiple Vasubandhus?

When this was is not entirely clear, and in fact the dating of Vasubandhu is still subject to dispute. Anacker dates him to *c.*316–96 CE,[29] Takakusu to 420–500, Mochizuki to 433–533, Hirakawa to 400–80.[30] We are thus looking at a span of 200 years, the fourth and fifth centuries, in which to place Vasubandhu. A suggestion that has introduced additional complications is one due to Erich Frauwallner, claiming that there were in fact two Vasubandhus rather than one.[31] Frauwallner argued that we would have to distinguish two writers with the name Vasubandhu who lived in close temporal proximity, an elder Vasubandhu who lived roughly between 320 and 380 CE, and a younger Vasubandhu who lived from about 400 to 480. If we take into account Vasubandhu's biography as we find it in the traditional accounts, it is evident where the motivation for this split comes from. Vasubandhu seems to have two very distinct sides to him: that of an Abhidharma scholar (again subdivided into a Sarvāstivāda scholar who composed the *Abhidharmakośa*, and a Sautrāntika who wrote the commentary), and that of a Mahāyāna teacher who authored some of the most spirited defences of the system of thought that later systematizers regard as the Yogācāra school of Buddhist philosophy. For Frauwallner, the older Vasubandhu is the Yogācārin, while the younger composed the *Abhidharmakośa*. Apart from arguments based on the earliest biographical accounts of Vasubandhu (which, Frauwallner claims, look as if two separate biographies have been spliced together), one of the main reasons for this split are occasional references by Yaśomitra, a commentator on the *Abhidharmakośabhāṣya* to an 'older Vasubandhu (*vṛddhācāryavasubandhu*)', which give the impression that Yaśomitra is himself referring to another author also called Vasubandhu who lived some time before the author of the *Abhidharmakośa*. Contemporary scholars do not regard these considerations as decisive enough to uphold the 'two Vasubandhus' hypothesis,[32] especially as it, though solving some interpretative problems, generates others. If the *Abhidharmakośa* was composed a whole century after such key Yogācāra works as the *Yogācārabhūmi*, why does this book, filled as it is with references to specific positions and authors, not refer to this school, and why does it use the term 'Yogācāra' in a way that clearly does not presuppose any doctrinal identity, but merely refers to practitioners of yoga? Moreover, there seem to be a variety of ways of explaining the references to the 'older Vasubandhu'. The term might here not literally mean older, but could have been used in an honorific sense,[33] or it could refer to an earlier stage in Vasubandhu's philosophical development,[34]

The split between the Ābhidharmika and the Mahāyāna scholar

Problems with the hypothesis of multiple Vasubandhus

[29] Anacker 2002: 23. [30] Tola and Dragonetti 2004: 154–5, n. 2.

[31] Frauwallner 1951.

[32] For some criticism see Jaini 1958; Bhikkhu Pāsādika 1991; an extended discussion is in Gold 2015a, 2–21.

[33] Anacker 2002: 24–6, n. 13. [34] Mejor 1989–90.

or finally, it may indeed refer to a different Vasubandhu, but in quite another way. Paramārtha's biography tells us that *all* the three sons of Vasubandhu's mother were called 'Vasubandhu', though two of them were also called by different names in order to tell them apart: Asaṅga ('no attachment') and Viriñcivatsa (child of Viriñci, another name of his mother Prasannaśīlā). In this case the term 'older Vasubandhu' could refer to the oldest of these three Vasubandhus, namely Asaṅga.

The main force behind the hypothesis

It seems as if the main force that makes the hypothesis of the two Vasubandhus attractive is one that often stands in the way of a nuanced understanding of the history of Buddhist philosophy: the view that Buddhist philosophers can be clearly divided into different schools of thought, that each of these schools of thought has a core set of unique beliefs that distinguishes them from all other schools, and that all of a philosopher's intellectual activity takes place within the limits of this framework. While there is no doubt that doxographic frameworks are propaedeutically useful for trying to explain the rough outlines of development of Buddhist thought (as they are used in the present work), the overly simplistic nature of their key assumptions is obvious once these are properly formulated. Buddhist philosophers did not compose their treatises in order to found new schools, and did not subsequently regard themselves as their chief exponents, but the identity of these schools is projected backwards with the benefit of historical hindsight, in order to stress certain similarities amongst the views of temporally contiguous sets of thinkers. These schools developed, often over considerable time, and their views developed with them; there is no fixed set of theses that is common to every work by every author ascribed to a given school and thereby constitutive of that school's intellectual identity. Finally, the views of philosophers change over the course of time, sometimes in radical ways, a fact that is as true today as it was in ancient India. To ascribe philosophical texts to authors on the basis of the fact that the positions described in them diverge, if at all, only in the most minimal fashion is unlikely to lead to a satisfactory account of authors and the development of their work. The fact that the framework incorporating these views is not simply regarded as propaedeutic tool but as authoritative in its own right lends support to the idea of 'splitting up' Vasubandhu into two, despite the fact that the traditional accounts always consider Vasubandhu to be a single author with a unified body of works. The split allows us to distinguish the Ābhidharmika Vasubandhu from the Yogācārin, ascribe to each a set of unique Abhidharma and Yogācāra beliefs, and consider their intellectual activity as wholly contained within these respective frameworks. However, once we question the intrinsic cogency of the framework motivating this split we realize that the justification for the division slips away, and that the historical evidence brought forward to support it can equally be explained in other ways.

Difficulties with doxographic frameworks

### *d. Stage 5: Later Yogācāra*

After Asaṅga and Vasubandhu the history of Yogācāra thought continued in India for about another seven centuries. Unfortunately we are not able to provide a detailed account of this intellectually very fertile period here, but have to limit ourselves to mentioning a few particularly noteworthy episodes. The most important thinkers of later Yogācāra were without question Diṅnāga, a disciple of Vasubandhu, and Dharmakīrti, a disciple of one of Diṅnāga's disciples. Both of them are known first and foremost for their work on logic and epistemology, in fact their works are often regarded as the foundation of a separate 'logico-epistemological school' alongside Madhyamaka and Yogācāra. We will discuss their ideas on reasoning, debate, and the theory of knowledge in more detail in the next chapter. In this chapter we will focus on some of their other works that are not primarily concerned with logico-epistemological matters.

Diṅnāga and Dharmakīrti

Diṅnāga's *Ālambanaparīkṣā*

Diṅnāga's most noteworthy treatise in this group is his *Ālambanaparīkṣā*, a work that we will meet again below in the context of the Yogācāra criticism of atomism.[35] This text is extremely short, consisting of only eight verses, together with a brief auto-commentary, a mere two-and-a-half Tibetan folios long (the Sanskrit original is lost).[36] Despite its brevity, this work of Diṅnāga's proved to be fairly influential, not just in terms of the later commentaries it attracted, but also by generating various responses from non-Buddhist thinkers.[37] As the title of the work indicates, it is an investigation (*parīkṣā*) of the support (*ālambaṇa*) of the perceptual state, that is, whatever it is in the world that makes a certain state a perceptual state. Diṅnāga argues that for something to act as a support of a perception, it must satisfy two conditions: it must be caused by it and it must exist in the way in which the perception makes it appear. If something does not enter into causal contact with our sensory apparatus it is hard to see how we could say that we perceive it. And if the way the something exists and the way it appears to us wholly diverge we should rather speak of a misperception than of a perception. Perception should not only hook us up with the world, it should also get the world more or less right. As we have will see below,[38] Diṅnāga argues that neither atoms nor conglomerates of atoms can fulfil both conditions, and for that reason they cannot be what we perceive. Is there anything that fulfils both conditions? Consider internal representations. Such representations are introduced by views according to which we are unable to perceive an object just as it is, but require the mediation of an internal intermediary, some representation that brings together all the different features of an object our different sensory

Conditions for supporting a perceptual state

Representations as supports

[35] See below, pp. 172–3.

[36] For a translation together with a set of Indian and Tibetan commentaries see Duckworth et al. 2016.

[37] Sastri 1942: xi–xii. [38] p. 172–3.

faculties have perceived. For this reason internal representations are causes of perception as well; they are closer to us than the object itself, but they are nevertheless part of the causal field that gives rise to the perception. Moreover, the internal representation exists in the way in which perception makes it appear; certainly more so than the external object itself.

Diṅnāga is thus runs a transcendental argument for idealism. He identifies what the preconditions for us to have any perceptions at all must be (there must be causes that exist in the way they appear), and argues that, given that we have perceptions, and given that the familiar candidates such as atoms and their conglomerates fail to fulfil this condition, what we really perceive are internal representations.

## 2. Proofs of Buddhist Doctrines

If we consider the development of Buddhist thought, and that of Yogācāra in particular, from the times of Diṅnāga onwards, it becomes apparent that Buddhist philosophy has entered a phase of increased debate and argumentative interactions with non-Buddhist schools. One manifestation of this is a series of proofs of specific Buddhist concepts that Indian Buddhist philosophers debated at the time. Such proofs would obviously be of little use in an intra-Buddhist debate, where the basic assumptions of Buddhism were not questioned, and the issue was rather how specific doctrinal disputes about the interpretations of concepts were to be resolved. But once Buddhists debated more extensively with non-Buddhists, the necessity to provide specific arguments establishing points of view that the opponent is unlikely to share becomes more pressing. We will be looking at three such proofs here: a proof of rebirth, a proof of the falsity of solipsism, and a proof of momentariness.

### *a. Rebirth*

This argument, which Dharmakīrti gives in the *Pramāṇasiddhi* chapter of his *Pramāṇavārttika*, is actually meant to establish two positions at the same time: the existence of rebirth and the non-material nature of the mental, that is, the establishment of a form of interactionist dualism. Dharmakīrti puts this argument forward in the context of arguing for the Buddha as a source of epistemic authority (*pramāṇabhūta*). The reason he provides is that the Buddha is infinitely compassionate. We might think this is a curious way of justifying an epistemic point by an ethical observation. After all, the fact that someone is very compassionate does not necessarily entail that he has a privileged insight into how the world works. However, as Indian commentators on this passage point out,[39] that

Arguing for the Buddha's epistemic authority

Infinite compassion during infinitely many lives

[39] See Franco 1997: 23–6.

the Buddha has practised compassion over the course of countless lifetimes means that he has invested all his powers in finding a way to liberate all beings from suffering and its cause. It is because of this that he has developed insight into the nature of reality that made it possible for the Buddha to become liberated himself and to show the way to liberation to others. Compassion, when pursued to the limit, will inevitably have epistemic consequences, and it is these consequences that justify regarding the Buddha as an authority about how to become free from saṃsāra.

Of course, if the Buddha's great compassion differs from the compassion ordinary beings may experience by having been cultivated over an infinite number of lifetimes, Dharmakīrti then has to say something establishing that the Buddha, and indeed all other beings, have lived through an infinite number of lives prior to this one. The background of his argument is the standard Abhidharma account of what there needs to be in order for a moment of consciousness to arise. This list includes four conditions, which include a properly functioning sensory faculty (*adhipatipratyaya*), an object of awareness (*ālambanapratyaya*), and an immediately prior moment of the same type of awareness (*samanatarapratyaya*). The final condition is the key. If for each moment of consciousness we need a prior moment to play a part in producing it, consciousness must stretch back infinitely backwards. This means it must have existed before we were born, thereby entailing both an unending succession of lives stretching back into the past, as well as the ability of the mental to exist without a physical basis (as there is nothing physical that has been transmitted from the body of my previous birth to this one, the mind must have existed in the intermediate state between the two births without any body supporting its existence). This latter claim is, of course, essential for a Yogācārin: if the mind could not exist without the physical we could hardly claim that everything physical is in fact only the mental in disguise without depriving the mental of its existential support. In fact all major religious and philosophical schools in India accepted the existence of rebirth and the existential independence of the mental in some form—all, that is, apart from the Cārvākas, a school of materialism that denied the existence of irreducibly mental phenomena. They argued that as the sound of a drum does not continue elsewhere when the percussionist stops playing,[40] but ceases, or as once the intoxicating properties of some alcohol[41] dissipate they do not become attached to another liquid, so the destruction of the body entails the destruction of the mind, not just its move to another locus. It is this kind of materialism, a theory nearly universal in the current sciences of the mind, yet

Conditions for the arising of consciousness

Infinite regression of consciousness

Cārvāka materialism

[40] Bhattacharya 2013: 6–7. [41] Bhattacharya 2002: 604, 612.

one that appeared uniformly absurd to the ancient Indian thinkers, that Dharmakīrti's arguments are chiefly directed against.

Two challenges

This is obviously not the place to go into a detailed discussion of the systematic prospects of Dharmakīrti's argument as a refutation of materialism,[42] but it is useful to briefly note two obvious challenges his argument faces.

Proof of past lives, not of rebirth

First of all, on its own it is strictly speaking not a proof of rebirth but a proof of past lives, since it attempts to show that the present mental moment had infinitely many mental predecessors, not that it is going to have infinitely many mental successors. Dharmakīrti was aware that inferring the cause from the effect is an altogether more satisfactory move than trying to infer effects from potential causes.[43] Other factors might intervene, and the 'cause' might never bring about the effect, and a given mind-moment might never cause its successor. In order to argue for the extension of mind into the future we would therefore need to argue that it is the nature of mind-moments to bring about their successor, and that because the relation of the immediately preceding mind-moment to the present one is essentially the same as that of the present mind-moment to the immediately succeeding one, the present moment will always produce a successor moment.

Accounting for unconsciousness

A second difficulty is connected with accounting for periods of unconsciousness, such as deep sleep or coma. If a person wakes up from a coma, their first waking moment would have to have been produced by the last pre-coma moment, since there are not any mind-moments in between. This leads to the curious consequence that the 'immediately preceding' mind-moment can be separated from the 'immediately succeeding' one by a considerable temporal distance. Yet Dharmakīrti's commentators point out that this is a consequence to be endorsed, since the only other alternative is that something in the body should restart consciousness, and in this case consciousness should always be able to re-arise in a body, which is manifestly not the case.[44] This argument might not strike us as too convincing (after all, we now believe that there is a *physical* difference between a dead body and one in a coma), but it is worthwhile to note that once we hold on to the idea that mental causation can be suspended by temporal gaps, it becomes straightforward to explain how the loss of consciousness at the moment of death could be followed by the re-arising of a causally successive consciousness in another body, simply because no transfer of physical matter, nor an unbroken connecting chain of mind-moments, is required for one episode of consciousness to be regarded as a continuation of another one.

[42] For some discussion of this see Franco 1997: 128–32; Arnold 2012.

[43] See Franco 1997: 109.

[44] See Arnold 2012: 39–40.

### *b. Other minds*

A second problem that is of considerable interest for Yogācāra philosophers is the problem of other minds. Solipsism, the position that there is only one mind, namely my own, and no others, is not *per se* a problem for idealism, since arguing that all is mind does not commit us to accepting that all is just *my* mind. But the issue becomes particularly pressing in the case of Yogācāra, since it is not just a denial of material objects. It also argues for a denial of external objects, as a way of undermining the duality between the subject (the self in here) and the objects (the world out there) that is supposed to lie at the root of our continuing transmigration through saṃsāra. Other minds are, of course, external objects too, and we might wonder whether the same unwelcome consequences the Yogācārin assumes to follow from the postulation of mind-independent objects cannot simply be reinstated by reference to mind-independent minds. If the subject–object duality can arise with respect to atoms and their conglomerates, can it not equally arise with respect to distinct mental states and their conglomerates? Yet it is evident that the acceptance of solipsism must appear as highly problematic from a Buddhist perspective. A relatively minor worry is that canonical sources tell us that one of the special powers the Buddha acquired as part of his enlightenment is the ability to know other minds directly. Yet if there are no other minds to know, what precisely would the Buddha's knowledge be knowledge of? Presumably the knowledge of his own mind would not qualify as the kind of knowledge that presupposes liberation for its obtaining. More importantly, the entire point of the Mahāyāna path seems to disappear on the solipsist picture of the world. If its aim is to lead all beings to liberation, how could this be any different from just liberating myself if there are no other beings whatsoever apart from me?

Solipsism as problematic for Buddhism

Dharmakīrti's *Santānāntara-siddhi*

To reject the appearance of an affinity to solipsism that one might ascribe to Yogācāra, Dharmakīrti composed a separate, short treatise, the *Santānāntarasiddhi*. In this text Dharmakīrti argues that knowledge of other minds does not arise in fundamentally different ways for the idealist and for the realist. The realist does not have direct knowledge of other minds, but infers their existence from the appearance of purposeful actions. The same is true for the idealist. He does not have direct access to other minds either, but receives a variety of impressions that are wholly mental in nature. Some of these are correlated with specific mental states that appear to him to be internal (e.g. my intention to move my arm, and the subsequent impression that my arm goes up), while others are not (the impression of your arm going up is not reliably preceded by specific intentions of mine). On the basis of this the Yogācārin can infer that in the same way in which my arm-lifting is preceded by a specific mental state, so is your arm-lifting, even though I cannot access it directly. The only difference seems to be that for the realist the impression of arms going up is to be regarded as an objective, external fact involving material objects, while the Yogācārin consider such facts to be wholly mental. An objection that is raised at this stage is that, according to the Buddhist understanding of mind, causation does not happen across separate mental streams. One mental event of mine can cause another event of mine, but a mental event of yours cannot directly cause a mental event of mine (such as the thought that you lift your arm because you intended to do so). Dharmakīrti points out that the connection is not one of direct causation, but of inference. If I see smoke on a distant mountain and infer the presence of fire, I do not know the fire because it entered into direct causal contact with my perceptual system. All the idealist and the realist can hope to achieve is inferential knowledge of other minds. What Dharmakīrti points out is that, to use modern terminology, we are justified to apply the intentional stance to other people, thereby treating their behaviour as if it was the result of their inner mental life. The belief that there is such an inner life counts as knowledge according to Dharmakīrti's epistemology, since it allows us carry out actions that fulfil our desires (in this case, we achieve the impression of successfully interacting with other people). Dharmakīrti's argument seems to be successful in preventing Yogācāra from sliding into solipsism, though we might wonder whether it does not provide a licence to attribute intentionality to all kinds of phenomena, such as plants, the weather, and even the random behaviour of a roulette wheel. If I am rewarded by the fulfilment of my desires with respect to these (as I may well be), would I not be equally justified in ascribing minds to them as I would be ascribing them to the people around me? The Yogācārin does not seem to be able to provide an external reason why we are more justified in one ascription than in the other, yet if all the reasons for differentiating between them are internal, the spectre of solipsism seems to rise once more.[45]

Our knowledge of other minds is inferential

Indeed, Dharmakīrti's argument was not able to put the issue of solipsism to rest for the Yogācārins. Towards the very end of the history of Buddhism in India, the eleventh-century scholar Ratnakīrti composed the *Santānāntaradūṣaṇa*, a short treatise on the refutation of the existence of other minds, and what appears to be a defence of solipsism. Ratnakīrti argues that there is no real possibility of differentiating consciousness as a whole into different streams, one for each mind, thereby establishing the existence of minds other than one's own. His key point is that mental events that occur in our mind do not specifically identify themselves as belonging to our own mental stream.[46] The simple reflexivity of consciousness, which the Yogācārins accept, is not enough here. Neither consciousness being aware of itself, nor the fact that I consider my thoughts to be mine, is sufficient for making them mine; there needs to be some internal way of identifying them as

Ratnakīrti's *Santānāntaradūṣaṇa*

[45] For this point see Reat 1985: 270. [46] See Ganeri 2007: 205–9.

mine and as not belonging to somebody else. Simply thinking of a thought that it is mine will not be sufficient, since another person will think the very same thing of their thought, and this will be theirs, not ours. We would therefore need a unique way of connecting each set of mental events with some kind of unique identifier, like 'JCW's thought', in order to regard them as mine. This kind of thought-tagging cannot just boil down to belonging to a specific set of mental events forming a maximally connected series, the standard Buddhist reductionist account of a person. This would not rule out solipsism, since if solipsism was true my thoughts would obviously belong to such a series, which would be the only one there is. Rather, the 'JCW' tag of each thought would need to be internally accessible, and distinguishable from the 'ABC' tag, the 'DEF' tag, and so on. But such branding of thoughts in terms of irreducibly distinct persons that have them is of course not possible within the Buddhist conception of the mind. If we are reductionists about persons, it seems, then we have to accept the consequence that we cannot really differentiate between different streams of consciousness. This theory does not entail all the problematic consequences for the Buddhist path, since Ratnakīrti confines the solipsistic picture to the level of ultimate reality.[47] At the level of conventional truth the division into individual minds, and all the ethical and soteriological consequences that come with it, still hold.

Solipsism at the level of ultimate reality

### c. *Momentariness*

The final notion we want to discuss here is that of momentariness, the idea that all existents only last for a moment and immediately disappear upon arising, so that our perception of temporally persisting objects is simply an illusion akin to that we experience every time we watch a film in the cinema. Like the idea of rebirth and the existence of other minds, momentariness has been the object of considerable attention by Yogācāra masters, though they were by no means the first who tried to provide argumentative support for this initially quite unintuitive concept.

We noted above that in addition to the argument for momentariness from the spontaneity of destruction we find in Vasubandhu's *Abhidharmakośa-bhāṣya*, there are two more forms of argument for momentariness that make their appearance in the history of Buddhist philosophy. These are the argument from the *momentariness of cognition* and the argument from *change*.

Argument from the momentariness of cognition

Arguments from the momentariness of cognition, put forward, amongst others, by Vasubandhu,[48] take as their premise the claim that all mental phenomena are momentary, and arise and cease moment by moment, without temporal thickness. Now these mental phenomena depend causally on their bases, which are the physical sense faculties, and thus the momentariness of the

[47] McDermott 1969: 1.

[48] In the *Mahāyānasūtrālaṅkārabhāṣya*, see von Rospatt 1995: 125.

mental phenomena must be inherited from the momentariness of the physical phenomena that give rise to them. An example sometimes used to illustrate this argument is that of a passenger in a carriage. The rise and descent of the passenger (the mind) is only due to the rise and descent of the carriage (the body), and the passenger's movement is nothing but a replication of the pattern of movement of the cart.[49] This argument derives its force from the generally accepted view within Buddhist philosophy that permanent and impermanent entities are fundamentally different kinds of thing, and so could not be connected by a causal relation. A permanent cause could therefore not bring about an impermanent effect. (Of course, this only helps in establishing momentariness if the impermanent is identified with the momentary, and the permanent with the non-momentary,[50] so that there could not be impermanent phenomena that are in fact non-momentary.)

Mental momentariness inherited from momentariness of percepts

An early form of the argument from change was put forward in Asaṅga's *Śrāvakabhūmi*. The best way of understanding the point Asaṅga makes in this text[51] is that entities change their properties unceasingly throughout time, and that such a change is not a substitution of one property by another on the basis of some persisting substance, but a replacement of one object (having the first property) by a distinct, though similar one (having the second property). If this is the case, the constant change of objects entails their inability to persist, since each instance of change is characterized by the cessation of one object and its substitution by another.

The argument from change

Further versions of arguments from change have been explored by Dharmakīrti, and later Ratnakīrti presents another development of them in his *Kṣaṇabhaṅgasiddhi*. Ratnakīrti puts forward an indirect and a direct argument. The indirect argument attempts to show that the assumption of the temporal thickness of objects, the idea that they last for more than one moment and are therefore extended in time, leads to a contradiction. Consider a material object that appears to be temporally extended, such as a pot. The pot at midday can be regarded as an effect of the pot at midnight, insofar as an object stays in existence by causing its later time-slices. But now consider the pot at two immediately successive moments, $t$ and $t'$. The pot at $t$ can bring about an effect at $t'$ that is either the same, or different, or it may bring about no effect at all. The last can be ruled out immediately, since Ratnakīrti understands existence precisely in terms of causal efficacy, as the ability to bring about effects. But if the pots at $t$ and $t'$ are the same, the former would bring about an effect that

Ratnakīrti's indirect argument

[49] Von Rospatt 1995: 126. Section II.II.B (122–52) presents a detailed discussion of various forms of this argument.

[50] See von Rospatt 1995: n. 334, 148 for a passage from Sthiramati's *Mahāyānasūtrālaṅkāravṛttibhāṣya* where he makes this very identification.

[51] See von Rospatt 1995: 153–5, and section II.II.C (153–77) for further discussion of arguments from change.

already exists, a position that is also not satisfactory. So the pots at the two moments have to be different. But since this argument applies to any two successive moments of the pot's existence, the pot cannot be temporally extended. This is the contradiction entailed by the denial of momentariness.[52]

Ratnakīrti's direct argument

Ratnakīrti's direct argument for the momentariness of an arbitrary object such as a pot proceeds as follows. As we have already seen, to exist means having causal efficacy. Ratnakīrti also argues that such efficacy, once present, is discharged immediately. We might consider this premise as not particularly plausible, since there are various existent, causally efficacious things that do not presently bring about an effect. Take a grain in the granary: it has the power to sprout, but it does not currently do so. But, we may argue, this is only because we conceive of it without the causal field (*sāmagrī*) of background conditions such as water, soil, warmth, and so on that make the arising of the effect possible. Without the causal field, the seed cannot produce any sprout, yet once all the constituents of the causal field are assembled, the effect is produced without delay. If we then consider a given pot at various successive moments in time, $t$, $t'$, and $t''$, it is clear that the pot at $t$ cannot bring about the pot at $t''$, since it has discharged its causal power immediately, bringing about the pot at $t'$. Only this pot at $t'$ has the ability to bring about the pot at $t''$. For Ratnakīrti, the causal capacities of an object are not only intricately connected with its existence, but also with being the kind of object it is. So if the pot at $t$ and the pot at $t'$ have different causal powers, they must be different kinds of thing. Therefore, as the theory of momentariness claims, there is not a single pot persisting throughout the three moments but a succession of pots that differ in nature, one causing, and thereby replacing, the next.[53]

## 3. Key Yogācāra Concepts

After this survey of the historical development of Yogācāra thought in India we will introduce some of its key concepts as described in the works of the three Yogācāra masters Maitreya, Asaṅga, and Vasubandhu. Three of them can be considered as constituting the conceptual core of Yogācāra thought: the idea that everything is wholly mental (*cittamātra*), the notion of a foundational consciousness (*ālayavijñāna*), and the doctrine of the three natures (*trisvabhāva*).

### *a.* cittamātra

If there is anything deserving to be called the signature doctrine of Yogācāra[54] it is the idea of 'consciousness-only' (*cittamātra*), the view that all things are

[52] See Feldman and Phillips 2011: 30–1, 67. [53] See Feldman and Phillips 2011: 34–7, 70.

[54] Certainly from the time of Vasubandhu onwards, though things look somewhat different if we consider earlier Yogācāra literature such as the *Yogācārabhūmi* (Kellner 2017a: 307).

merely mind. This view is, to put it mildly, somewhat unintuitive, not just from the perspective of contemporary Western naturalism, but also for any Buddhist trained in the Abhidharma framework that considers matter (*rūpa*), the first of the five *skandhas*, as one of the fundamental ontological categories. The Yogācāra thinkers have developed a variety of arguments to deny the existence of material objects.[55] Amongst them we can distinguish three main groups, correlated to three epistemic instruments (*pramāṇa*): arguments relating to the possibility of *inferring* material objects, arguments regarding their being established by *scriptural authority* accepted by the Buddhists, and arguments concerning the possibility of *perceiving* such objects.

Arguments against material objects

It appears as if our best theories of the world distinguish between entities that are only subjectively observable (such as dreams and illusions), and those that are objectively observable (such as tables and chairs), and that this epistemological distinction is matched by an ontological one between objects that are merely mental and external, material objects. The well-known discussions of illusory appearances we find in many Yogācāra texts challenge this assumption. Following the illusionistic doctrines of the *Prajñāpāramitā* texts and the examples they provide, Yogācāra writers point out the phenomenological indistinguishability of our everyday experience from dreams, magical performances, mirages, and visual illusions. The first in particular provides them with an example of a complex experience that shares key features with waking experience. Waking experience exhibits temporal and spatial structuring (events do not happen in a random order, or at random places, but follow a spatio-temporal trajectory), and so do events in a dream. Events in the waking world display causal efficacy (when we drink water, our thirst is quenched), but so do events within the dream.[56]

1. Inferring material objects

Dream example

But if we are unable to distinguish from the inside between a world in which all is mental and a world in which there is also matter in addition to mind, how could we make the inference from the appearance of matter to our senses to its existence? We could be in a phenomenologically indistinguishable situation (such as in a dream), and our inference would then be erroneous. Moreover, what is the advantage of postulating material objects? The Yogācārin argues that they are a mere idle wheel that does not confer any explanatory benefits.

Postulating matter as explanatorily idle

A related point can be made by reference to the well-known example of the 'three cups of liquid', which presupposes some specific beliefs about Buddhist cosmology. The idea is that when the same cup of water is presented to beings

Example of the 'three cups of liquid'

[55] For a concise discussion of five types of arguments against the existence of material objects associated with Dharmakīrti see Kellner 2017a, b.

[56] In fact dream events cannot only be causally efficacious with respect to dream effects, but can also bring about effects in the waking world, as Vasubandhu points out by his appeal to the example of wet dreams, in *Viṃśikā* 4, see Tola and Dragonetti 2004: 82.

born into different realms of existence they will perceive it as substantially different things. Human beings will see a cup of water, gods will see a cup of ambrosia, hungry ghosts will see a cup filled with blood, pus, and other unsavoury substances, while beings born in hell see a cup of molten metal.[57] Once more, the appearance of water does not warrant our inference that there is an external object with the properties of water out there. The properties water seems to have, of being cool, transparent, pleasant to the taste, and so on, appear to be artefacts of our cognitive system, since they disappear when other kinds of being apprehend it. But it is then difficult to explain what kind of external object there might be that has the ability to appear in these protean shapes. It cannot be hot, or cold, or sweet, or salty, or clear, or opaque; in fact, it is difficult to see how we could have knowledge of any of the properties such objects have by themselves.

Restriction to invariable co-cognition

Apart from the argument from illusion and considerations of how much our sensory capacities (which are ultimately due to our karmic potentials) influence our perception, we also sometimes find reference to a third argument, called *sahopalambhaniyama*. This 'restriction to invariable co-cognition', which is developed in detail by Dharmakīrti,[58] points out that objects of awareness (such as a blue patch) and acts of awareness (cognition of something blue) always go together. We can never catch any object in an unperceived state, since the very process of perceptually 'catching' it already implies some form of cognitive access to it. But this means that there is something problematic with inferring from our perception of the world mind-independent, eternal objects, that is, objects that could exist independent of them being cognized by anybody. If object and perception are invariably conjoined, what reason would we have to conclude that one of them could exist on its own? It might look as if this argument could easily backfire, since if blue and the awareness of blue are always combined, how could we infer, as the Yogācārin does, that there is only the *mental* half of the pair? The answer to this problem is that the Yogācārin has other reasons for denying that the 'blue'/'awareness of blue' pair could be reduced to the material factor, namely the rejection of the Cārvāka assumption that matter could give rise to mind.[59] Of course, mind cannot give rise to matter either, but it can at least give rise to the erroneous appearance of matter, which is all the Yogācārin needs in order to claim that the invariable concomitance should be considered as indicating that there really only is the right half of the pair. It would be mistaken to argue that in general the invariable

[57] While particularly vivid, the appeal to different realms of existence is not essential to the example. The *Bodhicittavivaraṇa* (ascribed to Nāgārjuna) mentions the example of the body of a woman being seen as a potential lover by a man, a walking corpse by an ascetic, and something to eat by a dog (20, Lindtner 1982: 190–1).

[58] Iwata 1991. [59] Bhattacharya 2002: 603–5.

concomitance of two entities implies that there is only one of them (that the stars in the Big Dipper always occur together does not mean that there is only one star there), but the argument does not make this general claim: in the case of the Big Dipper, the individual stars can be inspected in isolation; in the case of blue and the awareness of blue this is not possible.[60]

2. Scriptural authority and the existence of material objects

A clear argument for the existence of material objects that all Buddhists must accept, it seems, is based on the fact that the Buddha himself spoke in his discourses as if such things existed. When the Buddha speaks about the absence of a substantial self, and claims that there is only the mistaken superimposition of such a self on the five *skandha*s, he seems to acknowledge that there is a mind-independent, external *rūpa-skandha*, in accordance with the common-sense view and in contradiction with the Yogācāra position that there is only mind. The Yogācārin can, of course, respond (and this is in fact what Vasubandhu does) by pointing out that such teachings are to be understood as interpretable (*neyārtha*), not as definitive (*nītārtha*), that this, that they were given in a specific context to a specific audience that would have been insufficiently equipped to deal with the full complexities of the mind-only system. For this reason the Buddha spoke to them in a mere as-if manner, playing along with their mistaken idea that external objects exist. However, a defender of the traditional interpretation of these texts might not be very impressed by this move. Why, he will ask, do we have to choose this more convoluted explanation if we can have the simpler (and therefore theoretically preferable) explanation that the Buddha meant what he said when he referred to external things? Even if the previous argument about the difficulties of inferring the existence of external objects goes through, we have still the authority of the straightforward interpretation of the Buddha's own discourses to vouch for them. At this point the Yogācārin responds that the Buddha could not have meant his talk about matter literally, since when we analyse our best theories of matter they turn out to be internally contradictory. Vasubandhu[61] points out that there is something inherently problematic about the notion of an atom, since it is both supposed to be partless and should also collectively fill up space. Yet it is unclear how this could happen. If we line up three atoms in a row, the right side of the leftmost atom and the left side of the rightmost atom do not touch, since there is the middle atom between them—this is why we have a row three atoms long. But this means that the part of the middle atom where it touches the left side of the rightmost atom, and the part where it touches the right side of the leftmost atom cannot be the same, otherwise the left and right atom *would* touch each other. But this is already to admit that the middle atom

Interpretable vs. definite teachings

Atomism as internally contradictory

Lining up three atoms

[60] Chakrabarti 1990: 34–5.

[61] *Viṃśikā* 11–14. See Kapstein 2001.

can have two separate parts, which contradicts our initial assumption that atoms are partless.

More generally, the worry is that if we put a lot of atoms of zero spatial extension together we get another thing of zero spatial extension, in which case the theory of atoms could not explain how there can be an extended world of external objects.

Atoms and optics

A related difficulty can be expressed with reference to light and shade. If one atom blocks the light falling on another atom, so that the other atom is in the shade, the shading atom will have to have a light side and a dark side, and thereby two distinct parts. For if it did not, the back of the shading atom would be as bright as the front, where the light touches it, and so the shaded atom behind it would actually be in the light. Therefore, if we postulate partless atoms it seems impossible to account for familiar optical phenomena such as shade, a consideration that counts against adopting such a theory in the first place.

Atomism cannot be a basis for epistemology

In his *Ālambanaparīkṣāvṛtti* Diṅnāga raises a different worry for the materialist supporter of atoms. First, when we see a medium-sized object such as a cup, we obviously don't see the atoms that compose it. They are too small to be seen, and in any case they all look the same, whereas what we see in the world around us does not all look the same. Do we then see an agglomeration of atoms that is a cup? The difficulty with this suggestion is that it is not entirely clear to what extent we are here dealing with an *external* object, since picking out medium-sized objects does not seem to be possible without relying on mental constructs that distinguish one collection of atoms from another. Consider a simple example. In a black-and-white dot matrix picture the image is entirely composed of black dots. The dots are all the same, and too small to be seen with the naked eye. What we see when we see part of such a picture as a cup, another as a vase, and so forth are different arrangements of these indistinguishable dots. But how do we tell which set of dots represents the cup, which the vase, and which might not represent anything at all, because it is just part of the background shading? We already have to have an image of what cups and vases look like in order to identify the cup-collection, vase-collection, and so forth in the picture. But in this case we have not come up with something perceived that is wholly external, since we rely crucially on mental images to see anything at all in the picture, rather than just random visual noise. Therefore, Diṅnāga argues, what is supposedly external (the atoms) we do not perceive, and what we do perceive (the collections) is inextricably bound up with mental, and hence internal phenomena. Diṅnāga's point is not the same as Vasubandhu's, namely, that the notion of an atom is intrinsically contradictory; rather, he wants to point out that the atomist is not able to base a satisfactory theory of how we know the world around us on his atomistic theory. The Yogācārins present a set of reasons why theories of matter (and the chief ancient Indian representatives of these were atomistic theories) cannot be worked out in a satisfactory manner. For this reason the Buddha's references to material objects cannot be taken literally, but must be considered as interpretable, as intended to work on the basis of a mistaken assumption of the existence of matter that the audience shares.

3. Perceiving material objects

We might think that the strongest argument in favour of material objects is neither the fact that they can be inferred on the basis of our best theories of the world, nor that the Buddha said that there are such things, but that we can continuously and unambiguously observe them through our senses. Yet the Yogācārin will object that such sensory experiences are possible without the existence of external objects. Suppose you believe that external objects such as a cup exist because this cup was perceived by you. Yet when you think 'I saw this cup', you are not dealing with an external object, but with a mental object, a representational form (*ākāra*), since the cup-perception is already a thing of the past and is no longer present in front of you. What about when you are presently looking at a cup? This does not help, at least as long as we accept the theory of momentariness. If all things last only for an instant, since forming perception takes time the cup-moment that caused your cup-perception no longer exists when that perception arises. Your perception always lags behind reality. Since the perception of the cup you are presently experiencing cannot link you to a presently existent thing (as that cup-moment has disappeared), and since whatever might be presently existent (the current cup-moment) is not experienced, your present perceptions are always perceptions of something merely mental. So even if experience seems to provide us with strong evidence that we are in contact with external objects, the principle of momentariness shows this to be a mistake.

Representationalist argument

The Yogācārin can therefore argue that whichever one of the three epistemic instruments inference, scriptural testimony, or perception we want to rely on in order to establish the existence of external objects, we always draw a blank, and that for this reason the position of 'mind-only' (*cittamātra*) is established.

Reality of representational forms

It is worthwhile to note at this point that there was considerable discussion within Yogācāra about the degree of reality to be ascribed to the representational forms (*ākāra*). In Indian sources we find a doxographical distinction between those schools that believe perceptual cognition to take place via representational forms (*sākāravāda*) and those that deny the place of such forms in epistemology (*nirākāravāda*).[62] Examples of the former are

[62] The reader should be aware that amongst Indian authors there was no agreement on what precisely an *ākāra* was thought to be, and which thinkers were supposed to be subsumed under terms like *sākāravāda* and *nirākāravāda* (Funayama 2007: 189–90, Seton 2015). The outline I present in the following pages provides some guidance for navigating this very intricate and often confusing section of Indian Buddhist thought. Nevertheless, I had to simplify greatly and the resulting account is, unfortunately, imperfect in a variety of respects. Still, I believe that having an imperfect map is better than having none at all.

*sākāravāda* vs. *nirākāravāda*

Sautrāntika and Yogācāra,[63] both of which consider perception to be mediated by a representational form. *Nirākāravāda* theories like Nyāya or Sarvāstivāda, on the other hand, hold that cognition can access objects directly; the content of a cognition is settled by the object, the cognition itself is without form.[64]

*satyākāravāda* vs. *alīkākāravāda*

The *sākāravāda* approach may be in turn be subdivided into two positions, depending on the view they take concerning the nature of the *ākāra*. One considers representational forms to be true (*satya*, *bden pa*), the other takes them to be false (*alīka*, *rdzun pa*).[65] What precisely this division between these two takes on representational form, *satyākāravāda* and *alīkākāravāda*, amounts to is not entirely clear.[66] It is fairly straightforward to see why a representationalist like a Sautrāntika would be considered to follow the *satyākāravāda*. For him the representational form represents the external object of perception, and the form represents the object truly or accurately.

Since the Yogācārins deny the existence of external objects, it is not immediately obvious what role the notion of the 'truth' or 'accuracy' of an *ākāra* could play for them. If there is nothing out there that the representational form represents, how could it do so more or less accurately?

Yet even a Yogācārin could claim that our perception of a grey elephant, say, is only deceptive with respect to the externality ascribed to the elephant,[67] but not with respect to the phenomenal properties of appearing as grey or appearing as an elephant. This is what a *satyākāravādin* will assert; for him the representational forms are really present in consciousness.[68] In opposition to this *satyākāravāda* interpretation of Yogācāra, the *alīkākāravāda* reading denies the accuracy of representational forms. Here the forms that appear to the mind are taken to be simply the product of delusion; they do not succeed in accurately representing anything. What is real is the reflexive awareness

[63] Even though Yogācāra is commonly classified as belonging to the *sākāravāda*, Siderits (2016: 281–2) argues that a *nirākāravāda* reading of Yogācāra may be possible. According to this reading cognition happens without recourse to an *ākāra*, while the object of cognition is still wholly mental in nature. Such a view would deny material objects, but not that the nature of the object of cognition can be independent of being cognized by a cognition.

[64] See Kajiyama 1965: 429, Della Santina 2000, Komarovski 2011: 72–84.

[65] This way of grouping the schools was adopted by the 11th-century Tibetan rNying ma scholar Rong zom chos kyi bzang po. Needless to say, Tibetan scholars did not agree on the doxographical systematization of the different theories of *ākāra* (see Almogi 2013: 1334–5).

[66] Additional confusion between the terms may be avoided by being aware that even though we cannot simply conflate *satyākāravāda* and *sākāravāda*, and *alīkākāravāda* and *nirākāravāda* (McClintock 2014: 328), some authors treat them as synonymous or use the latter terms to indicate the former distinction (Ruegg 1981a: 123; 2010: 347, Della Santina 1992; 2000: 35, n. 2.). See also Tillemans 2008: 41, n. 91. Unlike the terms *sākāravāda* and *nirākāravāda*, the terms *satyākāravāda* and *alīkākāravāda* are reconstructions from Tibetan and are not found in extant Sanskrit sources (Moriyama 2014: 431, n. 4). This does not mean, of course, that the distinction they indicate is not present in Indian sources, but simply that (at least in the texts that have come down to us) this distinction was not drawn using terms denoting specific theories or *vādas*.

[67] Moriyama 1984: 11–12. [68] Dreyfus 1997: 433.

(*svasaṃvedana*), free from perceiver and perceived representational form, an awareness which is thus a non-dual form of cognition (*advayajñāna*).[69] The diversity of representational forms is a mistaken appearance superimposed on a singular phenomenon, the reflexive awareness of consciousness.

The difference between *satyākāravāda* and *alīkākāravāda* is not concerned with the question whether representational forms exist. As both are forms of *sākāravāda*, both accept that they do. The difference concerns the truth or accuracy of these forms, a difference that is obviously not cashed out in terms of their accuracy in representing external objects, but in terms of whether or not these representational forms exist in the way they appear. Do the representational forms appearing as grey or appearing as an elephant and so on exist as entities (*dngos po*)[70] within consciousness, or do they in fact have a different nature quite distinct from appearing as grey or as an elephant?

Representational forms and the three natures

The eleventh-century scholar Bodhibhadra underlines this way of drawing the distinction between *satyākāravāda* and *alīkākāravāda* in terms of the Yogācāra theory of the three natures,[71] pointing out that the *satyākāravāda* assumes that the representational forms should be subsumed under the dependent nature (*paratantra-svabhāva*), while the *alīkākāravāda* interpretation includes them amongst the imaginary nature (*parikalpita-svabhāva*).[72] What this alignment of the two accounts of representational form with the theory of the three natures is supposed to demonstrate is that, according to the *satyākāravāda* understanding, the *ākāra* is the really existent basis for the erroneous appearance of external objects, whereas for the *alīkākāravāda* the *ākāra*, despite appearing as a mistaken projection arising from a distinct basis, is fully non-existent.[73]

The debate about the status of representational forms is interesting not only because it attracted a considerable amount of scholastic discussion in India,[74] and subsequently in Tibet, but also because, despite being *prima facie* simply an internal Yogācāra debate, it raises intriguing questions about this school's relation to Madhyamaka. We will therefore come back to this debate below, when we examine the relationship between Yogācāra and Madhyamaka in more detail.[75]

[69] Moriyama 1984: 23. For more on *svasaṃvedana* see pp. 184–5 below.

[70] Dreyfus 1997: 557. [71] See below, pp. 182–4.

[72] Moriyama 1984: 10–11, Seton 2015: 144–5.

[73] This way of understanding the distinction between *satyākāravāda* and *alīkākāravāda* of course generates a tension with the above attempt to subsume both under *sākāravāda*. We might argue that if the *alīkākāravāda's ākāra* is fully non-existent in this way, *alīkākāravāda* should be considered to be a form of *nirākāravāda*.

[74] The Indian debate involves three 10th–early 11th-century thinkers all associated with Vikramaśīla monastery, Ratnākaraśānti (one of Atiśa's teachers) defending *alīkākāravāda* and Jñānaśrīmitra and Ratnakīrti arguing in favour of *satyākāravāda*.

[75] See pp. 206–12.

Is Yogācāra a form of idealism?

We now have some idea how Yogācāra can be understood as arising out of Sautrāntika representationalism, yet we might still be unsure what *kind* of theory Yogācāra is. In fact, what exactly the Yogācāra position amounts to is still a matter of debate. One way of understanding it is simply as a denial of the *rūpa-skandha*, as the thesis that there are no material objects. Others claim that Yogācāra's aim was not primarily ontological, but that its proponents were more interested in epistemological matters and did not consider themselves to be in the business of defending a uniquely correct theory of ontology. The first interpretation is usually what one has in mind when referring to Yogācāra as a form of idealism. Whether this is an altogether fortunate choice of terminology is debatable. Yogācāra certainly shows little more than superficial similarity with an idealism of the type Berkeley defended, and has even less in common with idealism of the Hegelian variety.

Ontology vs. epistemology

On the other hand, understanding what precisely the non-idealist understanding of Yogācāra amounts to is no straightforward matter.[76] The best interpretation of this reading seems to be the claim that Yogācāra authors were not seeking to prove the ontological statement that there are no material objects, but simply wanted to establish the epistemological statement that we have no good evidence for assuming that there are any such things. It seems, however, as if the gulf between the idealist and these non-idealist interpretations is not as wide as the authors of the latter assume. It is, after all, fairly easy to move from the epistemological to the ontological claim by appealing to principles that the ancient Indian authors were well aware of.

The 'lack of evidence' principle

If we focus on Vasubandhu and the *Viṃśikā*, which contains a particularly popular exposition of the *cittamātra* position, we can fruitfully compare the argument given there with the same author's rejection of a substantial person (*pudgala*) in the ninth chapter of his *Abhidharmakośabhāṣya*.[77] What Vasubandhu does there is to investigate various ways in which we could look for the person, and if there was a person we would expect it to show up. Perception and inference being our chief means of epistemic access to the world, a substantial self should be either perceivable or inferable. And if, as Vasubandhu's co-religionists do, we regard the Buddha's teachings as authoritative, his references to persons should establish their existence.

But because the self is neither perceivable and inferable, as Vasubandhu shows in detail, and because the Buddha's teachings in this respect need to be understood in relation to the specific context in which they were made, there is no route through epistemic instruments that leads to the self. If we are justified in concluding that Vasubandhu's position in the *Abhidharmakośabhāṣya* is

[76] Some contemporary authors who defend a non-idealist reading of Yogācāra include Kochumuttom 1982, Hayes 1988, Oetke 1992, and Lusthaus 2002.

[77] See Kellner and Taber 2014 for a sustained discussion of this comparison.

that there is no substantial self, can we not similarly conclude that, at least in the *Viṃśikā*, he wants to defend the position that there are no external objects? After all, in this text Vasubandhu points out that the various ways in which our epistemic instruments appear to provide evidence for external objects do not actually provide any evidence at all. By appeal to the principle that we are justified to infer that there is no *x* if there is no evidence for *x*, we are able to move from the epistemological reading of Yogācāra to the ontological interpretation.[78]

The principle of lightness

A second principle that can help us to bridge this gap is an appeal to the principle of lightness (*lāghava*). This principle says that if we are faced with two conflicting theories that explain the same facts, but one makes fewer ontological assumptions than the other, we should choose the former. In the *Viṃśikā*, Vasubandhu points out that even if we drop the assumption of external objects, we can still explain everything that the believer in such objects can explain. The Yogācārin's theory is therefore the lighter one, as it only assumes one kind of object (namely mental objects), while his opponent has to assume that there are two kinds of object, mental and physical ones. So metatheoretical principles such as the principle of lightness suggest that the epistemic statement that there is nothing in our experience properly understood that points towards the existence of external objects can be used to justify an ontological claim. This is the claim that a theory of the world that does not entail the existence of external objects is preferable.

Non-idealist interpretations and philosophical *zeitgeist*

It therefore looks as if the non-idealist interpretation, when made sufficiently precise, can lead to the idealist interpretation by appeal to some plausible and historically attested philosophical principles. It is interesting to speculate why the non-idealist interpretations are so popular in contemporary Western discussions of Yogācāra. One cannot help but suspect that this is a product of the philosophical *zeitgeist*. Idealism is, to understate matters, a minority position in contemporary philosophy. So it might appear as if there is a certain hesitation in attributing to the ancient Indian thinkers a philosophical position that seems to be so thoroughly discredited.[79] We might even support this by reference to the maxim of charity: if we should provide historical philosophical texts with the strongest reading possible, that is, interpret them in such a way that the arguments they make come out sound, should we not avoid reading the Yogācāra texts in a straightforwardly idealist manner?

[78] Of course this principle has to be qualified. The early Indian materialists argued against the existence of future lives by appeal to the same principle, saying that there is no perceptual evidence for them (see Preisendanz 1994: 530). This argument did not find much favour amongst Indian thinkers. There clearly are various things that we cannot perceive yet which still exist (the room behind the wall, subatomic particles, etc.). We therefore have to exclude that the non-perception is not simply due to some kind of obstruction between us and the object, or due to our sensory limitations, and we have to extend the reach of our argument to all the epistemic instruments to enable the non-evidence argument to carry substantial argumentative weight.

[79] Compare Schmithausen 2005: 49.

Wrong appeal to the maxim of charity

But a moment's reflection reveals that this idea, if it really is what motivates non-idealist interpretations of Yogācāra, is mistaken, and that its appeal to the maxim of charity is flawed. The principle does not suggest that we interpret historical philosophical texts according to whatever is the philosophical flavour of the day. Rather, once we have determined (by considering the text itself together with its cultural context) what position it is setting out to support, we reconstruct its arguments in such a way that they give the strongest possible support for that position. It would be very peculiar if the fact that contemporary philosophy is not particularly interested in idealism should have any bearing on what we think specific Indian authors wanted to establish when they composed their texts. The maxim of charity is useful when reconstructing individual arguments, but not when trying to determine what a text's overall position is likely to be.

Absence of explicit denial of material objects

Yet there remains one fact about early Yogācāra texts that needs explaining, and this may well have acted as a motivation for various non-idealist interpretations as well. The early Yogācāra authors do not say explicitly that there are no material objects.[80] Considering Vasubandhu's *Viṃśikā* as an example, we do not find him saying directly that there is no matter, but that there is only mind. Even his argument for the impossibility of atomism need not be understood as 'a metaphysical assertion of a transcendent reality consisting of "mind-only"', but can be taken merely as 'a practical injunction to suspend judgment' concerning the existence of anything beyond the perception.[81]

Ultimate reality only knowable through meditation

Why are the early Yogācārins such as Vasubandhu not more explicit in pointing out that they are making an ontological claim, rejecting the existence of matter, and postulating only mental objects in its place? One possibility is that this reticence is ultimately due to the belief that the true nature of reality can only be known through meditation. If there are aspects of the theory of mind-only that cannot be known in a purely discursive manner,[82] it is understandable that Yogācāra writers did not present their theory in a way that would convey the appearance that the proof of a specific ontological claim was all that was at issue.

[80] Though it is worthwhile in this context to ask how explicit 'explicit' has to be. Kellner and Taber (2014: 718–19) note that '[i]t is likely that any statement to the effect that "we are not aware of external objects", and possibly even any statement to the effect that "there are no external objects", will be able to be construed *phenomenologically*, as pertaining just to our experience, i.e., as meaning that *the things we are experiencing* are not external, physical objects, and not *ontologically*, as denying that there are material objects outside of consciousness . . .' If not even the explicit statement 'there are no external objects' could not rule out the non-idealist interpretation one may well wonder what would.

[81] Hayes 1988: 100, quoting Hall 1986: 18.

[82] It is obvious that there are, for Buddhism consistently distinguishes between the *intellectual insight* into a proposition and its *realization* at the experiential level (see Kellner and Taber 2014: 747–8).

Commenting on verse 10 of the *Viṃśikā*, Vasubandhu points out that the emptiness of all things (*dharma-nairātmya*) is to be understood as having an indescribable essence known only by enlightened beings,[83] and he concludes the work by saying that the notion of mind-only 'is not conceivable in all aspects, but is the Buddha's domain'.[84] One way of understanding this is by considering the Yogācāra arguments against matter, such as those found in the *Viṃśikā*, as having primarily the negative purpose of clearing away the wrong view of what *dharmas* are like, namely, that there is a sharp distinction between the mental and the physical, and between the perceiving subject and the perceived object. Yogācāra arguments examine the various reasons we could give for why external objects exist, and the theories we develop about the existence of these objects, and show that the reasons do not justify our beliefs and that the theories are intrinsically problematic. This, however, does not lead to a kind of sceptical position where we have just refuted the claim that we have any knowledge of external objects, and must now suspend judgment about their real nature. Instead, the Yogācārin holds that once the erroneous conceptions of reality have been cleared away, meditative practice will provide an avenue to gain a realization of their true nature. This, it seems, could be at least one of the reasons why the early Yogācāra texts are not as explicit about stating claims concerning the non-existence of external objects as we might expect. True philosophical insight, the Buddhist philosophers hold, does not come from studying a philosophical treatise, understanding its arguments, refuting objections, and assenting to its conclusions. What is at issue is the transformation of the way the world appears to us in our experience, not just of the way in which we think about the world that appears to us. Once again it has become clear that, in trying to understand Buddhist philosophy in India, we cannot just focus on the arguments and the doctrinal texts containing ideas that the arguments support and develop. We also have to take into account the dimension of meditative practice that such arguments and the views they defend are connected to. Only by being aware of this additional, extra-argumentative factor influencing Buddhist thought can we hope to develop a nuanced understanding of the positions the texts themselves defend.

Yogācāra arguments clearing away the wrong belief in matter

### *b.* ālayavijñāna *and the eight types of consciousness*

Yogācāra divides consciousness (*vijñāna*) into eight kinds (two more than most other Buddhist schools), five correlated with the sense powers, as well as thinking, namely visual consciousness (*cakṣur-vijñāna*), auditory consciousness (*śrotra-vijñāna*), olfactory consciousness (*ghrāṇa-vijñāna*), gustatory conscioueness (*jiḥva-vijñāna*), tactual consciousness (*kaya-vijñāna*), and mental

[83] *anabhilāpyenātmanā yo buddhānāṃ viṣaya*, Ruzsa and Szegedi 2015: 145.
[84] Verse 22: *sarvathā sā tu na cintyā buddhagocaraḥ*, Ruzsa and Szegedi 2015: 157.

consciousness (*mano-vijñāna*). In addition there is the defiled mind (*kliṣṭamanas*), and the foundational consciousness (*ālayavijñāna*). These eight kinds of consciousness are correlated with meditative states insofar as they gradually drop away as higher levels of meditative absorption are realized. The first five are obviously dependent on the various kinds of sensory data that constitute their objects. Mental consciousness arises continuously, except in special mental states such as deep sleep, coma, or deep meditative states such as the meditative absorption without perception (*asaṃjñisamāpatti*). Only after having attained the further state of meditative absorption without perception (*nirodhasamāpatti*), a state in which meditators are said to remain in a kind of suspended animation, unperturbed by blazing fires or dangerous animals approaching, will the defiled mind disappear as well. The foundational consciousness persists through all of these states.

Disappearance of consciousness in meditative states

The defiled mind

The defiled mind is directed at the foundational consciousness and mistakenly conceives of it as a self. By doing so it generates a split between the self as the subject and the various other phenomena as objects, and takes over the first six types of consciousness, with the result that their deliverances are also conceived of in terms of subject and object. As such it is the ultimate cause of the various unhealthy mental attitudes directed at the self, and thereby the cause of our continuous existence in saṃsāra. It only ceases once the meditator has attained the state of an *arhat*.

The foundational consciousness: explanatory benefits

1. Meditation and the continuity of consciousness

The eighth type of consciousness, the foundational consciousness, is an intriguing concept that brings with it a variety of theoretical benefits. First, the foundational consciousness makes it possible to explain how specific states of deep meditative absorption in which all sense consciousness and all thinking are said to cease are still a kind of conscious state. The state of *nirodhasamāpatti* ('attainment of cessation') is at the heart of the problem here. For if intentional mental events cease during this kind of absorption, and if consciousness is considered to be nothing but a chain of mental events, one causing the next, it is unclear how consciousness can ever get restarted once the meditator emerges out of the meditative state. The first successive mental event does not appear to have a predecessor that could have caused it. The idea of a continuing foundational consciousness can solve this problem.[85] As the foundational consciousness continues to run in the background, though all intentional mental events have ceased, in the post-meditative state new mental events can simply arise from it. Recent authors have argued that the full-blown notion of a foundational consciousness would not have been necessary for Yogācārins to account for the continuation of consciousness after *nirodhasamāpatti*. Buescher[86] introduces an idea with the rather cumbersome name

[85] For more on this see Schmithausen 1987. [86] Buescher 2008: 51–3.

'bi-polar *bīja*-model'.[87] According to this, sense-faculties and consciousness (*vijñāna*) can stand in a mutually causal relationship where they 'exist potentially within each other, with the capacity mutually to effect each other's re-arisal, or re-actualization, after the functional presence of any one of them had been interrupted for more or less extended periods of time'. The sensory organism produces consciousness when encountering sensory objects, but this organism also has the latent potentiality (*bīja*) for consciousness residing within it, so that once the meditator emerges from *nirodhasamāpatti* cognitive experiences can re-arise because the meditator's body is still present.

The 'bi-polar *bīja*-model'

Interestingly, the underlying idea of mutual causality (*sahabhūhetu*), found in the Sarvāstivāda Abhidharma,[88] where one item causes another, and the other causes the first (as the legs of a tripod keep each other standing up), is criticized by Vasubandhu in the *Abhidharmakośabhāṣya*, where he sets out to establish that causation only flows in one direction. It is interesting to speculate[89] that if Vasubandhu had already held Yogācāra views when composing the *Abhidharmakośabhāṣya*[90] he might have used this argument in support of the theory of foundational consciousness as the only satisfactory way of accounting for the continuation of consciousness after *nirodhasamāpatti*.[91]

2. Transmigration and karma

Second, once the Sarvāstivāda theory of the existence of the three times has been done away with, Buddhists obviously needed some way of accounting for the way the transmigration of consciousness and the law of karmic causality works. If consciousness is momentary, how can one mind take rebirth in a new body? And if the past mind-moment that has acted on a specific intention no longer exists, why does a later mind-moment manifest as an experience of the consequences of this intention? The notion of the foundational consciousness provides a way of accounting for both at the same time. It functions as a repository in which karmic seeds (*bīja*) can be deposited at the time of action, and from which they manifest once the result has ripened. Of course, since the foundational consciousness is as momentary as everything else, what we are really looking at here is a staccato succession of moments of foundational consciousness, each one causing the next. The entire collection of karmic seeds is (so to speak) copied onto each successive moment of foundational consciousness, as each gives rise to its following moment. Once a seed ripens in the foundational consciousness it leads to a perception in which the foundational consciousness splits into one part that is perceived as an external object, and

87 Buescher 2008: 53.

88 See Bhikkhu Dhammajoti 2003, 2009: 154–5, Tanaka 1985: 91–111, Ronkin 2005: 217.

89 Gold 2015a: 261–2, n. 69.

90 As is argued by Kritzer 2005.

91 Note, however, that the notion of simultaneous causation is accepted by several Yogācāra authors, such as Asaṅga (Bhikkhu Dhammajoti 2009: 159–60) and Digṅāga (Tola and Dragonetti 2004 46–9, n. 10) and plays an important role in Yogācāra thought, where *the ālayavijñāna* and *bīja* are considered as being related by simultaneous causation. See Bhikkhu Dhammajoti 2009: 121–3.

another that is perceived as a substantially existent subject that perceives the object. This response based on a subject/object duality leads to the deposition of further karmic seeds in the foundational consciousness which will ripen at a later time.

It is therefore evident that the theory of the eight types of consciousness is both motivated by meditative concerns, corresponding to a hierarchy of states of consciousness with varying degrees of subtlety, and explaining the continuity of consciousness after states of deep meditative absorption, as well as by doctrinal considerations, namely the need to explain the transmission of karmic seeds.

### c. trisvabhāva

Another highly important conceptual distinction within Yogācāra is that between the 'three natures' (*trisvabhāva*). It is discussed at length in the *Saṃdhinirmocanasūtra*, and Vasubandhu devotes one of his best-known works, the *Trisvabhāvanirdeśa*, exclusively to this topic. Given the very explicit rejection of the very idea of *svabhāva* by Madhyamaka, it might be surprising that Yogācāra is going to adopt not just one but three different forms of *svabhāva*. In fact, however, the theory of the three *svabhāva*s can be better understood as a theory of three ways in which *svabhāva* can be absent.[92] The three natures are the imputed nature (*parikalpita-svabhāva*), the dependent nature (*paratantra-svabhāva*), and the perfected nature (*pariniṣpanna-svabhāva*). A common way of explaining the distinction between them is by reference to a mirage seen in the desert. The imputed nature corresponds to the water the deluded traveller sees, while the dependent nature corresponds to what underlies the illusory appearance: a combination of air at different temperatures and light-waves refracted by it. The perfected nature is simply the fact that there is no real water anywhere in the combination of causal factors that underlies the illusory appearance.

Mirage example

Three kinds of absence

It is thereby evident that, far from postulating three kinds of substances (*svabhāva*), Yogācāra describes three kinds of absences. The imputed nature (the water) is simply not there, it is a mistaken superimposition of a subject/object duality, heavily reliant on linguistic conceptualization, and is wholly non-existent. The dependent nature is there, but it is not what it seems. Instead of water there is something else there, in our example a nexus of interdependent causal factors involving air and light that have nothing to do with water.

[92] See *Trisvabhāvanirdeśa* 26: 'The three natures are characterized as non-dual and as without support, because of the non-existence [of one], because of [the other's] non-existence like that [in the way it appears], [the third] is the nature of the non-existence [of one in the other]', *trayo 'pyete svabhāvā hi advayālambalakṣaṇāḥ | abhāvād atathābhāvāt tad-abhāva-svabhāvataḥ* (Anacker 2002: 465).

The illusory appearance is absent from it. The perfected nature, finally, is the fact that there is no imputed nature in the dependent nature. This, too, should not be conceptualized as a substantially existent thing (or even a substantially existent nature of the world), since its existence essentially involves a mistaken projection of something non-existent. We only need the concept of the perfected nature because we have the erroneous idea of an imputed nature in the first place.[93]

Three natures and two truths

The Yogācāra concept of the three natures can be fruitfully compared to the Madhyamaka notion of the two truths. Both sets of distinction are proposed in order to conceptualize the difference between the world as it appears to us, as possessing intrinsic nature, and the world as it is seen to be once analysed by the Buddhists' arguments, namely empty. While they share a common purpose, seeing how these two distinctions are supposed to line up is less straightforward. One way of comparing them is by identifying the conventional truth with the imagined nature and the ultimate truth with the dependent nature, with the perfected nature being simply a fact about the relation between the two, that is, the fact the conventionally imputed truth is in fact nowhere to be found once analysis investigating the ultimate truth is applied. This would be a way of understanding the Yogācāra distinction very much along Madhyamaka lines. We could equally argue that the three natures manage to fill a conceptual gap in the Madhyamaka picture of the two truths, particularly when understood in a semantic non-dualist way where it is assumed that the only truth there really is is the conventional truth. The three natures would instead present an account according to which there is a basis of appearance (the dependent nature) that exists conventionally, as well as an inconceivable ultimate reality (the perfected nature). In this way the Yogācārin can respond to what he considers the conceptually problematic non-foundationalist assumption of the Mādhyamika that it is 'appearances all the way down'. The appearances themselves (the imagined nature) can be considered to be strictly non-existent, but this does not have to entail that there cannot be a sufficiently real conventional nature that grounds all appearances, though it is not itself an appearance.

Three natures from a Madhyamaka perspective

Two truths from a Yogācāra perspective

Three further important concepts we should mention at this point are the idea of the reflexivity of consciousness (*svasaṃvedana*), the Yogācāra conceptualization of the structure of the Buddha's teaching as described in the

[93] In the *Trisvabhāvanirdeśa* Vasubandhu uses a different example, that of an elephant conjured into existence by a magician who speaks a *mantra* on a piece of wood, letting it appear as an elephant. In this example the imagined nature corresponds to the non-existent elephant seen, the dependent nature to the magic trick that brings it into existence, and the perfected nature to the absence of the elephant. The *mantra* corresponds to the *ālyavijñāna* and the wood to reality as such (*tathātā*). See Garfield 2002.

framework of the three turnings of the wheel of the doctrine, and the notion of Buddha-nature, or *tathāgatagarbha*.

### *d.* svasaṃvedana

The notion of *svasaṃvedana* denotes the ability of conscious states not only to be aware of the object of the state (as when our visual consciousness perceives something coloured red, for example), but at the same time of the conscious experience itself.[94] It is important to note that *svasaṃvedana*, or reflexive awareness, is not the same as introspective awareness aiming to observe one's own mental states.[95] If I drink a cup of tea and think 'I am now tasting the tea', I exercise introspective awareness. This awareness comes and goes, and in most cases our perceptions are not accompanied by a meta-level commentary of what is currently going on in our mind. Reflexive awareness, on the other hand, is always present when there is an object-directed instance of consciousness. It is considered to be what makes the consciousness of some object conscious in the first place,[96] and is also associated by some interpreters with the phenomenological quality, the 'what-it's-likeness' of an episode of consciousness.[97]

No fundamental division between minds

Yogācāra requires this idea of the reflexivity of consciousness since it denies the existence of external objects. If there is no apple the perception of an apple could be a perception of, the perception must ultimately be directed at a mental thing. For this reason, one mental object (the perceptive event) is directed at another one (the seemingly external apple). And as there is ultimately no distinction between different mental streams, one corresponding to me, one to the apple, this must be a case of the mind being directed at itself.[98] Once the fact that the superimposition of the subject/object duality is a mere superimposition is realized, the practitioner becomes aware that what he previously regarded as the perception of external things has in fact an underlying non-dual nature where the mind directly knows itself.

Of course, the fact that the Yogācāra denial of external objects requires the reflexivity of consciousness is not an argument for it unless we are already convinced of the truth of the Yogācāra position. Later Yogācāra authors therefore tried to develop arguments for reflexivity that did not rely on specific Yogācāra premises.

Diṅnāga presents several arguments aimed at establishing that each cognitive event is simultaneously aware of itself,[99] instead of suggesting (as the

[94] The existence of *svasaṃvedana* becomes a major point of contention in later Tibetan elaborations of Indian thought. See Williams 1998, Garfield 2006.

[95] Williams 1998: 7. See also Matilal 1986: 148.

[96] Śāntarakṣita (*Tattvasaṃgraha* 2021) argues that if an act of consciousness of some object $x$ was not reflexively self-aware, it could also not be conscious of $x$ (Jha 1991: 2. 1032).

[97] Ram-Prasad 2007: 54.

[98] Ram-Prasad 2007: 69–70.

[99] Kellner 2010: 210.

Naiyāyikas did) that reflexivity could be accounted for by appealing to a *second*, higher-order mental state that is aware of the first state.

Diṅnāga's regress argument

The first argument focuses on a straightforward infinite regress.[100] If a mental state becomes conscious by being the object of second-order state, we will then want to know what makes this second state conscious. For if it is not conscious itself, and therefore not cognitively available to us, the content of this second-order state, namely the first-order state, would not be available to us either. But then we need to assume the existence of a third-order state, and so on, without a chance of ever completing the chain in order to make any of the states in the chain conscious. In order to break the chain we have to assume that it is the first-order mental state itself that makes it cognitively available to us via its reflexive nature.

Diṅnāga's memory argument

Diṅnāga's second argument combines considerations of an infinite regress with references to memory.[101] Assume, for *reductio*, that there was a mental event M of me cognizing the teacup, as well as another, distinct event M*, of me cognizing me cognizing the teacup (i.e. cognizing M). For Diṅnāga these two mental events cannot happen at the same time, so when M* occurs, M* must involve M as a memory.

Now it seems fairly uncontroversial that you can only remember what you have experienced at an earlier time,[102] otherwise you are just dealing with a pseudo-memory, with a psychological illusion. M* is supposed to be the memory of your cognizing the teacup at an earlier time. But at that time your experience was not that of *cognizing* a teacup, it was just an experience of a teacup. The example seems to demand that you remember something that you did not experience. In order to fix this, we would have to assume that there was another mental event, M', between M and M*, where this is the event of experiencing cognizing the teacup, and the content of the memory at M*. But the relation between M and M' is just the same as the one between M and M* used to be, and we would have to insert another event, M'', between the two in order to ensure that M' is actually an act of memory. This procedure is obviously unending, and for that very reason unsatisfactory. Memory can only reproduce experiences we have had, but is not able to move our cognitions to a higher order. If all we had at time *t* is the experience of a teacup, no later memory will turn this into an experience of cognizing a teacup.

Since the higher-order view of cognition leads to an infinite regress, Diṅnāga argues that the only way we can account for the cognition of cognition is by assuming that one act of cognition can do both, cognize an object and cognize itself as well.[103]

[100] Hayes 1988: 141. [101] Kellner 2011: 414–16. [102] Matilal 1986: 153.

[103] In his criticism of the notion of *svasaṃvedana* Śaṅkara also refers to an infinite regress resulting from each cognition being cognized by another, but resolves it not by cognitions

### e. *Three turnings*

Yogācāra texts conceptualize the range of the Buddha's teaching in terms of three set of discourses, or 'turnings of the wheel of the doctrine' (*dharma-cakra-pravartana*). According to the *Saṃdhinirmocanasūtra*, the first contained the doctrine of the four noble truths (*catuḥsatya*) and comprises the teachings found in the non-Mahāyāna *sūtras*. The second, the 'wheel of signlessness' (*alakṣaṇa*), includes the teachings of emptiness in the Perfection of Wisdom texts that form the basis of the Madhyamaka, and the third, the 'wheel of good differentiation' (*suvibhakta*) or 'wheel for ascertaining the ultimate' (*paramārtha-viniścaya*), taught the doctrine of the three natures (*trisvabhāva*) characteristic of Yogācāra. The three turnings, which correspond to the sequence in which the corresponding texts appeared in the history of Buddhism, are also considered to represent an ascent in terms of philosophical sophistication and authoritativeness. The first two turnings belong to the interpretable teachings of the Buddha (*neyārtha*), while the final one is definitive (*nītārtha*). This is an example of a kind of doxographical framework extremely widespread in Indian philosophy, which simultaneously allows for the comprehensive description of an entire body of teachings (all teachings of the Buddha are supposed to find their place somewhere in this system) and lets the system that stands behind the description come out on top. Needless to say, Madhyamaka authors who adopt the system of the three turnings regard the second turning as definitive, and the other two as aimed at disciples endowed with less penetrating intellects, even though this means losing the ability of correlating philosophical sophistication with the order in which the teachings appeared.

Historical and philosophical sequence

### f. tathāgatagarbha *and Yogācāra*

It would be mistaken to regard the notion of the *tathāgatagarbha*, the 'essence' or 'womb' or 'container' (*garbha*) of the 'Thus-gone' (*tathāgata*), the Buddha, as a specific Yogācāra concept. The idea that there is a potential in all sentient beings to become a Buddha is rather a pan-Mahāyānist notion that is taken up by Buddhist philosophers across different schools.[104] There are, nevertheless, sufficiently many connections between this concept and the Yogācāra school to discuss it at this place. The concept is brought up in key Yogācāra texts such as the *Laṅkāvatārasūtra*, where it is identified with the foundational

cognizing themselves, but by reference to a witnessing self (*sākṣin*), an uncognized cognizer that terminates the regress of cognitions. See Śaṅkara's *bhāṣya* on *Brahmasūtra* II.2.28 (Darling 2007: 314–17).

[104] Within the Indian (and Tibetan) Buddhist tradition it does not make much explanatory sense to consider the *tathāgatagarbha* theory as a separate philosophical school. Things were different in Chinese Buddhism, where the *tathāgatagarbha* texts were sometimes regarded as the *fourth* turning after the three distinguished by Yogācāra. See Williams 2009: 103.

consciousness (*ālayavijnāna*).[105] The *sūtra* describes it in terms of a well-known acquatic metaphor:

> A great ocean's waves roll on continously, its body [i.e. the *ālayavijnāna*] is uninterrupted, free from the fault of impermanence, disassociated from a view of a self, perpetually pure in its substance.[106]

One of the central texts of the *tathāgatagarbha* theory, the *Ratnagotravibhāga*,[107] a text probably dating from the fourth century CE,[108] is regarded in the Tibetan tradition as one of the 'five works' that Maitreya revealed to Asaṅga; Asaṅga composed a commentary to it, the *Mahāyāna-uttara-tantra-śāstra-vyākhyā*. Furthermore, the notion of the *tathāgatagarbha* lines up more naturally with the characterization of ultimate reality we find in Yogācāra than with that we find in Madhyamaka. The latter's characterization of ultimate reality in terms of emptiness is a primarily negative one, it describes it in terms of what is not there (a substantially existent core, *svabhāva*),[109] while the former's is more positive, postulating a foundational consciousness that is the source of all appearance.

Conceptual predecessors of the concept of *tathāgatagarbha*

As with all concepts that rose to any prominence within Buddhist philosophy in India, that of the *tathāgatagarbha* has conceptual predecessors in the early Buddhist sources, predecessors that can be regarded as seeds that later sprouted into the diversity of concepts and theories that characterize Buddhist thought in India.

Natural purity of mind

One of these predecessors is the idea of the natural purity of mind that continues to exist in a defiled state. Versions of this can already be found in the early Buddhist *suttas*, when Buddha advises that 'this mind is luminous, O monks, but it is defiled by adventitious defilements'.[110] This can be understood as saying that luminosity is an inner or intrinsic property of the mind, to the extent that it illuminates or makes known the objects that are before the mind. Despite the fact that this luminosity is part of the mind's inner nature, it can be temporally impeded by factors such as the defilements that block its manifestation.[111] It is evident how this can be developed into the idea of an enlightened potential, or even a fully formed enlightened mind constituting the

[105] Suzuki 1932: 203.

[106] *mahodadhitaraṃgavannityamavyucchinnaśarīraḥ pravartate anityatādoṣarahita ātmavādavinivṛtto 'tyantaprakṛtipariśuddhaḥ*, Vaidya 1963: 90. See Suzuki 1932: 190, Red Pine 2012: 241.

[107] Holmes and Holmes 1985.

[108] Frauwallner 1956: 255 dates the text to the middle of the 3rd century CE. Despite the relatively early date of this text, the *tathāgatagarbha* theory only rose to greater philosophical prominence in India at a later time, around the 11th century (Williams 2009: 101).

[109] Takazaki 1974 argues that *tathāgatagarbha* theory has in fact arisen in opposition to the Madhyamaka theory of emptiness. See de Jong 1979: 585.

[110] *Aṅguttaranikāya* 1.10: *pabhassaram idaṃ bhikkhave cittaṃ tañ ca kho āgantukehi upakkilesehi upakkiliṭṭhaṃ*, Bikkhu Bodhi 2012: 97, Harvey 1995: 166–79, 217–26.

[111] For a version of this interpretation see Bikkhu Bodhi 2012: 1598.

core of all sentient beings, present even though their current status in cyclic existence means that this core is almost entirely hidden.

'transformation of the basis'

More specifically, in the Yogācāra context we find the idea that the eradication of defilements (*kleśa*) required for obtaining liberation brings with it a 'transformation of the basis' (*āśraya-parāvṛtti*). There are different ways of understanding what this 'transformation' amounts to. It is sometimes said to consist of the elimination (*prahīṇa*) of the foundational consciousness that contains the karmic potentialities responsible for the continued appearance of cyclic existence.[112] Sometimes the focus is on the eradication of the latent badness (*dauṣṭhulya*) inherent in the *ālayavijñāna* itself, and if the *ālayavijñāna* is seen as more than simply another term for this collection of bad potentialities,[113] we can conceive of the emergence of an understanding of the 'transformation of the basis' as one according to which the defilements and unwholesome karmic seeds contained in the *ālayavijñāna* are removed,[114] leaving behind an undefiled consciousness (*amalavijñāna*).[115] It is only a short step from this to the idea that an originally pure nature of the mind was present all along, and that bringing this nature to light is what liberation consists in.

*tathāgatagarbha* as a substitute self

A second predecessor of the *tathāgatagarbha* theory are attempts[116] to introduce a kind of substitute self, an entity that escapes the criticism of the Buddha's no-self theory but is at the same time robust enough to fulfil some of the theoretical roles sometimes played by the self. The Pudgalavāda's *pudgala* and the Yogācāra's *ālayavijñāna* can be seen as two similar attempts that go in the same direction. The *Mahāparinirvāṇasūtra*[117] explicitly identifies the *tathāgatagarbha* with the *ātman*,[118] and states that the *ātman* is real:

All things are not without self. The self is real, it is permanence, it is a [positive] quality, it is unchanging, it is firm, it is peace; thus, like the good milk remedy of the physician the Tathāgata also teaches in accordance with reality.[119]

[112] Schmithausen 1987: 499–500, n. 1337; King 1998: 5–17, 8.

[113] Unlike, for example, its portrayal in verse 18 of Vasubandhu's *Triṃśikā*: 'Consciousness is just all the seeds, and transformation takes place in such and such a way, according to a reciprocal influence, in which such and such a type of discrimination may arise', *sarvabījaṃ hi vijñānaṃ pariṇāmastathā tathā | yātyanyonyavaśād yena vikalpaḥ sa sa jāyate* (Anacker 2002: 423).

[114] Conze 1962: 230. [115] Radich 2008.

[116] See above, pp. 59–60.

[117] Habata 2013. This is a Mahāyāna text quite distinct from the *Mahāparinibbānasutta* preserved in the Pāli canon; see Radich 2015.

[118] 'the self is the nature of the Tathāgata', *bdag ces bya ba ni de bzhin gshegs pa'i snying po'i don to*, Habata 2013: sections 375–6.

[119] *chos thams cad ni bdag med pa yang ma yin te | bdag ni de kho na nyid do || bdag ni brtag ban yid do || bdag ni yon tan nyid do || bdag ni ther zug pa nyid do || bdag ni brtan pa nyid do || bdag ni zhi ba nyid do zhes sman pa bzang po'i 'o ma bzhin du de bzhin gshegs pa yang de kho na nyid dang ldan pa ston par mdzad do*, Habata 2013: section107.

Statements such as this are somewhat baffling in the light of the Buddhist non-self doctrine that explicitly denies the existence of a self. Such endorsements of a substantial self are qualified to some extent in texts like the *Śrīmālādevī-siṃhanādasūtra*, where it is pointed out that this 'self' is different from that postulated by other non-Buddhists. Nevertheless, the introduction of self-related terminology in the *tathāgatagarbha* texts remains puzzling.[120]

The *tathāgata-garbha* and the acceptance of an *ātman*

While we may not be able to resolve this puzzle altogether, two things are nevertheless worth noting. The first is the fact that the key *tathāgatagarbha* texts arose during the time of the Gupta empire (*c.*320–550 CE), a period sometimes described as the 'golden age' of India, marked by important developments in many fields commonly regarded as classical brahmanic culture. While it would be certainly too crude to explain the whole *tathāgatagarbha* theory as a kind of metaphysical 'keeping up with the Joneses', supplying Buddhism with a notion of self that its brahmanic critics might have seen as lacking, the texts themselves raise the point that the *tathāgatagarbha* theory was taught in order to convert non-Buddhists who would otherwise be scared off by the seemingly nihilistic character of a theory that does not allow for an *ātman* in whatever form. To this extent the teaching of Buddha-nature can be interpreted as yet another instance of expedient means (*upāya*), a teaching that aims at producing the intended result for a specific audience, not one that faithfully mirrors a transcendent reality.

In any case, the relationship of influence between Buddhist and brahmanical concepts is an intricate one, and one that in all likelihood was not one-way. While it may have been the case that a historical and intellectual context (such as India during the Gupta period) in which theories according a central place to the notion of an *ātman* were successful and well developed brought about the development of specific ideas already present in the Buddhist teaching, and resulted in something like the *tathāgatagarbha* teaching, it is also likely that there were statements within the Buddhist teachings that triggered developments in classical Indian thought.[121] One example of this may be Gauḍapāda's seventh-century commentary on the *Māṇḍūkya Upaniṣad*, one of the earliest texts on Advaita Vedānta. This is often considered to show 'a marked propensity for Buddhist arguments and terminology', being specifically influenced by ideas found in Madhyamaka texts.[122]

Positions that appear to conflict with the Buddha's teachings

Second, the embracing of the notion of the *ātman* by some *tathāgatagarbha* texts can be seen as part of a larger group of doctrines that arise at prominent positions at different points of the development of Buddhist philosophy in India, doctrines that appear to take up views directly opposite to those the Buddha taught. These include doctrines that seem to conflict with the Buddha's

[120] For further discussion see Jones 2014. [121] Ruegg 1989. [122] King 1997: 140.

Substantial self

rejection of the view of substantial existence (*astivāda*), in particular the rejection of the existence of the *ātman*. Some of the *tathāgatagarbha* texts are particularly clear examples, but the Pudgalavādin's *pudgala* and the Yogācārin's foundational consciousness can equally be regarded as attempts to reintroduce some kind of substantial entity into the void that the non-self teaching has left behind.

Nihilism

At the other extreme are the positions that appear to embrace nihilism (*nāstivāda*), which the Buddha also rejected. Mādhyamika philosophers have frequently been accused of being guilty of nihilistic tendencies,[123] but similar claims can also be found in Mahāyāna *sūtras*. The *Samādhirājasūtra*, for example, records the teachings of a Buddha called Abhāva ('non-existence'):

> As soon as he was born, he proclaimed, risen to the skies, the non-existence of all the dharmas.... And as many as there were sounds in that world, so manifold was the utterance of this Tathāgata, Leader of the world: 'All, indeed, is non-existent, nothing is existent.'[124]

Antinomian injunctions

Finally, we find ethical claims that appear to clash directly with the pronouncements in early Buddhist sources. These are frequently found in tantric texts; the following passage from chapter 2 of the *Hevajratantra* is not uncharacteristic:[125]

> [The bodhisattva] Vajragarbha said: 'What usage and observance should one follow?' The Lord replied:
>
> 'You should slay living beings,
> you should speak lying words,
> you should take what is not given,
> you should frequent others' wives.'

These doctrines were obviously not intended as refutations of the Buddhist positions, but as forms of the Buddha's teaching, in fact usually as a way of expressing its true intent. Yet in view of such very different understandings of what the Buddha's teaching was, some way of restoring consistency has to be found. An obvious way is to declare the texts in question mistaken and non-Buddhist. This strategy was comparatively rare. A more common strategy is to argue that the text, while authentic, is elliptical. In order to be understood

Hermeneutic strategies for restoring consistency

[123] Westerhoff 2016a.

[124] *sa jātāmatro gagane sthitvā | sarvāṇa dharmāṇa abhāvu deśayī* [. . .] *yāvanti śabdās tahi lokadhātau | sarve hy abhāvā na hi kaści bhāvaḥ | tāvantu kho tasya tathāgatasya | svaru niścarī lokavināyakasya*, Régamey 1990: 36–7.

[125] II.iii: 29: *vajragarbha āha || kena samayena sthātavyaṃ kena saṃvareṇeti || bhagavān āha || prāṇinaś ca tvayā ghātyā vaktavyaṃ ca mṛṣāvacaḥ || adattañ ca tvayā grāhyaṃ sevanaṃ parayoṣitaḥ*, Snellgrove 2010: I: 97, II: 56. See also ch. 5 of the *Guhyasamājatantra* (Gäng 1988: 132–5).

properly, specific qualifiers need to be inserted.[126] Most frequently, however, the apparent inconsistency is dissolved by reference to the distinction between interpretable (*neyārtha*) and definitive (*nītārtha*) teachings, arguing that one of the contradictory positions only holds provisionally, and was exclusively taught to a particular audience given its specific explanatory needs, while the other holds in an unqualified, ultimate manner.[127] These latter two hermeneutic strategies gave the Buddhist philosophical enterprise a surprising flexibility, while at the same time minimizing the need to label teachings that self-identify as Buddhist to be inauthentic. A commentator who regarded a position A as the final intent of the Buddha's teaching could also accept one reporting him as saying not-A at the interpretable level, as long as one could argue that there was a position even less conducive to liberation than not-A that the teaching of not-A was supposed to dispel, even if the view to be realized for achieving liberation was A.

The *tathāgatagarbha* in different modes: Madhyamaka and Yogācāra

Despite the conceptual connections between the *tathāgatagarbha* theory and Yogācāra, the theory can be interpreted both in Yogācāra and in Madhyamaka modes. A key difference between these two modes is the way the emptiness of the *tathāgatagarbha* is to be understood. According to the Madhyamaka understanding, the *tathāgatagarbha* is empty in the same way as everything else (including emptiness) is empty: lacking *svabhāva*, devoid of intrinsic nature, unable to stand existentially on its own. To this extent the *tathāgatagarbha* is not a kind of ultimate reality present at the core of every being, but a doctrine taught, like all teachings of the Buddha, in order to lead a specific audience to liberation, in this case an audience that needed a quasi-*ātman* to hold on to. As such, these teachings are not different in kind from those where the Buddha affirms the existence of a person in order to teach about the regularities of karma, regularities that some might see as presupposing the existence of a person to whom these regularities can apply. Both of these are teachings that require further interpretation (*neyārtha*).[128] What the *tathāgatagarbha* teaching emphasizes is that the mind's defilements are, like all properties of the mind, changeable. As such, each being has the potential to become a Buddha, insofar as the defiled nature of the mind can be changed, by continuous practice, into the enlightened nature of the Buddha's mind. To the

Madhyamaka: *tathāgatagarbha* as a conventional teaching

*tathāgatagarbha* as potential

[126] See above, pp. 119–20, for more discussion of the 'interpolation procedure' based on this assumption. In the tantric case the apparently antinomian statements are often accounted for not by interpolation but by giving them non-literal interpretations. In explaining the above passage the commentary *Yogaratnamālā* points out that 'taking of life' refers to the non-arising of thought, 'lying speech' to the fact that the beings the bodhisattva vows to liberate are not ultimately real, and so forth (Farrow and Menon 2001: 193–4).

[127] For more discussion of the stratification of philosophical views into inferior and superior ones this involves see Hacker 1983; Kiblinger 2005.

[128] Ruegg (1989: 53) is critical of this move as a means 'evacuating' the theory of *tathāgatagarbha* by confining it to the realm of the Buddha's provisional teachings.

extent that the defilements are not substantial the mind is intrinsically pure, and this purity can also be understood as permanent, insofar as, whenever there is mind at all, it will be accompanied by its impermanent nature which brings with it the possibility of transformation into the enlightened mind.

Yogācāra: *tathāgatagarbha* as emptiness of defilements

Understood in the Yogācāra mode, on the other hand, the emptiness of the *tathāgatagarbha* is not seen as an emptiness of intrinsic existence, but as an emptiness of defilements.[129] There is an intrinsically pure, eternal, and inherently existent ultimate nature of all sentient beings that remains the same in the unenlightened as in the enlightened. Its teaching is not merely provisional, but constitutes the Buddha's final teaching (*nītārtha*) on the nature of reality.

It is therefore clear that the division between different Madhyamaka and Yogācāra takes on the theory of Buddha-nature was not created by different views on the authenticity of the *tathāgatagarbha* scriptures. Neither side considered them to be inauthentic or created in a fraudulent manner. Rather, the division resulted from differences about which category of the Buddha's teaching they should be assigned to: to those that are to be taken literally, or to those that have to be interpreted relative to a specific context.

Self-emptiness vs. other-emptiness

The two interpretations of *tathāgatagarbha* theory competed with each other in the continuation of the history of Indian Buddhist thought in Tibet, where they were known as the teachings of 'self-emptiness' (*rang stong*) and 'other-emptiness' (*gzhan stong*). Even though our account cannot follow these developments here, it is worthwhile to note that the debate about which of the two interpretations should be accepted as correct can be spelt out in terms of the different factors contributing to the development of Buddhist philosophy we have discussed above. A *textual* dimension of this dispute concerns the question which group of Nāgārjuna's works, the texts comprising the *yukti*-corpus, or the set of hymns, expresses his final philosophical theory.[130] Another dimension of the discussion consists of the question which of the other two factors, *argumentative reasoning* or *meditative experience*, should have the final say. The proponents of the 'other-emptiness' were clear in asserting that philosophical reasoning (as embodied by the 'self-emptiness' theory) could only get you so far, and that the realization of the *tathāgatagarbha* lay beyond what could be accessed in this way, and was something that could only be realized by means of direct meditative insight.[131] It is important to note, however, that the difference between these two factors need not just be seen as a reflection of the opposition of an apophatic Madhyamaka understanding of emptiness and a kataphatic Yogācāra one. Rather, both approaches can be seen as *upāya*, as means that convey different kinds of practitioners to a

[129] Compare the characterization of the *tathāgatagarbha* in the *Śrīmālādevīsiṃhanādasūtra* (Wayman and Wayman 1974: 99). See also Ruegg 1969: 319–46.

[130] Ruegg 1968: 507.

[131] Williams 2009: 114–15.

specific realization that turns out, when properly analysed, to be the same liberating insight.[132]

## 4. Factors That Shaped Yogācāra Philosophy

At this point we might ask ourselves where these new and unusual Yogācāra ideas came from. Yogācāra presents a distinct step in the development of Buddhist thought in India, but it is not immediately clear what caused this step to be taken in the first place. In the Introduction we distinguished three different factors influencing the development of Buddhist philosophy: arguments, texts, and meditative practices. All three can be seen to play some part in the genesis of Yogācāra philosophy.

### *a. Argumentative factors*

First, Yogācāra might be regarded as a natural response to the arguments for universal emptiness that the Mādhyamikas have put forward. Because Madhyamaka does not allow for substantial entities at any level, there cannot be any ontological ground for founding phenomena anywhere. Throughout the history of Madhyamaka some of its opponents have considered this view as tantamount to nihilism. For if everything is only made up of something else, and therefore empty of intrinsic nature and 'not really there', there must be something not made up of anything else at the bottom of the chain, for otherwise nothing is 'really there'. Yogācāra can therefore be understood as a reaction to an argument they considered as taking the idea of the emptiness of emptiness found in the Perfection of Wisdom texts too far.[133] While Yogācāra still saw itself as providing a philosophical explication and argumentative defence of the claims the *Prajñāpāramitāsūtras* make, its proponents wanted to backtrack from the anti-foundationalist picture the Madhyamaka arguments introduced, and instead develop a theory of emptiness that could be considered compatible with some substantialist assumptions.

### *b. Textual factors*

Second, we can regard Yogācāra philosophy as driven by the appearance of specific texts. What the Yogācāra thinkers might have been trying to do is to provide a series of arguments to show how the claims of a set of new or newly discovered texts could be philosophically supported. Traditional accounts certainly place great emphasis on the role of texts in the origination and

[132] This stance was taken by the Tibetan scholar Shākya mchog ldan. See Brunnhölzl 2007: 52–3.

[133] This position is also taken by Masuda 1926: 25, though he locates the problem not in a general difficulty with non-foundationalism, but argues that Nāgārjuna also denies the existence of consciousness, and sees Yogācāra as an attempt to avoid this allegedly implausible result.

development of the Yogācāra school. The work of Asaṅga, the school's founder, is crucially influenced by the five treatises of Maitreya revealed to him. The *Daśabhūmikasūtra*, one of the two texts Asaṅga has his students read to Vasubandhu to convert him to Mahāyāna, contains a key claim of the Yogācāra position: 'All of this, consisting of the three spheres, is merely mind.'[134] According to this conception, the development of Yogācāra philosophy was not primarily pushed by the intention to counterbalance the position of the Mādhyamikas, but to develop a framework for making sense of a newly prominent set of Buddhist *sūtras*.

### c. *Meditative factors*

Finally, a third factor that may have influenced Yogācāra's development are meditative practices. The basic idea of those who believe in such meditative influence is that Yogācāra's aim was to provide a cogent systematization of the results of meditative practice and the phenomenology that goes with such practices. Without denying that argumentative dynamics or the responses to specific texts were essential for the development of Yogācāra, it will be useful to spend some time discussing the specific interrelation between philosophical development and meditative practice in Yogācāra,[135] as the latter is a factor that is often not sufficiently accounted for when discussing the history of Buddhist philosophy.

The 'practice of yoga'

A connection between Yogācāra and meditative practice is already evident from its name, a compound noun comprising *yoga* and *ācāra*, making it the school of the 'practice of yoga'. What exactly yoga was meant to denote at the time when the school's name was coined is not entirely straightforward, but it is uncontroversial to assume that it involved some techniques of mental training or cultivation. From the very beginning of Buddhism, Buddhists have employed a variety of meditative techniques as part of the path to liberation. Usually these techniques involve focusing one's attention on a specific object; this might be an outer object, such as a decomposing corpse (part of the 'meditation on the impure' (*aśubhabhāvanā*) employed to combat attachment), or an inner object such as the breath, or the flow of mental phenomena, as in *śamatha* and *vipaśyana* meditation. A natural question that arises is what kind of things the objects experienced in meditation are. In some Buddhist texts we find the idea that they are made of a specific subtle kind of matter, a kind of matter that

The nature of meditative experiences

[134] *cittamātram idaṃ yad idaṃ traidhātukam* (Vaidya 1967: 31). It is interesting to note that this is one of only two texts that Asaṅga quotes in his *Mahāyānasaṃgraha* as scriptural proof of the truth of the *cittamātra* doctrine (the other being the *Saṃdhinirmocanasūtra* ii, 7, Lamotte 1973: 2. 93–4).

[135] Deleanu (2006: 1. 158) considers a possible development of the Yogācāra tradition from 'an active community of meditation practitioners' in the Sarvāstivāda tradition: 'the birth of the *Śrāvakabhūmi* as well as much of the rest of the *Yogācārabhūmi* was most probably closely connected to such a yogic milieu' (159).

is not accessible to ordinary sense faculties. Later discussions also raise the possibility that these objects are of a purely mental nature.

In the *Saṃdhinirmocanasūtra*, a key Yogācāra text, the issue is raised by the bodhisattva Maitreya in a conversation with the Buddha:[136] Asked by Maitreya whether the image that is the focus of meditation is the same as the mind or different from it the Buddha replies:

Their merely mental nature

> Maitreya, it is 'not different'. Why is it not different? Because that image is simply cognition-only. Maitreya, I have explained that consciousness is fully distinguished by [the fact that its] object of observation is cognition-only.
>
> Bhagavan, if that image, the focus of *samādhi*, is not different from the physical mind, how does the mind itself investigate the mind itself?
>
> The Bhagavan replied: Maitreya, although no phenomenon apprehends any other phenomenon, nevertheless, the mind that is generated in that way appears in that way. Maitreya, for instance, based on matter, matter itself is seen in a perfectly clear round mirror, but one thinks, 'I see an image'. The matter and the appearance of the image appear as different factualities. Likewise, the mind that is generated in that way and the focus of *samādhi* known as the 'image' also appear to be separate factualities.
>
> Bhagavan, are the appearances of the forms of sentient beings and so forth, which abide in the nature of images of the mind, 'not different' from the mind?
>
> The Bhagavan replied: Maitreya, they are 'not different'. However, because childish beings with distorted understanding do not recognize these images as cognition-only, just as they are in reality, they misconstrue them.

The *sūtra* points out that the phenomena experienced in meditation are merely mental in nature,[137] and because of this the mind must be observing itself

[136] *byams pa tha dad pa ma yin zhes bya'o | | ci'i phyir tha dad pa min zhe na | gzungs brnyan de rnam par rig pa tsam du zad pa'i phyir te | byams ba rnam par zhes pa ni dmigs pa rnam par rig pa tsam gyis rab tu phye ba yin no | | zhes ngas bshad do | | bcom ldan 'das ting nge 'dzin gyi spyod yul gzugs brnyan de gal te gzugs sems de las tha dad pa ma lags na | sems de nyid kyis sems de nyid la ji ltar rtog par bgyid lags | bka' stsal pa | byams pa de la chos gang yang chos gang la yang rtog par mi byed mod kyi | 'on kyang de ltar skye pa'i sems gang yin pa de de ltar snang no | | byams pa 'di lta ste dper na | gzugs la brten nas me long gi dkyil 'khor zhin tu yongs su dag pa la gzugs nyid mthong yang gzugs brnyan mthong ngo snyam du sems te | de la gzugs de dang | gzugs brnyan snang ba de don tha dad par snang ngo | | de bzhin du de ltar skyes pa'i sems de dang | ting nge 'dzin gyi spyod yul gzugs brnyan zhes bya gang yin pa de yang de las don gzhan yin pa lta bur snang ngo | | bcom ldan 'das sems can rnams kyi gzugs la sogs par snang ba sems kyi gzugs brnyan rang bzhin du gnas pa gang lags pa de yang sems de dang tha dad pa ma lags zhes bgyi'am | bka' stsal pa | byams pa tha dad pa ma yin zhes bya ste | byis pa phyin ci log gi blo can rnams ni gzugs brnyan de dag la rnam par rig pa tsam de nyid yang dag pa ji lta ba bzhin mi shes pas phyin ci log tu sems so*, Powers 1995: 154–7.

[137] However, Asaṅga rules out the most obvious interpretation, namely that they are mere memory images, since phenomena experienced in meditation are experienced as present, while

during meditative practice. How this can happen is explained by the example of a mirror. As looking in a mirror can give the impression that there are two people in the room, myself and the person in the mirror, so the mind watching itself can give rise to a similar apparent split between observer and observed object, even though the separate existence of the observed object is merely illusory. What is more surprising is the next statement of the *Saṃdhinirmocanasūtra*, which says that *other* things, such as the bodies of sentient beings, are also not different from the mind. This is an astonishing generalization from an intuitively quite plausible claim about objects observed in meditation[138] to an intuitively considerably less plausible claim about tables and chairs. At this stage it is worthwhile to ask two different questions. First, why would this view seem attractive to Buddhists in the first place? And second, why would we think it is actually true—what are the arguments that can be given in its support? The second question is addressed extensively in the works of Yogācāra authors, and we have already considered some arguments for the 'merely mind' thesis above.

Generalization of this claim to include other objects

Meditative cognition as an epistemic instrument

Regarding the first question, one reason why this generalization might have seemed attractive is the fact that cognitions achieved through meditative training were considered as epistemic instruments of a special sort, as epistemic instruments that are distinguished from other such instruments by being non-conceptual (*nirvikalpa*) and able to conceive of the world without the habitually added conceptual overlay in a non-erroneous manner (*abhrānta*), since they could not be misled by this very overlay. If such an epistemic instrument investigates its objects and determines that they are mental in nature, there is a certain justification for arguing that its insights are also applicable to objects of other epistemic instruments (such as the objects of sense perception) as well, simply because this epistemic instrument is more

memory images reflect something that is past. Yet even if they were memory images this would not help the Yogācārin's opponent: since memory images concern things that are past (*atīta*) and therefore do not exist anymore, they are mere mentation (*vijñaptimātra*). The claim that they are memory images could not be used to support the thesis that there must be external objects these images are images of. (*Mahāyānasaṃgraha* ii, 8, Lamotte 1973: 2. 96–7).

[138] It is interesting to note in this context that the *Bhadrapālasūtra* (translated into Chinese in 179 CE) takes this view even about objects of meditation we might have thought Buddhists would ascribe a more objective existence to. In the context of visualizing the Buddha Amitābha and his paradise Sukhāvatī, the text underlines that there is no contact with the real Buddha Amitābha. Rather, the visions obtained are considered to be purely mind-made: 'The Buddha is mind-made, only the mind sees the Buddha. The Buddha is just my mind, the Tathāgata is just my mind' (*sems kyis sangs rgyas byed pa ste || sems nyid kyis kyang mthong ba'o || sems nyid nga'i sangs rgyas te || sems nyid de bzhin gshegs pa'o*), Schmithausen 1973: 175, n. 45. Schmithausen's views of the connection between meditative experience and metaphysics in Buddhism first described in his 1973 article encountered substantial criticism from Buddhist scholars (see Sharf 1995, Bronkhorst 2000), and the battle appears to continue. For the latest instalment see part 4 of Schmithausen 2014 (pp. 597–641), itself primarily a response to Franco 2009.

successful in seeing the world in the way it really is. This view of meditative perception as qualitatively superior to other epistemic instrument is also pointed out in the *Śrāvakabhūmi* section of the *Yogācārabhūmi*. Schmithausen notes that the

> contemplation process does not merely lead to a mental reproduction of the object that is so clear and vivid as if the object itself were directly perceived. Rather, the contemplation process culminates in a non-conceptualizing (*nirvikalpa*) perceptual cognition or insight (*pratyakṣaṃ jñānadarśanam*) that transcends the mental image and directly apprehends the respective object itself.[139]

Superiority of meditative perception over other epistemic instruments

Meditative perception aims not simply at replicating ordinary epistemic instruments (e.g. by producing a visualization of an object qualitatively indistinguishable from its visual perception), but strives at surpassing it by gaining a kind of knowledge of the object that is not possible for other instruments.[140]

The mind-only view thus coheres well with the conception of meditatively trained perceptions as highly authoritative. An additional consideration that renders the mind-only view attractive becomes apparent when we consider another meditative practice, also mentioned in the *Yogācārabhūmi*.[141] Here the aim is not just to produce a specific vivid meditative image, but to produce such images in order to supersede the ordinary appearances. Subsequently the practitioner will dissolve the meditative images. This is considered to lead not only to a disappearance of the objects of meditation, but at the same time to the disappearance of all other objects as well. The simile the text uses to illustrate this technique is to remove a big wedge by inserting another, smaller wedge. This meditative practice and the example illustrating it are very hard to make sense of unless we understand them against the background of a mind-only view. Meditative objects have the property that they can be produced and dissolved at will. But if all objects are of the same nature as meditative objects, that is, if they are all mental, then it is not unreasonable to assume that being able to dissolve one set of mental objects might also enable one to dissolve another set of mental objects. After the practitioner has dissolved the meditative images, he is left with the basis on which they arose, namely his own mind. Similarly, if the automatic superimposition of appearances that are ordinarily conceived of as external objects is stopped, the underlying basis of reality free from these superimpositions will appear.

Meditative perception and the dissolution of objects

139 Schmithausen 2007: 231–2.

140 See also Conze 1962: 53, 253, 256. Wayman (1965: 69) points out that it is a 'standard doctrine of Buddhism through all its periods that the person whose mind is stabilized or concentrated sees things as they really are. From the beginning, the theory was that an entity can be somehow visualized mentally in better, more real or truer form than in ordinary sense perception. To remove error and illusion, one has to do something about the foundation of mind, rehabilitate or transform it.'

141 Schmithausen 1973: 169–70.

The additional mental constructs that the practitioner has produced in his own mind correspond to the small wedge that can then be applied in order to drive out the larger wedge, which corresponds to the mental constructs that are commonly misconceived as mind-independent external things.

Yogācāra position based on meditative experience

That the Yogācāra perspective is intricately connected with meditative experience, rather than simply a philosophical position adopted because it appears to follow from specific philosophical arguments is also supported by the *Laṅkāvatārasūtra*, which notes that:

> Just as a physician provides medicine for the sick,
> So indeed do the Buddhas teach mind-only (*cittamātra*) to sentient beings.
> It is not an object for either philosophers (*tārkika*) or *śrāvaka*s, indeed the Lords (i.e. the Buddhas) teach it drawing on their own experience.[142]

In addition to stressing the soteriological importance of the Yogācāra doctrine for healing beings afflicted by suffering and its causes the *sūtra* points out that the position of mind-only has its basis in the direct experience (*pratyātma-gati-gocara*)[143] of enlightened beings, and is not just a position argued for by argumentatively skilled thinkers.

Yogācāra and tantra

It is thus apparent that the core Yogācāra belief of 'mind-only' is not only supported by the Buddhist view of meditation, but also renders certain meditative practices intelligible in the first place. In this context we should also briefly consider the connection between Yogācāra philosophy and tantra. Tantric texts began to appear in India in the seventh and eighth centuries CE. Whether they were also composed at this time is a complex question. According to the traditional account, the Buddhist *tantra*s were taught either by the historical Buddha or by some transcendent form of the Buddha, and were only revealed at a later stage when the conditions amongst the practitioners were considered to be optimal. These texts are characterized by reference to ritual formulae (*mantra*), symbolic descriptions of the abode of deities (*maṇḍala*), and ritual gestures (*mudra*), which are all brought together in the performance of a tantric rite after the practitioner has received an initiation (*abhiṣeka*) from his teacher. These rites would often involve visualizing the *maṇḍala*, visualizing oneself in the form of the deity, together with the transformation of one's surroundings into the deity's dwelling-place. With Yogācāra in mind, Stephan Beyer remarks that:

> [t]he Buddhist philosophers in India had long made an axiom of the 'softness' of reality and given an ontological status to the omnipotence of the imagination: it devolved upon

[142] *āture āture yadvad bhiṣag dravyaṃ prayacchati |*
*buddhā hi tadvat sattvānāṃ cittamātraṃ vadanti vai ||*
*tārkikāṇām aviṣayaṃ śrāvakāṇāṃ na caiva hi |*
*yaṃ deśayanti vai nāthāḥ pratyātmagatigocaram ||* (Vaidya 1963: 22.) See also the passage from the *Laṅkāvatārasūtra* quoted above on p. 149

[143] For further discussion of this term see Suzuki 1930: 421–3, Forsten 2006: 38–9.

them to explain not why imagery is private, but why reality is public. Much of Buddhist 'ontological psychology' is an attempt to explain in historical terms why we make a systemic epistemological error in our apprehension of the world, why we attribute to it a solidity that in fact it does not possess. In answering these questions, the philosophers planted many of the seeds that would flower in the Tantric manipulations of reality; they asserted the possibility and provided a model, but the Tantrics built a contemplative technique upon the structures of earlier meditation and gave it a new symbolic potency and the means of magic.[144]

Yogācāra as explaining the efficacy of tantric techniques

Yogācāra thought seems to provide a natural philosophical background for tantric rituals. If we want to explain why practices like the visualization of *maṇḍala*s, offerings, the mental transformation of one's environment into the pure abode of the deity, and even the visualization of oneself as the central deity in the *maṇḍala* are supposed to lead to progress on the path to enlightenment, rather than constituting a particularly ritualized form of daydreaming, we need to presuppose that the world we ordinarily inhabit, the world of atoms, tables, chairs, and galaxies, is of the very same nature as the constituents of tantric practice. If the entire world is fundamentally mental in nature it is easier to understand how it may be possible to transform it into a different world by purely mental techniques.[145] If, as the Yogācāra believes, how we perceive the world is crucially influenced by karmic imprints in our mind (that is, by purely mental phenomena), we can understand how one might attempt to transform the world of saṃsāra into the nirvāṇic world of a pure realm by trying to affect these imprints, and to replace them by others so that the world then naturally appears to us like a pure realm.

Of course, these tantric texts only appeared several centuries after the Yogācāra materials we are currently looking at. Yet, as we can explain the initial appeal of Yogācāra ideas by considering conceptions of meditative techniques that were practiced when the first Yogācāra texts appeared, so we can understand the ongoing attraction of Yogācāra thought in the Indian Buddhist philosophical world by taking into account how it forms a natural theoretical underpinning for the rituals practised in Buddhist tantra.

[144] Beyer 1988: 92.

[145] Beyer notes, regarding pre-tantric visualization techniques that arose at the beginning of the Common Era, that 'Buddhist writers have pointed out that there is a metaphysics implicit in the practice of eidetic visualization; it is the ontology of the vision and the dream. A universe of glittering and quicksilver change is precisely one that can be described as empty. The vision and the dream become the tools to dismantle the hard categories we impose upon reality, to reveal the eternal flowing possibility in which the bodhisattva lives. Such possibility exists only because everything—rocks, flowers, Buddhas, Buddhafields—is made of mind, and therefore empty. These *samādhis* are interpreted as teaching us to de-reify the world, obliterate the boundaries between the real and the imaginal, and see all our experiences as a Buddhafield—visionary, magical, and full of meaning.' <www.singingtotheplants.com/2014/01/visualization-before-tantra>.

## 5. Yogācāra and Other Schools of Buddhist Philosophy

Yogācāra and Abhidharma

On the face of it, Abhidharma and Yogācāra could be seen as fundamentally contradictory enterprises. One is distinctly dualist, postulating a variety of fundamental phenomena, some of which are physical and some of which are mental, while Yogācāra is a monist doctrine that considers *all* objects to be merely mental. On the other hand, key Yogācāra philosophers like Asaṅga and Vasubandhu also wrote important Abhiharma treatises, like the *Abhidharmasamuccaya* and the *Abhidharmakośa*, which were in turn commented on by influential Yogācāra commentators like Sthiramati. (Note, by contrast, that we have no evidence of Abhidharma treatises from Madhyamaka authors.) The Abidharma tradition is not simply limited to early Buddhism or to the early period of Buddhist scholastic philosophy, but continued through its later development, in particular through an interesting connection with Yogācāra. While it is clear that the Yogācāra position is very different from that of the Ābhidharmikas, the two systems are still connected not just in the biographies of philosophers such as Vasubandhu, who changed from an Abhidharma master to a Yogācāra master, but also systematically, to the extent that important Yogācāra ideas can be seen as developments of Abhidharma concepts.[146]

Mind-only

The notion of karma entails that our present experience is to a significant degree influenced by potentialities generated by past actions. One way of putting this is to say that the world we live in is the product of karma, and Vasubandhu in fact describes matters in this way in his *Abhidharmakośabhāṣya* when he notes that

> it is said that the world in its variety arises from karma. It is because of the latent dispositions (*anuśaya*) that actions accumulate, but without the latent dispositions they are not capable of giving rise to a new existence. Thus, the latent dispositions should be known as the root of existence.[147]

In Yogācāra this idea is developed further to the extent that the karmic formation of perception becomes so important that the world so formed drops away completely. The picture is no longer, as in the case of the Abhidharma, that of an experienced world shaped by karmic forces, but that of one entirely produced from such forces. To this extent the Yogācāra theory can be understood as an argumentative development of the representationalist

[146] See Schmithausen 1967.

[147] Commenting on *Abhidharmakośa* 4:1: *karmajaṃ lokavaicitryam ity uktam | tāni karmāṇyanuśayavaśādupacayaṃ gacchanti antareṇa cānuśayān bhavābhinirvarttane na samarthāni bhavanti | ato veditavyāḥ mūlaṃ bhavasyānuśayāḥ*, Pradhan 1975: 277: 3–6, Poussin and Pruden 1988–90: 2. 767.

epistemology in Sautrāntika Abhidharma by one further step. As we saw above,[148] for the Sautrāntika perception does not connect us directly with external objects, since these objects disappear even before we could have any knowledge of them. Instead, we perceive a mental object, a phenomenological aspect or representational form (*ākāra*) that resembles the external object, and that can serve as a basis for inferring the existence of such an external object as having caused our knowledge. The Yogācāra position can then be construed as simply accepting the existence of the mental representations, without assuming a necessity of inferring any entities behind them. According to its account, such mental representations, embedded within the framework of karmic causality, are sufficient to explain the entire world as it appears to us. External objects are simply an explanatorily idle wheel.

Foundational consciousness

Not only the idea of 'mind-only' (*vijñāptimātratā*) can be seen to have Abhidharma ancestors, but even such specific concepts as that of a foundational consciousness (*ālayavijñāna*) may be considered as developed from preexistent Abhidharma ideas.[149] Once more we can find roots in the Sautrāntika epistemology, specifically in the *anudhātu*[150] (a synonym of *bīja*, 'seed')[151] doctrine. Sautrāntika faces the difficulty of explaining how a specific mental episode or moment can constitute knowledge of a particular object, even though the object (as a momentary entity) has already passed out of existence, and even though the mental moment was not caused by the object but by the immediately preceding mental moment. They solve this by arguing that the causal history of each moment is present within that moment (it is 'perfumed' by it), and this history is passed on to its successor moment. The *anudhātu* therefore acts as 'the serial continuity of the person... *qua* the presently existing causal matrix that subsumes the total causal efficacies and content of consciousness passed on from the preceding moment'.[152] Each moment therefore has the potential for tracing our way back to the beginning of the causal chain, rather like going through a list of names on a book's flyleaf in order to identify the original owner. In this way the present instance of knowledge can be linked back to the object that caused it in the past (though this object no longer exists) due to traces left in the mental moment as it exists now. The conceptual distance between this idea of potentialities caused by past mental events that exist in the present mental moment, and the idea of a foundational consciousness as a repository of karmically caused potentials, is not vast.

*anudhātu*

[148] pp. 79–80. [149] See Waldron 1994–5.
[150] Bhikkhu Dhammajoti 2007b: 247. [151] Bhikkhu Dhammajoti 2007b: 265, n. 9.
[152] Bhikkhu Dhammajoti 2007b: 247.

*bījabhāva*

Moreover, in the *Abhidharmakośabhāṣya* we find the concept of the 'seed-state' (*bījabhāva*) described in a way that appears to clearly indicate a trajectory leading to the idea of an *ālayavijñāna*:

> By seed-state one should understand a specific power to produce the defilement, an ability belonging to the person under consideration and engendered by the previous defilement. Likewise, in a given person, there exists the power to produce a thought that remembers, a power engendered by a consciousness of perception, likewise, the power to produce rice, which belongs to the plant, sprout, stalk, etc. is engendered by the seed of the rice.[153]

Asaṅga also points out explicitly that early Buddhist schools (the Śrāvakayāna) already refer to the *ālayavijñāna*, even though they do so by means of synonyms such as 'root-consciousness' (*mūlavijñāna*) and so forth.[154]

These examples show that there is an important and substantial historical trajectory connecting Abhidharma theorizing in its Sautrāntika manifestation and Yogācāra philosophy.[155] The systems differ in some of their core conclusions about the nature of the world, yet specific Sautrāntika ideas can be regarded as the beginning of a conceptual road that, once travelled on in a specific direction, leads to ideas that show a considerable resemblance with some we find in Yogācāra.[156]

Yogācāra and Madhyamaka

One question that the consideration of Yogācāra's relation to other schools raises is that of the unity of the Mahāyāna philosophical outlook. We have seen that the Perfection of Wisdom texts, and the concepts of universal emptiness and illusionism they expound, play an important role for Madhyamaka as well as for Yogācāra. Still, the theories that Mādhyamikas and Yogācāracins have developed in explaining what these texts mean are very different. So we are faced with the question whether there is a philosophical divide within the Mahāyāna tradition, containing two contradictory accounts, that of Madhyamaka and of Yogācāra, or whether both are in fact only two different interpretative

Fundamental divide in Mahāyāna philosophy?

[153] Commenting on *Abhidharmakośa* 5:2: *ko 'yaṃ bījabhāvo nāma | ātmabhāvasya kleśajā kleśotpādanaśaktiḥ | yathānubhavajñānajā smṛtyutpādanaśaktiryathā cāṅkurādīnāṃ śāliphalajā śāliphalotpādanaśaktiriti*, Pradhan 1975: 278: 22–4, Poussin and Pruden 1988–90: 3. 770.

[154] *Mahāyānasaṃgraha* I: 11: *yang rnam grangs kyis kun gzhi rnam par shes pa nyan thos kyi theg par yang bstan te*, Lamotte 1973: 1. 7, 2. 26–8.

[155] King 1998: 9: 'many of the most important "new" Yogacara concepts... as utilised in the various Mahāyāna *śāstras* attributed to Vasubandhu, seem to be philosophical elaborations or extensions of concepts and themes already found in the *Abhidharmakośabhāṣya*.' Note, however, that whether we regard the relationship between Yogācāra and Sautrāntika as a germination of one from the other, or whether we conceptualize it in other ways remains a moot point. See our remarks above, pp. 81–3.

[156] As such, the doxographical label 'Yogācāra-Sautrāntika' sometimes applied to the school of Diṅnāga and Dharmakīrti is less perplexing than it might otherwise seem. If there is a conceptual trajectory from one to the other one, many, following Murti (Coward 1983: 288), understand this as the adoption of a Sautrāntika position at the level of conventional truth and of the Yogācāra position at the level of ultimate truth. On the idea of 'Yogācāra-Sautrāntika' see also Bhikkhu Dhammajoti 2007a: 23–31.

approaches that do not disagree in any fundamental way. If we consider the history of Yogācāra/Madhyamaka interactions, matters are far from clear.

Bhāviveka and the Yogācāra/ Madhyamaka distinction

On the one hand there is the position that Bhāviveka's criticism of the Yogācāra position in his *Madhyamakahṛdaya*[157] is not only the first uncontroversial example of the Madhyamaka/Yogācāra divide seen as a division between two schools with incompatible views, but that Bhāviveka is in fact responsible for the antagonistic confrontation between Madhyamaka and Yogācāra. Tāranātha points out that, 'before the appearance of these two masters [Buddhapālita and Bhāviveka] all the followers of Mahāyāna remained under the same teaching',[158] and that after the latter's death 'the followers of the Mahāyāna debated amongst each other, split into two schools'.[159] This passage can be taken to mean a variety of things. On the one hand it could say that before the sixth century followers of the Mahāyāna were not aware of the fundamental doctrinal incompatibilities between the two schools, and that it was only Bhāviveka's analysis that brought these out into the open. On the other hand it could be taken as indicating that the Mahāyāna position before Bhāviveka interpreted both Madhyamaka and Yogācāra in such a way that their doctrines did not conflict, and merely presented distinct, but complementary, ways of understanding the doctrines of the Great Vehicle. Bhāviveka's understanding of Madhyamaka then interpreted it in such a way that it would in fact appear as inconsistent with Yogācāra.

Bhāviveka certainly did not see matters in this way; for him, his work aims at responding to the Yogācāra charge of nihilism directed at the Mādhyamikas, so that it would have been the Yogācārins who not only regarded Madhyamaka and Yogācāra as incompatible, but also declared the former to be internally inconsistent.[160]

Yogācāra and Madhyamaka as inconsistent

It is, in fact, hard to overlook the fact that the mutual criticism of the two schools stretches through most of the period considered in this volume. The *Bodhicittavivarana*, a work not implausibly ascribed to Nāgārjuna,[161] contains a sustained discussion and criticism of Yogācāra concepts. In verse 27 the author points out that: 'The sage's doctrine that all is mere mind is intended to remove the fear of fools, it does not concern reality.'[162] Similarly, the

[157] Eckel 2008.

[158] *slob dpon 'di gnyis ma byon gyi bar du theg pa chen po mtha' dag bstan pa gcig tu gnas pa.*

[159] *legs ldan sku 'das pa'i 'og tsam nas theg pa chen po pa'ang nang du sde gnyis su gyes nas rtsod pa byung* ngo, Dorji 1974: fo. 133, Lama Chimpa 1970: 187.

[160] Eckel 2008: 66.

[161] Lindtner (1982: 11) considers this as one of twelve works ascribed to Nāgārjuna apart from the *Mūlamadhyamakakārikā* that 'must...be considered genuine' (see also the discussion in 1982:180–1). In fact it is one of the most frequently quoted works of Nāgārjuna in later Indian commentarial literature.

[162] *cittamātram idaṃ sarvam iti yā deśanā muneḥ | uttrāsaparihārārtham bālānāṃ sā na tattvataḥ*, Lindtner 1982: 192.

*Laṅkāvatārasūtra*, one of the key texts of the Yogācāra tradition, contains passages that seem to deny some Yogācāra positions.[163] We have already considered the criticism Asaṅga brought forward against the Yogācārins whom he suspected of falling into nihilism. On the other hand we also find relatively late treatises that appear to combine the standpoints of Yogācāra and Madhyamaka, such as Kambala's *Ālokamālā*.[164]

Foundationalism vs. non-foundationalism

If we focus on the philosophical contents of the two systems, it is clear that they propound incompatible metaphysical positions. The Yogācāra system describes a foundationalist scenario: the dependent nature is empty of the imagined nature, but the dependent nature, in the form of the foundational consciousness, is still there to act as the ultimate basis of all that exists. Even though there are no external objects, such as tables and chairs, there is the content of the foundational consciousness which, the Yogācārin claims, is grotesquely misunderstood as a world of external objects by the deluded mind. Contrast this with the non-foundationalist picture we find in Madhyamaka. Because emptiness itself is empty, there is no bottom level we could postulate that is not conceptually imputed on something else and that could therefore act as an objective foundation of all that exists in the world. A manifestation of this incompatibility is that both schools accuse each other of falling into *both* the extremes of nihilism and excessive realism at the same time. For Madhyamaka, Yogācāra is a nihilist position since it denies that the imagined nature is conventionally real. For the Yogācārin, the imagined nature is not something that exists in a lesser sense; it simpy fails to exist and constitutes a wholly false superimposition on the dependent nature. But since the Mādhyamika does not accept the dependent nature as substantially real, he considers the complete denial of the imaginary nature as equivalent to nihilism. It is this acceptance of the dependent nature as a ground of appearances that makes the Yogācāra theory (from the Madhyamaka perspective) also guilty of postulating substantial entities that do not exist, and thereby of falling into the other extreme view as well. The Madhyamaka's concept of the emptiness of emptiness does not allow for the existence of the kinds of ground that the dependent nature constitutes.

Mutual accusations of realism and nihilism

The Yogācārin, on the other hand, can just run these charges the other way round. He argues that the Mādhyamaka is a nihilist because he accepts no foundation like the dependent nature to ground the appearance of everyday

[163] See e.g. the denial of foundational consciousness in *Laṅkāvatārasūtra* 3: 48: *na svabhāvo na vijñaptirna vastu na ca ālayaḥ | bālairvikalpitā hyete śavabhūtaiḥ kutārkikaiḥ*, Vaidya 1963: 68 'There is no intrinsic nature, no conceptual construction, no substance, no foundational consciousness; these, indeed, are so many discriminations cherished by the ignorant who like a corpse are bad logicians.' Suzuki 1932: 145. This denial of foundational consciousness is not found in all Chinese versions of this verse, see Red Pine 2012: 196–7.

[164] 500–50?, Lindtner 2002.

reality that we see around us. But at the same time, he is not only denying too much but also accepting too much, because he wants to elevate what the Yogācārin regards as the non-existent and wholly false imagined nature to the status of conventional reality, that is, to something that exists, even if only in a manner of speaking.

At this point it would be easy to throw up our hands, suspecting that these reciprocal charges of falling into the two extremes are little more than the philosophical equivalent of name-calling. Yet the fact that each system can produce criticisms of the other that are exactly parallel gives us an indication that the two theories are actually closely related. It is not only the case that Madhyamaka and Yogācāra appear to be able to criticize each other with similar validity; the two systems can also interpret each other as being part of their own system.

Yogācāra as part of Madhyamaka

For this interpretation Madhyamaka uses the conceptual scheme of the Buddha's graded teaching, that is, the idea that the Buddhist doctrine forms a hierarchy of increasing philosophical sophistication, where each step was taught to members of a particular audience to work with their specific assumptions and preconceptions. In this context the Yogācāra system would succeed the teaching of the Abhidharma, with its basic tenets of karma and non-self. On the basis of this teaching, disciples would still believe in the substantial, independent existence of *dharma*s, and even though they may have abandoned attachment to their self, they might still develop attachment to these *dharma*s. At this stage the Yogācāra theory comes in, arguing that all these *dharma*s are in fact only mind-dependent and do not form part of an external reality. In addition, it introduces a further route to understanding the non-self doctrine by pointing out that if there is no objectively existent grasped *object* there also cannot be any *subject* that does the grasping. In doing so Yogācāra introduces some other substantialist assumptions (such as the existence of the foundational consciousness) which have to be removed by the next highest system, Madhyamaka, but this is not to deny that Yogācāra itself is a perfectly good tool for removing some of the misconceptions of the Abhidharma.

Śāntarakṣita's synthesis

This is the approach we find later in Śāntarakṣita's (725–88) attempt at synthesizing Madhyamaka and Yogācāra in his *Mādhyamakālaṃkāra*,[165] where he notes:

> By relying on the *cittamātra* system, know that external entities do not exist. And by relying on this [Madhyamaka] system, know that no self at all exists, even in that [mind]. Therefore by holding the reigns of reasoning, as one rides the chariots of the two systems, one becomes a real Mahāyānist.

[165] 92–3, Blumenthal 2004: 171–2. The main independent work of Śāntarakṣita's disciple Kamalaśīla, the *Madhyamakāloka*, also contains a detailed exposition of this synthetic approach.

The idea behind this syncretist approach is that Yogācāra is the best account of conventional truth, while the Madhyamaka theory of universal emptiness is the best account of ultimate truth. Both play a role in a gradual philosophical de-substantialization of the world. First the Yogācāra analysis does away with the conception of matter as we find it in the Abhidharma, and substitutes a fundamentally mental reality for it. The Madhyamaka arguments then pull the rug from under this idealist foundation, arguing that nothing, neither mind nor matter, can function as an ultimately real basis of existence.

Madhyamaka as part of Yogācāra

The Yogācārins simply reverse the picture the Mādhyamikas use to interpret Yogācāra by referring to the idea of the three turnings. This, we remind ourselves, has the Buddha teach Madhyamaka after Abhidharma but before Yogācāra (this view of the historical sequence also happens to do justice to the fact that the target of Nāgārjuna's Madhyamaka critique is primarily the Abhidharma). In this framework it is possible to conceive of Madhyamaka as an antidote to the teachings of the Abhidharma and their assumption of substantially existent entities. However, after the second turning the Buddha's teaching is not complete, for what has happened so far is merely clearing the ground of various false conceptions. Madhyamaka has shown how various concepts lead to contradictions when properly analysed, and therefore have to be discarded. But what is to be put in their place? This is where the Yogācāra teaching of the three natures comes in, specifying a basis of all appearances in the form of the dependent nature, which is the foundational consciousness.

The 2nd and 3rd turnings as not differing in content

A different, and somewhat more subtle, understanding of the three turnings attempting to unify Madhyamaka and Yogācāra is based on the idea that the second and third turnings do not actually teach a different kind of content. Both turnings concern ultimate reality as described in the Perfection of Wisdom literature, but they interpret the import of this teaching in different ways. According to the second turning, we have a theory, the theory of the emptiness of emptiness, that gives expression to ultimate reality; according to the third turning, ultimate reality is beyond all expressions. From the perspective of the third turning, the second turning does not misconstrue the theory of emptiness, but it misunderstands what kind of position this theory points towards: according to the second turning, it can be expressed by a set of philosophical statements, according to the third turning, it has to be understood as referring to something inexpressible by language and conceptualization, something that one can only become acquainted with through meditative practice.[166]

*ākāra*, Yogācāra, and Madhyamaka

In this context it is also worthwhile to consider how the notion of representationl form (*ākāra*) was used in order to conceptualize the relation between Yogācāra and Madhyamaka.

[166] For an interpretation of this kind see Gold 2015b: 230.

Śāntarakṣita rejects both accounts of representational forms

Śāntarakṣita describes and rejects both Yogācāra positions on the status of representational forms in the *Madhyamakālaṃkāra*.[167] One problem he raises for the *satyākāravāda* is that it appears inconsistent to assume that consciousness, which is fundamentally real, is a single thing,[168] and that the various representational forms are also fundamentally real, and that consciousness and the forms are the same thing.[169] If the manifold representational forms really exist, consciousness must be manifold, and hence not ultimately real, but if consciousness is not manifold, the diversity of forms must somehow only be apparent and they cannot exist in the way they appear. Śāntarakṣita then raises a series of eight absurdities in refutation of the *alīkākāravāda* position.[170] One of these concerns the fact that representational forms, because they are not fundamentally real, cannot be part of the causal network.[171] They do not act as causes, and they do not arise as effects. But this makes it very hard to explain why representational forms arise and cease in an orderly manner, rather than being present permanently, or flashing in and out of existence in random ways. The *alīkākāravādin* seems to be incapable of accounting for the phenomenology of the world as it in fact appears to us.

In familiar Madhyamaka manner, Śāntarakṣita argues that both views of the nature of representative forms must fail because they share a common erroneous underlying assumption: that there could be ultimate truths about the status of representational forms as they occur in consciousness.[172] As both the ultimate reality of consciousness in particular and the existence of ultimately true theories in general is rejected by the Mādhyamika, both *satyākāravāda* and *alīkākāravāda* turn out to be based on mistaken presuppositions concerning the ontological status of consciousness.

Ratnākaraśānti on *ākāra*

Later Indian authors like Ratnākaraśānti argue against Śāntarakṣita's criticism of the Yogācāra conception of representational form.[173] At the same time, Ratnākaraśānti also tries to forge an alliance between Yogācāra and Madhyamaka,[174] though, unlike Śāntarakṣita, he does this not by conceiving

[167] He treats *satyākāravāda* in verses 46–51 and *alīkākāravāda* in verses 52–60 (Blumenthal 2004: 117–39, 266–75. See also Moriyama 1984).

[168] Della Santina 200: 28. Yogācāra accepts the Abhidharma position that manifold or partite entities cannot be ultimately real. See Mipham 2005: 241.

[169] Blumenthal 2004: 121–2.

[170] Blumenthal 2004: 127–34. The problem mentioned here is the sixth absurdity (132). See Yiannopoulos 2012: 140 for a discussion of Ratnākaraśānti's response to this criticism of *alīkākāravāda*.

[171] Della Santina 2000: 31. For further discussion of causal efficacy as the mark of the real see below, Chapter 4, section 4, p. 000.

[172] Blumenthal 2004: 134–7, Mipham 2005: 261–3, see also McClintock 2014: 328.

[173] See e.g. his *Madhyamakālaṃkāropadeśa* (Yiannopoulos 2012: 223–49); Moriyama 2014.

[174] Ratnākaraśānti's approach has sometimes been labeled as 'Vijñapti-Madhyamaka' (*nam rig dbu ma*), and positioned explicitly against what was taken to be a misinterpretation of Nāgārjuna by Candrakīrti (*klu grub kyi dgongs pa 'chal ba*, Yiannopoulos 2012: 23). See also Ruegg 1981a: 122.

of Yogācāra as propaedeutic to Madhyamaka's ultimate point of view, but by focusing on the *alīkākāravāda* understanding of representational form. And indeed, there seem to be intriguing similarities between a position regarding representational forms as unreal and the Madhyamaka conception of emptiness. Tillemans notes that the *alīkākāravāda*'s negation of the reality of appearances is 'closer to those Svātantrika-Mādhyamikas who recognize an object-*qua*-appearance, one which is conventionally established, but ultimately illusory'.[175] Yet there remains the crucial difference that the *alīkākāravāda* still assumes representational forms, understood as belonging to the imaginary nature (*parikalpita-svabhāva*), to have an ultimately real basis on which their existence depends, namely reflexive awareness. The Mādhyamika, on the other hand, explicitly denies the existence of any ultimate foundation of unreal appearances.

*alīkākāravāda* and Madhyamaka

So does that mean that Yogācāra, in any form, has to be considered as a foundationalist theory and is as such intrinsically incompatible with the Madhyamaka theory of the emptiness of emptiness?

The answer to this question is not as clear as one might initially think. Note that we can regard the sequence of positions from Sautrāntikā-*satyākāravāda* through Yogācāra-*satyākāravāda* to Yogācāra-*alīkākāravāda* as a progressive evaporation of the ontological content of the respective theories. In the Sautrāntika case we still have a world of external objects causing and being mirrored by internal representational forms. Yogācāra lets go of these external objects in order to formulate a theory according to which 'the cause producing the aspect [i.e. the *ākāra*] is not an invisible external object but an internal propensity, and... reality consists of self-cognizing awarenesses mistaken for external perceptions'.[176] Yet this *satyākāravāda* version of Yogācāra still thinks of cognition as relating to objects, objects that are no longer external but have been replaced by internal objects, the representational forms that are considered as real enties. The Yogācāra-*alīkākāravāda* lets go of these objects as well, and analyses them as mistaken projections on reflexive awareness. It thereby rules out not only the duality of representational form and external object, but also that of perceiver and internal object.

Progressive evaporation of ontological content

This sequences maps nicely onto the first of the four stages (*bhūmi*) of yoga distinguished by Ratnākaraśānti.[177] Having moved through a sequence of epistemological accounts where the percept (*ālambana*) takes the form of external objects, internal representational forms, and non-dual cognition, respectively, there is yet a fourth stage to obtain, a stage that consists of 'direct comprehension of the *mahāyāna* consisting in residence in gnosis absolutely free from appearance (*nirābhāsa*), and in which *nāman* and *lakṣaṇa*

The four stages of yoga: Ratnākaraśānti

[175] Tillemans 2008: 42, n. 92. [176] Dreyfus 1997: 435.
[177] Yiannopoulos 2012: 175–85, Ruegg 1981a: 122–3.

as well as *grāhya* and *grāhaka* have disappeared'.[178] In his *Prajñāpāramitopadeśa*, Ratnākaraśānti describes this fourth stage as follows:

In the fourth stage, the yogis pass beyond the subtlest conceptualisation of phenomena. Without exertion and without conditioning, they realize experientially, through a direct perception, the suchness of all phenomena. They realise the complete vanishing of the marks of phenomena and the nature of phenomena, the enlightened wisdom, which is non-dual, free of appearances and apprehension, the supra-mundane non-conceptual calm abiding and penetrating insight.[179]

The four stages: Kamalaśīla

It is interesting to note that we encounter what looks like very much the same four-stage model in Kamlaśīla's *Bhāvanākrama*.[180] In both cases the exposition is connected with an identical set of verses from the *Laṅkāvatārasūtra*.[181] Kamalaśīla describes the final stage by noting that

things arise neither from their own selves nor from other things and when subject and object are unreal [*alīka*], the mind, being not different [from the two], cannot be true, either. Here, too, he must abandon attachment to ascribing reality to the cognition of non-duality [*advayajñāna*], and he must abide in the knowledge of non-manifestation of even nondual knowledge [*advayajñānanirābhāsa-jñāna*]. . . . When the yogin abides in the knowledge of nonmanifestation of nondual knowledge, he, being established in the highest truth, sees [the truth of] the Great Vehicle.[182]

Whether these two accounts describe two fundamentally different insights into reality that make a difference for Mahāyāna practice,[183] or whether they express the same state of realization, is a moot point. It may be that only those who have obtained this level of insight would be able to tell; in any case, it is evident that at least Ratnākaraśānti believed that the Yogācāra and the Madhyamaka understanding of the four stages are in fact the same.[184]

Tibetan developments of *alīkākāravāda*

Attempts to develop a common vision of Yogācāra and Madhyamaka based on *alīkākāravāda* and Ratnākaraśānti' s exposition of it continued in the later Tibetan development of Indian Buddhist philosophy. A prominent example of

[178] Ruegg 1981a: 123.

[179] Bentor 2000: 43. This translation is based on the Tibetan; the Sanskrit of the text is extant and has been edited by Hong Luo (see Luo 2013: 17), though it remains unpublished to date.

[180] Sharma 1997: 33–4, Driessens 2007: 48–51, see also Kajiyama 1991: 137–40.

[181] 10:256–8 (Ratnākaraśānti only cites the first two of the three verses): 'Having entered into mind-only, he would not conceptualize external objects, based on the foundation of suchness he would go beyond mind-only. Having gone beyond mind-only, he would go beyond signlessness, established in signlessness the *yogi* sees the Mahāyāna. This effortless state is peaceful and purified by vows, the highest knowledge is without self, being signless, it does not see', *cittamātraṃ samāruhya bāhyamarthaṃ na kalpayet | tathatālambane sthitvā cittamātramatikramet || cittamātramatikramya nirābhāsamatikramet | nirābhāsasthito yogī mahāyānaṃ sa paśyati || anābhogagatiḥ śāntā praṇidhānairviśodhitā | jñānamanātmakaṃ śreṣṭhaṃ nirābhāse na paśyati* (Vaidya 1963: 124, Suzuki 1932: 246–7).

[182] Kajiyama 1991: 139.

[183] Komarovski 2011: 80–1.

[184] Ruegg 1981a: 123–4. See also Seton 2015: 78.

this is the fifteenth-century Tibetan scholar Shākya mchog ldan.[185] He regarded *alīkākāravāda* as on the same level as Madhyamaka,[186] without, however, glossing over the various interesting distinctions in the ways Yogācāra and Madhyamaka presented their views of ultimate reality. He pointed out that while perceived through the argumentative dimension the two systems were very close, though not identical, yet they were one and the same when viewed through the meditative dimension: the understandings of reality achieved by those perfecting the paths of *alīkākāravāda* Yogācāra and Madhyamaka ultimately coincide.[187]

Mutual subsumption and the unity of Mahāyāna thought

The fact that Yogācāra and Madhyamaka are mutually interpretable in the way described above provides a route to understanding views about the original unity of the two systems such as we find in Tāranātha. For any Mādhyamika would be able to say that he accepts the truth of Yogācāra, and any Yogācārin could say that he accepts the truth of Madhyamaka if the relation between the two systems is understood such that either Yogācāra acts as a preliminary account leading up to Madhyamaka, or such that Madhyamaka essentially depends on Yogācāra meditative practice to achieve its liberating potential. Though it may seem as if the unity of the Mahāyāna has been preserved in this way, we might be justified in being suspicious. After all, the Mādhyamika and the Yogācārin have different views about what it means to accept the truth of both systems. For the former, Madhyamaka comes out as the final true theory, while for the other this is Yogācāra. While it might look as if the unity of the Mahāyāna meant that there are just different paths up the same mountain, we might wonder whether Madhyamaka and Yogācāra do not actually disagree about what is at the top and what is further down the mountain. In this case the mountains they describe could be the same, but would have to be two distinct peaks.

Yogācāra and Madhyamaka as aiming at the same inexpressible truth

Apart from this argument from mutual subsumption, there is a different position one may adopt in order to establish the fundamental unity of Madhyamaka and Yogācāra. Yogācāra has traditionally placed much emphasis on the claim that ultimate reality is inexpressible. Considering the background assumptions of this school, this is understandable. Yogācāra emphasizes how our view of the world is inevitably coloured and distorted by concepts, and puts great emphasis on a perceptual shift caused by meditative practice. In order to become acquainted with the way things really are, we therefore have to go beyond the set of concepts we employ, and since they provide the framework in which all our linguistic expressions take place, such a move implies that we

[185] Sometimes believed to be a reincarnation of Ratnākaraśānti (Komarovski 2011: 50).

[186] Komarovski 2011: 83.

[187] Komarovski 2011: 79, 154–5. The 19th-century Tibetan scholar Mi pham rgya mtsho seems to have shared this position (Komarovski 2011: 80–1).

must go beyond the realm of what is expressible. Such a way of perceiving the world is also the one used by the Buddhas, who have completed their meditative training and moved beyond the distortions of subject/object duality to comprehend a reality that cannot really be expressed in terms of such a distinction.

Yet if we consider the Madhyamaka perspective, we also find various remarks that it does not express a thesis,[188] or that one should not hold the theory of emptiness as an established philosophical position (*dṛṣti*).[189] Theses and philosophical positions are of course linguistically expressed entities, and if the conclusion of the Madhyamaka arguments cannot be rendered in terms of these, we might be justified in suspecting that it is not something that lends itself to linguistic expression. So Madhyamaka would accept the inexpressibility of ultimate truth as well, and since there is no sensible way of differentiating between a pair of inexpressible positions, Madhyamaka and Yogācāra would then appear to aim at the same position with regard to ultimate truth, namely that it is inexpressible. They differ, of course, when it comes to specifying the way in which the realization of ultimate truth is to be obtained. For Yogācāra it is the attainment of a non-dual state of consciousness by sustained meditative practice, for Madhyamaka it is the use of arguments, that is, a form of conceptualization, in order to bring an end to conceptualization.

Different conceptions of inexpressibility

While this approach[190] avoids the difficulties of the mutual subsumption approach we saw earlier, it not entirely clear that it manages to present a faithful representation of both positions. While it is true that for the Mādhyamika there is no thesis, philosophical position, or other linguistic item that could express ultimate truth, his reason for this view is not that conceptualization necessarily distorts the reality it sets out to represent, as the Yogācārin would have it, but a global anti-realism about truth. For the Mādhyamika there is no way things are ultimately; for the Yogācārin there is such a way, but it is inexpressible. When the Mādhyamika asserts that ultimate reality is inexpressible (*anabhilāpya*) and non-conceptual (*nirvikalpaka*), he does not mean that there might be some other way of epistemic access to this reality, one that does not go via expressions or concepts, but that there is no access by expressions and concepts because there is nothing for them (or any other epistemic instrument) to access here: there is no ultimate reality, no way things are 'no matter what'.[191] It therefore appears as if the difference between thinking that

[188] Such as verse 29 of Nāgārjuna's *Vigrahavyāvartanī*, see Westerhoff 2010: 63–5, Huntington 2003: 72–3.

[189] *Mūlamadhyamakakārika* 13:8, Siderits and Katsura 2013: 145–6.

[190] For further discussion see the essays by Siderits and Gold in Garfield and Westerhoff 2015.

[191] These expressions are therefore to be understood as incorporating non-implicative negations (*prasajya-pratiṣedha*), negations that reject an important presupposition of the proposition to be negated, as the negation in 'the number 5 is not red' rejects the presupposition that numbers could be coloured at all.

there is no ultimate reality, and the global anti-realism about truth that comes with it, and thinking that ultimate reality is inexpressible marks the crucial divide between Madhyamaka and Yogācāra,[192] a divide that seems to be unbridgeable by all the attempts we have so far encountered. Our only options seem to be to accept that there are two definite (*nītārtha*) incompatible philosophical positions within the Mahāyāna, or that there is just one, subsuming the other, and that this second one must therefore be in need of contextual interpretation (*neyārtha*).

## 6. Yogācāra and Vedānta

Amongst the relations of Yogācāra with non-Buddhist schools of Indian thought that with Vedānta is particularly interesting. Not only do the two systems share a certain surface familiarity, insofar as they are both frequently labeled as forms of idealism, the seventh-century thinker Gauḍapāda, author of the *Māṇḍukyakārikā* (itself a commentary on the *Māṇḍukya Upaniṣad*) and Śaṅkara's supposed *paramaguru*, or teacher of his teacher,[193] is often supposed to have been substantially influenced by Yogācāra (and, to an extent, by Madhyamaka).[194]

Early Vedānta and Yogācāra

Gauḍapāda describes the world as similar to a dream (*svapna*) and an illusion (*māya*): 'Other creation-theorists, on the other hand, consider creation to be the manifestation of divine power (*vibhūti*), creation is conceived by [yet] others as having the same nature as a dream and an illusion.'[195] This echoes similar characterizations we find in Yogācāra texts.[196] For the Yogācārin, the world as it appears to us, that is, the imagined nature (*parikalpita-svabhāva*), is wholly unreal, and hence fittingly characterized by similes like dreams and illusions, where what the dream or the illusion shows is wholly non-existent. Over and above such general Mahāyāna themes, like the illusoriness of the

Dreams and illusions

[192] Gold (2015b: 237) disagrees. For him difference between these two positions 'may be considered merely one of framing'.

[193] Some scholars date Gauḍapāda as early as the middle of the 6th century, in which case his role as Śaṅkara's grand-teacher would be more doubtful. See Joshi 1969: 11.

[194] Dasgupta 1922: 1. 423: 'I believe that there is sufficient evidence in his *kārikās* for thinking that he was possibly himself a Buddhist, and considered that the teachings of the Upaniṣads tallied with those of the Buddha'; Mayeda (1968: 87) notes that the fourth chapter or *prakaraṇa* of the *Māṇḍukyakārikā*, called *Alātaśānti*, 'extinction of the wheel of fire', which makes up nearly half of the 215 verses of the text, 'may well be regarded as a Buddhist text'. Whether all the four chapters were indeed composed by the same author is contested, see King 1997: ch. 1. For a discussion of some textual parallels between the *Māṇḍukyakārikā* and Mahāyāna works see Joshi 1969.

[195] *Māṇḍukyakārikā* I:7: *vibhūtiṃ prasavaṃ tv anye manyante sṛṣṭicintakāḥ | svapnamāyāsarūpeti sṛṣṭir anyaiḥ vikalpitā*, Swāmī Nikhilānanda 1974: 38.

[196] *Laṇkāvatārasūtra* 10: 251, 279, 291, Vaidya 1963: 124–6, Suzuki 1932: 246, 249–50.

world in which we live,[197] the *Māṇḍukyakārikā* also takes up more specific Yogācāra motives.

Identity of knower and known

One such motive is the identity of knowledge (*jñāna*) and the known (*jñeya*),[198] or of the perceiver (*grāhaka*) and perceiving (*grahaṇa*), illustrated by the example of the 'wheel of fire' that gives the fourth chapter of the *Māṇḍukyakārikā* its name: 'Just as a firebrand, when in motion, appears straight, crooked, etc., so consciousness in motion (*vijñāna-spandita*) appears as perceiver and perceived.'[199] When a torch is moved around in a circle various static shapes such as glowing circles or ellipses can be seen, even though there is no illuminated circular or elliptical object in front of us. In the same way, consciousness can generate the appearance of perceiver and perceived, even though no such things should be accorded any ontological status.

*vijñāna-spandita*

The notion of the motion, 'oscillation', or 'vibration' of consciousness (*vijñāna-spandita*), which denotes the activity of consciousness that brings out the indicated duality (corresponding to the motion of the torch that produces the visual illusion) constitutes a close parallel to the Yogācāra idea of the 'transformation of consciousness' (*vijñāna-pariṇāma*) that explains the apparent split of the manifest world into the appearance of a substantial self (*ātman*) and the objects this self perceives (*dharma*).[200]

*asparśayoga*

The rejection of this epistemic dualism between knower and known also appears to form the background of the notion of *asparśayoga*, the 'yoga of no contact' that Gauḍapāda refers to. Instead of simply understanding it as a specific meditative technique,[201] it may also be taken to be a specific epistemic

[197] We find similar characterizations also in Prajñāpāramitā texts, for example in the *Aṣṭasahāsrikāprajñāpāramita*: 'For illusions and beings are not two different things, and for dreams and beings are not two different things. All *dharmas* and gods are also like an illusion, like a dream', *māyā ca sattvāś ca advayametadadvaidhīkāram iti hi svapnaś ca sattvāś ca advayametadadvaidhīkāram | sarvadharmā api devaputrā māyopamāḥ svapnopamāḥ* (Vaidya 1960b: 20, see Conze 1994: 98.), and there are interesting connections between the *Māṇḍukyakārikā* and Madhyamaka (some of the phrasing of the illusionistic descriptions in fact follow very closely similar characterizations in Nāgārjuna's *Mūlamadhyakakārikā* (compare *Māṇḍukyakārikā* II: 31: *svapnamāye yathā dṛṣṭaṃ gandharvanagaraṃ yathā* (Swāmī Nikhilānanda 1974: 116) with *Mūlamadhyakakārikā* VII: 34: *yathā māyā yathā svapne gandharvanagaraṃ yathā*). For further discussion see King 1997: ch. 4, Bronkhorst 2011b: 62–3.

[198] *Māṇḍukyakārikā* III: 33: 'It is asserted that knowledge that is free from imagination and unborn is not distinct from the knowable', *akalpamajaṃ jñānaṃ jñeyābhinnaṃ pracakṣate*, Swāmī Nikhilānanda 1974: 187.

[199] *Māṇḍukyakārikā* IV: 47 *ṛjuvakrādikābhāsam alātaspanditaṃ yathā | grahaṇagrāhakābhāsaṃ vijñānaspanditaṃ tathā*, Swāmī Nikhilānanda 1974: 260.

[200] See e.g. the opening verse of Vasubandhu's *Triṃśikā*: 'The figures of speech (*upacāra*) "self" and "nature", functioning in so many ways, arise in the transformation of consciousness', *ātma-dharmopacāro hi vividho yaḥ pravartate vijñānapariṇāme*, Anacker 2002: 422.

[201] Such as the withdrawal of the mind from sensory objects; see *Bhagavadgītā* 2: 58, 5: 21–2, 27 (Feuerstein 2014: 113, 153–5).

state brought about by such techniques.[202] This state would be a realization of the absence of contact (*sparśa*) between the perceiving mind and the perceived object, since the external objects fail to be present in the first place.[203] There is a noteworthy parallel here with the goal of Yogācāra practice, an approach aiming at the removal of the wrong superimposition of externality to objects that fail to exist in a mind-independent way, and at the attainment of a way of cognizing the world that is not subject to such superimpositions.

Vedānta criticism of Yogācāra

Despite the intriguing historical and systematic connection between Yogācāra and Vedānta, central Vedānta thinkers such as Śaṅkara launched a sustained attack on Yogācāra thought.[204] One point Śaṅkara raises towards the beginning of his discussion is how the Yogācāra's idea of objects appearing 'as if' they were external could be made sense of, given that they assume that there are no external objects in the first place.[205] How can something be like another thing, if the second thing does not exist? Could a person behave like the son of a barren woman behaves?

How can mental objects be like external objects?

Our arguments must not undermine the epistemic instruments

A second point Śaṅkara mentions concerns the relation of the Yogācāra position to the epistemic instruments (*pramāṇa*).[206] An understanding of these 'instruments' that provide us with an epistemic grip on the world is usually taken to be at the very beginning of any philosophical inquiry. But if we accept an epistemic instrument like perception, which seems to acquaint us with entities external to our mind, how could any amount of Yogācāra arguments subsequently convince us that such objects fail to exist? We determine what can and what cannot exist on the basis of the epistemic instruments, and if our subsequent philosophical conclusions appear to undermine one of the presuppositions of these instruments, we would cut off the very epistemological branch on which our conclusion is supposed to rest.

Qualified and qualifier must differ

Śaṅkara also argues that the Yogācāra identification of the supposed external object with a mental image leads to problems in differentiating different parts of the world.[207] When we distinguish a white cow from a black cow we identify both as cows, though we tell them apart by different qualifications. Analogously, Śaṅkara argues, a mental image of a jar and a mental image of a pot are both perceptions, though they are differentiated by what they are mental images of. In both examples the qualified (*viśeṣya*) is the same ('cow', 'mental image'), but

[202] Gauḍapāda (*Māṇḍukyakārikā* III: 39) notes that 'it is difficult for all yogins to attain it', *asparśayogo vai nāma durdarśaḥ sarvayogibhiḥ*, Swāmī Nikhilānanda 1974: 197.

[203] King 1997: 148, Hixon 1976: 217, 234–5.

[204] Śaṅkara's main criticisms of Yogācāra are set out in his *Brahmasūtrabhāṣya* (II.2.28–32, Date 1973: 1. 325–34). For an analysis of these, as well as the perspective of other Vedānta thinkers on them, see Darling 2007. A close paraphrase of Śaṅkara's criticism is given by Kher 1992: 506–10. Ingalls (1954: 298–9, 303) argues that, unlike the preceding arguments against the Abhidharma metaphysics (II.2.18–27), which reflect traditional criticisms of the Buddhist tradition, the arguments against Yogācāra are original to Śaṅkara.

[205] Date 1973: 1. 328. [206] Date 1973: 1. 328. [207] Date 1973: 1. 328–9.

its qualification (*viśeṣaṇa*, 'black'/'white', 'of a pot'/'of a jar') differs. If the qualification was not different from the qualified a white cow would be the very same thing as a black cow, as both are cows. Since this is not so, the mental image (the qualified) must also be distinct from its object (the qualification), contrary to what the Yogācārin asserts.

Foundational consciousness and momentariness are incompatible

A fourth point raised concerns the coherence of the principle of momentariness, which all Buddhist schools accept, with the specific Yogācāra position. Śaṅkara claims that the postulation of a foundational consciousness is incompatible with the principle of momentariness.[208] If the foundational consciousness is itself permanent, this contradicts the Buddhist conception that all compounded phenomena (*saṃskṛta*) are impermanent,[209] and are indeed only momentary existents.[210] On the other hand, if the foundational consciousness is momentary, how can it act as a receptacle of habitual tendencies (*vāsanā*) that is supposed to span several lifetimes? For Śaṅkara, this underlines the necessity to postulate a permanent entity, a witnessing self (*sākṣin*) 'connected with the three times', in order to explain phenomena such as memory based on habitual tendencies.[211]

Madhva on momentariness

Later Vedānta authos such as Madhva identify a somewhat different problem for the compatibility of Yogācāra and the theory of momentariness, arguing that the problem is not a conflict with the notion of a foundational consciousness, but with the fact that internal and external objects have different properties, and therefore cannot be identical: 'The momentariness of cognition and the permanence of things have been asserted, hence there is a discordance.'[212] Since internal representations, *qua* mental phenomena, pass into and out of existence at a rapid pace due to their momentariness, and since external objects remain for a longer duration, Madhva argues that they cannot be the same thing.

Obviously the Yogācārin has some reply to each of these challenges; we will not investigate them here, as doing so would take us deeper into the Yogācāra–Vedānta debate than is possible in a historical survey such as this.

[208] Date 1973: 1. 332–3, Ingalls 1954: 302.

[209] Abhidharma metaphysics accepts some exceptions to the principle of universal momentariness, in the case of uncompounded (*asaṃskṛta*) phenomena such as space and nirvāṇa (see Bhikkhu Dhammajoti 2009: 38–9, 471–99). However, these phenomena are, unlike the *ālaya* with its continuous planting and ripening of seeds, unchanging, and, at least according to some interpretations, mere absences, so that it is plausible to assume that they may constitute exceptions to universal momentariness.

[210] 'Yet when there is a permanent nature the tenet of [momentariness connected with] the foundational consciousness is abandoned.', *sthirasvarūpatve tvāyalavijñānasya siddhāntahāniḥ*, *Brahmasūtrabhāṣya* ad II.2.31, Joshi 2011: 2. 557.

[211] Date 1973: 1. 333, Kher 1992: 508–9, Ingalls 1954: 301. Instead of postulating a witnessing self, Buddhist thinkers like Diṅnāga explain the existence of memory in terms of reflexive awareness, arguing that if one cognition was cognized by another cognition (rather than by itself) we would end up with an infinite regress (see pp. 184–5 above). Śaṅkara is not convinced by this point, however, arguing that his witnessing self does not need another to establish it, and can thereby stop the regress.

[212] *jñānaṃ kṣaṇikam arthānāṃ ca sthāyitvam uktam || ataś ca naikyam*, Darling 2007: 359.

Reasons for Śaṅkara's attitude towards Yogācāra

A question that remains, however, is why Śaṅkara does not adopt a doxographically more inclusive line towards the Yogācāra views he describes. In the familiar tradition of the doxographic hierarchy, Śaṅkara could have described Yogācāra as an incomplete approximation of the final truth of Advaita Vedānta, rather than as a deficient view to be refuted. Yet while Vedānta and Yogācāra may appear relatively close from a contemporary perspective, with their rejection of material objects and their emphasis on the illusoriness of the world as it appears to us,[213] the crucial reason why Śaṅkara would not want to regard the Yogācārin (or any Buddhist, for that matter) as a philosophical fellow-traveller is the latter's rejection of the existence of an *ātman*. Vedānta doxographies, such as the medieval *Sarvadarśanasaṃgraha* by Mādhava,[214] characteristically assign the second-lowest place to Buddhist theories, excelled in their distance from the truth of Vedānta only by the materialist Cārvāka system.

Rather than constituting a philosophical runner-up, Śaṅkara sees the Buddhist no-self theory as making a fundamental mistake, and as at best deceptively and misleadingly similar to Vedānta ideas.[215] For this reason it is essential for him to stress the difference between the two systems, demonstrating both the superiority of the Vedānta approach and its distance from the Buddhist theory.

[213] Śaṅkara has sometimes been accused of being a crypto-Buddhist (*prachanna-bauddha*) who introduced Buddhist elements into the interpretation of Vedānta. See Darling 2007: 118–22.

[214] Cowell et al. 2006.

[215] I therefore disagree with Ingalls (1954: 304), who argues that the difference between Śaṅkara's Vedānta and Yogācāra is to be spelt out 'psychologically and historically', rather than metaphysically.

# 4

# The School of Diṅnāga and Dharmakīrti

## 1. The Lives of Diṅnāga and Dharmakīrti

Dates of Diṅnāga and Dharmakīrti

Diṅnāga and Dharmakīrti form part of a lineage of teachers and disciples that starts with Vasubandhu (Diṅnāga's direct teacher) and continues via Diṅnāga's disciple Īśvarasena to Dharmakīrti. This gives us some limited help in dating them, since we can assume that they all lived roughly in the two centuries following the death of Vasubandhu. Diṅnāga is commonly dated to 480–540 CE; in the case of Dharmakīrti there is still considerable debate over whether he should be placed in the sixth or in the seventh century. Frauwallner[1] dates him to the period of 600–60 CE, based mainly on the fact that the Chinese pilgrim Xuanzang, who visited India around the middle of the seventh century, did not mention Dharmakīrti, though Yijing, who visited at the end of the seventh century, did. This evidence is hardly decisive, however, and there are arguments for dating Dharmakīrti considerably earlier, in the sixth century.[2] Based on the discussion of Dharmakīrti in Jaina sources, Balcerowicz suggests that he lived between 550 and 610 CE.[3]

The traditional accounts of Diṅnāga's life tell us that he was ordained as a monk in the Pudgalavāda tradition. Having grown dissatisfied with their theory of persons he left his teachers and eventually studied with Vasubandhu. In these accounts we also find a colourful story of how Diṅnāga composed his main work, the *Pramāṇasamuccaya*.[4] Before he left on his alms-round, Diṅnāga wrote the introductory verse on a piece of rock with a piece of chalk in the cave where he was living at the time:

Diṅnāga's *Pramāṇasamuccaya*

Having bowed down to Him, who embodies the epistemic instruments, who seeks the benefit the world, the teacher, the well-gone, the protector,
I here make a single compendium of my various scattered [writings],
to establish epistemic instruments.[5]

[1] Frauwallner 1961. [2] Balcerowicz 2016: 475–6. [3] Balcerowicz 2016: 477.

[4] Lama Chimpa 1970: 183–4, Bu ston 2013: 247–8.

[5] *pramāṇabhūtaya jaggadhitaiṣiṇe praṇamya śāstre sugatāya tāyine | pramāṇasiddhyai syamatāt samuccayaḥ kariṣyate viprasṛtād ihaikataḥ*. For further discussion of this verse see Jackson 1988; Hattori 1968: 73–6.

In his absence a non-Buddhist teacher called Kṛṣṇamunirāja became aware of Diṅnāga's undertaking and erased the verse. Diṅnāga wrote it down again, only to find it again erased on his return. This repeated itself a couple of times until Diṅnāga and Kṛṣṇamunirāja finally met and started to debate. Diṅnāga defeated him in debate, but was no match for Kṛṣṇamunirāja's magical powers. Flames shot out of his mouth and burned Diṅnāga's robes and all his belongings. Obviously very depressed by this turn of events, Diṅnāga threw the piece of chalk up into the air, resolving to give up his motivation to work for the sake of all living beings once it hit the ground. But it never did, since the bodhisattva Mañjuśrī caught it in mid-air, encouraging him, and assuring him that the work he was about to compose, the *Pramāṇasamuccaya*, would in time become 'the sole eye for all the other treatises'.

We encounter some of these motives from Diṅnāga's life-story (defending one's position in a debate, adversarial encounters with non-Buddhist teachers) in the accounts of Dharmakīrti's life again. Dharmakīrti studied Diṅnāga's *Pramāṇasamuccaya* with the latter's disciple Īśvarasena, who realized that Dharmakīrti's understanding not only surpassed his own, but was in fact equal to that of his teacher Diṅnāga, and encouraged him to compose a commentary on it.[6] This was to become his *magnum opus*, the voluminous, though unfinished, *Pramāṇavārttika*, expounding Diṅnāga's ideas using various conceptual innovations that were, as far as we know, not anticipated by his teacher Īśvarasena or by Diṅnāga himself.[7]

Dharmakīrti's *Pramāṇavārttika*

Dharmakīrti's life-story includes some animated episodes that pitch him against some of India's greatest non-Buddhist philosophers, including the Mīmāṃsakā Kumārila Bhaṭṭa and the Advaita Vedāntin Śaṅkara. Kumārila, who engaged very critically with the teachings of Diṅnāga, is said to have studied for a time at Nālandā, and hence had intimate acquaintance with Buddhist doctrines[8] and skill in countering them in debate. Dharmakīrti is supposed to have joined his household incognito as a servant, in order to learn

Dharmakīrti and Kumārila

[6] Lama Chimpa 1970: 229, Bu ston 2013: 249.

[7] These two works, Diṅnāga's *Pramāṇasamuccaya* and Dharmakīrti's *Pramāṇavārttika*, are central for understanding the key ideas of the logico-epistemological school, and will also be central for our exposition in the following pages. Though they are related to one another as root text and commentary we should not think that they form a monolithic doctrinal block. The two works are better conceived of as being like overlapping circles. There are some positions of Diṅnāga's that Dharmakīrti does not share, and the other way round, as well as a large overlap of common positions. The position is complicated by the fact that Diṅnāga's works appear to have been thoroughly destroyed at the time of the decline of Indian Buddhism (Warder 2000: 426–7), making it necessary to rely on translations instead of the original Sanskrit. Describing in detail how Dharmakīrti's system developed out of Diṅnāga's is unfortunately beyond the scope of a work such as this. We will focus on ideas that are common to both authors, sometimes noting points of disagreement between them as we go along.

[8] According to some sources Kumārila studied with various non-orthodox teachers (including Buddhists) for twelve years. See Verardi 2014: 207.

all his doctrines so as to be able to refute the non-Buddhist teachers more easily. He first worked on Kumārila's fields, and was later permitted to hear him teach, and even questioned Kumārila's wife and children to learn his most secret teachings that nobody else was permitted to hear.[9] Equipped with all he wanted to know, he then made his escape, ready to face Kumārila during a debate at a later time. Kumārila is supposed to have suggested that whoever lost the debate should be killed, but once Dharmakīrti had defeated Kumārila he and all his disciples converted to Buddhism.

Dharmakīrti and Śaṅkara

Dharmakīrti's biography also tells us that he defeated Śaṅkara in debate, who was so distressed by this that he drowned himself in the river Ganges.[10] He was, however, reborn as the son of Śaṅkara's disciple who, when the time was ripe, also challenged Dharmakīrti in debate, was also defeated, and drowned himself in the Ganges. The whole process repeated itself one more time, with the difference that this third incarnation of Śaṅkara did not kill himself after being defeated by Dharmakīrti at the very end of the latter's life, but converted to Buddhism.

Increased importance of debate with non-Buddhists

What is interesting about the content of these two biographies is what they reveal about the intellectual background against which the philosophical theories of Diṅnāga and Dharmakīrti were formulated. First, we note an increasing importance put on the ability to defend their interpretation of the Buddhist doctrine in a debate. The greater part of their biographies does not focus on their accomplishments as meditators or teachers, but on their success as debaters. Second, these debates were usually not intra-Buddhist disputes between different Buddhist schools but public debates, often involving high stakes, in which the Buddhist doctrine had to be defended against well-trained non-Buddhist opponents.[11]

Focus on logic and epistemology

Within this context several features of Diṅnāga's and Dharmakīrti's theories will appear less peculiar than they would otherwise have done. First, there is a very strong emphasis on discussions of epistemology and logic. When challenging an opponent in a debate, it is first of all important to have a clear conception of what possible sources of knowledge are acceptable, and ideally to

[9] Bu ston's version of this story (2013: 249–50) is peculiar. The teacher is not named here, but identified as Dharmakīrti's maternal uncle. Asking the teacher's wife for the answers to difficult questions about her husband's philosophical system, she agrees to put these questions to her husband while having sex with him. Dharmakīrti, apparently listening in, then steers the conversation as he 'tied a cord around her leg and pulled on it when difficult subjects were broached. After he understood thoroughly, he left.'

[10] Lama Chimpa 1970: 233.

[11] Stcherbatsky (1994: 1. 35) regards the account of Dharmakīrti's encounter with Kumārila and Śaṅkara as 'an indirect confession that these great brahmin teachers had met with no Dharmakīrti to oppose them. What might have been the deeper causes of the decline of Buddhism in India proper and its survival in the border lands, we never perhaps will sufficiently know, but historians are unanimous in telling us that Buddhism at the time of Dharmakīrti was not on the ascendancy, it was not flourishing in the same degree as at the time of the brothers Asaṅga and Vasubandhu.' For further discussion of the decline of Buddhism in India see Verardi 2014.

reach a consensus with the opponent about which sources either side may appeal to. Obviously it would not do for each side to cite the sacred scriptures of their respective school as authoritative, for the other side is unlikely to accept them so a debate could not even get started. It is therefore essential to establish some common ground both parties think can be legitimately appealed to in order to resolve a dispute.

More arguments for Buddhist claims

Second, it becomes clearer why in the tradition following Diṅnāga and Dharmakīrti we encounter an unprecedented number of arguments that set out to establish key Buddhist claims, such as arguments for the Buddha as a source of authority, his omniscience, the law of karma, rebirth, and so forth. Such topics would not have to be supported when speaking to a Buddhist audience, but in a situation in which Buddhist teachers engaged in debates with non-Buddhist teachers who shared very little of their religiously motivated beliefs, the ability to defend them in a way that had a chance of convincing the as-yet unconverted was a highly desirable feature.

## 2. Epistemology

In accordance with the strong epistemological focus of this school, Diṅnāga begins his *Pramāṇasamuccaya* with a chapter on perception, setting out some of the key epistemological distinctions of his system.[12] In the salutation that begins the work (quoted above) Diṅnāga addresses the Buddha by the term *pramāṇabhūta*, 'embodying the epistemic instruments'. This does not mean that the Buddha should be regarded as authoritative simply because of his enlightened status,[13] but rather that his enlightenment is the fruit of, and therefore flowing in its nature from, the correct application of epistemic instruments.

*svalakṣaṇa* and *sāmānyalakṣaṇa*

He first points out that there are only two kinds of veridical cognition brought about by epistemic instruments, perception (*pratyakṣa*) and inference (*anumāna*). This distinction is nicely mirrored at the ontological level by a distinction between two kinds of objects, the *svalakṣaṇa* (literally 'self-marked') and the *sāmānyalakṣaṇa*[14] ('generally marked'). According to the

[12] See Hattori 1968.

[13] This attitude would be rather uncharacteristic of how the Buddha himself thought of the epistemic role of authority, advising his disciples to test his words like the purity of gold is tested: 'Monks, just as experts examine gold by heating, cutting, and rubbing, so is my teaching to be accepted, but not out of reverence for me', *tāpāc chedāc ca nikaṣāt suvarṇam iva paṇḍitaiḥ | parīkṣya bhikṣavo grāhya madvaco na tu gauravāt*. This verse is found, *inter alia*, in Śāntarakṣita's *Tattvasaṃgraha* (verse 3588) and in the *Jñānasārasamuccaya* attributed to Āryadeva (see Hattori 1968: 73, and, more generally, Mimaki 2008).

[14] *sāmānyalakṣaṇa* is also frequently translated as 'universal' or 'property', though it should be more precisely understood as an *object* marked by a general quality (as is entailed by understanding the term *sāmānyalakṣaṇa* as a *bahuvrihi* compound). The idea is that such 'objects in general' can be known without standing in direct contact with any specific instance. I can infer from the sound

most common interpretation, the former are momentary particulars and the latter are objects in general, particulars being exclusively accessed by sense perception, while objects in general are apprehended by inference.

Diṅnāga describes these *svalakṣaṇa* entities as free from conceptual construction (*kalpanāpodha* or *nirvikalpaka*) and indescribable, because they are not associated with any name. Perception 'yields a total but unconceptualized, prelinguistic image of this object: perception does not determine or ascertain anything'.[15] If we read Diṅnāga's theory as a version of the Abhidharma project, we can consider the *svalakṣaṇa* entities to be the fundamental *dharmas* and perception as a route that gives us access to them. (Again, *dharmas* can here be usefully conceptualized as particularized properties or tropes.) Conceptual construction (*kalpanā*, literally 'ordering' or 'arranging'), on the other hand, only works on groups of *dharmas*, assembling them together as a property (e.g. by disregarding the distinctions between different very similar blue-tropes) or an individual object (e.g. by putting together a blue-trope, a shape-trope, and so on). Perception is therefore never perception of the kind of medium-sized dry goods of our everyday acquaintance, such as tables and chairs.[16] On this interpretation the *svalakṣaṇa* entities are sometimes compared to the sense data of twentieth-century Western epistemology.[17] This idea is helpful to the extent that both are taken to be immediate objects of acquaintance. However, the analogy carries us only so far. Sense data are supposed to really have the properties they appear to have (thereby providing a foundation for our knowledge of the world), yet for Diṅnāga there are no properties at the level of *svalakṣaṇas*.

Relation to the Abhidharma project

The theory of perception that the logico-epistemological school defends faces the following apparent difficulty. On the one hand, perception is understood as non-conceptual (*kalpanāpoḍha*), non-erroneous (*abhrānta*), and directed at what is ultimately real, namely the *svalakṣaṇa* entities. It also can only perceive aggregates (*saṃcita*) of ultimately real objects, such as infinitesimal particles (*paramāṇu*).[18] They cannot be perceived in isolation, but only once they form a collection together with other such particles. On the other hand, the logico-epistemological school of Diṅnāga and Dharmakīrti, cohering with the mereological reductionism we find in other Buddhist traditions, does not accept collections or aggregates as ultimately real. As the example of the chariot and its parts shows us, a whole is something that is conceptually superimposed upon the ultimately real parts, but nothing that is ultimately real itself. This is obviously a problem for the account of perception described here, for if perception perceives aggregates, and aggregates are conceptual constructs,

Perception and ultimate reality

How can perception access the impartite non-conceptual?

that my neighbour owns a piano (a 'piano in general'), though any particular piano could have given rise to that instance of knowledge.

[15] Eltschinger 2010: 407. [16] Hayes 1988: 138. [17] Hayes 1988: 134.

[18] Dunne 2004: 99, 102, 109.

then how can perception provide us with access to the non-conceptual? Perception is seen here as based on a structural isomorphism between perception and the perceived,[19] but if a cognitive image (which is singular) can only ever be an image of an aggregate (which is plural), since only aggregates can be perceived, how could the two be structurally identical?[20]

Not a singular entity, but a singularity of effect

Later authors have tried to solve this difficulty by arguing that the cognitive image does not correspond to a single infinitesimal particle, or to a whole made of many such particles, but to the fact that many particles together produce the effect of being perceived. On the mental side we have the singularity of appearance, and on the side of the object we do not need to accept a singular entity, that is, an entity that somehow is one, despite having many parts, but it is sufficient that there is a singularity of effect, or a singularity of causal function. If this procedure works, we seem to be able to maintain that 'the object of perception is a real, physical entity which, although ultimately singular, somehow encompasses physical components that are ultimately multiple'.[21] However, this solution does not suffice for giving the defender of the logico-epistemological school everything he wants. The problem simply arises once more if we consider the case of a mental object. Such an object can be a single mental image, despite being phenomenologically variegated (*citra*; consider, for example, the image of a multicoloured butterfly's wing). In the case of infinitesimal particles the 'unity in multiplicity' is split across two levels. The perception is unified, though the object is variegated. But in the mental case there is no level we can turn to in order to repeat this trick. Both the unity and the variegation have to be attributed to the perception in question.

Dropping realism about external objects

Does this now mean that the logico-epistemological school has to drop its account of perception? Interestingly, this is not what happens. What they drop is *the overarching framework* in which this theory of perception is located, namely realism about external objects. We will discuss the background of this in more detail in our discussion of the 'sliding scales of analysis', but, to put it briefly, the external realist position, with its demand of a structural isomorphism between perceptions and external infinitesimal particles, is not to be considered to be the school's final view, but is to be replaced by an idealistic ontology on Yogācāra lines. If we accept this, then the crucial premise that we can only perceive aggregates disappears, as the notion of aggregation only covers the realm of the physical, a realm the idealist conception dispenses with.

It is also worth noting in passing, with regard to the question how the theories of Diṅnāga and Dharmakīrti relate to those of the Madhyamaka school, that the difficulty with the theory of perception just described can equally be interpreted

[19] Eltschinger 2010: 408.

[20] For a detailed discussion of this problem see Dunne 2004: 98–113.

[21] Dunne 2004: 110.

as supporting the claim that any perception is by necessity intrinsically bound up with conceptualization. That perception can only access aggregates, and that such aggregates are conceptual superimpositions, demonstrates that there cannot be any direct perceptual contact that is based on a structurally isomorphic reflection of the conceptualization-independent entities, a thesis that is at the very centre of the Mādhyamika's philosophical vision.

Perception, conceptualization, and Madhyamaka

We understand the logico-epistemological school's theory of *svalakṣaṇa* and *sāmānyalakṣaṇa* as pursuing a reductionist project. Its aim is to construct a theory based on a minimum of entities we have to consider as fundamentally real, constructing everything else on the basis of these entities. Understood in this way, it is tempting to understand it as a form of epistemological foundationalism.[22] Such projects consider particular parts of our knowledge as immune to sceptical doubt, and they proceed to reconstruct the rest of our knowledge on the basis of such an unshakeable foundation. In the present case this basis is supposed to consist of the momentary particulars, identified with the *svalakṣaṇa* entities. One reason that supports this idea is that for Dharmakīrti, perception is by its very nature immune from error.[23] The object of perception causes an internal representation, a form (*ākāra*) or appearance (*ābhāsa*) that corresponds to the object.[24] Diṅnāga criticizes the Nyāya definition of perception for incorporating the property of being inerrant (*avyabhicārin*), because this property is already part of what it means to be a perception, and not anything that needs to be included specifically in a definition.[25] The apprehension of a momentary particular by a perception cannot be mistaken, since the perception cannot deviate from what it is in contact with.[26] In order to make this claim cohere with the fallibility of human knowledge, all errors must be relegated to the mind.[27] Part of the price to pay for error-proofing

Epistemic foundationalism?

Perception as immune from error

What still counts as perception?

[22] The project is also ontologically foundationalist insofar as the *svalakṣaṇa* entities ground the existence of all other objects. They are the point where the process of ontological reduction stops.

[23] *Pramāṇaviniścaya* 1.4: *pratyakṣaṃ kalpanāpoḍham abhrāntam*, Steinkellner 2007: 7. Eltschinger (2010: 410) notes that Dharmakīrti's theory of perception has the curious consequence that, 'as far as perception is concerned, there is no difference between an ordinary mind and one that is liberated'. Once liberation has been obtained, the awakened being finds itself in direct, un-erroneous perceptual contact with reality (*tattvadarśana*) a contact that is free from conceptuality. It is only when teaching other beings that the Buddha would then again resort to concepts in his interaction with the world.

[24] Perception is thus connected with the world both through causation (as the external object causes the *ākāra* via the relevant sensory faculty) and through resemblance (as the *ākāra* has the form of the external object). This view of perception is commonly associated with the Sautrāntikas (see Kellner 2014).

[25] Hayes 1988: 139.

[26] If we follow the interpretation in Hayes 1988: 139 Diṅnāga, even though, unlike Dharmakīrti, he did not include immunity from error (*abhrānta*) in the definition of perception, still held that 'cognition born of faculty–object contact is necessarily non-erroneous', as Diṅnāga's criticism of the Nyāya definition implies.

[27] This is a position of Diṅnāga's that Dharmakīrti did not share.

perception in this way is that hardly anything of what we would usually classify as perception can be considered to be so by the present account. In particular, our ordinary perceptions of medium-sized dry goods like shoes, and ships, and sealing-wax do not count as perceptions.

Connection with Nāgārjuna's criticism of epistemic instruments

Some scholars have argued that the motivation for this foundationalist project can be found in Nāgārjuna's criticism of epistemic instruments in his *Vigrahavyāvartanī*.[28] The idea is that, after Nāgārjuna's argument that the epistemic instruments could not be established by themselves, by something else, by both, or neither, Diṅnāga's project constitutes an 'exasperated attempt to secure the possibility of valid cognition',[29] defending the possibility of epistemology against the 'onslaught of Nāgārjuna's dialectics that crumbled the old foundations that used to support the entire Buddhist religion'[30] by his notion of perception. Nāgārjuna's critique, it is argued, is based on the idea that all our cognitions are inevitably tarnished by a conceptual overlay (*samāropa*), and if Diṅnāga can establish that there is some sort of untainted epistemic access to the world that manages to avoid contamination by conceptualization he would have found a way to avoid Nāgārjuna's sceptical criticism. Diṅnāga's supposed reply would embrace an externalist conception of knowledge, where even though we might not *know* that our beliefs are justified, we would still *be* justified, because below the distorting user-interface of conceptualization there would be a level of epistemic access to the world that both provided the raw material for conceptualization, and also connected with things in a direct way, without a mistaken superimposition of entities that fail to be there in the first place.

Nāgārjuna does not pursue a sceptical agenda

I am not entirely convinced by this supposed connection between Nāgārjuna and Diṅnāga, primarily because I do not consider it to be very likely that in the *Vigrahvyāvartanī* Nāgārjuna was in fact pursuing a sceptical agenda.[31] It is true that Nāgārjuna argues against a foundationalist conception of the epistemic instruments, a picture according to which these instruments by their nature (*svabhāvatas*) deliver authoritative knowledge. But an argument that knowledge cannot be grounded in this way is not an argument that there cannot be any knowledge at all, which is the position the sceptic would want to argue for. Nor does it undermine the foundations of the Buddhist religion. In fact, Nāgārjuna makes the point[32] that it is precisely the assumption that auspicious phenomena, phenomena leading to liberation and so on, exist with intrinsic nature that undermines the Buddhist path, since it is otherwise unclear how these could be developed where they are not present.[33]

[28] Franco 1986: 86. [29] Franco 1986: 86. [30] Franco 1986: 89.
[31] For further discussion of my interpretation of this text see Westerhoff 2010.
[32] *Vigrahavyāvartanī* 52–6. [33] Westerhoff 2010: 94–104.

Three kinds of perception

At this stage it is worthwhile to note that there are various cognitive processes that Diṅnāga subsumes under the notion of perception. So far we have just referred to sensory perception with the five external senses, but in the Indian context perception is always understood to also include the cognition of mental events in a manner that is as direct and immediate as the sensory cognition of external objects. In addition to the perception of external and of mental objects, Diṅnāga also includes yogic perception (*yogipratyakṣa*) as a third kind of perception. This is a form of perception that apprehends a thing in itself (*arthamātra*) without any form of conceptual construction based on scriptural authority (*āgama*).[34] Could the interpretation that *svalakṣaṇa*-type objects cannot be known with more authoritative force than those with *sāmānyalakṣaṇa* argue that it is yogic perception instead that puts us into direct contact with how things are at the fundamental level? We shall come back to this question when we have a closer look at the notion of yogic perception in section 6 of this chapter.

## 3. Inference

Inference and conceptual construction

The second epistemic instrument other than perception that Diṅnāga discusses is inference (*anumāna*). In the logico-epistemological school inference extends much further than we would normally expect it to. What we would otherwise call a perceptual judgment (say, 'this tomato is red') becomes the result of an inference for Diṅnāga, since neither the property of redness nor the temporally extended tomato are considered to be available for perceptual access. The former is constructed via the process of exclusion,[35] the latter by running together a series of quickly succeeding tomato-moments.[36] But in addition to the form of inference that mediates between the world and us, there is also the realm of those inferences we employ in debating with others. Diṅnāga and Dharmakīrti are the philosophers who contributed in the most significant way to the explication of rules of inference within the Buddhist theoretical enterprise. They built on the work of earlier Buddhist authors such as Vasubandhu,[37] but it is only during their time, a time of intense debate between Buddhist and non-Buddhist thinkers, that the study of inferential patterns occupied centre-stage in the Buddhist philosophical world. The focus on the theory of

Inference and debate

[34] Hattori 1968: 27. There is some disagreement on whether these three are all the forms of perception Diṅnāga accepted, or whether reflexive awareness (*svasaṃvedana*) should be added as a fourth, rather than just being considered as a form of mental perception. See Franco 1993; Yao 2004.

[35] See the section on *apoha* below (pp. 235–8).

[36] To this extent the notion of *anumāna* also covers what we would more commonly refer to as 'conceptual construction'.

[37] Such as his *Vādavidhi*, see Anacker 2002: 29–48.

knowledge that is characteristic of the school of Diṅnāga and Dharmakīrti links up clearly with the new prominence of inter-doctrinal debates.[38] Not only would conducting such debates presuppose an agreement on what sources of knowledge could be seen as authoritative in general, there also needed to be specific agreement on which argumentative patterns would be accepted by both parties as carrying probative force.

Characteristics of inferences

Diṅnāga considered inference to be based on the idea that certain observed features could be indicative of other unobserved ones, such as when we infer an unobserved fire on a distant mountain pass, because we observe smoke there. Such indicative relations cannot always be successfully appealed to, though. That the ground is wet might be because it has rained recently, but we cannot use the wetness to infer the rain, as there are other possible reasons (somebody might have emptied a pot of water, for instance). In order to exclude such cases, Diṅnāga defined acceptable inferences to be those characterized by a triple mark (*trairūpya*).[39] In the context of the smoke–fire example mentioned above the three characteristics are:

The triple mark

1. *pakṣadharmatā*: the subject of the inference (*pakṣa*), the mountain, is characterized by the reason (*hetu*), smoke;
2. *anvaya*: there is at least one similar entity (*sapakṣa*) characterized by the reason, smoke, and the property to be established (*sādhya*), fire;
3. *vyatireka*: there is no dissimilar entity (*vipakṣa*) characterized by the reason, smoke, and lacking the property to be established (*sādhya*), fire.

Pervasion

The relation between the reason and the property to be established encoded in these conditions is termed 'pervasion' (*vyapti*); in a fully formulated inference pervasion is spelt out in terms of examples that establish the second and third conditions. Establishing the second condition requires a similar or congruent example such as kitchen stove, where there is smoke and fire, the third a dissimilar or incongruent example such as a lake, where there is neither smoke nor fire. In the case of the spurious rain inference just mentioned, the second characteristic does not obtain. There are examples of the ground being characterized by the reason (wetness), but without it having rained recently.

*anumāna* is not formal logic

Inferences that exemplify the triple mark are formally valid, yet it is unsatisfactory to regard the theory of *anumāna* put forward by the logico-epistemological school simply as an attempt to construct a formal logic.[40] Epistemological considerations play an important role in the thought of Diṅnāga

[38] In addition, inference concerns phenomena that are not immediately accessible to the senses, and these are particularly likely to give rise to differing opinions.

[39] See Hayes 1988: 112–31.

[40] We sometimes even find the tradition of Diṅnāga and Dharmakīrti as a whole described as 'Buddhist logic' (this is, for example, the title of Theodore Stcherbatsky's 1930–2 pioneering study of this tradition).

and Dharmakīrti, and failing to appreciate this leads to an inevitable misunderstanding of their tradition, resulting in criticism of them for failing to carry through a project they were never engaged with in the first place. Their conception of *anumāna* incorporates formal features at a central place, but is not restricted to them.

Inference for oneself and others

Diṅnāga argued that there are two kinds of inference based on the *trairūpya* model, inferences 'for oneself' (*svārthānumāna*) and inferences 'for others' (*parārthānumāna*). The former are inferences performed in one's own mind to acquire inferential knowledge of some matter. The latter are inferences put forward in a public context so that another person can use them to acquire their own inferential knowledge based on them. The difference between the two is not simply one of perspective. An inference for oneself is simply the knowledge of the property to be established in the subject, since there is the right kind of reason. It only involves two members, subject and reason, whereas an inference for others involve three, the subject, the reason, and the two examples. It might appear that the difference between them is little more than a difference in formulation, and that in any case the logical structure of an inference in its form 'for oneself' and 'for others' is the very same.[41] This overlooks, however, that the inference 'for oneself' is about a sequence of psychological states that lead to an inferential cognition, while the inference 'for others' is about the proper way in which such a sequence is to be expressed in language. A helpful way of conceptualizing the difference between the two types is by understanding the inference for oneself in terms of a mental model.[42] The idea is that the reasoner constructs a model in his mind (a model that might well be not linguistic, but, for example, pictorial), a model of situations that satisfy all the premises in order to test whether the conclusion holds in all of them. If it does, the inference is valid. This insight can then be expressed by putting all the premises and the conclusion in proper linguistic form for the sake of conveying the inference to another speaker.

Mental models

Inference 'for oneself' is obviously the most important of the two, since it delivers the aim of inference, inferential cognition, whereas inference 'for others' merely fulfils the function of allowing others to create a similar cognition in their own minds. Nevertheless, in order to study the form inference takes in the Indian discussion we need to look at its public form as inference 'for others'. Different Indian logical traditions differ on how much of the above structure has actually to be stated in the proper expression of an inference. The Nyāya conception of inference stands at one end of the scale, distinguishing

Ways of formulating 'inference for others'

[41] Prasad 2002: 36.

[42] See Chatterjee and Sirker 2010. The authors also argue that the theory of mental models provides a good template for understanding the purpose of one of Diṅnāga's logical treatises, the *Hetucakraḍamaru*.

five essential parts in what is essentially the pattern described above, including stating the statement to be proven ('there is fire on the mountain') twice, at the beginning of the inference, as a thesis to be argued for, and at its end, as a thesis just established. Dharmakīrti's conception is at the parsimonious end of the scale, requiring just two parts, the assertion of the subject having the establishing property (*pakṣadharmathā*, 'there is smoke on the mountain') and the assertion of the pervasion (*vyapti*) of the establishing and the established property ('wherever there is smoke there is fire'). That the inference does not even require stating the thesis to be argued for coheres well with Dharmakīrti's conception of the inference 'for others' as a means (*sādhana*) for generating an inferential cognition in an audience, not as a self-sufficient, comprehensive proof.

Inferences as tokens

From the preceding discussion of inferences 'for oneself' and 'for others' it is evident that both kinds of inference are tokens, not types. The first is a sequence of specific mental events in one's mind, the other a sequence of speech acts intended to bring about such a sequence of mental events in the mind of another. The sequence of mental events, the inference 'for oneself', is obviously the most important one. Yet this may suggest that Diṅnāga's and Dharmakīrti's theory incorporates a kind of psychologism that Western logic explicitly sets out to reject. From the Western perspective, logic does not deal with things that go on in the mind but with abstract structures of implication. This is important, since the force of logical succession is altogether greater than that of psychological succession. In my mind I can make any thought follow a given other thought, but only certain conclusions follow from a given set of premises. For this reason, understanding logical sequences in terms of psychological sequences is bound to lead to problems. However, the logico-epistemological school does not assume that all there is to a sound inference is what goes on in the reasoner's head. Rather, it is the underlying facts in the world that determine whether an inference like the one from smoke to fire is successful. The thesis established (*pratijñā*, 'there is fire on the mountain') is not an abstract object towards which the act of inference is directed, but the structure of the result of a mental act that is underwritten by how things are in the world. If the properties in the world are not aligned in the way specified by the three characteristics the inference will not achieve its epistemic aim.[43]

The role of examples in inferences

Apart from the fact that the logico-epistemological school does not conceive of inferences as abstract objects but rather as concrete tokens, there is another fact that highlights a crucial difference between the Indian theory of inference

[43] This fact holds for the Indian logical tradition more generally, though opinions differ over what the 'underlying facts in the world' amount to. For a Naiyāyika it will be the way universals are related to each other and to the objects they instantiate; for the followers of Diṅnāga and Dharmakīrti it will be spelt out as involving *apoha*-based *ersatz* constructions.

and the study of logic as it is familiar from the Western context. This is the use of examples to spell out the similar and dissimilar cases. If the argument we are considering is deductively valid, there is no need to introduce examples, apart from heuristic purposes. The introduction of examples is more characteristic of inductive arguments that attempt a proof by cases ('because these representative examples have a property, others have too').

Logical and epistemological dimension of *anumāna*

What these differences indicate is that the Indian *anumāna* is to be considered as distinct from its Western relative insofar as it merges a logical and an epistemological dimension. The three characteristics of the reason indicate a specific way in which properties in the world are related, and if they are so related, making the associated inference ('there is fire, because there is smoke') will result in knowledge. The purpose of the examples is to maximize the likelihood that the person who draws the inference is really doing so in a situation in which the properties are related as described.[44]

Positive example

The positive example assures us that the property to be established, and the property that is to act as its indicator, are indeed real. In the case of fire and smoke this is obviously not very contentious, but in the case of inferences involving less straightforwardly empirical objects matters might not be so clear. For properties to be taken ontologically seriously they must be instantiated in some place or other,[45] and clearly the instantiation of the two properties referred to in the inference cannot be used to settle this point, since the inference is the very thing under dispute.[46]

Negative example

The negative example,[47] on the other hand, is in place to show that we have applied due diligence in ascertaining that the threefold characteristic really obtains in the world. The example of the lake illustrates this well. One might well think that the mist rising from a lake is an instance of something that looks very much like smoke, though it arises entirely without fire. Having understood the nature of mist, however, and its difference from smoke, we can be assured

[44] For further discussion of this understanding of *anumāna* see Siderits 2016a.

[45] The reason that makes the tradition of Indian logic not particularly interested in pure validity, divorced from soundness (namely, that inferences are supposed to generate inferential knowledge about the objects of debate, rather than being of interest merely as abstract structures) may also be what explains its lack of interest in uninstantiated properties.

[46] See Dunne 2004: 32.

[47] There is debate about whether both examples need to be present in all cases. A situation where this demand is problematic is when inferences establish a universal property (such as, in the Buddhist case, 'everything is impermanent' or 'everything is empty'). If these conclusions are true the arguments establishing them could not refer to *vipakṣa* cases, as there would then be nothing permanent or non-empty. (See Dunne 2004: 30–1, n. 39.) Very early Indian discussions of formal inferences do not mention the counterexample. One explanation of this fact is that one would usually expect the discussion of counterexamples to come from the opponent in the debate, not from the proponent. If this is the case, including the two kinds of example in the inference might indicate that the form of inference changes over time as the conception of inference changes, from something regarded as belonging primarily to a debating context, involving a proponent, to something mainly seen as what individual epistemic agents do. (See Siderits 2016a: 124, n. 83).

that in the lake both smoke and fire are absent. Adducing the negative example indicates that we have checked for potential cases that indicate that the inference we have drawn might, after all, not be supported by the way the world is.

Pseudo-reasons

This explanation also provides a good way of understanding the list of 'pseudo-reasons' (*hetvābhāsa*) we find discussed in most Indian texts on logic and debate. One way of seeing them is just as a list of defects in the construction of an argument that turn it into a fallacy and imply that the offender has lost the debate. Another way of understanding them is to consider them as a list of inferential pitfalls reasoners are prone to make. Taken in this way they could function as a basis for checking that the most likely mistakes in constructing an inference have been ruled out.

Fallibilism and externalism

Of course, despite our best efforts to determine how the property to be established and the establishing property are related, we could still be mistaken in our view. There might be cases where the establishing property exists without the property to be established that we have overlooked. The Indian theory of *anumāna* considers it as fallible—a clear contrast with the Western notion of a deductive inference, which is not fallible (though it may be based on false premises).

The *anumāna* is also a good indicator of the externalist background of much of ancient Indian epistemology, Buddhist and non-Buddhist. For an externalist, knowledge comes from standing in a specific relation to the object known, whether or not one knows that this relation obtains. For the internalist, on the other hand, knowledge requires knowing that we know. Reliable routes of epistemic access are not enough for them, we also need to *know* that these routes are reliable. The externalist conception renders the fallibilist conception of inference unproblematic. We do not engage in inference in order to acquire knowledge we know to be indefeasible in every possible way. What assures us that our inferentially gained belief is knowledge is that the three characteristics that describe the inference also hold true of the way the respective properties are related in the world. When engaging in inference we attempt to make it likely that we are in an epistemic situation where this relation of properties obtains, and the two examples are means we employ to increase the likelihood of being in that situation.

'good reasons' and validity

It has now become clear that the ideal of a good reason (*saddhetu*) the tradition of Diṅnāga and Dharmakīrti describes encompasses more than simply formal validity. Formal considerations are of course present, the statement that there is smoke on the mountain, together with the statement of pervasion, encapsulates the (formally valid) *modus ponens* inference: 'if there is smoke there is fire, there is smoke on the mountain, so there is fire on the mountain.' But a good inference needs not just to be valid, it must also be sound, that is, have true premises. Otherwise the argument cannot give rise to an inferential cognition, and for this reason factual considerations form an essential part of appraising the status of arguments. In addition, for a reason to be good there needs to be a relevant doubt (*saṃśaya*) together with the desire to know (*jijñāsā*),[48] so epistemic considerations about who knows and doubts what must be taken into account as well. Finally, the fact that the contestants in a debate must be in certain epistemic states for a reason to be a good reason entails that there are also strategic considerations about when to make an argument that need to be considered. If a contestant does not have the requisite doubt or desire to know, giving an argument is pointless, even though the argument's intrinsic features have not changed.

Trying to understand the Indian theory of inference as doing substantially the same as logic developed in the Western tradition therefore inevitably fails to do justice to the complexity of the enterprise, and its connection with the wider Indian philosophical and religious landscape. While the two endeavours overlap at important points, we achieve the most nuanced description of the theory of *anumāna* by considering it as a *sui generis* intellectual project.

## 4. Metaphysics

Causal efficacy

A crucial distinction that Dharmakīrti (though not Diṅnāga) draws between *svalakṣaṇa*- and *sāmānyalakṣaṇa*-type entities is that only the former, but not the latter, have causal efficacy (*arthakriyāsamārtha*). Such efficacy has ontological import, as it is the mark of the real. This point is made very clearly in his *Pramāṇavārttika* 3:3, here presented with the commentator Manorathanandin's additions in brackets:

> Whatever has causal powers, that really exists in this context [i.e. when we examine reality]. Anything else is declared to be [just] conventionally existent [because it is practically accepted through mere conceptual fictions]. These two [i.e. the real and the conventional] are [respectively] particulars and objects in general.[49]

The possession of causal power (*śakti*) and the ability to act on and influence other entities is therefore the tell-tale sign that distinguishes the real from the unreal. This position has far-ranging implications for the whole of Dharmakīrti's philosophy. An immediate consequence is that because objects in general or object-types, failing to have a unique spatio-temporal location, fail to be causally efficient in this way Dharmakīrti regards them as not real.

Momentariness and causal efficacy

A characteristic of real things that, for Dharmakīrti, coincides with causal efficacy is momentariness. Clearly, if what is efficacious is momentary and vice

[48] This is a view that Dharmakīrti shares with the Nyāya tradition. See Dunne 2004: 16, n. 4.

[49] *arthakriyāsamartham yat tad atra [vastuvicāre] paramārthasat | anyat saṃvṛtisat proktaṃ [kalpanamātravyavahāryatvāt] | te [paramārthasaṃvṛtī] svasāmānyalakṣaṇe*, Miyasaka 1971–2: 42; Pandeya 1989: 64.

versa, objects in general cannot be efficacious (and hence not real) because they do not change from moment to moment—the very idea of an object in general entails its trans-temporal existence. It is important to note that Dharmakīrti's criticism applies both to what we might call 'horizontal' objects in general, as well as to vertical ones. Objects in general as trans-temporal, non-spatial objects such as redness or being extended obviously fail to satisfy the momentariness requirement for reality, but so do temporally extended objects, such as a red vase. They, too, are nothing but superimpositions on momentary particulars, and for that reason not fundamentally real.

Dharmakīrti's arguments for momentariness

What are Dharmakīrti's reasons for the thesis of universal momentariness? He puts forward two arguments, an 'argument from cessation' (*vināśitvānumāna*), a version of the argument from the spontaneity of destruction going back to Vasubandhu we met earlier, and an 'argument from existence' (*sattvānumāna*), a form of the argument from change.

Argument from cessation

The first argument starts from the empirically plausible premise that all things perish sooner or later. This presents us with two possibilities: either the perishing of an object is caused, or things perish without a cause. A straightforward example is the destruction of a pot (the effect) brought about by striking it with a hammer (the cause). However, when properly analysed, what the stroke brings about is a collection of shards, on which the non-existence (*abhāva*) of the pot is superimposed. Vasubandhu and Dharmakīrti argue more generally that absences (such as the absence of the pot) are not real things, and as such cannot enter into causal relations.[50] This leaves us with the second possibility, that things perish spontaneously (*ākasmika*). And this perishing, it is argued, has to happen immediately after the thing has arisen. If it perished only after some time there would have to be some cause responsible for it perishing *just then*, rather than at another time. We then need to postulate a real cause of a mere absence, and the difficulty of how we can have a two-place causal relation relating an existing cause to something that is not real arises once more.

Argument from existence

The argument for momentariness 'from existence' argues that real things are always causally efficacious in some way, though their effects might not always be noted by us. One effect that even the most seemingly inert objects produce is the existence of a closely resembling object at the next moment in time. But, Dharmakīrti argues, if things are always producing effects they must always be changing. Why? If an object persisted permanently (*nitya*) through periods of time, what would explain that it produced a series of effects, and produced effects that differ from one another? If a permanent object produced first effect *a*, then effect *b*, and if *a* and *b* are distinct, the permanent cause cannot be responsible for this, as it has not changed between the time of producing *a* and

[50] For this reason absences could also not cause anything. Rather than a fire going out because of the absence of oxygen, the real cause would be the presence of something else (such as nitrogen).

the time of producing *b*. The obvious reply would be that a persistent thing generates different effects successively, simply by being put into different causal surroundings. The same litmus solution turns red when mixed with an acid and blue when mixed with a base. However, this view does not seem to sit well with the way in which we actually analyse causal scenarios. When we compare two situations such that an effect has arisen in one but not in another, we consider the crucial causal factor to be precisely what is different between the two situations, not what is identical.

Thus, if causally efficacious objects continuously change, and if we do not assume that there is a constant substratum that underlies the change, we will be dealing with a succession of different though closely resembling objects that arise and cease in quick succession.

Consequences of rejecting objects in general

Dharmakīrti's identification of the real, the causally efficacious, and the momentary allows him to exclude objects in general from the realm of the real. At first sight this rejection of objects in general might appear to us as a fairly technical point of little consequence outside of the scholastic world of Buddhist metaphysical theorizing. This appearance is deceptive, however. First of all, note that this view has important implications for putting the Buddhist position in sharp opposition to most of its non-Buddhist rivals. The argument that permanent entities cannot enter into causal relations has obvious consequences both for the conception of a permanent soul (*ātman*), as well as for any theistic view that postulates the existence of a creator god. The eleventh-century scholar Mokṣākaragupta argues against the existence of a soul by pointing out that the occurent cognition of the self or soul (*ahaṃkārajñāna*) arises only intermittently; it is sometimes present, and sometimes absent. Therefore, as in the case of other kinds of cognitions that are sometimes present, sometimes absent (like, for example, cognition of lightning, which is only present when lightning is), we should infer that it must have a cause that is also sometimes present, sometimes absent, and not a cause that is permanent.[51] Inferring a permanently existent self on the basis of an intermittent sense of self is as faulty as inferring the existence of a permanently existent bolt of lightning on the basis of the momentary perception of its flash.

*ātman*

The creator god

Ratnakīrti, another member of the logico-epistemological school, argues that momentariness is wholly incompatible with the characteristics of a creator god,[52] implying not only that because such a god is permanent he could not have created the world, but also that because he is not causally efficacious he cannot be real.

Caste

In addition, the rejection of objects in general has important implication for the Buddhist view of the brahmanical concept of caste. Another term

[51] Kajiyama 1998: 141. [52] Patil 2009: 199, 333.

for object-types, *jāti*, can also denote caste, and connections between the non-existence of objects in general or object-types and the non-existence of caste were explicitly made by later commentators on Dharmakīrti. A defining feature of castes, according to the brahmanical understanding, is that they are natural kinds, divisions of the world that do not have a human origin but are grounded in the very nature of reality. Arguing for their non-existence allows Buddhists following the logico-epistemological school to distance themselves from other traditions and the social structures that come with them on strictly ontological grounds.[53]

Finally, the rejection of objects in general not only had important consequences for the Buddhist position in distinguishing it from other strands of Indian thought, it also created pressing questions for the Buddhists themselves.

The bifurcation of knowledge

Diṅnāga's distinction of two kinds of epistemic instrument and two kinds of epistemic object corresponding to them led to a curious bifurcation of knowledge. Suppose we infer the existence of fire on some distant mountain by observing smoke, and assume there is no smoke without fire. Later, when we climb the mountain and perceive the fire by sight, we do not achieve (contrary to what we might intuitively assume) a second epistemic perspective on the same fire that we previously inferred. For Diṅnāga, perceived and inferred objects are radically distinct. He rejects, in a word, what other schools of Indian philosophy refer to as *pramāṇasamplava*, the mixing of epistemic instruments to make it possible that several instruments produce cognitions of the same object. This somewhat unintuitive position is not simply a consequence of his rejection of the reality of objects in general, for these *sāmanyalakṣaṇa* are, for Diṅnāga, all that inference operates on, but also has a source in the Abhidharma background of the logico-epistemological school. This developed the theory that sensory perceptions such as sight, touch, and so on all only apprehended their particular objects. Diṅnāga can be seen as having taken up this 'epistemological atomism', combining it with the ontological split between particulars and objects in general, to end up with a theory in which each epistemic instrument only has access to one kind of object.[54]

Having created a theory with such a significant gap amongst the objects of knowledge, Diṅnāga and Dharmakīrti obviously needed some way of bridging it. We have the impression that when we perceive a fire that we have previously inferred, we access the same fire from two epistemic perspectives, though,

[53] Eltschinger 2012. In assessing the political dimension of the logico-epistemological school more generally it is worthwhile to note how the logico-epistemological school (as well as Buddhist tantra) can be regarded as arising from the 6th century social dynamics where Buddhism felt mounting pressure from its brahmanical opponents. In this context both epistemology and tantra can be understood as constituting Buddhism's attempt to fight back, in dialectical and ritual terms, against increasingly powerful Brahmin adversaries (Eltschinger 2013; 2014: 174).

[54] Dreyfus 1997: 298.

according to Diṅnāga and Dharmakīrti this is not the case, and we believe that when we think and talk we refer to objects in general, even though Diṅnāga and Dharmakīrti deny that such things are real. Supposing the logico-epistemological school is right about its revisionist project, we still need some account of how our mistaken ideas about epistemology relate to the ways we really acquire knowledge, and how these ways can be successful, given the constraints imposed by Diṅnāga's and Dharmakīrti's theory.

## 5. Language

*apoha* theory

A key conceptual tool for building such a bridge between the manifest image of the world and the austere reductionist vision of the logico-epistemological school is the theory of exclusion (*apoha*) developed by Diṅnāga and Dharmakīrti. They needed to provide some account of just what it is that we are talking about when we talk about the blue colour of a blue vase. Clearly they could not spell this out in the relatively straightforward manner of, for example, the Naiyāyikas, by saying that we refer to the object-type blue that is present (via an instantiation relation) in this particular vase. Since objects in general are not admitted as part of the theory's ontology, we require some kind of *ersatz* notion that can play the role of such objects without incurring all the metaphysical criticism that Diṅnāga and Dharmakīrti have voiced. This is what the notion of exclusion is supposed to provide. Instead of identifying blueness with the collection of individuals that all instantiate the property blue, we understand it as those individuals that the term non-blue excludes.

At first sight it is difficult to see what might be gained by this. If we divide our world into blue things and non-blue things, those things that the latter excludes (the complement of the set of non-blue things) are just all the blue things. All we have done, it seems, is to provide a cumbersome way of talking about the set of all blue things.

Absences as less real than presences

Two things need to be taken into account at this point. First, Diṅnāga and Dharmakīrti appear to rely here on a general Buddhist intuition that absences are less real than presences. If something turns out to be an absence, it is more straightforward to understand it as a conceptual construction (and hence not as fundamentally real) than if it happens to be a presence.[55] An empty table is both the absence of an orange, and the absence of an apple, and what distinguishes the two absences is that the first situation is one in which we were looking for an orange and failed to find one, while in the second we were looking for an apple. The very identity of an absence therefore turns out to

[55] Compare Cox 1988: 67.

depend essentially on something mind-made, namely our expectation to find something there which turns out to be absent.

*apoha* and two kinds of negation

Second, the notion of *apoha* indeed looks redundant if we understand it just as applying negation twice over, as two negations that cancel each other out. There is, however, a better way of understanding what the *apoha* construction was meant to achieve, if we consider a difference between two kinds of negation Indian scholars appealed to.[56] We have already mentioned these above; the first, implicative negation (*paryudāsa-pratiṣedha*), was used to negate an attribute of an individual while implying that a different attribute like it would apply, for example, by saying that someone is not a Brahmin while believing that he belongs to one of the other three castes. The second, non-implicative negation (*prasajya-pratiṣedha*) makes no such assumptions. If we say, for example, that a tree is not a Brahmin, we do not imply that is perhaps belongs to the *kṣatriya* or *vaiśya* caste. We can now use these two distinctions in the *apoha* construction by considering, for example, the non-implicative negation of 'being blue', then form the implicative negation of this negation, and treat the resulting complex as an *ersatz* for the object-type 'being blue'. What is the motivation for this? Non-implicative negations do not preserve certain assumptions about the *negandum* (in the above example, that whatever is not a Brahmin must belong to one of the other castes), stating that the thing negated does not have the property in question, nor another of the same kind. If we therefore form the non-implicative negation of the set of blue things, we end up with the set of non-blue things, but without assuming that this set is unified by another object-type, in the way in which the blue objects are unified by the object-type of blueness. Implicative negation claims that the *negandum* does not have the property in question, but another of the same kind. Forming the implicative negation of the non-implicative negation of the set of all blue things preserves the assumption that there is nothing unifying all the objects in the set, but returns us to the set of blue objects. It is evident that because two different negations have been applied in this context we cannot just assume that they cancel each other out.[57] We also see how moving through the two kinds of negation the metaphysical assumption that the set of all the blue objects is what it is because all the objects instantiate the object-type of blueness has been left behind. Diṅnāga can therefore employ the 'exclusion of what is other' (*anyāpoha*), that is, the implicative negation of the non-implicative negation of the original set as a substitute for object-types. When we speak about blueness and other properties we can simply consider this talk as referring

The two negations do not cancel each other out

[56] This interpretation of *apoha* semantics is explained in greater detail in Siderits 2016b.

[57] The fact that double negation elimination does not apply to mixed sequences of implicative and non-implicative negations is a key feature employed to explain certain puzzles connected with the tetralemma (*catuṣkoṭi*). See Westerhoff 2009: 68–89.

to the unproblematic exclusion, rather than to the ontologically dubious objects in general.

*apoha* and causal power

In Dharmakīrti's exposition of *apoha* theory the notion of causal power, which appears to be almost entirely absent from Diṅnāga's account, occupies a prominent role. By doing so, Dharmakīrti can address an important question arising in connection with the *apoha* construction: where does the original conception of blue objects, which is then processed by the machinery of two negations, come from? We obviously cannot assume that it is due to some property that all blue objects share, since these properties are precisely what this account is trying to do without. Dharmakīrti argues that what the blue objects share is a causal power, an ability to bring about certain effects which other objects lack. Yet we might ask whether this is not itself indicative of a shared property amongst all the blue objects, thereby reintroducing objects in general through the back door? Dharmakīrti is not committed to this problematic consequence, however, since he argues that the causal power of objects is to be conceptualized relative to our desires. All particulars are unique and without resemblance to any other particulars. Still, certain particulars may all fulfil some of our desires. Every fire-particular, for example, is distinct from every other one: some may be a wood fire, some may be caused by cow-dung, some may be smoky, some may be without smoke, some have red flames, some blue flames, and so on. Nevertheless, they all fulfil our desire when we want to warm ourselves. The needs at the root of our desires are usually sufficiently unspecific to allow a whole range of objects to satisfy them, and this makes it possible for us to group them all under the same concept 'fire'. We therefore see how these causal powers are crucially dependent on human conceptualization: they are picked out relative to human interests, and not by any characteristics of the objects separate from such interests. Still, does this not merely show that the objects instantiate certain causal powers, even though these powers are only *named* relative to human concerns? Dharmakīrti denies that a group of objects that answers to a specific human need can only do so if each member instantiates a common underlying property. The example he gives are antipyretic drugs. These all answer to the human need for a medicine that lowers fever, but they do so in causally different ways. Dharmakīrti takes this as indicating that there is nothing more behind grouping these objects together than that they satisfy a human need. We need not assume a resemblance in the objects themselves, and thereby some kind of object-type they all instantiate.

Causal power relativized to human desires

The role of conceptualization

When considering the theory of Diṅnāga and Dharmakīrti and the role that is played by a conceptual overlay superimposed on a set of fundamental entities we might think that their view of concepts and conceptualization is mainly negative, seeing it as something that stands between us and a direct, conceptually untainted view of the world. The theory of *apoha* shows that this is far from the case. Concepts are taken very seriously by Diṅnāga and Dharmakīrti, and the theory of exclusion goes to great length in describing how, despite the unreality of objects in general, concepts can still play a role in our everyday epistemic interaction with the world. Another reason for the importance of concepts that we have not discussed so far and will address in the next section is the role they play in yogic perception.[58]

## 6. Scriptural Authority and Yogic Perception

### *a. Scriptural authority*

We mentioned earlier that the development of Buddhist philosophy in India was influenced by three major factors: the necessity to conform with the teaching of the Buddha and the teachings of the later Buddhist masters, the need to develop its positions in a way that was rationally defensible in an argument with an opponent, and the fact that Buddhist philosophy formed part of a larger enterprise of meditative training that was ultimately intended to lead to the liberation from cyclic existence. How the thinking of Diṅnāga and Dharmakīrti was influenced by the need to defend the Buddhist doctrine against non-Buddhist opponents has become clear from our discussion so far. But the logico-epistemological school also has interesting things to say on the other two factors, scriptural authority and meditative practice. In keeping with their dominant epistemic interests, both of these factors are analysed with respect to their ability to act as authoritative sources of knowledge. Are they able to be appealed to as epistemic instruments that can be applied on the way to liberation?

Given that Diṅnāga and Dharmakīrti are Buddhist writers, their epistemological system has to have something to say on the status of religious texts, Buddhist and non-Buddhist, as a source of knowledge. The status of scripture in this respect is particularly problematic since religious texts purport to give us insight into non-empirical matters, though they do not allow for cross-checking this against other epistemic instruments. While I can sometimes confirm inferential cognitions perceptually (going to the mountain to see whether there really is a fire) or perceptions inferentially (I can confirm that the cup I see in front of me is no hallucination because I can infer from my memory that I put it there), in the case of claims made by religious scriptures this is generally not possible. This on its own would not be too problematic if there was not also a considerable divergence between what different sets of scriptures assert.

For this reason it is necessary to understand the nature of scripture as a purported epistemic instrument. In the ancient Indian context we find two different ways in which this done, by investigating the source of the scripture, and by considering its intrinsic qualities.

[58] Dunne 2011: 103.

Authority of texts arising from their source

There are two different strategies authors have pursued in order to establish the reliability of religious texts based on their source. The first is to argue that the author of the scripture has various properties that make him trustworthy, and for this reason we should trust the scripture he has produced. The second is the claim that the scripture has precisely no author, and therefore no source that could in any way be tainted by human imperfections. Its perfection resides in the fact that, unlike all other kinds of text we know, it is authorless, and this perfection is the reason that we should trust it. The first strategy is pursued by the Buddhists, as well as by Nyāya, Sāṃkhya, Vaiśeṣika, and Jainism; the latter is famously defended by Mīmāṃsā, who argue that the Vedas are eternal and without a human author (*apauruṣeya*). This idea is criticized by the Buddhists by pointing out that an uncreated text could not have a speaker's intention behind it; it would be neither true nor false.[59]

Diṅnāga's praise of the Buddha

Dharmakīrti formulates his argument for the reliability of the Buddha by a detailed unpacking of the epithets that Diṅnāga employs in his praise to the Buddha in the verse of homage (*namaḥśloka*) that begins the *Pramāṇasamuccaya*, which we cited above. We remember that the Buddha is described there as one who 'embodies the epistemic instruments' (*pramāṇabhūta*), 'seeking the benefit of the world' (*jagaddhitaiṣin*), is a teacher (*śāstṛ*), a well-gone (*sugata*), and a protector (*tāyin*). Dharmakīrti believes that these are not just generic terms of praise for the Buddha, but that they actually embody an argument for his reliability. 'Seeking the benefit of the world' refers to the Buddha's great compassion, directed at the end of eventually becoming a protector of all living beings. In order to do so he has practised the means leading to liberation for a long time to become a teacher. This led to his becoming a *sugata*.[60] Dharmakīrti elsewhere telescopes this argument by simply saying that 'compassion is the proof'[61] of the Buddha embodying an epistemic instrument. The idea is that the Buddha's compassion caused him to seek ways to help others, acquiring the knowledge that would do so and the means of teaching it effectively.[62]

[59] See Karṇakagomin's *Pramāṇavārttikavṛttiṭīkā* 405: 24–407: 9 (Sāṅkṛtyāyana 1943). I discuss this point further below, in section 8b.

[60] Dharmakīrti reads this term as specifically applying to the Buddha's knowledge (Franco 1997: 19–20).

[61] *Pramāṇavārttika* 2: 34: *sādhanaṃ karuṇa*, Miyasaka 1971–2: 8.

[62] Tillemans (2008: 23, n. 59) suggests that the attempt to establish the authority of the Buddha not only had a theoretical function, but included 'important sociological and political dimensions'. One motivation for establishing the authority of a teacher in general, he suggests, was to 'defuse opponents' criticism about the impropriety of his behaviour or the questionable behaviour of certain monks'. At least Candrakīrti's commentary on Āryadeva's *Catuḥśataka* XII: 294, referring to 'erroneous views ... after having focused chiefly on the Buddhists' temples, food, monk's robes and the like' (Tillemans 2008: 130), might be understood like that (though it may equally be an injunction not to confuse the qualities of the message with those of some of its messengers). The supposedly cozy living conditions in Buddhist monasteries are mentioned repeatedly in satirical

Scriptural authority arising from internal characteristics

Dharmakīrti also mentions criteria for the authority of scripture that are based on characteristics of the texts themselves,[63] rather than on their origin. Later Tibetan scholastics referred to these as the 'threefold analysis' (*dpyad pa gsum*). This analysis amounts to checking whether the scripture in question contradicts perception, inference, or other propositions inferred from scripture, that is, whether it is in conflict with either of the two epistemic instruments identified by the logico-epistemological school, and whether it is consistent. In fact we find that this 'threefold analysis' forms the basis for an inductive argument for the reliability of scripture.[64] Within the logico-epistemological school we are presented with an exhaustive division of phenomena into three epistemic classes: the manifest (*pratyakṣa*), the imperceptible (*parokṣa*), and the radically inaccessible (*atyantaparokṣa*). Manifest objects are those literally 'in front of our eyes' (*prati-akṣa*), like tables and chairs; the imperceptible cannot be accessed by the senses, but can be inferred. The fire on the distant mountain that we infer from the presence of smoke is a case in point, but the Buddhist tradition also subsumes metaphysical theses such as momentariness and universal emptiness under this class. The radically inaccessible finally include topics such as the lifespans of gods in the various heavens of traditional Buddhist cosmologies, or the precise karmic connections between actions and their results. Facts about these are inaccessible to human reason, and to know them requires reliance on a qualified informant with greater cognitive power than mere humans (such as a Buddha).

Three degrees of epistemic distance

Inductive argument for long-distance reliability

The argument is then that, because the scriptures turn out to be correct in cases that can be checked (that is, they are confirmed by, and do not contradict, perception and inference, and do not lead to conflicting implications), they should also be deemed to be correct when talking about radically inaccessible things. A source that has been shown to be reliable as far as we can see should, according to this reasoning, also be considered as reliable when considering what lies beyond what we can see.

It is interesting to note that this argument already goes back at least as far as Āryadeva, who points out in his *Catuḥśataka* notes that:

> Whoever doubts what the Buddha said
> About that which is hidden
> Should rely on emptiness
> And gain conviction in him alone.

literature. See e.g. Bhaṭṭa Jayanta's *Āgamaḍambara*, Dezső 2005: 55–9, as well as pp. 13–14 of the extended notes to this volume available at <http://claysanskritlibrary.com/excerpts/CSLMuchAdoAnnotation.pdf>.

[63] It is worth noting that in this context Dharmakīrti does not draw a distinction between scripture in the narrower sense (*āgama*) and *śāstra*, commentaries and treatises more generally. The same procedures are to be applied to assess the reliability of both. See Tillemans 2008: 23, n. 58.

[64] Tillemans 1999a: 30.

Those who find it hard to see
This world are ignorant of others.
Those who follow them will be
Misled for a very long time.[65]

The idea here is that emptiness is one of the Buddha's teachings that can be demonstrated by reasoning,[66] and its correct explication by the Buddha should give us confidence in also accepting his teachings about what is imperceptible.[67] Other doctrines, according to this approach, are not even empirically adequate; they do not give a faithful representation of the world as we can grasp it via the senses and reasoning, so, *a fortiori*, they also cannot be trusted when it comes to making pronouncements about what is beyond this world.

Scripture as subsumed under inference

These considerations lead us to the view that Buddhist scriptures should be regarded as producing knowledge in an inferential way,[68] thereby subsuming scripture (*āgama*) under the epistemic instrument of inference. There is no need to postulate an additional epistemic instrument, testimony (*śabda*), as various non-Buddhist schools do. Instead of accepting the Buddha's pronouncement just on the basis of the fact that it was said by the Buddha, we can combine this fact as a premise with the claim of the Buddha's authoritativeness previously argued for in order to infer the statement itself.

[65] 12: 5–6: *buddhokteṣu parokṣeṣu jāyate yasya saṃśayaḥ | ihaiva pratyayas tena kartavyaḥ śūnyatāṃ prati || loko 'yaṃ yena durdṛṣṭo mūḍha eva paratra saḥ | vañcitās te bhaviṣyanti suciraṃ ye 'nuyānti tam*, Lang 1986: 111–12.

[66] It is interesting to note that all of the 'three marks of existence' (*trilakṣaṇa*), suffering, impermanence, and no-self, are included amongst the manifest and the imperceptible, and are therefore accessible to the conjoined forces of perception and reason. If it makes sense to speak of a 'conceptual core' of the Buddhist teaching, the *trilakṣaṇa* is probably one of best candidates for inclusion in it. The examples of knowledge that is radically imperceptible we find in the Buddhist sources are located on the periphery of the teachings. They are certainly not things one has to know in order to achieve liberation.

[67] This form of argumentation is also put forward by Nyāya authors like Gautama and Vātsyāyana. They argue that because the Vedas are reliable when it comes to matters that can be empirically tested (such as the efficacy of medical knowledge (*āyurveda*) and spells (*mantra*)) they are also to be trusted when it comes to non-empirical matters. (Tillemans 2008: 32). The information the Vedic texts provide on such practical matters not only testifies to their authors' good intention to help others, but also to their ability to turn this intention into successful practice. As such, their claims on matters that are not as readily observable as those relating to medicine and so forth should be considered as equally motivated by a combination good intention and ability. (Hayes 1984: 652.) This position differs, however, from the one put forward by Dharmakīrti, insofar as the latter wants to restrict the authority of scripture exclusively to radically imperceptible matters, whereas Nyāya does not. Verbal testimony (*śabda*), one of the four epistemic instruments that the Naiyāyika accepts, includes scripture and can, according to *Nyāyasūtra* 1.1.8, pertain both to empirical and to non-empirical matters. This leaves open the possibility of cases where scriptural testimony can provide knowledge even though the same matter is already settled by perception or inference, a possibility that Dharmakīrti rejects.

[68] See Dharmakīrti's *Pramāṇavārttika* 1: 216: 'Since the statements of a credible person are generally trustworthy, a cognition arising from them is an instrumental inference', *āptavākyā-viṣamvādasāmānyād anumānatā,* (Gnoli 1960: 109).

A different kind of inference?

The question arising at this point is precisely what kind of inference this inference could be. The paradigmatic kinds of inference for Dharmakīrti are inferences underwritten by how things stand in the world (*vastubalapravṛtta*), that is, inferences supported by the way entities such as fire and smoke are related to one another. Inferences based on scripture do not appear to belong to this kind, as the probative element in these seems to be not how two kinds of properties are related, but what a specific religious text says.

The later Tibetan commentarial tradition attempts to minimize this apparent difference, arguing that scriptural inferences are to be considered just like any other inference. The inference is simply taken to say that some scripture *x* is correct in teaching some (radically inaccessible) fact *y* because *x* is characterized by the triple mark of a reliable scripture mentioned above. We then just have to confirm that the subject has the property that constitutes the reason, and that there is the necessary pervasion: whenever there is a triply marked scripture the statements it makes are true.[69]

The Indian tradition, however, is considerably more cautious when it comes to assessing the status of scripturally based inference. Dharmakīrti cautions us against taking scripturally based inferences to be full-fledged epistemic instruments, and his commentator Śākyabuddhi in fact claims that it is not actually instrumental.[70]

Scepticism about appealing to the Buddha's authority

The reason for scepticism towards making a case for scriptural inference on the basis of the authority of the Buddha is that nobody can actually know that a specific person, such as the Buddha, in fact has the properties that make him an epistemic instrument when it comes to matters of liberation. Dharmakīrti notes that those specific mental attitudes that would ensure such authoritativeness are supersensible (*atīndriya*), and so:

> they would have to be inferred from physical and vocal behaviour that arises from them. And most behaviour can also be performed deliberately in a way other than the mental state they seem to reflect because those behaviours occur as one desires and because those behaviours may be intended for various aims. Thus, there is an overlap of the alleged evidence for faults and faultlessness.[71]

Appearances can be deceptive, and the display of a certain behaviour does not give us certain knowledge of the source of the behaviour.

Scepticism about appealing to the internal characteristics of texts

Basing our support of scriptural inferences on the internal characteristics of religious texts is not going to help us much either in securing the former's

[69] For further discussion see Tillemans 1999b: 37–41, 48, n. 4.

[70] Dunne 2004: 241.

[71] *Svavṛtti* on *Pramāṇavārttika* 1: 218–19: *svaprabhavakāyavāgvyavahārānumeyāḥ syūḥ | vyavahārāś ca prāyaśo buddhipūrvam anyathāpi kartuṃ śakyante puruṣecchāvṛttitvāt teṣāṃ ca citrābhisandhitvāt*, Gnoli 1960: 218–19, Dunne 2004: 244.

status. One reason for this is that Dharmakīrti is sceptical about the pervasion underlying a scripturally based argument since there is no necessary relation of words to their objects.[72] But if the connection between words and objects is merely due to human convention, then the force of an argument based on a scriptural passage must also be partially based on human conventions, and therefore cannot be considered to be purely founded in facts (*vastubala*).

Conventionality of language

The other reason is that the consideration of the triple characteristic, being an inductive argument, is not able to deliver certain knowledge. That someone has been reliable in the past, or is reliable on matters other than the ones presently discussed, does not imply that he is also reliable now, or is reliable regarding the matter at hand.[73] Dharmakīrti stresses his scepticism towards inductive arguments by pointing out that we cannot determine that all the rice in some pot is cooked merely by sampling and determining that individual grains, or even most of the grains, are cooked.[74] In the same way, the correctness of scripture regarding matters that can be determined by perception or inference does not guarantee its truth when it comes to matters that cannot be so determined.

Scepticism about induction

What, then, is the status of scripturally based inference? Later commentators such as Karṇakagomin and Śākyabuddhi point out that such inferences cannot be regarded as objective (*vastutas*); unlike the paradigm examples of inferential knowledge (such as inference from smoke to fire), they do not draw their epistemic power from a factual basis. Rather, they are inferences due to the thought of the people having them (*puṃso 'bhiprāyavaśāt*) because these people want to follow the Buddhist path.[75]

Scripturally based inferences cannot be objective

The picture emerging from this seems to be that scriptural authority is a source that practitioners need to rely on in order to set out on the spiritual path as a matter of practical necessity. There is no need for the path to the liberating truth the Buddha discovered to be rediscovered by every Buddhist on their own. Those who want to engage in Buddhist practices can, and should, rely on scriptural authority, simply because of the absence of any other way (*agatyā*)[76] leading to the aim of liberation. Someone who aspires to this goal 'cannot proceed without relying on the validity of scripture'.[77] Yet there is no objective

Practical necessity of relying on scriptures

[72] *Pramāṇavārttika* 1: 213, *Svavṛtti* ad 1:217, Gnoli 1960: 107, 109; Tillemans 1999a: 41–2.

[73] Śākyabuddhi makes this very clear in his *Pramāṇavārttikaṭīkā*: 'though we might observe that people are non-belying on certain objects, we also observe deviance [i.e. that they are in error] concerning other objects' (Tillemans 1999a: 50, n. 9).

[74] *Svavṛtti* on *Pramāṇavārttika* 1.13, Tillemans 1999a: 50, n. 9.

[75] Tillemans 1999a: 43.

[76] *Svavṛtti* on *Pramāṇavārttika* 1.217, Tillemans 1999a: 42.

[77] *nāyaṃ puruṣo anāśrityāgamaprāmāṇyam āsituṃ samartho*, *Svavṛtti* on *Pramāṇavārttika* 1.213.

fact, independent of human interests and concerns, that underlies the authority of Buddhist scriptures as epistemic instruments.[78]

No necessity for a leap of faith

However, this should not be understood as saying that scriptures need to be accepted by a leap of faith, and that such a leap is what makes Buddhist scriptures authoritative and supports inferences drawn from them. The view of the logico-epistemological school is not to accept beliefs for which we have no evidence, just to be able to enter the Buddhist path. Rather, the idea is that the would-be practitioner realizes that other beings have obtained certain results, that they have done so following certain practices, and that he, should he want to obtain the same results, should follow the same practices. Like someone who wants to be able to drive a car, observing that all other drivers are able to do so because they have practised with a driving instructor, then signs up with a driving instructor himself, so the Buddhist practitioner will accept scripture on pragmatic grounds.[79] There is no guarantee that the desired results will be obtained,[80] just as taking driving lessons does not guarantee that we will ever be able to drive a car. But if there is any possibility of obtaining this goal, it is this. As Dharmakīrti notes, 'if one engages oneself on the basis of scripture, it is better to engage oneself in this way [based on a scripture that shows all the internal evidence of being reliable]'.[81] The inferences we make on the basis of scripture are not supported by the power of fact (*vastubala*) but are the product of a rationally defensible choice, a choice which is responsible, insofar as we have done our epistemic duty in checking the triple characteristics of the scripture in question, but a choice that remains, nevertheless, fallible.[82]

Historical context of the critical view of scriptural authority

This view of religious scripture may appear quite surprising from the perspective of a writer as obviously committed to the truth of the Buddhist teachings as Dharmakīrti was. Yet at least part of its motivation appears more transparent when we consider the historical and intellectual context in which Dharmakīrti worked. His was not an era of intra-doctrinal debate, where most of the discussions were between Buddhist and Buddhist, trying to clarify the minutiae of the interpretation of the Buddha's words. It was a time of vivid

[78] This view appears to be reflected in Bhāviveka's critical remarks on the status of scripture (*āgama*) in *Madhyamakahṛdayakārikā* 9:19: 'If scripture has the status of scripture simply because it has been handed down without interruption, then it is established that all [the 363 doctrines listed in the *Sūtrakṛtāṅgasūtra*] are scripture. One should hold on to what is true', *saṃpradāyānupache-dād āgamasyāgamatvataḥ | sarvasyāgamatāsiddheḥkiṃ tattvam iti dhāryatām*, Lindtner 2001. For a survey of editions and translations of the various chapters of the *Madhyamakahṛdayakārikā* see Eckel 1992: 243–4.

[79] Tillemans 1999a: 46.

[80] For this reason the inference is inconclusive (*śeṣavat*, literally 'with remainder'). See Eltschinger 2010: 420.

[81] *varam āgamāt pravṛttāv evaṃ pravṛttir iti*, *Svavṛtti* on *Pramāṇavārttika* 1: 217, Gnoli 1960: 109.

[82] It is therefore reason (*yukti*), rather than authority that should have the last word in these debates (Eltschinger 2010: 420).

debate between different Indian systems of thought, and Buddhism was clearly interested in joining in with the debate. That the motivations for this were entirely un-Buddhist[83] is at least not obvious. While the social, and indeed material, dimensions of dialectical success in the arena of ancient India debating cannot be denied, it is likely that Buddhist authors were aware that setting out to defend one's position in a debate, in particular to defend it against somebody who might disagree with very fundamental assumptions, will not only provide an opportunity for refining one's arguments but also for increasing one's own understanding of the problem debated.

Purpose of the arguments for the Buddha's authority

We might wonder at this point what the purpose of Diṅnāga's, and especially Dharmakīrti's, extended arguments for establishing the authority of the Buddha was, given that they conclude that scriptural inferences cannot be classified as inferences fully grounded in reality. Why argue for the reliability of the Buddha if reliance on him is then not considered as a separate epistemic instrument? We might find an answer in an argumentative figure employed already by Vasubandhu. Given the diversity of interpretations of the Buddhist scripture, we cannot simply rely on one specific one. Yet at the same time the Buddha's words should still be considered as reliable, as without him there would be no Buddhism as we know it. Vasubandhu's answer is to conceptualize the Buddha as a perfect source of knowledge to which we have only imperfect access.[84] The reason for the divergence of interpretations lies in the fallibility of contemporary commentators, not in its source. These commentaries can be used as a guide to arrive at the Buddha's message, but they cannot be automatically taken as authoritative in themselves, but must be scrutinized by perception and inference. In the same way, the logico-epistemic tradition considered it as valuable to establish the Buddha's trustworthiness, even though this would not entail that reliance on the word of the Buddha could just replace appeal to perception and argument. Appeal to scripture is a shortcut on the path to liberation, but the fact remains that perception and argument are the means we need to employ in order to access the knowledge the Buddha obtained and which led to his liberation. This coheres well with the externalist outlook of the logico-epistemological school, that sees justification as flowing from a combination of facts that obtain in the world (the authority of the Buddha), and our doing our epistemic duty by appealing to reliable

Imperfect access to a perfect source of knowledge

Coherence with externalist outlook

[83] Conze (1962: 256) claims that it is '[a]t variance with the spirit of Buddhism, it can indeed be tolerated only as a manifestation of "skill in means". Logic was studied "in order to vanquish one's adversaries in controversy", and thereby to increase the monetary resources of the Order. Its methods implied a radical departure from the spirit of *ahiṃsā* and tolerance . . .' He remarks in addition, with reference to Dharmakīrti, that 'this branch of studies produces people who are boastful and inclined to push themselves forward.' Conze's remarks need to be assessed keeping in mind the increased pressure on Buddhism from its brahmanical opponents at the times of Diṅnāga and Dharmakīrti. See Verardi 2014.

[84] Hayes 1984: 653–4.

forms of confirmation (such as the three marks of scripture). The fallibility of scripturally based inference is not a defect, but a reflection of our general epistemic predicament in attempting to acquire knowledge about the world.

The double nature of the logico-epistemological school

It therefore becomes clear that the position of the logico-epistemological school as developed by Dharmakīrti and his successors has a double nature. One side of it shows a considerable openness towards non-Buddhist schools and a desire to engage in debate with them. It is worthwhile to keep in mind in this context that roughly up to the seventh century the division between the different schools of Indian philosophy (or what would later be classified as such schools) was somewhat fluid. Borrowings of concepts and entire collections of concepts were frequent.[85]

Interpenetration of philosophical schools

In the development of the literature on debate (*vāda*), discussion goes backwards and forwards between Buddhist and non-Buddhist traditions; Nyāya incorporated the whole scheme of Vaiśeṣika categories into its own account, Diṅnāga even composed an entire treatise by lifting a set of verses from the non-Buddhist grammarian Bhartṛhari, changing a few words and adding his own dedication.[86]

Maximizing impact on non-Buddhist audience

Given this philosophical give-and-take across different traditions, it is understandable that Dharmakīrti saw some real potential for his ideas having import outside of the Buddhist tradition by presenting them in a way that did not make the entire enterprise hang on the acceptance of specific texts, but was open to examination on the basis of epistemic instruments, perception and inference, that his interlocutors, Buddhist or non-Buddhist, were likely to share. Some have argued that Dharmakīrti presented his theory of epistemic instruments by using concepts familiar to and acceptable to non-Buddhist traditions, to maximize the likelihood of them being taken up by different traditions, and that he occasionally employs concepts used by other traditions but gives them a different sense, achieving at least the appearance of conceptual continuity with some of these other traditions.[87]

'double reading' of Dharmakīrti's arguments

These are not the only cases of potential 'double readings' of Dharmakīrti's text; in other cases he phrases his position in such a way that it can be given both a Sautrāntika and a Yogācāra reading, leaving it to the interpreter to decide which understanding he wants to bring out as dominant.

Apologetic character of Dharmakīrti's writings

The other side of this double nature is the clearly apologetic character of much of his writings, initiating a tradition that set out to establish not only the authority of the Buddha, but also other basic claims of the Buddhist worldview, like the four noble truths, the law of karma, rebirth, momentariness, the Buddha's omniscience, the existence of an innate Buddha-nature, and so on. Whether it was for this reason that his reputation amongst Buddhists is the

[85] Franco 1997: 38.

[86] For discussion of the *Traikālyaparīkṣā* see Frauwallner 1982a: 821–8; Houben 1995: 272–324.

[87] Franco 1997, ch. 2. In this way Dharmakīrti's approach to non-Buddhist traditions would resemble Nāgārjuna's approach to rival Buddhist traditions, such as the Mahāsaṅghikas. See pp. 47–8.

direct opposite of his repudiation by members of non-Buddhist schools is debatable. It is evident, however, that rather than convincing Nyāya, Vaiśeṣika, Mīmāṃsa, and other thinkers of the merits of his system, their reaction to Dharmakīrti was clearly negative, a reaction that may have contributed to the formation of a more fixed system of philosophical 'schools' with relatively inflexible boundaries.[88] Some have argued that it is possible to consider the lineage of the logico-epistemological schoool as moving more and more from the direction of open philosophical inquiry into the defence of Buddhist orthodoxy.[89] While Diṅnāga's theory of epistemology was phrased in a relatively neutral way (a neutrality we would expect, for example, from a theory of medicine or grammar), his successors successively moved into a greater integration of these epistemological ideas with Buddhist doctrine, using them as a tool for establishing the validity of core Buddhist beliefs. Whether the idea of a 'genuinely disinterested philosophical investigation'[90] that underlies this interpretation is a useful concept for understanding ancient Indian thought appears to me at least questionable. It is likely, though, that the interlinkage of epistemological, logical, and doctrinal matters in its presentation did not exactly help it in achieving a sympathetic reading from non-Buddhist philosophers.

Negative reactions

Neutrality vs. orthodoxy

Dharmakīrti's opening and closing verses of the *Pramāṇavārttika* are likely to be a reflection on the fact that his work had limited success among his non-Buddhist contemporaries. He points out that ordinary beings, attached to common things, have only limited understanding, and are therefore unable to grasp the profundity of his thought. Like the water of the sea, his work will remain in itself, without being absorbed by anybody.[91]

## b. *Yogic perception*

Yogic perception is mentioned quite briefly by Diṅnāga as one of the kinds of perception, and it is characterized as a form of perception that is not associated (*avyatibhinna*) with the teacher's instruction[92] and perceives the thing as it is (*arthamātra*). The commentator Jinendrabuddhi explains this latter phrase as 'without erroneous superimposition'.[93] Dharmakīrti expands on this concise

Its characteristics

[88] Franco 1997: 38. [89] Hayes 1984: 665–6. [90] Hayes 1984: 666.

[91] Frauwallner 1982b: 685–6. Frauwallner speculates that this sense of disappointment may have been responsible for the fact that Dharmakīrti left the *Pramāṇavārttika* incomplete. For a poem in a similar melancholy vein sometimes attributed to Dharmakīrti see Franco 1997: 39. Whether the poet Dharmakīrti is identical with the philosopher Dharmakīrti is a moot point (Brough 1968: 17), though some of his poems show a definite acquaintance with Buddhist philosophical ideas (see e.g. Brough 1968: 134).

[92] Hayes (1984: 655–6) sees this qualification as an expression of Diṅnāga's 'suspicion towards scripture in general'. The teacher's instruction invariably influences the way we perceive reality, and yogic perception is supposed to go beyond this, allowing us to experience phenomena without influence of a doctrinally constructed conceptual overlay. This qualification appears to include all instructions, including those that make up the Buddha's teachings.

[93] *mātraśabdo' dhyāropitārthavyavacchedārthaḥ*, Torella 2012: 474.

characterization of yogic perception (*yogipratyakṣa*) by explaining it as the final one of a three-stage process beginning with intensity (*prakarṣa*) and termination (*paryanta*).[94] The first stage, intensity, consists of the meditator's persistently bringing the object of meditation before his mind. As a result of this it appears to his mind more and more vividly until, at the stage of termination, it appears almost as vivid as something perceived by the senses. Stage three, yogic perception is obtained when the appearance of the object has achieved the same level of vividness as sensory perception.

Yogic perception as epistemic super-power

Descriptions of yogic perceptions can be found in nearly all Indic philosophical traditions, and they often take the form of epistemic super-powers, such as seeing things that take place at great distance. In the Vaiśeṣika system yogic perception enables the practitioner to have direct acquaintance with the categories of Vaiśeṣika ontology, qualities, actions, universals, and so forth.[95] Yogic perception is therefore a kind of enhanced perception that allows us to perceive aspects of reality that are too subtle to be apprehended by our senses, much in the way a microscope lets us see very small things and a telescope things at great distance. What makes these epistemic super-powers authoritative is that they detect real, though very subtle, features of the world around us. This, however, is not the view of yogic perception we find in Dharmakīrti. For him, yogic perception is not a kind of epistemic super-power[96] or mystical gnosis of the underlying nature of being, nor directed at a momentary particular out there in the world, but at a concept—this is what the meditator tries to bring to mind in a vivid manner. Yet concepts are, for Dharmakīrti, unreal objects par excellence. We should also note that Dharmakīrti sees yogic perception as something that is very much part of a continuum on which other cognitive states can be located too. He points out that: 'A trustworthy awareness that appears vividly by the force of meditation—similar to cases such as the fear [induced by something seen in a dream]—is a perception; it is nonconceptual.'[97] Dharmakīrti elucidates what is meant by vivid appearance in this context by further examples: 'Those confused by [states] such as derangement due to

Dharmakīrti: directed at concepts

[94] Woo 2003: 440. [95] Isaacson 1993: 146–7.

[96] Dharmakīrti is very critical of such powers as having anything to do with the search for liberation. In *Pramāṇavārttika* 2: 31–2 he notes that 'persons longing for liberation should not look for someone who, like vultures, perceives distant or even all things (*sarvasya vedakaḥ*), up to the total number of insects, (*kīṭasaṃkhyā*)' (Miyasaka 1971–2: 8; Eltschinger 2010: 421).

[97] *Pramāṇaviniścaya* 1.28: *bhāvanābalataḥ spaṣṭaṃ bhayādāviva bhāsate | yaj jñānam avisaṃvādi tat pratyakṣam akalpakam*, Steinkellner 2007: 27. How yogic perception can be both directed at concepts and non-conceptual is certainly somewhat puzzling. One possible answer is that it is the vividness of yogic perception that subsumes it (like sensory perception) under cognitions free from conceptual construction (Woo 2003: 443). Another possibility is to point out that the yogic perception of the first noble truth, for example, perceives the instance of suffering (understood as a property-particular) present in each *svalakṣaṇa* without having to rely on the *sāmanyalakṣaṇa*, or object in general, of suffering. As such it can be non-conceptual and yet directed at something conceptually expressed by the first noble truth.

Yogic perception and deluded states of mind

desire, grief or fear, or those confused by dreams of thieves and so on, see things, although unreal, as if they were in front of them.'[98] What is curious about these examples is that they seem to suggest that yogic perception can share characteristics with clearly deluded states of consciousness.[99] A lover who concentrates intensely on the features of his beloved might in the end be able to see her as vividly as if she were standing in front of him, but what does this fact have to do with yogic perception?[100] If yogic perception is directed at objects that are no more real than thieves in a dream, or romantic fantasies, and is, moreover, characterized by a vividness it shares with various unwholesome and deceptive states of mind, to what extent can it be regarded as an epistemic instrument? This is precisely the criticism Mīmāṃsaka philosophers like Kumārila bring forward against the Buddhist notion of yogic perception. If yogic perception is directed at a mental object, like wishing something or remembering something, how can it be regarded as epistemically authoritative?[101]

Mīmāṃsā criticism of yogic perception

That the idea of yogic perception became a hotly contested topic in the debate between the Mīmāṃsā school and the school of Diṅnāga and Dharmakīrti is hardly surprising. A chief aim of Mīmāṃsā was to defend the authoritativeness of Vedic revelation, a set of texts that were taken to derive their authority from their clearly non-human status due to their authorless origins. And if human epistemic capacities could be enhanced in the way envisaged by the notion of yogic perception, accessing the previously hidden, the justification for Vedic revelation might seem threatened.[102] Yogic perception would provide a means of gaining epistemic access to what lies behind the reach of perception and inference, and in this case Vedic revelation could no longer be seen as the sole interpreter of this radically different realm. On the contrary, yogic revelation would then open up a way to liberating knowledge that does not rely on revelation, a position in tension with a school like Mīmāṃsā that regards Vedic revelation as the only route to such knowledge.

It is clear that for Dharmakīrti the source of the authoritativeness of yogic perception cannot lie in the fact that it gets the world right at the most fundamental level. Unlike the Vaiśeṣika, who takes yogic perception to be a means to access the most fundamental aspects of the structure of the world, Dharmakīrti's version is not validated by revealing the ultimate features of the world, so it is necessary to find another way of explaining that it is nonetheless non-erroneous (*abhrānta*). Its validation comes through the goal of yogic perception. This goal is, of course, the obtaining of liberation, and the status

Yogic perception as validated through its goal

[98] *Pramāṇaviniścaya* 1.29: *kāmaśokabhayonmādacaurasvapnādyupaplutāḥ | abhūtān api paśyanti purato 'vasthitān iva*, Vetter 1966: 74, note 3; Steinkellner 2007: 28; Dunne 2006: 517.

[99] It is, as Dunne (2006: 497) points out 'phenomenologically akin to hallucination'.

[100] See Kajiyama 1998: 54, n. 124.

[101] Woo 2003: 441. See also Kajiyama 1998: 54, where the opponent raises this very point.

[102] See Torella 2012: 473, 477.

of yogic perception as epistemically authoritative comes from the ability to bring about this result.[103] As such, there is no difference *in kind* between it and the vividly appearing dreams and fantasies mentioned above, though there is a difference with respect to their results. The former trap us more and more deeply in saṃsāra, while the latter provide us with a way of escaping from it. This fact has implications for the soteriological efficacy of yogic perception considered in isolation. If yogic perception is not authorized by linking us to the basic structure of the world but by its effect in achieving liberation, the practitioner needs to be sure that he is engaging in the right kind of yogic perception, that is, yogic perception directed at the right kind of object (the main example Dharmakīrti refers to are the four noble truths). This guidance on what yogic perception should properly be directed at has to come from the instruction of earlier authorities and thus, ultimately from the authority of the Buddha. Yogic perception therefore cannot be considered to be on its own sufficient for generating liberating insight; it needs to be combined with scriptural authority in order to achieve this effect.

Yogic perception needs to be properly directed

## 7. How to Classify Diṅnāga's and Dharmakīrti's Philosophy

Did Diṅnāga and Dharmakīrti form a distinct school?

We have mentioned before that the division of Indian Buddhist philosophy into schools is at best to be understood as a hermeneutic device that allows us to dig some conceptual trenches through a complex field of arguments, and not as a system of doctrinal allegiance the Indian thinkers would themselves have adhered to in any straightforward manner.[104] This is particularly noticeable in the case of the school Diṅnāga and Dharmakīrti. Even though contemporary authors sometimes refer to it as the 'logico-epistemological school', it had no name in ancient India (the convenient term *pramāṇavāda* is a modern coinage), and it is quite unclear whether Diṅnāga, Dharmakīrti, and their followers would have regarded themselves as members of a specific school of Buddhist thought distinct from other schools. They certainly did not form a separate ordination lineage, and even the question of their doctrinal distinctness (at least when considered from their own perspective) is unclear.[105] Doxographers sometimes classify these thinkers by the curious epithet 'Yogācāra-Sautrāntika'

[103] We find here another example of the important place causal efficacy plays in Dharmakīrti's system. In the Sarvāstivāda Abhidharma *karitrā* indicated what was both real and present, here *arthakriyākāritva* is the mark of the real and supplies the characteristic of the authoritativeness of yogic perception.

[104] Hayes 1986: 167–8.

[105] It is also worthwhile to note that while the Abhidharma, Madhyamaka, and Yogācāra each regarded themselves as spelling out the teachings of a specific set of Buddhist *sūtras*, there is no such set of texts associated with the logico-epistemological school.

(on which more below), indicating that they combined specific Abhidharma and Mahāyāna beliefs, rather than defending a radically new position.

What kind of thinker was Dharmakīrti?

Classifying Dharmakīrti's thought in relation to other schools of Indian Buddhist thought is a notoriously complex enterprise. Some have argued that he should be included in the Sautrāntika school (and hence belonged to the Abhidharma traditions).[106] One of the difficulties with this idea is that it is not clear what we mean by Sautrāntika. The school left no literary remains, and although we have some information on its views from sources of rival traditions, the greatest part comes from Vasubandhu's *Abhidharmakośabhāṣya*, and, as we noted above, it is questionable whether this can be regarded as a faithful representation of the Sautrāntika position that preceded him.

Sautrāntika?

Dharmakīrti and the Mahāyāna schools

While there is little in Dharmakīrti's works that conveys an explicit Mahāyāna flavour,[107] there are parts that convey a clear Yogācāra message. In the *pratyakṣa* chapter of the *Pramāṇavārttika*,[108] for example, he discusses the ultimate identity of perceiver and perceived, a view that leads to a mere-mind (*vijñaptimātra*) view of ultimate reality.[109] Later commentators, such as Jitāri and Mokṣākaragupta, who lived at the end of the first to the beginning of the second millennium, consider Dharmakīrti as a Mādhyamika,[110] and we also find traditional accounts that consider him to be a tantric practitioner.[111] It now looks as if association with every single one of the Buddhist schools has been ascribed to Dharmakīrti. In fact, the aim of trying to resolve this issue is not so much attempting to determine the correct box into which we should put Dharmakīrti (after all, the often fluid nature of these schools and failure of most Indian Buddhist philosophers to self-identify as members of one or the other makes this an enterprise unlikely to yield much by way of important insight into Dharmakīrti's thought), but to find a way of accounting for the apparently inconsistent positions incorporated into Dharmakīrti's system that form the basis for ascribing him to some of these schools. The strongest cases can be made for associating Dharmakīrti's position with Abhidharma and with Yogācāra views, but how can any consistent system include both? How could

106 See Singh 1984, 1995, and the highly critical review of the former in Hayes 1984.

107 Such as quotations from the major Mahāyāna *sūtras*, discussion of the Bodhisattva ideal, a focus on omniscient Buddhahood rather than *arhat*ship as the goal of the path.

108 3: 320–73, 532–5 (Miyasaka 1971–2: 84–90, 110).

109 See e.g. Dreyfus and Lindtner 1989: 27–52. We noted above (pp. 82–3, 200–1) there is a case to be made for locating Sautrāntika and Yogācāra as points on the same philosophical trajectory. In the Tibetan doxographic literature we sometimes find an association of Sautrāntika both with Yogācāra and with the system of Dharmakīrti via the division of Sautrāntikas into those 'following scripture' (*lung gi rjes su 'brangs pa*) and those 'following reasoning' (*rigs pa'i rje su 'brangs pa*), the former being based on works by Vasubandhu, the latter on works by Dharmakīrti (Geshe Lhundup Sopa and Hopkins 1976: 92, Klein 1991: 22–3, Jackson 1993: 112).

110 Steinkellner 1990.

111 Tsonawa 1985: 49, Jackson 1993: 113.

one be both a Sautrāntika and accept the existence of mind-independent objects and be a Yogācārin who denies precisely such things?

The Abhidharma consensus

One reason for the Abhidharma flavour of much of Dharmakīrti's exposition is that he regarded this position as a kind of lowest common denominator of several strands of Buddhist thought. The disagreements between Abhidharma schools nonwithstanding, the intersection of their beliefs constitutes a significant portion of basic doctrinal assumptions shared by different Buddhist schools.[112] To this extent Dharmakīrti might have tried to achieve a maximum of agreement with his philosophical position by formulating them in a way that would not immediately disengage his audience by exposing them to Mahāyāna or tantric beliefs that they might not share, and that are moreover irrelevant for the success of the argument under consideration. This intuition has been recently expanded by ascribing to Dharmakīrti a set of 'sliding scales of analysis'.[113] This explains how a philosopher could hold a set of different, mutually inconsistent positions without collapsing into overall inconsistency. The key idea is that for Buddhist philosophers theories can (and frequently do) diverge in terms of philosophical accuracy and soteriological efficacy. Even if out of two mutually inconsistent theories one is philosophically more accurate, the other may have greater success in moving a specific audience closer to liberation, for example, because the conceptual resources used by the first theory exceed the comprehension of the audience. For this reason both theories would be part of the philosopher's overall account, even though they would never be taught at the same time to the same audience, thereby preventing inconsistency. This idea of 'graded teaching' (*anuśāsana*) has a long history in Buddhist thought, going back to the very early distinction between the teachings of the Buddha that were considered definitive (*nītārtha*) and those that were considered in need of contextual interpretation (*neyārtha*). Verse 18:8 of Nāgārjuna's *Mūlamadhyamakakārikā* ('All is so, or all is not so, both so and not so, neither so nor not so. This is the Buddha's teaching')[114] is generally considered as an example of a theory at four different levels of conceptual sophistication.[115] In his *Ratnāvalī*, Nāgārjuna compares the Buddha to a grammarian who will even teach some of his students something as basic as the alphabet, in accordance with their different intellectual capacities.[116]

'sliding scales of analysis'

Graded teaching

[112] With the exception of Madhyamaka, which does not share the Abhidharma's metaphysical foundationalism. Yet even here the possibility remains open to conceive of the Abhidharma's metaphysical analyses as restricted to the level of conventional truth only.

[113] Dunne 2004: 53–79. The term was first introduced in McClintock 2003.

[114] *sarvaṃ tathyaṃ na vā tathyaṃ tathyaṃ cātathyam eva ca | naivātathyaṃ naiva tathyam etad buddhānuśāsanaṃ.*

[115] See Ruegg 1977: 5–7. Further references to graded teaching by Nāgārjuna can be found in his *Ratnāvalī* 3:94–6 and *Yuktiṣaṣṭikā* 30.

[116] *yathaiva vaiyākaraṇo mātṛkām api pāṭhayet | buddho 'vadat tathā dharmaṃ vineyānāṃ yathākṣamam*, Hahn 1982a: 128.

In his *Bodhicaryāvatāra*, Śāntideva explicitly refers to a hierarchy of successively more sophisticated philosophical positions when he points out that the perspective of the ordinary person is refuted by that of the yogin, and that this is in turn refuted by the perspectives of higher and higher yogins.[117] In expounding theories lower down the chain, the Buddhas therefore 'close one eye' to simplify their more sophisticated perception for the sake of a less conceptually refined audience.[118]

Four levels of philosophical analysis

For explaining Dharmakīrti's approach it is necessary to distinguish four levels of philosophical analysis in ascending order of sophistication.[119] At the lowest level we begin with the *perspective of ordinary, unenlightened beings*. Their view of the world is not to be faulted to the extent to which it is largely pragmatically successful: it allows them to successfully interact with the world. However, from a philosophical perspective it leaves much to be desired, as it is characterized by the chief fault of *satkāyadṛṣṭi*, the mistaken superimposition of a substantial self where there is none, both in the case of persons, as well as in the case of other phenomena. At the second level of the scale we come to the *reductionist view* that we find exemplified in the Abhidharma. Both persons as well as other partite objects are analysed and found to be nothing but convenient verbal designations sitting on top of what is ultimately real, namely conglomerations of fundamentally existing *dharmas*. At this level, some elements are still characterized by spatial, temporal, or conceptual extension. Some objects, such as colours, are spread out in space, some objects have temporal extension, and, most importantly, some qualities of objects are shared across different instances of them: all earth-atoms are solid, all water-atoms wet, and so on.[120] By and large this perspective accords with the Sarvāstivāda view we find in Vasubandhu's *Abhidharmakośa*. At the third level the reductionist perspective is further refined into a form of *particularism*. According to this position all three forms of extension are given up because they are considered to be the products of cognitive errors. We perceive objects as spatially extended because we confuse qualities of the mental image of the object with qualities of what gives rise to the mental image. The assumption of temporal extension is an artefact of the slowness of our perceptual system. Because we cannot keep up with the rapid succession that marks the change of things, we simply group together various successive phenomena that form part of a single causal chain

1. Ordinary beings

2. Reductionism

3. Particularism

[117] 9:3b–4a *tatra prākṛtako loko yogilokena bādhyate | bādhyante dhīviśeṣeṇa yogino 'pyuttarottaraiḥ*, Vaidya 1988: 183–5.

[118] As Dharmkakīrti points out in his *Pramāṇavārttika* 3: 219: 'Therefore the Buddhas, disregarding the ultimate, close one eye like an elephant and propagate theories that involve external objects merely in accord with worldly conceptions', *tad upekṣitatattvārthaiḥ kṛtvā gajanimīlana | kevalaṃ lokabuddhyaiva bāhyacintā pratanyate* (Miyasaka 1971–2: 70).

[119] Our exposition follows Dreyfus 1997: 98–9 and Dunne 2004: 53–79.

[120] Dunne 2004: 57–8, 70–1.

and construe it as one temporally persisting object. The same happens in the case of shared objects in general or object-types. Even though every particular is different from any other particular, we are often not able to register the differences between distinct things. As in the case of temporal resolution, the comparative coarseness of our conceptual resolution causes us to lump together various distinct, though similar things. So despite the fact that all there is out there in the world is a variety of things such as earth-atoms that are distinct from one another, on account of some similarity we put them all together and argue that they all instantiate the same object-type of solidity. This view is often referred to as a Sautrāntika position, and the emphasis on the extremely short-lived nature of all objects seems to justify this, even though, as noted before, it is difficulty to be precise about the distinction between this form of Sautrāntika, the form that we find in Vasubandhu, and those coming from sources preceding Vasubandhu.[121] This particularist stance is the philosophical position from which Dharmakīrti constructs most of his arguments. This is a curious fact, since it does not represent his final view, the position he wants to endorse after discussing various other positions that are all in some way defective. For if we push our philosophical analysis yet further we get to a fourth level, an *idealist theory*, according to which the duality between the perceiving subject and the non-material perceived object is illusory. All phenomena have only one nature, and this nature is mental. The affinity of this view with Yogācāra positions is obvious, and many commentators do in fact gloss this as a Yogācāra position. Despite the fact that this is the position Dharmakīrti wants to endorse, in the end it does not dominate his philosophical exposition. In fact there is only one substantial section of the *Pramāṇavārttika* where he employs it consistently as a background for his argumentation.

4. Idealism

Historical and systematic significance of the four levels

This sequence of four positions along the sliding scale of analysis is interesting for a number of reasons. On the one hand it mirrors the historical development of Buddhist thought in India, from the confrontation with non-Buddhist believers in a substantial *ātman* through Abhidharma reductionism, a thoroughgoing form of particularism, up to the idealism of Yogācāra. Yet this sequence is at the same time considered to be a conceptual hierarchy, an ascent to better and better philosophical theories or, what amounts to the same thing in the Buddhist context, a hierarchy of views that result in less and less erroneous superimposition (*samāropa*). It is obvious how the Abhidharma reductionism is supposed to remove clinging to the mistaken belief in a substantial self where there is none. Yet, as the particularist stage argues, the

[121] The unclarity of what precisely counts as a Sautrāntika position was inherited by later Tibetan commentators. Dunne (2004: 71) points out that we can find instances of them subsuming any of the three positions just described under the label 'Sautrāntika'.

reductionist is still bound by superimposing spatial, temporal, and conceptual extension to a world consisting of non-extended, momentary, and utterly distinct particulars. Removing those frees us from further superimpositions, and thereby from the potential for further clinging, clinging that in turn leads to suffering and continuing entanglement in cyclic existence. However, seen from the idealist perspective this is still not enough. Further superimposition takes place when the appearance of external objects is superimposed on some purely mental phenomena, thereby creating the particularist picture in the first place. A thoroughgoing removal of superimpositions must also dispense with the erroneous distinction between perceiving subject and perceived object.

The neither-one-nor-many argument

A single argumentative pattern can be understood as the driving force behind the movement through the four different levels. This is the neither-one-nor-many argument, well known throughout the history of Buddhist philosophy.[122] When applied to the perspective of ordinary beings, this argument begins with the question whether an object and its parts are identical or different. It appears that they cannot be identical (since the object is one and the parts are many, and one thing cannot have contradictory properties), and that they cannot be different (as the whole is never found as a separate entity distinct from the parts). The reductionist argues that we should conclude from this that wholes are not real in the first place, but merely conceptually constructed pseudo-entities. The same considerations can then be applied to particulars and properties they supposedly share (here a key argument is that distinct shared properties would have to be permanent, conflicting with the principle of momentariness), and to the perceiving object and perception (if they are distinct, why do we never encounter one without the other?).[123]

We might wonder whether stage four, idealism, is a necessary stopping-point for the application of the neither-one-nor-many argument, or whether it could be applied here too, moving to a fifth stage, and, more generally, whether it could be applied to *any* stage in the analysis, leaving *no* level as the final view. This question leads to the historically and systematically intriguing question concerning the relationship between Dharmakīrti's system and Madhyamaka, an issue we will return to below.[124]

Specific features of the 'sliding scales of analysis' model

In the meantime, though, note another curious feature of the system of these sliding scales of analysis, a feature that distinguishes Dharmakīrti's case from that of other instances of historico-conceptual hierarchies of philosophical views in Buddhist texts. Dharmakīrti argues mainly from a particularist perspective (only one of four chapters of his *Pramāṇavārttika* consistently takes up the idealist point of view), and thus from a perspective he knows to be false. This is peculiar, insofar as the appeal to the hierarchy of views is usually

[122] Tillemans 1983, 1984, Dunne 2004: 63.
[123] Chakrabarti 1990.
[124] p. 257.

Particularism is not Dharmakīrti's final view

intended to let the author's own view come out on top in terms of conceptual sophistication. Yet in Dharmakīrti's case the particularist perspective is not his final word, and in the end needs to be replaced by the idealist one. One possible reason for this is that he considered the particularist perspective to be the lowest common denominator, the best balance between conceptual sophistication and widespread acceptance. Some claim that as we ascend the series of views the positions get more and more counterintuitive,[125] and Dharmakīrti would probably have agreed with this, if 'intuitions' are to be understood as the conceptual superimpositions (*samāropa*) that the stages of analysis are supposed to successively remove. As during Dharmakīrti's times there was a much greater degree of debate with non-Buddhist opponents, it is evident that the preservation of a certain degree of broader appeal for one's system would be very beneficial to make sure that discussions are not ruled out from the start due to lack of shared assumptions.

Heuristic use of particularism

That the particularist position is not Dharmakīrti's final view also means that he does not have to have worked out every detail of the system, nor would he have to be prepared to defend every aspect of it. Like a teacher who explains a physical phenomenon by an atomic theory he knows, strictly speaking, to be false, he can accept that there are certain fatal objections to the theory, or that there are some of its aspects that cannot be satisfactorily worked out. What is important about explanations drawn from such a theory is not that they are completely right about the way the world is, but that they get us to the next level of understanding.

Dharmakīrti on the reality of causation

Causation plays a central role in Dharmakīrti's philosophical system. It is the one property that functions as the mark of the real. In answering the question which of the many things we think or talk about should be taken ontologically seriously, Dharmakīrti looks for those entities that affect other things and bring about a change in them.

Criticism of the causal relation

What, however, about the status of the causal relation itself? Given the central role it plays in Dharmakīrti's system characterizing the real, we should assume that it is considered to be real itself. Curiously, this is not the case. The causal relation is affected by Dharmakīrti's criticism in the same way as all other objects in general.[126] Relations are affected by the neither-one-nor-many arguments in the same way as object-types such as redness or heaviness. In his *Pramāṇavārttika-svavṛtti*,[127] Dharmakīrti asks whether a relation between two objects is identical with the two objects or distinct from them. Since either option leads to problems, this reinforces the picture of an austere ontology of particulars in which relations have no place. This results in a curious dialectical situation. The main reason for the particularist picture's ontological split

[125] Dreyfus 1997: 49, Dunne 2004: 67.
[126] See Dunne 2004: 79, n. 37.
[127] ad 1: 236–7, Gnoli 1960: 118–19.

between real particulars and unreal objects in general lies in their difference of causal powers. But if the causal relation is unreal by the lights of the particularist's own system, how can it be appealed to in order to establish that very system? One way of addressing this puzzle (apart from simply saying that Dharmakīrti's system is inconsistent) is to point out that, given the system of sliding scales of analysis, Dharmakīrti is not obliged to defend the particularist position against all charges of inconsistency; in fact he can agree that the particularist's belief in the real existence of causal relations has to be dropped once we reach a more sophisticated level of philosophical analysis.

Dharmakīrti and Madhyamaka

Some later commmentators have argued that the rejection of the reality of causal relations would act as support for the claim that Dharmakīrti adopted a Madhyamaka position. The passage from Dharmakīrti's *Pramāṇavārttika* usually appealed to in this context has an opponent respond to Dharmakīrti's equation of the causally efficacious, ultimately real, and the particular by pointing out that nothing has causal efficacy. Dharmakīrti replies that this is manifestly not true, as seeds have the causal capacity to bring about sprouts and so on. But the opponent replies that 'such things are considered to have such a capacity conventionally, not ultimately'.[128] Dharmakīrti's laconic (and somewhat enigmatic) response to this is *astu yathā tathā*, 'be that as it may'.

Denial of the ultimate reality of causation

What is clear, however, is that commentators like Devendrabuddhi understood Dharmakīrti here as conceding the opponent's point, arguing that he might as well call causation *only* conventional, given that all he needs for his purposes is the conventional reality of causation.[129] It appears to be uncontroversial that the opponent here is a Madhyamaka, holding that ultimately there is no causal efficacy, even though causation does exist at the conventional level.[130] What there is disagreement about is whether Dharmakīrti here takes the Madhyamaka position on board, or whether he considers this as an interesting response, but one that is of little relevance for his present purposes. Apart from the denial of the ultimate reality of the causal relation, two other kinds of consideration are brought into play in order to argue for Dharmakīrti's support of the Madhyamaka position. The first is a passage from the *Pramāṇavārttika*[131] that may be interpreted as saying that—contrary to the assumption that the fourth, idealist level of analysis is Dharmakīrti's final view—consciousness itself is not ultimately real. The final reason is connected

[128] 3:3–4: *arthakriyāsamarthaṃ yat tad atra paramārthasat anyat saṃvṛtisat proktaṃ te svasāmānyalakṣaṇe | aśaktaṃ sarvam iti ced bījāder aṅkurādiṣu dṛṣṭā śaktiḥ matā sā cet saṃvṛtyā* (Miyasaka 1971–2: 42).

[129] Dunne 2004: 392–3, n. 3.

[130] Steinkellner 1990: 75. For further discussion of the ramifications of the unreality of causation in Buddhist thought see Siderits 2011b: 288–91.

[131] 3: 359 (Miyasaka 1971–2: 88), see Steinkellner 1990: 78–9.

with Dharmakīrti's frequent use of the neither-one-nor-many argument,[132] an argument that is primarily known from its use in Madhyamaka arguments.

Motivation for reading Dharmakīrti in a Madhyamaka way

Nevertheless, in the context of our discussion of the question whether Dharmakīrti 'really' was a Madhyamaka (a question that we might find similarly unsatisfactory as such questions as whether the Buddha 'really' was an empiricist or the author of the *Viṃśikā* 'really' was an idealist) is less interesting than what the attempts by Indian authors to interpret his thought in this way show us about the forces that shaped the formation of Indian Buddhist thought.

What we can observe here is the interplay of appeal to scriptural authority and employment of philosophical argument to establish a specific point of view within the Buddhist philosophical context. As mentioned above, in the context of a religiously shaped philosophical tradition such as the Buddhist one it is not just important to come up with an argument; the views the arguments support need also be linked back to the tradition itself. The tradition does not simply consist of the words of the Buddha as recorded in various *sūtras*, but includes the works of the luminaries of the Buddhist philosophical tradition such as Dharmakīrti. Like a wildflower meadow, these works contain a variety of seeds that can sprout under different conditions, and putting particular emphasis on given features of a text allows it to be read in the light on one tradition or another. What we find here in the attempts of Jitāri and Mokṣākaragupta to interpret Dharmakīrti with a Madhyamaka spin is an attempt to support the Madhyamaka set of philosophical arguments by arguing how ideas in the work of one of the authoritative figures of Buddhist philosophy can be used to develop his thought in a Madhyamaka direction (and possibly arguing that this shows that this development is what the author himself had intended and would have said more clearly had he expressed his views at greater length). Based on the idea that causation is not ultimately real, one could argue that the particularist stance on the basis of which Dharmakīrti constructs many of his arguments can be regarded just as an expedient expository device with propaedeutic potential, but without ontological import. If the key concept that confers ontological status, the causal relation, and with it the notion of causal efficacy is not itself fundamentally real, but a mere convention, the reality of the entities labelled real in this way cannot reach beyond the conventional status of whatever it is that constitutes their reality. Despite its prominence in

Lack of final level of analysis

Dharmakīrti's thought, the particularist level cannot be his final view, and he himself acknowledges as much in eventually replacing the particularist by the idealist stance. But if we accept that consciousness is not ultimately real, then the idealist stage cannot be the final view either, but must be replaced by something that analyses the mental away in the same manner as the mental

[132] Steinkellner 1990: 76–8.

analysed the particulars away. Now it looks as if this process could go on forever, and this is precisely what—according to this interpretation—the reference to the neither-one-nor-many argument would suggest. If it can be used to move us through all the levels of the sliding scales of analysis, from the everyday perspective all the way up to idealism, could it then not equally be applied to the idealist stage? If it can, then it seems to be the case that we will never arrive at a level of analysis that provides us with an ultimate ground for all the other levels, and this, of course, is precisely what the Madhyamaka analysis would imply. It appears that, using ideas found in Dharmakīrti's works, a case for developing or expanding his ideas in a Madhyamaka direction can be made, and that it is in this way, as an attempt at doing philosophy on the basis of texts regarded as authoritative rather than as an exercise in doxographic categorization, that the claims of commentators like Jitāri and Mokṣākaragupta are best understood. However, a difficulty for this reading is that, for Diṅnāga and Dharmakīrti, any stage after the idealist one will be non-dual and inexpressible (*anabhilāpya*), and this is a characterization of ultimate truth the coherence of which the Mādhyamikas regard as dubious (it is, after all, a position saying something about that of which nothing can be said).[133] To the extent that, according to Diṅnāga's and Dharmakīrti's account, the last thing we can say about reality before inexpressibility rules out all further philosophical assertion is that it is 'mind only', characterizing their position as idealist may seem to be the best of all possible choices.

Philosophical development rather than doxographic categorization

## 8. The School of Diṅnāga and Dharmakīrti and Its Relation to Mīmāṃsā

Regardless of our view of the historicity of Dharmakīrti's encounter with Kumārila, we can at least see the account as a representation of the sustained philosophical opposition between the logico-epistemological school represented by Dharmakīrti and Mīmāṃsā represented by Kumārila. The seventh-century Kumārila was one of the main exponents of Mīmāṃsā, founding a variety of Mīmāṃsā called Bhāṭṭa Mīmāṃsā (*bhaṭṭa*—'lord' or 'master'—is an epithet sometimes used for Kumārila), though the tradition itself is generally taken to go back to the beginning of the first millennium BCE, when Jaimini is said to have composed the school's foundational text, the *Mīmāṃsāsūtra*.

The interaction between Mīmāṃsā and Buddhist philosophy was sustained and extensive.[134] Kumārila responds to Diṅnāga's criticism of the Mīmāṃsā position in the *Pramāṇasamuccaya*, especially in his *Ślokavārttika*.[135] Dharmakīrti

Debate between the two schools

[133] See our discussion on pp. 210–12. [134] Verpoorten 1987: 23–30.
[135] Hattori 1968: 15–16, Iyengar 1927: 603–6, Rani 1982.

subsequently defended the Buddhist position against Mīmāṃsā criticism,[136] and in his encyclopedic *Tattvasaṃgraha* Śāntarakṣita gives a detailed account and criticism of Mīmāṃsā.[137] The frequent citing of Kumārila's works by Buddhist authors even allows us to get a reasonable idea of the contents of his lost works from the fragmentary quotations they give.[138]

Mīmāṃsā's aim

*dharma* and the Vedas

In the *Mīmāṃsāsūtra*, Jaimini describes the 'desire to know *dharma*' (*dharmajijñāsā*)[139] as the aim of the Mīmāṃsā enterprise. This *dharma* is characterized as the 'purpose specified by a Vedic injunction',[140] and 'connects a person with the highest good';[141] the route to the knowledge of *dharma* is through the Vedas. The main focus of the Mīmāṃsā is their establishment of the authoritative status of Vedic injunctions (*codanā*), themselves an instance of the epistemic instrument of verbal testimony (*śabda*). For Mīmāṃsā, *dharma* is something that is continuously 'yet to be' (*bhaviṣyat*).[142] One aspect of it is the good existence in an afterlife (*svarga*), an aim that Mīmāṃsā argues is to be accomplished by sacrifice.[143] (Unlike other schools of classical Indian thought, liberation from saṃsāra was not the aim of Mīmāṃsā soteriology).[144] This goal is obviously something not presently available and therefore 'yet to be'. Another aspect of the *dharma* to be achieved is the continuous renewal of the world by the performance of the Vedic rites. This performance is not just considered to yield positive results for the performer; it also has the more comprehensive function of continuously bringing into being the ritual world, though never completing this process.[145]

136 Dreyfus 1997: 15. For Dharmakīrti's criticism of the the Mīmāṃsā theory of language see Eltschinger, Krasser, and Taber 2012.

137 See e.g. Ratie 2014.

138 Frauwallner 1962: 78–90. Kumārila is supposed to have composed this work as a response to Dharmakīrti's criticism (Raja 1991: 109).

139 *Mīmāṃsāsūtra* 1.1.1, Thadani 2007.

140 *codanālakṣaṇo 'artho dharmaḥ, Mīmāṃsāsūtra* 1.1.2, Thadani 2007.

141 *sa hi niḥśreyasena puruṣaṃ saṃyunakti iti pratijānīmahe, Śābarabhāṣya* on *Mīmāṃsāsūtra* 1.1.1, Frauwallner 1968.

142 Arnold 2012: 201–2.

143 As expressed in the famous injunction that 'one desirous of heaven should perform sacrifice' (*svargakāmo yajeta*. See Frauwallner: 1968, n. 16). Compare also *Śābarabhāṣya* on *Mīmāṃsāsūtra* 6.1.1: 'It follows that heaven is something that could (or should) be accomplished, . . . and sacrifice would be the instrument to accomplish it', *svargasya kartavyatā gamyate* [. . .] *yāgas tasya karaṇaṃ syāt*, Nyāyaratna 1889.

144 '[T]he Mīmāṃsā carries the heritage of the "pre-karmic" past of the Indian tradition into an epoch for which karma and saṃsāra have become basic premisses. As well as their counterpart, *mokṣa*, the concepts of karma and saṃsāra do not play any role in the *Mīmāṃsāsūtra* and remain neglibible in its oldest extant commentary, Śabara's Bhāṣya' (Halbfass 1991: 301). *Svarga* (also termed *niḥśreyasa* ('something than which there is no better') is the aim of the Mīmāṃsā path, rather than simply an elevated inner-worldly state short of the goal of liberation (see Bronkhorst 2007: 4, n. 3).

145 Clooney 1990: 129–61. See also Arnold 2005: 238–9, n. 15.

Mīmāṃsā's defence of the authority of the Vedas rests on two main pillars. One is constituted by its epistemology, the other by its philosophy of language. The two positions are independent of one another (accepting one does not commit us to accept the other too). It is only by putting them together that Mīmāṃsā constructs an argument for warranted belief in Vedic injunctions. Mīmāṃsā and the 'logico-epistemological' school of Diṅnāga and Dharmakīrti share interests in similar areas of philosophy (logic/philosophy of language and epistemology), though the theories they advance in these fields are vastly different.

### *a. Mīmāṃsā epistemology*

One way of understanding the direction Mīmāṃsā epistemology takes is by asking what makes an epistemic instrument an epistemic instrument, that is, what is it about a *pramāṇa* that makes it suitable for generating knowledge. Is it something about the epistemic instrument itself, or is it the possession of some additional qualities?

Kumārila argues that the second possibility leads to considerable philosophical problems. Consider the Buddhist proposal of appealing to the cognition of the ability of fulfil its function (*arthakriyājñānam*)[146] in order to settle the trustworthiness of the deliverance of some epistemic instrument. Here the Buddhists would, for example, say that the specific instance of perception[147] of a lake is veridical, rather than illusory (as in the perception of a mirage), if the water thus perceived can in fact fulfil its functions, such as quenching thirst. However, Kumārila points out, if we settle the status of the first perception by appealing to a second perception (the perception confirming that water is causally efficacious), we have not actually made any progress, for the status of the second perception is not any more secure than that of the first. Both perceptions appear to be in exactly the same situation when it comes to justifying their status as epistemic instruments.[148]

*pramāṇas* cannot be established by other *pramāṇas*

There are various ways in which the defenders of Diṅnāga and Dharmakīrti can respond here.[149] First, note that there are cases where the trustworthiness of the second perception will not have to be settled by appeal to a third, but the ability of the object cognized to fulfil its function is part and parcel of having the cognition in the first place. When we appear to see a fire in a distance we

Possible responses to the regress

[146] As Dharmakīrti notes in *Pramāṇavārttika*, 'trustworthiness is the cognition of the ability to fulfil its goal', *arthakriyāsthitiḥ | avisaṃvādanam* (Miyasaka 1971–2: 2). See Dunne 2004: 280–1; Arnold 2005: 98.

[147] Note that in this discussion the term *pramāṇa* can be used both to refer to a specific epistemic practice (such as visual perception) and well as to particular instances of this (such as seeing a lake).

[148] See Dunne 2004: 274.

[149] See Dunne 2004: 272–8 for a further discussion of these ideas.

might go closer to it to feel its warmth. We then do not need to appeal to anything else to justify the trustworthiness of the warmth we feel, since given that our aim was to warm ourselves at the fire in the first place, we are justified in taking the perception (that of the fire) as veridical.[150] Second, we might consider solving the regress problem by establishing a minimal notion of causal efficacy, namely the ability of a mental state to have other mental states as effects. A perception of water would then be considered efficacious simply because it leads to other mental states, even if this is just the doubt whether the first perception is veridical. (Of course we would then need to appeal to other criteria to distinguish the trustworthy from the illusory perceptions, such as distinguishing this minimal sort of causal efficacy of the water-perception from a more substantial one that involves effects such as the quenching of thirst.)[151]

*pramāṇas* as intrinsically authoritative

Be this as it may, Kumārila regards his criticism as sufficiently weighty to support choosing the first alternative instead and argue that it is something about the epistemic instruments themselves that allows them to produce knowledge, arguing that 'the validity of all epistemic instruments should be accepted as intrinsic; for a capacity not already existing by itself cannot be produced by anything else'.[152] Of course, this should not be taken to mean that anything that some epistemic instrument delivers should therefore be considered as authoritative—the existence of perceptual and cognitive illusions makes it clear that this would let all sorts of erroneous cognitions in. Rather, the intrinsic authoritativeness of a veridical perception means that the causes of its veridicality are among the causes of the cognition's arising in the first place. We still need to rule out whatever extrinsic factors cause a cognition to be non-veridical (like, for example, perceptual distortions or cognitive biases), but once these are excluded, a cognition is to be considered as authoritative by default. As long as some piece of information is delivered by some epistemic instrument, and as long as no other epistemic instruments undermine it (as our tactile sense would, for example, once we try to touch the water we see in a mirage), our belief in whatever the instrument suggests there is will be justified.

*pramāṇas* produce justification, not knowledge

Note that we speak about justification, not about knowledge.[153] This might suggest watering-down our epistemic standards, but in fact a case can be made that all we could ever need (or perhaps even all we could ever get) in our endeavours to find out about the world is an entitlement to believe something to be true. If we additionally demand that all possible defeaters are ruled out, so that we are assured that all kinds of illusion-inducing circumstances do not obtain, we end up in a situation in which practically nobody could be taken to know anything.

[150] Dunne 2004: 274, 278. [151] Dunne 2004: 275–6.

[152] *svataḥ sarvapramāṇānāṃ prāmāṇyam iti gamyatām | na hi svato 'satī śaktiḥ kartum anyena śakyate*, *Ślokavārttika*, *codanā sūtra* verse 47, Kataoka 2011.

[153] See Arnold 2005: 61.

While I would be reluctant to refer to the Mīmāṃsā system as a form of 'common-sense realism',[154] given that in many senses their conclusions are so far removed from what is commonsensically assumed to be common sense, there is a fundamental trust in the deliverances of the epistemic instruments that is absent in the thought of Diṅnāga and Dharmakīrti. According to them, our everyday, untrained awareness of the world is not to be relied on, and matters of reality have to be settled by appeal to notions like the ability to fulfil its function. For Kumārila, on the other hand, information coming in through the six sense faculties can usually be accepted as showing just what it purports to show.

Fundamental trust in *pramāṇas*

### *b. Mīmāṃsā philosophy of language*

The second pillar in the Mīmāṃsā enterprise of justifying the authority of the Vedas, the only way of knowing *dharma*,[155] is their philosophy of language. They do not build this defence on the establishment of the authority of the texts' presumed author, Īśvara,[156] as the Naiyāyikas do,[157] but on the fact that the Vedas precisely have no author.[158] This argument from authorlessness (*apauruṣeyatva*) to authoritativeness might strike us as curious, since we would generally regard the fact that some piece of language had no author (if it was produced by some randomizing device, say) as speaking against it having any meaning, without even considering the further question of its truth. However, in the Mīmāṃsā context the implication between these two properties is supported by the peculiar position that 'the relation between words and their referents is primordial'.[159]According to this view, the link between an entity in the world and a piece of language (in fact, even a specific Sanskrit phoneme) is not anything established by the force of a conventional agreement between speakers. The connection of the term *gotva* with the property of being a cow is not derived from convention, but is written into the nature of existence.[160]

Vedas as authorless

Primordial connection between words and referents

[154] As e.g. Dan Arnold does in his entry on 'Kumārila', The Stanford Encyclopedia of Philosophy (Winter 2014 Edition), <http://plato.stanford.edu/archives/win2014/entries/kumaarila>.

[155] '*dharma* is stipulatively defined, or rather posited without argument, as a transcendent entity, and so is unknowable by any form of knowledge not itself transcendent', Pollock 1989: 607.

[156] The Mīmāṃsā philosophers do not believe there are any arguments for the existence of such divine being like Īśvara. Their arguments against theism bear interesting similarities with those of the Buddhists. See Krasser 1999: 215–23.

[157] Jacobi 2010: ch. 3; Patil 2009: 31–99.

[158] One Mīmāṃsā argument for the authorlessness of the Vedas is again routed in their common-sense epistemology: everybody who has ever learned the Vedas has learned them from a teacher who in turn learned them from his own teacher, never from the author. Postulating the existence of an unobserved author instead of the backwards infinite series of transmission would mean disregarding the output of an epistemic instrument like perception without good reason.

[159] *autpattikas tu śabdasya-arthena saṃbandhanaḥ*, *Mīmāṃsāsūtra* 5, Thadani 2007.

[160] Although this view of the convention-independent connection between words and meanings finds its most elaborate formulation in the Mīmāṃsā theories, parallels exist in the works of Sanskrit grammarians such as Patañjali's *Mahābhāṣya* (2nd cent. BCE), 115–16 (Joshi and Roodbergen 1986).

It is this natural connection between word and world[161] that provides us with the knowledge of *dharma*.[162] The main difficulty Mīmāṃsā sees in the intuitively more plausible view of language based on speaker agreement (which is also the position of the Buddhists) is that it is unclear how such an agreement could have ever gotten off the ground: if two speakers agree to use a certain term in a certain way, they first have to have a framework in which they can communicate their agreement, which would then have to be established by further conventions, and so on *ad infinitum*.[163]

How could conventions ever have begun?

Dharmakīrti disagrees with this view of language for a variety of reasons.[164] He points out that if the connection between word and meaning was indeed grounded in the nature of reality, would it not be reasonable to expect that then any listener could understand the meaning of given word immediately, without having ever learned it?[165] This is manifestly not the case; one does not understand the meaning of Sanskrit words without having studied Sanskrit. The defender of the Mīmāṃsā account might reply that, despite the fact that the connection between word and meaning is not *constituted* by convention, convention is still necessary to *know* this connection. Convention would then be an assisting factor in knowing the objective word–referent relation in much the same way in which light is required to see an object placed in front of us. Then, however, the 'natural connection' looks increasingly like a metaphysical postulate that is epistemically idle, something that does not cohere well with the Mīmāṃsā approach to epistemology. In addition, the introduction of a set of conventions telling us which word denotes which meaning threatens to introduce a divide between the status of the Vedas as authoritative texts and

Convention needed for knowing the word–world link?

Possibility of misunderstanding the Vedas

[161] Mīmāṃsā can therefore argue that a term like *svarga*, even though it does not form part of the world we live in (because no one has ever observed anyone going to heaven), must still refer since it occurs in the Veda. It is the primordial nature of language, not a set of speaker conventions that determines that an expression has a referent. See Wilke and Moebus 2011: 557.

[162] See Śabara's commentary on *Mīmāṃsāsūtra* 5, Abhyankar and Jośī: 1970–4: 24: 3–15.

[163] This problem has been worrying philosophers of language up to the present. See e.g. Lewis 1969: 2.

[164] For a detailed account of Dharmakīrti's criticism of the Mīmāṃsā theory of Vedic authority see Taber 2012: 119–66. Even though the Mīmāṣā view of language and the kind of conventionalism we find in most Buddhist thinking about language represent opposite ends of the philosophical spectrum, it is worthwhile to be aware that there is at least one Buddhist account of language that bears certain similarities with Mīmāṃsā and is likely to have been influenced by it. The Sarvāstivāda has developed the notion of the *nāma-kāya*, an entity that is not identical with speech in its spoken or written form, but is made manifest by sounds or letters, and conveys their meaning. The *nāma-kāya* is impermanent (it is a *saṃskāra*), though in the case of the Buddha's words it is also authorless (*apauruṣeya*). It might strike us as peculiar to characterize the teaching of a historical person such as the Buddha as authorless. Nevertheless, the Sarvāstivādins most likely wanted to stress that the teaching of the *dhātu*, *āyatana*, and *skandha* was not just an accidental discovery of a historically contingent character, but a trans-temporal truth, an insight taught by each Buddha anew, and therefore to a certain extent comparable to the Mīmāṃsā notion of authorless Vedic authority. For further discussion of these matters see Jaini 1959.

[165] *Pramāṇavārttika* 1: 227, Gnoli 1960: 113.

our ability to use them correctly for ritual purposes. For even though some word may be objectively connected with some entity in the world, if we have to interpret the word according to a system of conventions, we might systematically misinterpret the words of the Veda. Nothing precludes one from taking the famous injunction, 'one desirous of heaven should perform [the *agnihotra*] sacrifice' as saying 'one should eat dog meat'.[166] That the world settles the relation between word and world is not going to help us as long as we still need conventions to establish the relation between word and thought.

Moreover, the Mīmāṃsā conception of language is diametrically opposed to the *apoha* theory of Diṅnāga and Dharmakīrti. The point of the *apoha* theory is to explain how linguistic reference to phenomena like cowhood could still occur in the absence of any features in the world that function as stable, non-momentary objects in general that would not be able to participate in causal processes that characterize the world as we know it. Mīmāṃsā, on the other hand, defends an extreme realism about language that not only postulates an abstract level of linguistic structure behind an ephemeral reality of token utterances made in different languages, but links the very phonemes of Sanskrit to the fundamental structure of reality. This view has the immediate benefit of giving us some way of explaining the purported efficacy of the ritual use of language, such as we find in the Vedas, for if the structure of the world is intrinsically connected with the sounds of Sanskrit, it is at least conceivable that these very sounds can then be used to manipulate the world by the use of some of these sounds.

Mīmāṃsā and efficacy of rituals

Once we have accepted that there is an objective, speaker-independent, permanent connection between a language and the world, it follows that a grammatically well-formed set of statements in that language must be meaningful, since the structure we find in the expression is directly indicative of the structure of the reality expressed, and as long as a piece of language indicates how reality could be it is meaningful. Moreover, the expressions of the Vedas are not just meaningful, but also true. For falsity in some statements a speaker expresses results from some form of defect in the speaker, his limited epistemic powers, drawing a mistaken inference, or downright untruthfulness. But none of these defects can apply in the case of the Vedas, since they have no author.

Why the truth of the Vedas is implied

Dharmakīrti objected to the view by pointing out that in the same way the falsity of a view derives from defects in the speaker, so the truth of a view also derives from his reliability, which is based on other good qualities in turn (such as, in the Buddha's case, compassion). A statement that had no author at all would then either be false, since it is not backed by a reliable person that composed it, or it would lack any meaning at all.[167]

Dharmakīrti: truths need to be backed by speakers

[166] *Pramāṇavārttika* 1: 312–18, Gnoli 1960: 165–7, Dreyfus 1997: 222–3, Taber 2012: 126–7.

[167] *Svavṛtti* ad *Pramāṇavārttika* 1: 225; Gnoli 1960: 112.

Connection of Mīmāṃsā epistemology and philosophy of language

In any case, we can see at this point how the epistemology of Mīmāṃsā links up with its philosophy of language to support the authority of the Vedas.[168] According to the former, we are justified in believing claims backed up by some epistemic instrument, as long as there is no other evidence undermining them. The Vedas are an instance of one such epistemic instrument (*śabda*, testimony), and they inform us of various matters, such as *dharma*, or the ability to join the heavenly realms conditional on the execution of suitable sacrifices. But since the subject matter of the Vedas is transcendent and can *only* be revealed through them,[169] it is inaccessible to the other epistemic instruments,[170] and therefore can never be undermined. That the supposed result of a sacrifice is not observed, for example, does not mean that the epistemic instrument of testimony is undermined by that of perception. Frits Staal observes that:[171]

> When a ritual performance is completed, no fruit is seen. The Yajamāna, on whose behalf the rites have been performed, does not raise up, and go to heaven. Rather the opposite: he returns home and is, as the texts put it, the same as he was before.... The Mīmāṃsā concluded, quite logically, that the fruit of ritual activity is—temporarily—unseen. It will become apparent only later, e.g., after death.

*arthāpatti*

Mīmāṃsā introduced a specific epistemic instrument (*arthāpatti*, presumption, otherwise regarded as a form of inference) to help with this issue. A presumption is made in order to allow for the proper explanation of a given phenomenon. Given that Mīmāṃsa infers on the basis of its philosophy of language that the Vedas make meaningful claims, we must presume that there is something they are about, and since this is, while accessible to perception, not perceptible now, it must be accessible later.[172]

[168] We only have time to note, though not time to investigate, a potential tension between the Mīmāṣā epistemology and philosophy of language. The tendency towards common-sense realism we observe in their epistemology is certainly no longer present when it comes to Vedic exegesis: here how people ordinarily use a word is no guide to what it means in the Vedas. Taber (2012: 123) notes that 'mundane usage (*lokavāda*, *prasiddhi*) cannot be resorted to as a criterion for determining the meaning of Vedic statements, least of all by the Mīmāṃsakas, who like to point out that what ordinary humans say is for the most part untrue—hence, surely, how they commonly employ words cannot serve as any kind of *pramāṇa*—and who also routinely deviate from common usage themselves in their Vedic interpretations.'

[169] Pollock 1989: 607.

[170] *Mīmāṃsasūtra* 1.1.4 considers the inability of perception to know *dharma*: 'When there is a connection of the sense-faculties [with an object], a cognition arises for a person. That is perception. [It is] not the cause [for knowing *dharma*], because because it is the apprehension of that which is present', *satsamprayoge puruṣasyendriyāṇāṃ buddhijanma tat pratyakṣam animittaṃ vidyamānopalambhanatvāt*, Thadani 2007: 1. On the interpretation of this *sūtra* see also Taber 2006: 63–83.

[171] Staal 1996: 122.

[172] The notion of presumption is not restricted to the context of the efficacy of ritual action. Mīmāṃsā argues, for example, that we cannot make sense of our use of language without presuming the existence of language-independent universals our terms refer to (Arnold 2014: section 3.3).

If none of the other *pramāṇas* can therefore undermine the claims that the epistemic instrument of testimony (in the form of the Vedas) makes, we are justified in believing their claims, and the authority of the Vedic texts is thereby established.

## *c. Mīmāṃsā, historiography, and history*

Sheldon Pollock has developed the interesting claim that the particular philosophical position Mīmāṃsā developed in its defence of Vedic authority had important consequences for the way Indians wrote their own history, and for the role historical information played in Indian intellectual life in general. It is certainly peculiar to observe how little historical information we can find in many Indian texts.[173] There are works on statecraft that do not mention a single historical state, works on literary criticism that do not mention the names of poets or their works, and indeed, 'we can read thousands of pages of Sanskrit on any imaginable subject and not encounter a single passing reference to a historical person, place, or event—or at least to any that, historically speaking, matters'.[174] One important reason for explaining this, Pollock argues, is the Mīmāṃsā construal of Vedic texts as fundamentally ahistorical: they have no date of composition, no author, no context in which they arose, resembling timeless laws of nature more than collections of texts. Their immensely important status, and the fact that most kinds of learning in classical and medieval India saw itself as in one way or other derived from the Vedas,[175] led to the claim that any text describing these branches of knowledge was also composed in a manner resembling the Vedas, that is, by systematically downplaying the historical context of the work, its nature as an artefact that arose at a specific point, composed by specific authors, in order to portray it instead as an example of timeless authority. The lack of historical references and historical emphasis of much of classical Indian literature is perhaps less perplexing if we realize the philosophical background of construing the very lack of historical situatedness as a mark of excellence rather than as a defect.

The (ahistoric) Vedas as a model of excellence

It is instructive to put the Mīmāṃsā and the Buddhist philosophical approaches side by side, so to speak, located, as they are, at two different ends of the philosophical spectrum. Mīmāṃsā epistemology defends a position that approaches the deliverances of untrained epistemic instruments and the inferences usually drawn from them (also known as common sense) with a great degree of trust, arguing that justified belief is to be found in parallel with them. Buddhism, on the other hand, approaches the very same epistemic source with a great degree of wariness. As ignorance is the primary cause

Mīmāṃsā and Buddhist thought: the big picture

Epistemic optimism vs. pessimism

[173] For some discussion of the cliché that 'India has no history' see Franco 2013: 18–19.

[174] Pollock 1989: 606.

[175] A culture-wide process that Pollock labels 'vedicization' (Pollock 1989: 609).

that keeps beings trapped in cyclic existence, our untrained epistemic approach to the world is shot through to such an extent with questionable default assumptions and mistaken cognitive reflexes that we should be very suspicious of whatever knowledge of the world it proposes to deliver.[176] In this way Mīmāṃsā cannot only argue that much of the world is the way it seems to us, but also that *we* really are as we seem to us, namely, existing as permanent, substantial selves. We are entitled to believe that terms like 'being a cow' refer to what they seem to refer to (the abstract property of being a cow), not only because this is taken to be the best explainer for our use of such terms in language, but because for Mīmāṃsā, all our perceptions are concept-infused. Perceptions disclose things to us as falling under concepts (such as cowness, or whiteness), and if there is not evidence to the contrary we are justified in believing that the referents of these properties are real. Similarly, the way memory appears to us, for example, is such that we seem to recognize that the currently remembering subject is the very same as the one involved in the experience remembered. As there are no other epistemic instruments undermining this view of a persisting subject, we are justified in accepting it.

The Buddhists, and specifically the school of Diṅnāga and Dharmakīrti, vehemently disagree with all of this. They reject an enduring self for the same reductionist reasons we already find in the Abhidharma, and argue that despite appearances, there is no such thing. Abstract properties might appear theoretically useful, but it is entirely unclear how these, *qua* permanent, unchanging entities, can interact with mental and physical phenomena characterized by momentariness. Furthermore, the conceptual overlay that seems to come with every perceptual act is a problem, given the falsifying roles conceptualizations play, and not a guide to what there is.

Historical background of this disagreement

While I believe that we have to be quite cautious in trying to explain philosophical positions from the social and political conditions in which their proponents happened to find themselves, it is hard not to observe a certain congruence between the general philosophical outlooks of Mīmāṃsā and the school of Diṅnāga and Dharmakīrti described in this very broad way, and the social role of Brahmins and Buddhists in seventh-century India. Brahmins as a group occupied a role of power at the royal courts and acted as political advisors, in addition to offering spiritual advice and protection through *mantras*[177] and

[176] If we restrict our attention to the period roughly up to the middle of the first millennium CE a difference like this might even be considered to characterize the non-Buddhist and Buddhist schools of thought more generally, not just Mīmāṃsā and the school of Diṅnāga and Dharmakīrti: 'roughly until the middle of the first millennium CE . . . all Buddhist philosophers denied the reality of the world of our every-day experience, and all brahmanical philosophers accepted it.' Bronkhorst 2011a: 171.

[177] This included the pronouncement of curses, a task that the Buddhists were unwilling to perform (see Hahn 1982b: 331).

rituals, as well as astrological expertise and the interpretation of signs for predicting the future. Like the Brahmins, the Buddhists were dependent on the royal courts as a source of protection and donation,[178] but Buddhism placed little emphasis on ritual and prophecy, and was altogether less naturally suited for giving political advice than Brahmanism. The Brahmins had clear ideas about the nature of society and how it should be governed, while Buddhism was not greatly interested in developing a view of the right social order, but was a path to individual liberation from the unsatisfactoriness of saṃsāra.[179] Even the Buddha himself, when speaking to kings, was reluctant to give them political advice.[180]

Brahmins and Buddhists at royal courts

Switching to Sanskrit as a Buddhist doctrinal language some time in the second century BCE may have been an attempt to minimize the disadvantage the Buddhists had relative to the Brahmins in their connections with bearers of political power.[181] More importantly, however, the Buddhists had a different tale to tell, a philosophical outlook describing a route to spiritual perfection and liberation aimed at each individual being, including kings. Of course, this tale competed with the account given by the Brahmins, but it is interesting to note that underneath the surface disagreements in religious matters is an underlying epistemological message questioning the very philosophical assumptions on which the Brahmins based their power. This message is a form of scepticism towards the commonsensical appearance of the world. Being less invested in a position that emphasized the *status quo*, a position where the way the world appeared to ordinary observers (including the social and religious status of the Brahmins) was the way the world really was, and the way the world should be according to the most fundamental structures of reality, the Buddhists defended a philosophical outlook embodying distrust of a world conceived according to the certainties of common sense. Their account, doubting the results of untrained epistemic instruments, is more congruent with being a theory that finds itself disconnected from the structures of power

Different degrees of philosophical emphasis on the *status quo*

[178] In the Buddhist case the establishment of monasteries brought with it the requirements of 'upkeep and maintenance; such maintenance required donations beyond mere subsistence; such donations required the further maintenance of long-term relationships with donors.' Schopen 2007: 61.

[179] It is interesting to compare in this context brahmanical texts with advice on governance, such as the *Arthaśāstra* and the *Mānava Dharmaśāstra* or *Manusmṛti* with Buddhist texts such as Nāgārjuna's *Ratnāvalī* or the *Suhṛlekha*. The advice the latter provide is arguably more suitable for a king emulating the monastic ideal on the throne than for navigating the treacherous waters of *realpolitik*. (See Bronkhorst 2011a: 104–5). It is also noteworthy to note the absence of Buddhist treatises on other fields of knowledge intimately connected with the Brahmins' position of power, such as astronomy, astrology, and mathematics.

[180] Bareau 1993: 38.

[181] Bronkhorst (2011a: 129) argues that the need to interact with Brahmins in the defence of their interests at the royal court explains the Buddhist adoption of Sanskrit as a textual language. In order to engage with the Brahmins at a doctrinal level the Buddhists had to be able to use their tongue.

affirmed by these very instruments, than with being one that derives an important part of its legitimacy from considering that the world is more or less the way most people take it to be.[182] Congruence is, of course, not causation, but in order to achieve a nuanced understanding of the opposition between a Mīmāṃsā common-sense realism and fundamental distrust in conceptualization *à la* Diṅnāga and Dharmakīrti it is important to note that there are more dimensions to their respective positions than just the philosophical one.

## 9. The End of Buddhist Philosophy in India

The last 500 years

There is some justification for dating the end of the long tradition of Buddhist scholastic philosophy in India that began with the composition of the great Abhidharma treatises at the beginning of the Common Era as coinciding with the destruction of the great monastic universities of Nālandā and Vikramaśilā around the year 1200. This means that from the time of Dharmakīrti there are at least five more centuries of Buddhist philosophical activity on Indian soil.

A decline in quality?

Tāranātha is quite pessimistic about the state of philosophical sophistication achieved during this period, claiming that nothing in Indian Buddhism that came after the period of the 'six ornaments' (*rgyan drug*, Nāgārjuna, Āryadeva, Asaṅga, Vasubandhu, Diṅnāga, and Dharmakīrti) could quite compare to their brilliance:

> Before the great *ācārya* Dharmakīrti, the law of the Buddha was as bright as the sun. After him, generally speaking, there were many great *upādhyāya*s who worked excellently for the law. But there was practically none equal to the older *ācārya*s.... During the period of the six ornaments, the Mahāyāna *ācārya*s were great scholars of the doctrine and the *saṃgha* remained disciplined.... From this period on, the law became gradually weaker in the south and there eventually became extinct.... In other places, it survived in a scattered and feeble form.[183]

If we look at the amount and quality of philosophical work produced by Indian Buddhist scholars after the time of Dharmakīrti, Tāranātha's judgment seems unreasonably harsh. Yet we might at least agree with him that at this

[182] This point is raised by Bronkhorst (2011a: 171–2). He notes that 'Brahmins... were much more involved in courtly life and policy decisions than Buddhists: a political counselor is likely to lose much of his credibility if he maintains at the same time that the world of our every-day experience does not really exist' (2013: 359). Bronkhorst also argues, however, that the illusionistic doctrines of Buddhism are not found 'in the teaching of the Buddha as traditionally handed down' (2011a: 171) and are later introductions. I believe that, as with all concepts that acquired any prominence in the Buddhist philosophical discussion, seeds for the illusionistic ideas can already be found in the earliest Buddhist texts, even though the way these different seeds have sprouted was highly dependent on the constitution of the intellectual soil onto which they would later fall.

[183] Chimpa and Chattopadhyaya 1970: 255–6.

time all the major players have entered the stage.[184] The various positions of Madhyamaka, Yogācāra, and the logico-epistemological school continued to be developed, often with great philosophical sophistication, yet no further school of similar philosophical status emerged during the final five centuries of Buddhist thought in India. While the performance did not stop, the actors would be familiar to anyone knowledgeable about what had happened in Buddhist philosophy up to the time of Dharmakīrti.

Continuing performance but no new characters

We mentioned above that within the confines of this account we are not able to go beyond casting a quick glance at some of the more noteworthy figures who shaped philosophical activity during this time. A few of the major scholars of this last period of Indian Buddhist philosophy, such Śāntarakṣita, Kamalaśīla, Ratnākaraśānti, and Ratnakīrti we have already met. In this section we will add some brief discussion of two further important philosophers from this final period we have not discussed so far, Śāntideva and Atiśa.

## a. *Śāntideva*

Śāntideva's life

Śāntideva is most likely to have flourished some time between 685 and 763 CE. He was a Buddhist monk, and is commonly associated with the monastic university of Nālandā. The traditional accounts of his life[185] introduce a motive familiar from the life of the Buddha: born as a son of a king and destined to inherit the throne, Śāntideva nevertheless sees the spiritual dangers coming from life as a ruler and flees the kingdom. In addition, Śāntideva receives teachings from the very highest level from an early age. At the age of 6 he is said to have been initiated into the practice of the bodhisattva Mañjusrī, a bodhisattva specifically associated with wisdom, who appears to him in visions and teaches him directly.

During his time at Nālandā he was regarded as somewhat lazy by his fellow monks, who quipped that instead of the three activities prescribed for monks,[186] study, meditation, and service to the monastery, all Śāntideva was ever observed doing was eating, sleeping, and digesting. In order to show him up they requested him to recite a text he had memorized. When the time came, Śāntideva declared he would recite something never heard before, and began to recite the *Bodhicaryāvatāra*, a text that would become his most famous work, and one of the most well-known, and best-loved, Mahāyāna *śāstra*s. When reciting verse 34 of the ninth chapter, on the Perfection of Wisdom: 'When neither entity nor non-entity remains before the mind, since there is no other

[184] It is interesting to note that for Bu ston the history of Buddhism in India also appears to end in the eighth century. The last philosopher he discusses before moving from the development of Buddhism in India to its development in Tibet is Śāntideva (Bu ston 2013: 257–75). See also Chattopadhyaya 1967: 82.

[185] See Tsonawa 1985: 60–4.

[186] Crosby and Skilton 1995: 118.

mode of operation, grasping no objects, it becomes tranquil',[187] Śāntideva is said to have risen from his throne and ascended into the air until he could no longer be seen, even though his voice was still audible until he had finished the recitation of his work.

The *Bodhicaryāvatāra*

The *Bodhicaryāvatāra*, a long work of about 900 verses,[188] of immense popularity and prominent status in Buddhist literature, constitutes an extended investigation into the notion of the awakening mind (*bodhicitta*) characterizing a bodhisattva. It is not a particularly uncommon type of work, belonging to the kind of text that gives an account of the Buddhist path and the associated practices that a bodhisattva follows from the preparatory stages to its final goal.[189] It begins with praise of the treatise's subject matter, the awakening mind, in the first chapter, in order to set out the motivation for pursuing the path described later in the text. This is followed by preparing the ground for the practice, by generating merit through going for refuge and the confession of faults (chapters 2 and 3), and by teachings on how to uphold one's resolve in the bodhisattva path (chapter 4). The remainder of the text then follows the set of the six perfections (*pāramitā*): generosity (*dāna*), morality (*śīla*) (both discussed in chapter 5), patience (*kṣānti*, chapter 6), effort (*viryā*, chapter 7), meditation (*dhyāna*, chapter 8), and wisdom (*prajñā*, chapter 9). The text concludes in chapter 10 by the dedication of merit and a series of vows (*praṇidhāna*). Particularly well known are the sixth chapter, on the Perfection of Patience, where Śāntideva presents various arguments for developing the basis of the bodhisattva's great compassion, and the ninth chapter on the Perfection of Wisdom, containing an intricate discussion of the nature of emptiness set up as a debate between Mādhyamikas and proponents of various other Buddhist and non-Buddhist schools, most prominently Yogācārins.

Whatever our views on the facticity of the account of Śāntideva's first recitation of the *Bodhicaryāvatāra* are, it provides an apt illustration of the transformational potential the spiritual path described in it is supposed to have. As the bodhisattva works his way up to the realization of emptiness set out in the ninth chapter, the superimposition of a substantial self that constitutes the bondage to cyclic existence dissolves into thin air, though his compassionate activities continue to resonate in the world.

Śāntideva and Nālandā

Like many thinkers discussed in these pages, Śāntideva was connected with the great monastic university of Nālandā. This major monastic centre (together

[187] *yadā na labhyate bhāvo yo nāstīti prakalpyate | tadā nirāśrayo 'bhāvaḥ kathaṃ tiṣṭhenmateḥ puraḥ*, Vaidya 1988: 204.

[188] This version is sometimes referred to as the 'canonical rencension'. There is another version, about 200 verses shorter, discovered amongst the Dūnhuáng manuscripts. Research into the relation between the two is ongoing, see Saito 1993.

[189] Compare e.g. Āryaśūra's *Pāramitāsamāsa* (Meadows 1986) and Atiśa's *Bodhipathapradīpa* (Geshe Sonam Rinchen 1997).

with others, such as Vikramaśīla, Odantapurī, and Takṣaśīla) was one of the key locations where much of the development of Indian Buddhist philosophy took place. Nālandā was founded by King Śakrāditya of Magadha, usually identified with Kumāragupta I, who ruled around the period 415–55 CE,[190] and flourished subsequently under the patronage of the Gupta and Pāla dynasties. Traditional accounts describe how some of the greatest Mahāyāna scholars lived and taught at Nālandā; besides Śāntideva this illustrious list includes Asaṅga, Vasubandhu, Dharmakīrti, Dharmapāla, Candrakīrti, Sthiramati, Śāntarakṣita, Kamalaśīla, and Nāropa.[191] Apart from archaeological evidence, most of our information on how Nālandā functioned as a monastic university comes from descriptions by Chinese pilgrims travelling to India in search of Buddhist texts during the seventh century. Xuanzang (*c*.602–64)[192] spent about two years in Nālandā, and Yijing (635–713),[193] whose travels took altogether twenty-five years, lived there for about a decade.

Nālandā's curriculum

Though Nālandā is commonly referred to as a Buddhist university, there were many sides to it that were not specifically or exclusively Buddhist. Its Gupta patrons were not Buddhists but followers of Brāhmaṇism.[194] Nor was the Nālandā curriculum restricted to training in Buddhist subjects. In addition to the study of the eighteen schools of Abhidharma and the Mahāyāna, students were trained in grammar, logic, the Vedas, medicine, Sāṃkhya philosophy, and Sanskrit literature.[195] Of the 'five sciences' (*pañcavidyā*) that occupy a central place in monastic learning,[196] comprising grammar, prosody, synonymics, and poetic forms (*śabdavidyā*), logic (*hetuvidyā*), medicine (*cikitsāvidyā*), fine arts and crafts (*śilpakarmasthānavidyā*), and the study of Buddhist texts (*adhyātmavidyā*), only the last is specifically and directly

[190] Dutt 1988: 329.

[191] Joshi 1967: 171. Smith (1908–26: 9. 127) even claims that 'a detailed history of Nālandā would be a history of Mahāyānist Buddhism'. Early authors also connect scholars with Nālandā who lived considerably earlier than its foundation, or at any rate earlier than its foundation as a *mahāvihāra*—most famously Nāgārjuna and Āryadeva. For some discussion of this and the associated idea of the 'Nālandā tradition' see above, pp. 25, 32–3.

[192] Beal 1884. [193] Takakusu 1896.

[194] The religious loyalties of Indian kings are a complex issue. King Harṣavardhana (*c*.600–50 CE) is described as 'loading the Brahmans with gifts, and in his works he himself declares that he is a worshipper of Śiva.... But the personal sentiments of the monarch were clearly Buddhist, and of the Mahāyāna school. In the Mahāyāna even, his sympathies appear to have attached him to the Yogācāra school, as it was taught in the monasteries of Nālandā...' (Bronkhorst 2011a: 111).

[195] Dutt 1988: 332–3. Interestingly, astronomy or mathematics is not mentioned in this context (on the other hand, see Joshi 1967: 161). See also n. 179 above, and Bronkhorst 2011a: 118, n. 64.

The diversity of the Nālandā curriculum might not simply have been an expression of broad-mindedness or tolerant inclusivism. Another factor to take into account is that during a time when there was considerable external pressure on Buddhism from Brahmanism it was essential for the Buddhists to be familiar with the brahmanical systems so as to be able to defend their claims in debate. (Bouthillette 2017: 69).

[196] The five sciences are mentioned by Yijing, Xuanzang (Dutt 1988: 324), and Bu ston (2013: 42–7), see also Joshi 1967: 161.

concerned with Buddhist doctrinal matters. The importance of all five is underlined by a verse from Asaṅga's *Mahāyānasūtrālaṃkāra*:[197]

> Without diligence in the five fields of knowledge
> Even the noblest person cannot obtain omniscience.
> Therefore, to defeat challenges, to care for others,
> And for complete understanding, persevere in these.

Grammar and logic are associated with the first of the three aims mentioned here, to defeat challenges from opponents; medicine and the fine arts are part of caring for others; and the study of Buddhism is directed at attaining full understanding.

Nālandā and its patrons

There may well be a connection between the extent of royal patronage and the width of the Nālandā curriculum. We might consider it puzzling why non-Buddhist rulers treated a Buddhist institution with quite as much generosity as the Guptas treated Nālandā. One reason may be that they did not perceive Buddhism as in opposition to their own brahmanic beliefs. Buddhist and brahmanic practices for the worship of images show significant similarity,[198] and the Gupta period might have provided the foundation for the later incorporation of the Buddha into the Hindu pantheon.[199] But another, perhaps more important reason may be that they did not regard Nālandā as simply a Buddhist institution providing teaching of exclusive interest to Buddhists, but as a seat of learning and centre of instruction covering a wide range of subjects, from a Buddhist perspective but without an exclusive restriction to the Buddhist canon.[200]

Nālandā and the *Bodhicaryāvatāra*

Does the *Bodhicaryāvatāra* show any traces of being composed in Nālandā? Indian Buddhist treatises are not known for incorporating a great amount of historical and contextual information. Nevertheless, there are some connections we can find. First, Nālandā was of course a monastery, and Śāntideva was therefore addressing an exclusively male audience of monks. This does not imply that there would have been no women on the premises, though—Yijing mentions that during ritual ablutions of the Buddha image in Indian monasteries 'a band of girls plays music there'.[201] Men, however, were his primary audience, and Śāntideva's extensive remarks on the repulsive qualities of the human body (*aśubhabhāvanā*), which constitute a set of meditations to act as

[197] 11.60: *vidyāsthāne pañcavidhe yogamakṛtvā sarvajñatvaṃ naiti kathaṃcitparamāryaḥ | ityanyeṣāṃ nigrahaṇānugrahaṇāya svājñārthaṃ vā tatra karotyeva sa yogam*, Bagchi 1970. This verse is quoted by Bu ston (2013: 43).

[198] Dutt 1988: 196.

[199] In the *Daśāvatāracaritam* composed by Kṣemendra in the 11th century the Buddha appears as one of the 10 *avatāras* of Viṣṇu.

[200] Dutt 1988: 198. [201] Takakusu 1896: 147–8.

an antidote for a meditator overcome by sexual desire, describe in great detail the unattractive qualities of the female body.

Second, chapters 2 and 3 of the *Bodhicaryāvatāra* set out a Mahāyāna liturgy referred to as 'supreme worship' (*anuttarapūjā*). Śāntideva did not invent this liturgy, a version of which can already be found in the *Gaṇḍavyūhasūtra*, which dates from the fourth century CE or earlier. The liturgy aims to move the practitioner through a series of mental states, beginning with praise of and making offerings to the Buddhas, going for refuge, followed by the confessions of one's own shortcomings, rejoicing in the merits of others, requesting the Buddhas to teach, dedication of the merit generated, culminating in the generation of the awakening mind (*bodhicittotpāda*).

It is highly likely that the description of ritual actions described in these chapters corresponds to rites carried out by the monks at Nālandā on a daily basis, and that Śāntideva's audience was intimately familiar with them. It is certainly the case that the ritual actions concerning worship and offerings Śāntideva describes at the beginning of the second chapter, including the bathing of Buddha images, dressing them in fine cloths, offering perfumes, flowers, and incense to them accompanied by music and the singing of hymns, acts of prostration, and *stūpa* worship correspond closely to practices Yijing describes as having observed in Nālandā and other Indian monasteries at the time.[202]

A third connection between Śāntideva's texts and Nālandā, their place of composition, concerns his other major work, the *Śikṣāsamuccaya*, or 'Compendium of Training'.[203] This text consists of a set of twenty-seven verses on the training of the bodhisattva, together with a prose commentary and a selection of Mahāyāna *sūtras* illustrating and supporting the points Śāntideva makes. In this work he quotes about a hundred different texts; these quotations are particularly interesting, not only because they give us an idea which *sūtras* Mahāyāna scholars at Śāntideva's time studied, but also because the original Sanskrit version of many of these texts, apart from the quotations Śāntideva preserves, have been lost. It is likely that Śāntideva had memorized most of the texts he quoted there, but in order to get hold of them in the first place he would have needed access to a fairly well-stocked library. Nālandā, of course, was very well provided in this respect. Its library was a depository where visiting scholars could acquire authoritative copies of texts; Yijing alone departed from Nālandā with copies of 400 Sanskrit works.[204] Tibetan accounts relate the existence of three library buildings, called Sea of Jewels (*ratnodadhi*),

[202] Compare verses 2: 1–25 of the *Bodhicaryāvatāra* and Takakusu 1896: 147–66.

[203] Bendall and Rouse 1922, Goodman 2016. Whether the *Śikṣāsamuccaya* was composed before the *Bodhicaryāvatāra* or afterwards is unclear. The latter mentions the former, but this passage may be a later interpolation. For further discussion see Saito 2013.

[204] Joshi 1967: 170.

Ocean of Jewels (*ratnasāgara*), and Jewel-adorned (*ratnarañjaka*), and like all legendary libraries of antiquity they perished in flames.[205]

### b. *Atiśa Dīpaṃkaraśrījñāna*

Atiśa's early life

The second later Indian Buddhist philosopher we will consider here is Dīpaṃkaraśrījnāna, frequently referred to as Atiśa.[206] Born into a royal family in Bengal, Atiśa was ordained as a Buddhist monk comparatively late, at the age of 29. Sources on what he did before this time vary, but there is considerable evidence that he studied and practiced tantric teachings.[207] According to one account, he even spent three years in Oḍḍiyāna (a place sometimes identified with the Swat valley in today's Pakistan), taking part in tantric feasts in the company of *dākiṇīs*.[208] Oḍḍiyāna was a great centre of tantric studies, well known as the birthplace of Padmasambhava, the Indian tantric adept crucial to the early dissemination (*snga dar*) of Buddhism to Tibet in the time of King Khri srong lde bstan during the eighth century CE.

Atiśa was ordained as a monk in the Mahāsaṃghika school, according to some sources at Nālandā, after seeing a vision of Buddha Śākyamuni in a dream.[209]

His studies

In 1012, at the age of 31 and only two years after his ordination, Atiśa set out to travel to Suvarṇadvīpa (current Sumatra and Java), then a major centre of Buddhist learning. The journey, which Atiśa undertook in the company of merchants, and which included an encounter with sea-monsters along the way, took altogether fourteen months. His aim was to study in Suvarṇadvīpa with a well-known teacher called Dharmakīrti (not identical with Diṅnāga's grand disciple discussed above).[210] Tibetan translations of six works of this 'Dharmakīrti Suvarṇadvīpi' are preserved in the Tibetan commentarial canon (*bstan 'gyur*). His major work is a substantial commentary on Maitreyanātha's *Abhisamayālaṃkāra* (more than twice the length of Atīśa's *Bodhipathapradīpa* together with its auto-commentary), a work that is sometimes considered as 'one of the most outstanding representatives of the Mahāyāna philosophy of the 10th–11th century'.[211] This text confirms Dharmakīrti Suvarṇadvīpi's standing as an extraordinary scholar. Further evidence of his status is provided by the fact that most of the training of the scholar that Atīśa himself came to be must be due to Dharmakīrti Suvarṇadvīpi; Atīśa's previous monastic education before coming to Suvarṇadvīpa only lasted for two years, while his stay with

[205] Dutt 1988: 343. Tibetan records also relate that many books were saved from the conflagrations by an early miraculous sprinkler system: water rushing forth from the *Guhyasamāja* and *Prajñāpāramitā* texts kept in the upper floors of the building.

[206] Atiśa is an abbreviation of *atiśaya* ('outstanding'). See Eimer 1977: 17–22. For accounts of Atiśa's life see Chatthopadyyaya 1967; Eimer 1977, 1979.

[207] Eimer 1979: 191.

[208] Chattopadhyaya 1967: 74–5.

[209] Chattopadhyaya 1967: 77, Eimer 1979: 192–3.

[210] Eimer 1979: 194–5.

[211] Chatthopadhyaya 1967: 94.

Dharmakīrti stretched for twelve years. Atiśa is recorded as having been extraordinarily fond of Dharmakīrti, through whose instruction alone, he claims, he understood the concepts of love, compassion, and *bodhicitta*. Whenever he heard about Dharmakīrti later in life, Atiśa wept.[212]

Teacher at Vikramaśīla

After this extended period of training Atiśa, now in his mid-forties, returned to India to teach. Atiśa is primarily associated with the other great Buddhist monastic university in India apart from Nālandā, Vikramaśīla.[213] Vikramaśīla was founded considerably later than Nālandā, in the late eighth or early ninth century; for this reason we have no records from the early Chinese pilgrims that provided us with such detailed information about Nālandā. There are, however, Tibetan accounts of life at Vikramaśīla. As one of the leading centres of Buddhist scholarship in India it attracted a considerably number of foreign visitors, and is said to have had special residential quarters just for Tibetan students. At Vikramaśīla Atiśa's abilities as a scholar were recognized and he reached the position of an *upādhyāya* (*mkhan po*), which, though not actually the administrative head of the monastery,[214] constituted a role of academic leadership, possibly similar to a university's academic head. Another position that is attributed to him is that of an *upadhivārika* (*dge skos*), a kind of deanship that appears to have involved the disciplinary supervision of a group of monks.

The voyage to Tibet

Atiśa stayed in India for one-and-a-half decades, before, now nearly 60 years old, he embarked on what must have been his most ambitious journey, even for somebody as well-travelled as him: the voyage to Tibet. Buddhism had already arrived in Tibet in the seventh century, a period referred to as the early dissemination (*snga dar*) of the teachings. However, after two centuries the expansion of Buddhism stopped under the persecution of King gLang dar ma, beginning with him killing his brother and predecessor in 838. When gLang dar ma was assassinated in turn, the Tibetan empire fragmented, and after one-and-a-half centuries of decline Tibetans started to rekindle the Buddhist tradition by reconnecting with its roots in India. Part of this undertaking was to invite outstanding Indian scholars to teach in Tibet. King Byang chub 'od (984–1078), king of the ancient Tibetan kingdom of Guge in Western Tibet, and himself a Buddhist monk, sent out a search party to India to invite a *paṇḍita* to come to Tibet. The invitation of Atiśa was not an entirely straightforward matter, as Vikramaśīla was reluctant to let him go and initially only agreed to grant him leave of three years.[215] In the end his expected return never

[212] Eimer 1979: 195.

[213] Although he seems to have spent some time at Nālandā too. A colophon to a Tibetan translation indicates that he completed it there together with a Tibetan translator (Chatthopadhyaya 1967: 100).

[214] Chattopadhyaya 1967: 129–31.

[215] Chatthopadyaya 1967: 133.

happened: Atiśa spent the rest of his life in Tibet, and died at sNye thang just south of Lhasa in 1054 at the age of 73, having lived in Tibet for thirteen years.

His work in Tibet

After a year's journey up to Kathmandu and further on through Nepal, Atiśa arrived at Tho ling, the capital of the kingdom of Guge, at the age of 60. This year, 1042, is commonly regarded as the beginning of the later dissemination (*phyi dar*) of Buddhism into Tibet. Atiśa's activities in Tibet were manifold, and included teaching disciples,[216] blessing temples,[217] and translating and authoring texts. Best known of the works originating in Tibet is his *Bodhipathapradīpa*, which he composed during the first three years of his stay at the special request of King Byang chub 'od. Though only sixty-six verses long, Atiśa also wrote a comprehensive auto-commentary on it, the *Bodhimārgapradīpapañjikā*.

While the details of Atiśa's stay in Tibet, interesting as they are in themselves,[218] are of less direct relevance to a history of Indian Buddhist philosophy, there are two aspects of his life that deserve particular attention in the context of our present account.

Indian Mahāyāna's ambivalence towards tantra

The first is the way in which his life illustrates the ambivalence of Indian Mahāyāna towards tantra.[219] On the one hand, tantric and non-tantric Buddhist practices are taken to share a common goal: the attainment of Buddhahood. Tantric practices are considered to be a particularly swift path to this destination. On the other hand the tantric practices are also considered to be dangerous, as they make particularly high demands on the practitioner, and, if not carried out with the right motivation, can by their very antinomian nature lead not towards, but further away from enlightenment.[220] In addition, despite the fact that tantra is supposed to be particularly able to bring about rapid progress on the path to enlightenment, its sexual practices made it unsuitable for ordained monks,[221] thereby relegating the path of the monk to something that appeared, at least from the perspective of soteriological efficacy, second-rate.[222]

Atiśa's connection with tantra

As we saw, Atiśa began his spiritual life as a tantric practitioner before his ordination as a monk, and continued tantric practices in later life.[223] During his

[216] Chatthopadyaya 1967: 357–66. [217] Davidson 2004a: 102.

[218] For an account of the complex political situation Atiśa found himself in during his stay in Tibet see Davidson 2004a: 108–12.

[219] This doctrinal tension between sūtra and tantra had interesting political ramifications in the Tibetan society of Atiśa's time. See Samuel 1993: 471–3.

[220] We should note that the non-tāntrika's suspicion that tantra is likely to lead to ethical profligacy is matched by the tāntrika's worry that the non-tantric scholastic approach is likely to lead to greater acquaintance with the words than with the meanings of the Buddha's doctrine. A classic example of this is constituted by the life-story of Nāropa, a contemporary of Atiśa's and himself a famous scholar at Nālandā before his transformation into a tantric practitioner (Samuel 1993: 227–8).

[221] Davidson 2004b: 199–200. [222] Snellgrove 1987: 483–4, Ruegg 1981b.

[223] Samuel (1993: 468) describes Atiśa in his combination of sūtra and tantra practice as 'perhaps a typical product of the Indian monastic universities of the early eleventh century'.

time in Vikramaśīla he agreed to the expulsion of a tantric adept who was found in the possession of alcohol, though he claimed this was to be used for ritual purposes in propitiating a *yoginī*.[224] While this gives the impression of Atiśa as defending monastic discipline, which forbids the consumption of alcohol, against the antinomian practices of tantra, the further development of this account actually describes the expelled monk as a bodhisattva and as innocent of any breach of monastic discipline (using his spiritual powers he leaves the monastery by walking through a wall), and Atiśa as accumulating significant bad karma by acquiescing in his expulsion. In order to purge this karmic debt Atiśa is then considered to have taken the decision to teach the Mahāyāna in Tibet.[225]

Tantra in Tibet

A key reason for inviting him to Tibet seem to have been the desire on the Tibetan side to counteract certain developments of tantric practices then found in Tibet.[226] 'Gos lo tsā ba notes in the *Blue Annals*, a central Tibetan historical work, for example, that:

> notwithstanding the fact that some of the tantric precepts were to be found [in Tibet], tantric practices became defiled. Meditation on the ultimate reality was abandoned, and many coarse practices made their appearance, such as *sbyor sgrol* ('union and liberation', ritualized forms of sex and violence),[227] *gtad ser* (curses and magically produced hailstorms), and others.[228]

In order to remedy this situation the Tibetan kings 'sent invitations to numerous learned *paṇḍitas*, who were able to remove these obstacles by placing living beings on the path of purity'.

Atiśa on the suitability of tantric practices

One reason Byang chub 'od requested the composition of the *Bodhipatha-pradīpa* may have been to provide a theoretical underpinning, coming from the tradition of Indian Buddhism itself, for the rejection of such tantric practices.[229] What Atiśa actually says in the text is far more nuanced, however, treading the middle way, as befits a Mādhyamika. On the one hand he points out in verse 64 that initiations involving meditative exercises with a (visualized or actual) female partner are unsuitable for ordained monks,[230] yet on the other hand, in his commentary in this verse he is equally critical of those doubting the efficacy of tantric practice, pointing out that it is 'the heart of the Buddha's teaching. And he who condemns it as a field of activity for those who have the capacity, disposition, and development for it is going to hell—have no doubt

224 Eimer 1979: 212. 225 Eimer 1979: 212–13. 226 Eimer 1979: 216.

227 For more on the symbolic and literary dimensions of these terms see Samuel 1993: 467.

228 Roerich 1979: 204.

229 See Snellgrove 1987: 481–4, Samuel 1993: 470.

230 'The secret and wisdom initiations should not be taken by religious celibates, because it is emphatically forbidden in the *Ādi-buddha-mahā-tantra* (i.e. the Kālacakra-tantra)'. Sherburne 2000: 293, 317.

about it—because he is belittling the word of the Tathāgata and rejecting his profound doctrine'.[231] Atiśa thus points out that the tantric practices are the authentic teaching of the Buddha, and can be very efficacious for practitioners who have the necessary abilities (and who are not following the path of a Mahāyāna monk), though, as becomes clear in the remainder of the *Bodhipathapradīpa*, any Buddhist practice, including tantra, must place a clear emphasis on the teaching of the Mahāyāna *sūtras*: the teaching of the two *bodhicittas*, great compassion and the realization of emptiness. Certainly Atiśa himself translated[232] and wrote on a number of tantric texts, and remained himself a tantric practitioner who put particular emphasis on devotion to the goddess Tārā.[233]

Political dimension of the status of tantra

Far from being a purely doctrinal issue, the perceived tension between the antinomian dimension of tantra and the monastic (and more generally ethical) regulatory framework of Mahāyāna had a political side to it as well. In India as well as in Tibet the magical abilities exercised by the tantric practitioner were seen both as a way of legitimizing political royal power and—due to their transgressive nature—as a potential threat to this power.[234] The Tibetans who invited Atiśa were primarily concerned with the latter, a concern which constituted a major reason for requesting him to come to Tibet and teach. It would be mistaken, however, to view Atiśa's discussion of tantra solely in terms of the agenda of his hosts. It should rather be understood as a reflection of a more general tendency, in Buddhist and non-Buddhist thought, to reconceptualize tantra in a less antinomian manner, stressing the soteriological rather than the magical aspect of tantra, and removing or changing the more transgressive elements from the actual to the symbolic level.[235]

Buddhist scholasticism beyond India

The second aspect of Atiśa's life we should point out here is the extent to which he, more clearly than any of the Buddhist philosophers we have discussed so far, embodies the connection of Indian Buddhist scholastic culture

[231] Sherburne 2000: 297. [232] Jackson 2004: 111. [233] Samuel 1993: 471, Beyer 1988.

[234] For extensive discussion of this point see Samuel 1993, 2008. It is worthwhile to keep in mind that the political dimension of Buddhist tantra is no unique Tibetan phenomenon, but goes back to the history of tantra in India. One aspect that is likely to have supported development of tantra in India was its conceptualisation as a means of defending Buddhism against the increasing pressure from Brahmanism. Tantric ritual provided a route to establishing royal protection, something the Brahmins, with their ability to provide astrological and divinatory services, as well as advice on government in general were much better equipped for.

The martial dimension of Buddhist tantra in its fighting back against Brahmanism as that which 'by defeating the outsiders, removes the obstacles to the path toward liberation' (Eltschinger 2014: 174) is hard to overlook; the depiction of Buddhist deities trampling on members of the brahmanic pantheon or holding the severed heads of Brahma (Beer 1999: 309) is one of its immediately obvious manifestations. (Though this iconographic aggression seems to have gone both ways: we also find representations of the goddess Cāmuṇḍā seated on the corpse of the Buddha: Verardi 2014: 289–92.)

[235] Samuel 2008: 324–38.

with the world beyond the Indian subcontinent. By the eleventh century this culture had already spread considerably beyond India itself, and it becomes more appropriate to speak subsequently of an *Indic* rather than Indian Buddhist scholastic tradition.

In Atiśa's own life this is evident in his formation as a scholar. Most of his training in Buddhist philosophy did not take place at one of the great Indian monastic universities but in Suvarṇadvīpa, a long way from the Indian subcontinent. Atiśa then brought the learning he had acquired during those twelve years back to Vikramaśīla, and during the final years of his life set out to develop the spread of the Buddhist scholastic tradition in the remote and culturally, politically, and socially wholly different Himalayan realm.

Looking back from Tibet

The firm establishment of Buddhist learning in Tibet at the time of the 'later dissemination' seems to be a good point to end our discussion of the most important centuries of the development of Buddhist philosophy in India. Looking back from here we realize that our knowledge of the Indian Buddhist philosophical world would be considerably more fragmentary without the abundance of texts that have been preserved through the wholesale Tibetan adoption of Indian philosophical culture and the large-scale translation effort covering the entire canon of root texts and commentaries.

More importantly, the Tibetan tradition has maintained the continuation of Indian Buddhist scholastic debate up to the present day, by thinking along with their sources 'in a style and along lines that are *typologically* Indian without being *historically* Indian'.[236] This is not to say that the particular philosophical game that is scholastic Buddhism has not been shaped and changed in many ways by its transmission to a different cultural sphere, and most importantly, perhaps, by the fact that this sphere included no non-Buddhist opponents. Nevertheless, it is not least because of this continuity of the development of Tibetan Buddhism that the scholar of Indian Buddhist philosophy is able to encounter it not as a series of exhibits in the museum of the history of ideas, but as a living tradition.

[236] Ruegg 2004: 328.

# Concluding Remarks

The preceding pages constitute one account of the main trajectories of Indian Buddhist thought during the first millennium CE. There is much we had to leave out, and many thinkers, concepts, and dialectical exchanges deserve a much more detailed treatment than we could provide here. Despite the inevitably partial nature of this account, three main conclusions about the Buddhist philosophical enterprise have emerged that are worth repeating here.

First, it has become apparent that assessing different parts of Buddhist philosophy according to whether they accord with 'what the Buddha really taught' is not particularly helpful. By this I do not mean to discourage research into the earliest Buddhist sources. Rather, I want to suggest that we can understand more about Buddhist thought if we do not try to draw a dichotomy (as we might do in the case of a pearl) between an original 'inner core' of Buddhist thought and a later 'coating' of subsequent doctrinal developments. Instead, I have suggested a 'germination' model according to which a variety of conceptual seeds was present in Buddhism's earliest teachings, arguing that the different philosophical systems of Buddhist philosophy then arose from a selective emphasis on some of these seeds over others. As such, the task of the student of Buddhist philosophy is not to 'strip away' all the external layers in order to find the core of the pearl, but to understand how a given tradition and the particular intellectual climate in which it was located developed its specific views by focusing on certain aspects of the Buddha's teachings rather than others, letting some intellectual seeds grow to philosophical greater height than others. Nor do we have to assume that the focus of one tradition is more justified than that of another. From its very beginning the Buddhist tradition did not understand the Buddha's *dharma* as a single canonical exposition opposed to all others. Instead, the Buddha taught to a multiplicity of audiences in a variety of ways, and often on the basis of very different assumptions. It was not that one exposition was more authoritative than another, but that each was designed to meet the specific soteriological needs of its audience. We can think of the subsequent development of Buddhist thought along similar lines. That a specific set of concepts is stressed by a particular tradition at a particular time can be seen as indicating that the resulting version of the Buddha's *dharma* met the specific soteriological needs of the audience receiving it.

Those were the teachings that the practitioners and thinkers at that time and place perceived as providing the best means for making progress along the path to liberation.

Second, it has become abundantly clear above that Buddhist philosophy is not just about thinking. It is not even just about thinking in response to and within the context of Buddhist texts. Buddhist philosophy has been considered by all its proponents as part of the path to enlightenment and the liberation from suffering, and it has never been suggested that one can obtain this goal by thinking or philosophical analysis alone. The reason for this is that the unliberated state is not simply a product of false beliefs, even though false beliefs form an important part of this state. The Buddhist thinkers were not of the opinion that we could always simply get rid of a given false belief by encountering, analysing, and finally assenting to an argument that demonstrated its opposite. This is because certain beliefs (such as beliefs in a substantial self, or in intrinsically existent objects) are so deeply ingrained due to habitualized tendencies that keep reasserting themselves independent of the results of our philosophical deliberations. For this reason philosophical analysis has to be supplemented by a set of cognitive exercises that aim at weakening and finally removing the mental reflexes that bring about the constant and near-automatic reassertion of beliefs that our philosophical investigations have found to be deficient.

This does not mean, however, that such cognitive exercises or meditative techniques are merely intended to eradicate conclusions that philosophical analysis has previously undermined. The influence between philosophical investigations and meditative exercises is not one-way. From the classification of phenomena in the Abhidharma up to meditative exercises for the dissolution of visualizations associated with Yogācāra, we have seen examples of meditative techniques and their results influencing the development of philosophical theorizing. The philosophical and the meditative elements of the Buddhist path are mutually supporting. Meditative exercises are used to turn beliefs about the world supported by philosophical analysis into a deeply ingrained comportment towards the world, while philosophical analyses provide a conceptual background for experiences encountered during meditative training.

As such, the Buddhist philosophical tradition differs in an important way from the Western one, at least if the latter is conceived as primarily providing answers to puzzles about specific fundamental features of reality, an exercise of reason for its own sake, independent of the authority of specific texts or traditions.[1] Of course, there are certain elements of the Buddhist philosophical enterprise resembling such an understanding of philosophy, but I believe that

[1] For a different take on the Western philosophical tradition see Hadot 1981.

the preceding historical discussion will have convinced the reader that it is not possible to achieve a comprehensive understanding of the Buddhist philosophical tradition without taking into account aspects like its meditative dimension, features which do not play a large role in the way the philosophical enterprise is understood in the West.

The third point I want to stress that has emerged from the brief survey of Indian Buddhist thought I could offer here is the importance of a systematic engagement with the problems and concepts the Indian texts are concerned with. By this I mean the unwillingness to restrict our inquiry to what a specific ancient Indian philosopher or text said, but to investigate whether the arguments presented are valid, whether the position can be defended against obvious and not-so-obvious objections, and whether the overall picture emerging is an attractive one that we might be inclined to defend. I therefore recommend *doing philosophy* with ancient texts. Why this should be of interest to *historians* of philosophy is at least not entirely obvious. We would not necessarily expect the literary historian to compose novels, or the art historian to paint. But I believe that in the case of ancient Indian philosophical texts the connection between writing the history of philosophy and doing philosophy is particularly pertinent.

When studying ancient Indian philosophical texts, it is often not wholly evident how a particular argument is to be understood. This is partly due to the highly compressed *sūtra*-style of presentation, which provides an account of a philosophical system that is not meant to be understood without a commentary. But such commentaries may be lost, or only preserved in translations in different Asian languages, or may have been composed much later. So in order to make sense of a *sūtra* and its associated commentaries we need to create a framework of the different interpretative options, a map of different possible arguments or solutions to a philosophical problem a given work could present, in order to determine which of these provides the best possible reading of the text.[2] The only way to develop such a framework is by thinking through a philosophical question against the horizon of the given ancient text or tradition. This allows us to explore the different theoretical options available when setting out to answer a given philosophical question.

We can draw a comparison between the history of philosophy and the history of technology here. The historian of technology might not be content with finding out how the ancient authors envisaged a machine to be constructed, but may also want to know whether such a machine would have in

[2] We need not commit ourselves to the claim that there is only one such 'best' reading (Garfield 2015: 322–30). In fact, the boundary between a commentarial exposition of a text, drawing out what the text says, and a philosophical engagement with its contents, bringing it to life for a contemporary audience, was already fluid in the Indian scholastic context (Ganeri 2011: 115).

fact worked. In order to do so, assessing the ancient constructions from the perspective of modern engineering, or building a working model following the description in the text, would be essential steps. But even if questions regarding the actual technological feasibility of machines described in ancient texts is not at the forefront of our minds, and we simply want to focus on trying to understand what the texts say, attempting to solve an engineering problem by means of technological methods known and available to an ancient author could be of crucial importance. This is because such a hypothetical construction could guide our interpretation of the text, suggesting to us what the text might be saying.[3] As knowledge of and engagement with engineering is essential for the historian of technology, so knowledge of and engagement with the systematic discussion of philosophical problems is essential for the historian of philosophy. In the case of Indian thought, and its often highly condensed and elliptical mode of presentation in particular, such an engagement is in fact an indispensable hermeneutic tool. In order to reach a sophisticated understanding of Indian philosophical texts, philological and historical accuracy need to be combined with argumentative acuity and philosophical creativity.

[3] Assuming, that is, that the author had indeed succeeded in constructing the machine he describes. This assumption is a simple equivalent of the maxim of charity in interpretation: we assume that the author had some valid argument in mind when setting out his exposition, or at least we try our best in attempting to interpret the text as if he did.

# Bibliography


Kashinath Vasudev Abhyankar and Gaṇeśaśāstrī Ambādāsa Jośī (eds.): *Śrīmajjaimini-praṇīte Mīmāṃsādarśane*, Ānandāśrama, Puṇya, 1970–4.

Orna Almogi: 'Yogācāra in the writings of the eleventh-century Rnying ma scholar Rong zom chos kyi bzang po', in Ulrich Timme Kragh (ed.): *The Foundation for Yoga Practitioners: The Buddhist Yogācārabhūmi Treatise and Its Adaption in India, East Asia, and Tibet*, Harvard University Press, Cambridge, Mass., 2013: 1330–61.

William Ames: 'Bhāvaviveka's own view of his differences with Buddhapālita', in Dreyfus and McClintock 2003: 41–66.

William Ames: Review of Malcom David Eckel: *Bhāviveka and His Buddhist Opponents*, H-Buddhism, H-Net Reviews, Sept. 2009, <http://www.h-net.org/reviews/showrev.php?id=25526>.

Stefan Anacker: *Seven Works of Vasubandhu, the Buddhist Psychological Doctor*, Motilal Banarsidass, Delhi, 2002.

Bikkhu Anālayo: *The Dawn of Abhidharma*, Hamburg University Press, Hamburg, 2014.

Dan Arnold: *Buddhist, Brahmins, and Beliefs: Epistemology in South Asian Philosophy of Religion*, Columbia University Press, New York, 2005.

Dan Arnold: *Brains, Buddhas, and Believing: The Problem of Intentionality in Classical Buddhist and Cognitive-Scientific Philosophy of Mind*, Columbia University Press, New York, 2012.

Dan Arnold: 'Kumārila', *Stanford Encyclopedia of Philosophy* (Winter 2014 edition) <http://plato.stanford.edu/archives/win2014/entries/kumaarila, 2014>.

Shwe Zan Aung and Caroline A. F. Rhys Davids: *Points of Controversy, or Subjects of Discourse, Being a Translation of the Kathā-vatthu from the Abhidhamma-piṭaka*, Pali Text Society, London, 1915.

Sitansusekhar Bagchi: *Mahāyāna-Sūtrālaṅkāra of Asaṅga*, Mithila Institute, Darbhanga, 1970.

Piotr Balcerowicz: 'On the relative chronology of Dharmakīrti and Samantabhadra', *Journal of Indian Philosophy* 44, 2016: 437–83.

André Bareau: 'Le bouddha et les rois', *Bulletin de l'École Française d'Extrême-Orient* 80:1, 1993: 15–39.

André Bareau: *The Buddhist Schools of the Small Vehicle*, University of Hawaii Press, Honolulu, 2013.

Samuel Beal: Si-Yu-Ki. *Buddhist Records of the Western World.* Translated from the Chinese of Hiuen Tsiang AD 629, Trubner & Co, London, 1884.

Robert Beer: *The Encyclopedia of Tibetan Symbols and Motifs*, Shambala, Boston, 1999.

Cecil Bendall and William Henry Denham Rouse: *Śikshā-samuccaya, A Compendium of Buddhist Doctrine*, J. Murray, London, 1922.

Yael Bentor: 'Fourfold meditation: outer, inner, secret, and suchness', in *Religion and Secular Culture in Tibet: Tibetan Studies II: Proceedings of the Ninth Seminar of the*

*International Association for Tibetan Studies*, International Association of Tibetan Studies, Leiden, 2000: 41–58.

Stephan Beyer: *Magic and Ritual in Tibet: The Cult of Tara*, Motilal Banarsidass, Delhi, 1988.

Kamaleswar Bhattacharya: *L'ātman-brahman dans le bouddhisme ancien*, École française d'Extrême-Orient, Paris, 1973.

Ramkrishna Bhattacharya: 'Cārvāka Fragments: A New Collection', *Journal of Indian Philosophy* 30: 6, 2002: 597–640.

Ramkrishna Bhattacharya: 'Development of Materialism in India: the pre-Cārvākas and the Cārvākas', *Esercizi Filosofici* 8, 2013: 1–12.

Sibajiban Bhattacharya: 'Some features of the technical language of Navya-Nyāya', in Roy W. Perrett (ed.): *Indian Philosophy: A Collection of Readings. Logic and Philosophy of Language*, Routledge, London, 2001.

James Blumenthal: *The Ornament of the Middle Way: A Study of the Madhyamaka Thought of Śāntarakṣita*, Snow Lion, Ithaca, NY, 2004.

Bhikkhu Bodhi: *The Connected Discourses of the Buddha*, Wisdom, Boston, 2000.

Bhikkhu Bodhi: *The Middle Length Discourses of the Buddha*, Wisdom, Boston, 2001.

Bhikkhu Bodhi: *The Numerical Discourses of the Buddha*, Wisdom, Boston, 2012.

Karl-Stéphan Bouthillette: 'Battle for middle way: Bhāviveka's dialectical strategy in context', *Distant Worlds Journal* 3, 2017: 67–79.

Johannes Bronkhorst: 'Nāgārjuna and the Naiyāyikas', *Journal of Indian Philosophy* 13, 1985: 107–32.

Johannes Bronkhorst: *Karma and Teleology: A Problem and its Solutions in Indian Philosophy*, International Institute of Buddhist Studies, Tokyo, 2000.

Johannes Bronkhorst: 'Vedānta as Mīmāṃsā' in Johannes Bronkhorst (ed.): *Mīmāṃsā and Vedānta: Interaction and Continuity*, Motilal Banarsidass, New Delhi, 2007: 1–92.

Johannes Bronkhorst: *Buddhist Teaching in India*, Wisdom, Boston, 2009.

Johannes Bronkhorst: *Buddhism in the Shadow of Brahmanism*, Brill, Leiden, Boston, 2011 (2011a).

Johannes Bronkhorst: *Language and Reality: On an Episode in Indian Thought*, Brill, Leiden and Boston, 2011 (2011b).

Johannes Bronkhorst: 'Periodization of Indian ontologies', in Eli Franco (ed.): *Periodization and Historiography of Indian Philosophy*, de Nobili Research Library, Vienna, 2013: 357–63.

John Brough: *Poems from the Sanskrit*, Penguin, Harmondsworth, 1968.

Karl Brunnhölzl: *In Praise of Dharmadhātu*, Snow Lion, Ithaca, NY, 2007.

Karl Brunnhölzl: *Gone Beyond: The Prajñāpāramitā Sūtras, The Ornament of Clear Realization, and its Commentaries in the Tibetan Kagyü Tradition*, Snow Lion, Ithaca, NY, 2010.

Hartmut Buescher: *The Inception of Yogācāra-Vijñānavāda*, Verlag der Österreichischen Akademie der Wissenschaften, Vienna, 2008.

Bu ston rin chen grub: *Butön's History of Buddhism in India and its Spread to Tibet: A Treasury of Priceless Scripture*, Snow Lion, Boston, 2013.

José Ignacio Cabezón: *Buddhism and Language: A Study of Indo-Tibetan Scholasticism*, State University of New York Press, Albany, NY, 1994.

José Ignacio Cabezón: 'Two views on the Svātantrika-Prāsaṅgika distinction in fourteenth-century Tibet', in Dreyfus and McClintock 2003: 289–315.

Amber Carpenter: 'Persons keeping their karma together', in Yasuo Deguchi, Jay Garfield, et al. (eds.): *The Moon Points Back*, Oxford University Press, Oxford, 2015: 1–44.

Arindam Chakrabarti: 'On the purported inseparability of blue and the awareness of blue: an examination of the sahopalambhaniyama' in Doboom Tulku (ed.) *Mind Only School and Buddhist Logic*, Tibet House, New Delhi, 1990: 17–36.

Amita Chatterjee, Smita Sirker: 'Diṅnāga and mental models: a reconstruction', *Philosophy East and West* 60: 3, 2010: 315–40.

Alaka Chattopadhyaya: *Atīśa and Tibet*, Motilal Banarsidass, Delhi, 1967.

Lama Chimpa, Alaka Chattopadhyaya: *Tāranātha's History of Buddhism in India*, Indian Institute of Advanced Study, Simla, 1970.

Chodrung-ma Kunga Chodron: 'Accounts of the biography of Śāntideva: some observations concerning the effect of culture', in Upender Rao, Chodrung-ma Kunga Chodron, and Michelle Dexter (eds.): *Śāntideva and Bodhicaryāvatāra*, Eastern Book Linkers, Delhi, 2013: 14–52.

Francis X. Clooney: *Thinking Ritually: Rediscovering the Pūrva Mīmāṃsā of Jaimini*, Institute für Indologie der Universität Wien, Vienna, 1990.

Stephen Collins: *Selfless Persons*, Cambridge University Press, Cambridge 1982.

Edward Conze: *Selected Sayings from the Perfection of Wisdom*, Buddhist Society, London, 1955.

Edward Conze: *Buddhist Thought in India: Three Phases of Buddhist Philosophy*, George Allen & Unwin, London, 1962.

Edward Conze: *The Prajñāpāramitā Literature*, 2nd edn., Reiyukai, Tokyo, 1978.

Edward Conze: *A Short History of Buddhism*, George Allen & Unwin, London, 1980.

Edward Conze: *The Perfection of Wisdom in Eight Thousand Lines and Its Verse Summary*, Sri Satguru Publications, New Delhi, 1994.

Edward Conze: *Buddhist Texts through the Ages*, Oneworld, Oxford, 1995.

Lance Cousins: 'Samatha-yāna and Vipassana-yāna', in Gatare Dhammapala, Richard Gombrich, et al. (eds.): *Buddhist Studies in Honour of Hammalava Saddhātissa*, University of Sri Jayewardenepura, Nugegoda, 1984: 56–68.

Harold G. Coward: *Studies in Indian Thought: Collected Essays of Prof. T. R. V. Murti*, Motilal Banarsidass, Delhi: 1983.

E. B. Cowell, A. E. Gough, and K. L. Joshi (eds.): *Sarvadarśana-Saṃgraha of Mādhavācārya*, Parimal Publications, Delhi, 2006.

Collet Cox: 'On the possibility of a nonexistent object of consciousness: Sarvāstivādin and Dārṣṭāntika theories', *Journal of the International Association of Buddhist Studies* 11, 1988: 31–87.

Collett Cox: *Disputed Dharmas. Early Buddhist Theories on Existence*, International Institute for Buddhist Studies, Tokyo, 1995.

Collett Cox: 'Abhidharma', in R. E. Buswell (ed.): *Encyclopedia of Buddhism*, Macmillan, New York, 2004: vol. 1, 1–7.

Kate Crosby and Andrew Skilton (trans.): *Śāntideva: The Bodhicaryāvatāra*, Oxford University Press, Oxford, 1995.

Gregory Darling: *An Evaluation of the Vedāntic Critique of Buddhism*, Motilal Banarsidass, Delhi, 2007.

Surendranath Dasgupta: *History of Indian Philosophy*, Cambridge University Press, Cambridge, 1922.

V. H. Date: *Vedānta Explained. Śaṁkara's Commentary on the Brahma-Sūtras*, Munshiram Manoharlal, Delhi 1973.

J. W. de Jong: *Buddhist Studies*, Asian Humanities Press, Berkeley, 1979.

Ronald M. Davidson: *Tibetan Renaissance: Tantric Buddhism in the Rebirth of Tibetan Culture*, Columbia University Press, New York, 2004 (2004a).

Ronald M. Davidson: *Indian Esoteric Buddhism: A Social History of the Tantric Movement*, Motilal Banarsidass, Delhi, 2004 (2004b).

Florin Deleanu: *The Chapter on the Mundane Path (Laukikamārga) in the Śrāvakabhūmi: A Trilingual Edition (Sanskrit, Tibetan, Chinese)*, International Institute for Buddhist Studies, Tokyo 2006.

Peter Della Santina: 'Sākāra-Nirākāravāda controversy', in Albrecht Wezler and Ernst Hammerschmidt (eds.): *Proceedings of the XXXII International Congress for Asian and North African Studies Hamburg* (*Zeitschrift der deutschen morgenländischen Gesellschaft*, Supplement 9), Franz Steiner Verlag, Stuttgart, 1992: 174–5.

Peter Della Santina: 'The Sākāra–Nirākāravāda controversy', *Journal of Indian Philosophy and Religion*, 5, 2000: 26–36.

Csaba Dezső: *Much Ado about Religion*, New York University Press, New York, 2005.

Bhikkhu K. L. Dhammajoti: 'The Sarvāstivāda doctrine of simultaneous causality', *Journal of Buddhist Studies* 1, 2003: 17–54.

Bhikkhu K. L. Dhammajoti: *Abhidharma Doctrines and Controversies on Perception*, Centre of Buddhist Studies, Hong Kong University, Hong Kong, 2007 (2007a).

Bhikkhu K. L. Dhammajoti: 'Ākāra and direct perception (pratyakṣa)', *Pacific World* 9, 2007 (2007b): 245–72.

Bhikkhu K. L. Dhammajoti: *Sarvāstivāda Abhidharma*, 4th revised edn., Centre of Buddhist Studies, University of Hong Kong, Hong Kong, 2009.

Tseten Dorji (ed.): *Five Historical Works of Tāranātha*, Tibetan Nyingma Monastery, Camp No. 5, Dist. Lohit, Arunachal Pradesh, 1974.

Keith Dowman: *Masters of Mahāmudrā: Songs and Histories of the Eighty-four Buddhist Siddhas*, State University of New York Press, Albany, NY, 1985.

David Drewes: Revisiting the phrase '*sa pṛthivīpradeśaś caityabhūto bhavet*' and the Mahāyāna cult of the book', *Indo-Iranian Journal* 50:2, 2007: 101–43.

David Drewes: 'Early Indian Mahāyāna Buddhism', *Religion Compass* 4:2, 2010: 55–65.

Georges Dreyfus: *Recognizing Reality: Dharmakīrti's Philosophy and its Tibetan Interpretations*, State University of New York Press, Albany, NY, 1997.

Georges Dreyfus and Christian Lindtner: 'The Yogācāra philosophy of Dignāga and Dharmakīrti', *Studies in Central and East Asia Religions* 2, 1989: 27–52.

Georges Dreyfus and Sara McClintock (eds.): *The Svātantrika-Prāsaṅgika Distinction*, Wisdom, Boston, 2003.

Georges Driessens: *Kamalashila: Les étapes de la méditation*, Éditions du Seuil, Paris, 2007.

Douglas Duckworth, Malcolm David Eckel, Jay L. Garfield, John Powers, Yeshe Thabkhas, and Sonam Thakchöe (eds.): *Dignāga's Investigation of the Percept: A Philosophical Legacy in India and Tibet*, Oxford University Press, New York, 2016.

John Dunne: *Foundations of Dharmakīrti's Philosophy*, Wisdom, Boston, 2004.

John Dunne: 'Realizing the unreal: Dharmakīrti's theory of yogic perception', *Journal of Indian Philosophy* 34, 2006: 497–519.

John Dunne: 'Key features of Dharmakīrti's *apoha* theory', in Mark Siderits, Tom Tillemans, and Arindam Chakrabarti (eds.): *Apoha: Buddhist Nominalism and Human Cognition*, Columbia University Press, New York, 2011: 84–108.

Sukumar Dutt: *Buddhist Monks and Monasteries of India: Their History and Contribution to Indian Culture*, Motilal Banarsidass, Delhi, 1988.

Swami Dwarikadas Shastri: *Ācārya Yaśomitraṁ kṛta sphuṭārthā vyākhyopetam ācārya Vasubandhu viracitam svopajñabhāṣyasahitam abhidharmakoṣam*, vol. 1, Bauddha Bharati, Varanasi, 1970.

David Eckel: *To See the Buddha: A Philosopher's Quest for the Meaning of Emptiness*, HarperCollins, New York, 1992.

David Eckel: *Bhāviveka and His Buddhist Opponents*, Department of Sanskrit and Indian Studies, Harvard University, Cambridge, Mass, 2008.

Helmut Eimer: *Berichte über das Leben des Atiśa (Dīpaṃkaraśrījñāna): eine Untersuchung der Quellen*, Harrassowitz, Wiesbaden, 1977.

Helmut Eimer: *Rnam thar rgyas pa. Materialien zu einer Biographie des Atiśa (Dipamkaraśrījñāna)*, Harrassowitz, Wiesbaden, 1979.

Mircea Eliade: *Yoga: Immortality and Freedom*, Princeton University Press, Princeton, 1969.

Vincent Eltschinger: 'Dharmakīrti', *Revue internationale de philosophie 3*: 253, 2010: 397–440.

Vincent Eltschinger: *Caste and Buddhist Philosophy: Continuity of Some Buddhist Arguments against the Realist Interpretation of Social Denominations*, Motilal Banarsidass, Delhi, 2012.

Vincent Eltschinger: 'Buddhist esoterism and epistemology: two sixth-century innovations as Buddhist responses to social and religio-political transformations', in Eli Franco (ed.): *Periodization and Historiography of Indian Philosophy*, de Nobili Research Library, Vienna, 2013: 171–273.

Vincent Eltschinger: *Buddhist Epistemology as Apologetics: Studies on the History, Self-Understanding and Dogmatic Foundations of Late Indian Buddhist Philosophy*, Verlag der Österreichischen Akademie der Wissenschaften, Vienna 2014.

Vincent Eltschinger, Helmut Krasser, and John Taber: *Can the Veda speak? Dharmakīrti against Mīmāṃsā Exegetics and Vedic authority*, Verlag der Österreischen Akademie der Wissenschaften, Vienna, 2012.

Artemus B. Engle: *The Bodhisattva Path to Unsurpassed Enlightenment: A Complete Translation of the Bodhisattvabhūmi*, Snow Lion, Boulder, CO, 2016.

Harry Falk and Seishi Karashima: 'A first-century Prajñāpāramitā manuscript from Gandhāra - parivarta 1 (Texts from the Split collection 1)', *Annual Report of the International Research Institute for Advanced Buddhology at Soka University for the Academic Year 2011–2012*, 15, 2012: 19–61.

G. W. Farrow and I. Menon: *The Concealed Essence of the Hevajra Tantra, with the Commentary Yogaratnamālā*, Motilal Banarsidass, Delhi, 2001.

Joel Feldman and Stephen Phillips: *Ratnakīrti's Proof of Momentariness by Positive Correlation*, American Institute of Buddhist Studies, New York, 2011.

Georg Feuerstein: *The Bhagavad-Gītā. A New Translation*, Shambala, Boston and London, 2014.

Aucke Forsten: *Between Certainty and Finitude: A Study of Laṅkāvatārasūtra Chapter Two*, LIT Verlag, Münster, 2006.

Eli Franco: 'Once again on Dharmakirti's deviation from Dignāga on *pratyakṣābhāsa*', *Journal of Indian Philosophy* 14, 1986: 79–97.

Eli Franco: 'Did Dignaga accept four types of perception?', *Journal of Indian Philosophy* 21: 3, 1993: 295–9.

Eli Franco: *Dharmakīrti on Compassion and Rebirth*, Arbeitskreis für Tibetische und Buddhistische Studien, Vienna, 1997.

Eli Franco: 'Meditation and metaphysics: on their mutual relationship in South Asian Buddhism', in Eli Franco and Dagmar Eigner (eds.): *Yogic Perception, Meditation, and Altered States of Consciousness*, Verlag der Österreichischen Akademie der Wissenschaften, Vienna, 2009: 93–132.

Eli Franco: 'On the periodization and historiography of Indian philosophy', in Eli Franco (ed.): *Periodization and Historiography of Indian Philosophy*, de Nobili Research Library, Vienna, 2013: 1–34.

Erich Frauwallner: 'Der arische Anteil an der indischen Philosophie', *Wiener Zeitschrift für die Kunde des Morgenlandes* 46, 1939: 267–91.

Erich Frauwallner: 'On the date of the Buddhist master of the law Vasubandhu', *Instituto Italiano per il Medio ed Estremo Oriente*, Rome, 1951.

Erich Frauwallner: *Die Philosophie des Buddhismus*, Akademie-Verlag, Berlin, 1956.

Erich Frauwallner: 'Landmarks in the history of Indian logic', *Wiener Zeitschrift für die Kunde Süd- und Ostasiens* 5, 1961: 125–45.

Erich Frauwallner: 'Kumārila's Bṛhaṭṭīkā', *Wiener Zeitschrift für die Kunde Süd- und Ostasiens* 6, 1962.

Erich Frauwallner: *Materialien zur ältesten Philosophie der Karma-Mīmāṃsā*, Verlag der Österreichischen Akademie der Wissenschaften, Vienna, 1968.

Erich Frauwallner: 'Dignaga, sein Werk und seine Entwicklung', in Gerhard Oberhammer and Ernst Steinkellner (eds.): *Kleine Schriften*, Franz Steiner, Wiesbaden, 1982 (1982a): 759–846.

Erich Frauwallner: 'Die Reihenfolge und Entstehung der Werke Dharmakīrtis', in Gerhard Oberhammer and Ernst Steinkellner (eds.): *Kleine Schriften*, Franz Steiner, Wiesbaden, 1982 (1982b): 677–89.

Erich Frauwallner: *Studies in Abhidharma Literature and the Origins of Buddhist Philosophical Systems*, State University of New York Press, Albany, NY, 1995.

Toru Funayama: 'Kamalasila's distinction between the two sub-schools of Yogācāra. A provisional survey', in Birgit Kellner, Helmut Krasser, Horst Lasic, Michael Torsten Much, and Helmut Tauscher (eds.), *Pramāṇakīrtiḥ. Papers Dedicated to Ernst Steinkellner on the Occasion of his 70th Birthday*, part 1, Vienna 2007: 187–202.

Jonardon Ganeri: *The Concealed Art of the Soul*, Oxford University Press, Oxford, 2007.

Jonardon Ganeri: 'Towards a formal regimentation of the Navya-Nyāya technical language I', in Mihir Chakraborty, Benedikt Löwe, Madhabendra Nath Mitra, and Sundar Sarukkai (eds.): *Logic, Navya-Nyāya and Applications: Homage to Bimal Krishna Matilal*, College Publications, London, 2008.

Jonardon Ganeri: 'Sanskrit philosophical commentary', *Journal of the Indian Council of Philosophical Research* 27, 2010: 187–207.

Jonardon Ganeri: *The Lost Age of Reason: Philosophy in Early Modern India 1450–1700*, Oxford University Press, Oxford, 2011.

Peter Gäng: *Das Tantra der Verborgenen Vereinigung*, Eugen Diederichs Verlag, Munich, 1988.

Jay Garfield: 'Vasubandhu's Treatise on the Three Natures: a translation and commentary', in *Empty Words: Buddhist Philosophy and Cross-Cultural Interpretation*, Oxford University Press, Oxford, 2002: 128–51.

Jay Garfield: 'The conventional status of reflexive awareness: what's at stake in a Tibetan debate?', *Philosophy East and West* 56: 2, 2006: 201–28.

Jay Garfield: *Engaging Buddhism: Why It Matters to Philosophy*, Oxford University Press, Oxford, 2015.

Jay Garfield and Graham Priest: 'Mountains are just mountains', in Mario D'Amato, Jay Garfield, and Tom Tillemans (eds.): *Pointing at the Moon: Buddhism, Logic, Analytic Philosophy*, Oxford University Press, Oxford, 2009: 71–82.

Jay Garfield and Jan Westerhoff (eds.): *Madhyamaka and Yogācāra: Allies or Rivals?* Oxford University Press, New York, 2015.

Rupert Gethin: 'The mātikās: memorization, mindfulness, and the list', in Janet Gyatso (ed.): *In the Mirror of Memory: Reflections on Mindfulness and Remembrance in Indian and Tibetan Buddhism*, State University of New York Press, Albany, NY, 1992.

Raniero Gnoli: *The Pramāṇavārttikam of Dharmakīrti: The First Chapter with the Autocommentary*, Instituto italiano per il Medio ed Estremo Oriente, Rome, 1960.

Jonathan Gold: *Paving the Great Way: Vasubandhu's Unifying Buddhist Philosophy*, Columbia University Press, New York, 2015 (2015a).

Jonathan Gold: 'Without karma and nirvāṇa, Buddhism is nihilism: the Yogācāra contribution to the doctrine of emptiness' in Garfield and Westerhoff 2015: 213–41.

Richard Gombrich: *What the Buddha Thought*, Equinox, London and Oakville, Conn., 2009.

Luis Gómez: 'Buddhism in India', in Joseph Kitagawa (ed.): *The Religious Traditions of Asia: Religion, History, and Culture*, Routledge, London, 2002.

Charles Goodman: *The Training Anthology of Śāntideva: A Translation of the Śikṣā-samuccaya*, Oxford University Press, New York, 2016.

Emmanuel Guillon: *Les Philosophies bouddhistes*, Presses Universitaires de France, Paris, 1997.

Hiromi Habata: *A Critical Edition of the Tibetan Translation of the Mahāparinirvāṇa-mahāsūtra*, Dr Ludwig Reichert Verlag, Wiesbaden, 2013.

Paul Hacker: *Inklusivismus: Eine Indische Denkform*, De Nobili Research Library, Vienna, 1983.

Pierre Hadot: *Exercices spirituels et philosophie antique*. Études Augustiniennes, Paris, 1981.

Michael Hahn: *Nāgārjuna's Ratnāvalī. The Basic Texts (Sanskrit, Tibetan, Chinese)*, *Indica et Tibetica*, Hamburg, 1982 (1982a).

Michael Hahn: 'Kumāralātas Kalpanāmaṇḍitikā Dṛṣṭāntapaṅkti, Nr. 1: Die Vorzüglichkeit des Buddha', *Zentralasiatische Studien* 16, 1982 (1982b): 309–36.

Wilhelm Halbfass: *Traditions and Reflection: Explorations in Indian Thought*, State University of New York Press, Albany, NY, 1991.

Bruce Cameron Hall: 'The meaning of vijñapti in Vasubandhu's concept of mind', *Journal of the International Association of Buddhist Studies* 9:1, 1986: 7–23.

Paul Harrison: 'Buddhānusmṛti in the Pratyutpanna-buddha-saṃmukhāvasthita-samādhi-sūtra', *Journal of Indian Philosophy* 6, 1978: 35–57.

Paul Harrison: 'Who gets to ride in the great vehicle? Self-image and identity among the followers of the early Mahāyāna', *Journal of the International Association of Buddhist Studies*, 10: 1, 1987: 67–89.

Paul Harrison: *The Samādhi of Direct Encounter with the Buddhas of the Present: An Annotated English Translation of the Tibetan Version of the Pratyutpanna-buddha-saṃmukhāvasthita-samādhi-sūtra*, International Institute for Buddhist Studies, Tokyo, 1990.

Peter Harvey: *The Selfless Mind: Personality, Consciousness and Nirvana in Early Buddhism*, Curzon Press, London, 1995.

Masaaki Hattori: *Dignāga, On Perception*, Harvard University Press, Cambridge, Mass., 1968.

Richard Hayes: 'The question of doctrinalism in the Buddhist epistemologists', *Journal of the American Academy of Religion* 52:4, 1984: 645–70.

Richard Hayes: Review of Singh 1984, *Journal of the International Association of Buddhist Studies*, 9:2, 1986: 166–72.

Richard Hayes: *Dignāga on the Interpretation of Signs*, Kluwer Academic Publishers, Dordrecht, 1988.

Maria Heim: *The Forerunner of All Things: Buddhaghosa on Mind, Intention, and Agency*, Oxford University Press, New York, 2014.

Akira Hirakawa: 'The rise of Mahāyāna Buddhism and its relationship to the worship of stūpas', *Memoirs of the Research Department of the Toyo Bunko*, 22, 1963: 57–106.

Akira Hirakawa: *A History of Indian Buddhism*, University of Hawaii Press, Honolulu, 1990.

Alexander Hixon: 'Mahāyāna Buddhist Influence on the Gauḍa School of Advaita Vedānta', Ph.D dissertation, Columbia University, 1976.

Ken Holmes and Katia Holmes: *The Changeless Nature: Mahayana Uttara Tantra Sastra by Arya Maitreya and Acarya Asanga*, Karma Drubgyud Darjay Ling, Eskdalemuir, 1985.

Jeffrey Hopkins: *Buddhist Advice for Living and Liberation. Nāgārjuna's Precious Garland*, Snow Lion, Ithaca, NY, 1998.

Jan E. M. Houben: *The Saṃbandha-Samuddeśa (Chapter on Relation) and Bhartṛhari's Philosophy of Language*, Egbert Forsten, Groningen, 1995.

Johan Huizinga: *Homo Ludens: A Study of the Play-Element in Culture*, Routledge, London, 1949.

Clair W. Huntington: 'The Akutobhayā and Early Indian Madhyamaka', Ph.D dissertation, University of Michigan, 1986.

Clair W. Huntington: 'Was Candrakīrti a Prāsaṅgika?' in Dreyfus and McClintock 2003: 67–91.

D. H. H. Ingalls: 'Śaṅkara's argument against the Buddhists', *Philosophy East and West* 3:4, 1954: 291–306.

Harunaga Isaacson: 'Yogic perception (*yogipratyakṣa*) in early Vaiśeṣika', *Studien zur Indologie und Iranistik* 18, 1993: 139–60.

Takashi Iwata: *Sahopalambhaniyama. Struktur und Entwicklung des Schlusses von der Tatsache, dass Erkenntnis und Gegenstand ausschliesslich zusammen wahrgenommen werden, auf deren Nichtverschiedenheit*, Franz Steiner, Stuttgart, 1991.

R. Iyengar: 'Kumārila and Dignāga', *Indian Historical Quarterly* 3, 1927: 603–6.

H. R. Rangaswamy Iyengar: *Pramāṇa samuccaya*, Government Branch Press, Mysore, 1930.

Roger Jackson: 'The Buddha as *pramāṇabhūta*: epithets and arguments in the Buddhist "logical" tradition', *Journal of Indian Philosophy* 16:4, 1988: 335–65.

Roger Jackson: *Is Enlightenment Possible? Dharmakīrti and rGyal tshab rje on Knowledge, Rebirth, No-Self and Liberation*, Snow Lion, Ithaca, NY, 1993.

Hermann Jacobi: *Die Entwicklung der Gottesidee by den Indern und deren Beweise für das Dasein Gottes*, Shaker Verlag, Aachen, 2010.

Padmanabh S. Jaini: 'On the theory of the two Vasubandhus', *Bulletin of the School of Oriental and African Studies* 21, 1958: 48–53.

Padmanabh S. Jaini: 'The Vaibhāṣika Theory of Words and Meanings', *Bulletin of the School of Oriental and African Studies* 22, 1959: 95–107.

Padmanabh S. Jaini: *The Jaina Path of Purification*, University of California Press, Berkeley 1979.

Padmanabh S. Jaini: 'On the ignorance of the Arhat', in Robert Buswell and Robert Gimello (eds.): *Paths to Liberation: The Mārga and Its Transformation in Buddhist Thought*, University of Hawaii, Honolulu, 1992: 135–45.

Ganganatha Jha: *The Tattvasaṅgraha of Śāntarakṣita with the Commentary of Kamalaśīla*, Oriental Institute, Vadodara, 1991.

Christopher Jones: 'The Use of, and Controversy Surrounding, the Term *ātman* in the Indian Buddhist *tathāgatagarbha* Literature', D.Phil. dissertation, Oxford University, 2014.

K. L. Joshi: *The Brahmasūtra Śāṅkara Bhāṣya*, Parimal Publications, Delhi, 2011.

Lal Mani Joshi: *Studies in the Buddhistic Culture of India (during the 7th and 8th Centuries A.D.)*, Motilal Banarsidass, Delhi, 1967.

Lal Mani Joshi: 'Gauḍapāda's rapprochement between Buddhism and Vedānta', *Ṛtam, Journal of Akhila Bhāratīya Sanskrit Parishad*, 1:1, 1969: 11–22.

S. D. Joshi and J. A. F. Roodbergen: *Patañjali's Vyākaraṇa-Mahābhāṣya*, University of Poona, Pune, 1986.

Yuichi Kajiyama: 'Controversy between the *Sākāra-* and *Nirākāra-vādins* of the Yogācāra school—some materials', *Indogaku Bukkyogaku Kenkyu* 14:1, 1965: 26–37.

Yuichi Kajiyama: 'Later Mādhyamikas on epistemology and meditation', in Minoru Kiyota (ed.): *Mahāyāna Buddhist Meditation: Theory and Practice*, Motilal Banarsidass, Delhi, 1991.

Yuichi Kajiyama: *An Introduction to Buddhist Philosophy: An Annotated Translation of the Tarkabhāṣā of Mokṣākaragupta*, Arbeistkreis fur Tibetische und Buddhistische studien Universitat Wien, Vienna, 1998.

David Kalupahana: *Mūlamadhyamakakārikā of Nāgārjuna: The Philosophy of the Middle Way*, Motilal Banarsidass, Delhi, 1991.

David Kalupahana: *A Sourcebook on Later Buddhist Philosophy*, Dehiwala, 2008.

Matthew Kapstein: *The Tibetan Assimilation of Buddhism: Conversion, Contestation, and Memory*, Oxford University Press, Oxford, 2000.

Matthew Kapstein: 'Mereological considerations in Vasubandhu's "Proof of Idealism"', in *Reason's Traces: Identity and Interpretation in Indian and Tibetan Buddhist Thought*, Wisdom, Boston, 2001: 181–96.

Matthew Kapstein: 'Gter-ma as Imperial Treasure: The 1755 Beijing Edition of the Padma bka' thang', *Revue d'Etudes Tibétaines* 31, 2015: 167–87.

Seishi Karashima: 'Was the *Aṣṭasāhasrika Prajñāpāramitā* compiled in Gandhāra in Gāndhārī?', *Annual Report of the International Research Institute for Advanced Buddhology at Soka University for the Academic Year 2012–2013*, 2013: 171–88.

Kei Kataoka: *Kumārila on Truth, Omniscience, and Killing, Part 1: A Critical Edition of Mīmāṃsā-Ślokavārttika ad 1.1.2 (Codanāsūtra)*, Verlag der Österreichischen Akademic der Wissenschaften, Vienna, 2011.

Birgit Kellner: 'Self-Awareness (*svasaṃvedana*) in Dignāga's *Pramāṇasamuccaya* and *-vṛtti*: a close reading', *Journal of Indian Philosophy* 38, 2010: 203–31.

Birgit Kellner: 'Self-awareness (*svasaṃvedana*) and infinite regresses: a comparison of arguments by Dignāga and Dharmakīrti', *Journal of Indian Philosophy* 39, 2011: 411–26.

Birgit Kellner: 'Changing frames in Buddhist thought: the concept of *ākāra* in Abhidharma and in Buddhist epistemological analysis', *Journal of Indian Philosophy* 42, 2014: 275–95.

Birgit Kellner: 'Proving idealism: Dharmakīrti', in Jonardon Ganeri (ed.): *The Oxford Handbook of Indian Philosophy*, Oxford University Press, Oxford, 2017 (2017a): 307–26.

Birgit Kellner: 'Proofs of idealism in Buddhist epistemology: Dharmakīrti's refutation of external objects', in Jörg Tuske (ed.): *Indian Epistemology and Metaphysics*, Bloomsbury, London, 2017 (2017b): 103–28.

Birgit Kellner and John Taber: 'Studies in Yogācāra-Vijñānavāda idealism I: The interpretation of Vasubandhu's *Viṃśikā*', *Asia* 68:3, 2014: 709–56.

Johan Hendrik Kern: *The Saddharma-Puṇḍarīka or The Lotus of the True Law*, Dover, New York, 1963.

Chitrarekha Kher: *Buddhism as Presented by the Brahmanical Systems*, Sri Satguru Publications, Delhi, 1992.

Kristin Kiblinger: *Buddhist Inclusivism: Attitudes Towards Religious Others*, Ashgate, Aldershot, 2005.

Franz Kielhorn, Kashinath Vasudev Abhyankar, and Vāsudevaśāstrī Abhyankara (eds): *The Paribhāṣenduśekhara of Nāgojībhaṭṭa*, 2nd edn., Bhandarkar Oriental Research Institute, Poona, 1960–2.

Wan Doo Kim: 'The Theravādin Doctrine of Momentariness: A Survey of its Origins and Development', D.Phil. dissertation, University of Oxford, 1999.

Ryukan Kimura: *A Historical Study of the Terms Hīnayāna and Mahāyāna and the Origin of Mahāyāna Buddhism*, University of Calcutta, Calcutta, 1927.

Richard King: *Early Advaita Vedānta and Buddhism. The Mahāyāna Context of the Gauḍapādīya-kārikā*, Sri Satguru Publications, Delhi, 1997.

Richard King: '*Vijñaptimātratā* and the Abhidharma context of early Yogācāra', *Asian Philosophy* 8: 1, 1998: 5–17.

Anne Klein: *Knowing, Naming and Negation: A Sourcebook on Tibetan Sautrāntika*, Snow Lion, Ithaca, NY, 1991: 22–3.

Thomas Kochumuttom: *A Buddhist Doctrine of Experience: A New Translation and Interpretation of the Works of Vasubandhu, the Yogacarin*, Motilal Banarsidass, Delhi, 1982.

Yaroslav Komarowski: *Visions of Unity. The Golden Paṇḍita Shakya Chokden's New Interpretation of Yogācāra and Madhyamaka*, State University of New York Press, Albany, NY, 2011.

Helmut Krasser: 'Dharmakīrti's and Kumārila's refutations of the existence of god: a consideration of their chronological order' in Shōryū Katsura (ed.): *Dharmakīrti's Thought and Its Impact on Indian and Tibetan Philosophy* (Proceedings of the Third International Dharmakirti Conference, Hiroshima, Nov. 4–6, 1997), Verlag der Österreichischen Akademie der Wissenschaften, Vienna, 1999: 215–23.

Embar Krishnamacharya (ed.): *Tarkabhāṣa of Mokṣākara Gupta*, Oriental Institute, Baroda, 1942.

Robert Kritzer: *Rebirth and Causation in the Yogācāra Abhidharma*, Arbeitskreis für Tibetische und Buddhistische Studien, Vienna, 1999.

Robert Kritzer: 'Sautrāntika in the *Abhidharmakośabhāṣya*', *Journal of the International Association of Buddhist Studies* 26:2, 2003 (2003a): 331–84.

Robert Kritzer: 'General Introduction', *Journal of the International Association of Buddhist Studies*, 26: 2, 2003 (2003b): 202–24.

Robert Kritzer: *Vasubandhu and the Yogācārabhūmi: Yogācāra Elements in the Abhidharmakośabhāṣya*, International Institute of Buddhist Studies, Tokyo, 2005.

Étienne Lamotte: 'Sur la formation du Mahāyāna,' in J. Schubert and U. Schneider (eds.): *Asiatica. Festschrift Friedrich Weller*, Harassowitz, Leipzig, 1954.

Étienne Lamotte: *La somme du Grand Vehicule d'Asaṅga*, Institut Orientaliste Louvain-la-neuve, Louvain, 1973.

Étienne Lamotte: *History of Indian Buddhism: From the Origins to the Śaka Era*, Peeters Press, Louvain and Paris, 1988.

Karen Lang: *Āryadeva's Catuḥśataka: On the Bodhisattva's Cultivation of Merit and Knowledge*, Akademisk Forlag, Copenhagen, 1986.

Bimala Churn Law: *The Debates Commentary (Kathāvatthuppakaraṇa-aṭṭhakathā)*, London, Pali Text Society 1969.

Bimala Churn Law: *The Life and Work of Buddhaghosa*, Pilgrims Publishing, Varanasi, 2007.

Berthold Laufer: 'Indisches Recept zur Herstellung von Räucherwerk', *Verhandlungen der Berliner Gesellschaft für Anthropologie, Ethnologie und Urgeschichte* 18, 1896: 394–8.

Sylvain Lévi: *Mahāyānasūtrālaṃkāra, Exposé de la doctrine du Grand Véhicule*, vol. I, H. Champion, Paris 1907.

David Lewis: *Convention*, Harvard University Press, Cambridge, Mass., 1969.

Geshe Lhundup Sopa and Jeffrey Hopkins: *Practice and Theory of Tibetan Buddhism*, Grove Press, New York, 1976.

Rongxi Li: *The Great Tang Dynasty Record of the Western Regions*, Numata Center for Buddhist Translation and Research, Berkeley, 1996.

Xuezhu Li: '*Madhyamakāvatāra-kārikā* Chapter 6', *Journal of Indian Philosophy* 43:1, 2015: 1–30.

Christian Lindtner: *Nagarjuniana: Studies in the Writings and Philosophy of Nagarjuna*, Akademisk Forlag, Copenhagen, 1982.

Christian Lindtner: 'The *Laṅkāvatārasūtra* in early Indian Madhyamaka literature', *Asiatische Studien* 46, 1992: 244–79.

Christian Lindtner: *Bhavya on Mīmāṃsā: Mīmāṃsātattvanirṇayāvatāraḥ*, Adyar Library and Research Centre, Chennai, 2001.

Christian Lindtner: *A Garland of Light: Kambala's Ālokamālā*, Asian Humanities Press, Fremont, Calif., 2002.

Trevor Ling: *The Buddha: Buddhist Civilization in India and Ceylon*, Temple Smith, London, 1973.

Joseph Loizzo: *Nāgārjuna's Reason Sixty with Chandrakīrti's Reason Sixty Commentary*, American Institute of Buddhist Studies, New York, 2007.

Donald S. Lopez, Jr.: *A Study of Svātantrika*, Snow Lion, Ithaca, NY, 1987.

Donald S. Lopez, Jr.: *The Madman's Middle Way: Reflections on Reality of the Tibetan Monk Gendun Chopel*, University of Chicago Press, Chicago, 2006.

Hong Luo: 'The opening verses of Ratnākaraśānti's *Prajñāpāramitopadeśa*', *Maitreya Studies* 1, 2013: 17–29.

Dan Lusthaus: *Buddhist Phenomenology: A Philosophical Investigation of Yogācāra Buddhism and the Ch'eng Wei-shih lun*, RoutledgeCurzon, London and New York, 2002.

Anne MacDonald: *In Clear Words. The Prasannapadā, Chapter One*, Verlag der Österreichischen Akademie der Wissenschaften, Vienna, 2015.

Jiryo Masuda: *Der individualistische Idealismus der Yogācāra-Schule: Versuch einer genetischen Darstellung*, Heidelberg, Harrassowitz, 1926.

Bimal Matilal: 'Reference and existence in Nyāya and Buddhist logic', *Journal of Indian Philosophy* 1, 1970: 83–110.

Bimal Matilal: *Perception: An Essay on Classical Indian Theories of Knowledge*, Oxford University Press, Oxford, 1986.

Walter H. Maurer: 'The origin of grammatical speculation and its development in India', *Indo-Pacifica, Occasional Papers*, 1, Honolulu: University of Hawaii Department of Indo-Pacific Languages, 1981: 1–27.

Sengaku Mayeda: 'On the author of the *Māṇḍūkyopaniṣad* and the *Gauḍapādīyabhāṣya*', *Adyar Library Bulletin* 31–2, 1968: 73–94.

Sara McClintock: 'The role of the "given" in the classification of Śāntarakṣita and Kamalaśīla as Svātantrika-Mādhyamikas', in Dreyfus and McClintock 2003: 125–71.

Sara McClintock: 'Kamalaśīla on the nature of phenomenal content (*ākāra*) in cognition: a close reading of TSP *ad* TS 3626 and related passages', *Journal of Indian Philosophy* 42, 2014: 327–37.

A. C. Senape McDermott: *An Eleventh-Century Buddhist Logic of 'Exists'*, Reidel, Dordrecht, 1969.

James McHugh: *Sandalwood and Carrion: Smell in Indian Religion and Culture*, Oxford University Press, New York, 2012.

Carol Meadows: *Ārya-Śūra's Compendium of the Perfections: Text, Translation and Analysis of the Pāramitāsamāsa*, Indica et Tibetica, Bonn, 1986.

Marek Mejor: 'The problem of the two Vasubandhus reconsidered', *Indologica Taurinensia* 15–16, 1989–90: 275–83.

Annette Meuthrath: *Untersuchungen zur Kompositionsgeschichte der Nyāyasūtras*, Oros Verlag, Altenberge, 1996.

Annette Meuthrath: *Die Nāgārjuna zugeschriebene Vigrahavyāvartanī und die Nyāyasūtras. Eine Untersuchung des Verhältnisses beider Texte zueinander*, Dr Inge Wezler Verlag, Reinbek, 1999.

Katsumi Mimaki: '*Jñānasārasamuccaya* kk 20–28. *Mise au point* with a Sanskrit manuscript', in Jonathan Silk (ed.): *Buddhist Studies: The Legacy of Gadjin M. Nagao*, Motilal Banarsidass, Delhi, 2008: 233–44.

Jamgön Mipham: *The Adornment of the Middle Way*, Shambala, Boston and London, 2005.

Yūsho Miyasaka: '*Pramāṇavarttika-Kārikā* (Sanskrit and Tibetan)', *Acta Indologica* 2, 1971–2: 1–206.

Seitetsu Moriyama: 'The Yogācāra-Mādhyamika refutation of the position of the Satyākāra and Alīkākāra-vādins of the Yogācāra school. Part 1: A Translation of Portions of Haribhadra's *Abhisamayālaṃkārālokā Prajñāpāramitāvyākhyā*', *Bukkyō Daigaku Daigakuin kenkyū kiyō* 12, 1984: 1–58.

Shinya Moriyama: 'Ratnākaraśānti's theory of cognition with false mental images (**alīkākāravāda*) and the neither-one-nor-many argument', *Journal of Indian Philosophy* 42, 2014: 339–51.

Hajime Nakamura: *A History of Early Vedānta Philosophy*, Part I, Motilal Banarsidass, New Delhi, 1983.

Gyaktsen Namdol: *Bhāvanākramaḥ of Ācārya Kamalaśīla*, Central Institute of Higher Tibetan Studies, Sarnath, 1984.

Bhikkhu Ñāṇananda: *The Magic of the Mind. An Exposition of the Kālakārāma Sutta*, Buddhist Publication Society, Kandy, 1974.

Ngawang Gelek Demo (ed.): *Tāranātha's Life of the Buddha and His Histories of the Kālacakra and Tārātantra*, New Delhi, 1971.

Geshe Ngawang Samten: *Illuminating the Threefold Faith: An Invocation of the Seventeen Great Scholarly Adepts of Glorious Nalanda*, Central University of Tibetan Studies, Sarnath, 2011.

Swāmī Nikhilānanda: *The Māṇḍūkyopaniṣad with Gauḍapāda's Kārikā and Śaṅkara's Commentary*, Sri Ramakrishna Mission, Mysore, 1974.

Maheśachandra Nyāyaratna: *The Mīmānsā Darśana: One of the Six Systems of Hindu Philosophy, Or, an Exposition of the Ceremonial Rites of the Vedas by Jaimini, with the Commentary Śavara-Svāmin*, Asiatic Society of Bengal, Calcutta, 1889.

Gerhard Oberhammer: 'Ein Beitrag zu den Vāda-Traditionen Indiens', *Wiener Zeitschrift für die Kunde Süd- und Ostasiens* 7–8, 1963–4: 63–103.

Claus Oetke: *'Ich' und das Ich: Analytische Untersuchungen zur buddhistisch-brahmanischen Ātmankontroverse*, Franz Steiner, Stuttgart, 1988.

Claus Oetke: 'Doctrine and Argument in Vijñānavāda-Buddhism', *Wiener Zeitschrift für die Kunde Südasiens* 36, 1992: 217–25.

Patrick Olivelle: Upaniṣads, Oxford University Press, Oxford, 1996.

Janardan Shastri Pandey: *Bauddha-stotra-samgraha: A Collection of One Hundred and Eight Old Buddhist Hymns*, Motilal Banarsidass, Delhi, 1994.

Ram Chandra Pandeya: *The Pramāṇavārttikam of Ācārya Dharmakīrti with the Commentaries Svopajñavṛtti of the Author and Pramāṇavārttikavṛtti of Manorathanandin*, Motilal Banarsidass, Delhi, 1989.

Bhikkhu Pāsādika: 'Once again on the hypothesis of the two Vasubandhus', in V. N. Jha (ed.): *Prof Hajime Nakamura's Felicitation Volume*, Delhi, 1991.

Parimal Patil: *Against a Hindu God: Buddhist Philosophy of Religion in India*, Columbia University Press, New York, 2009.

Daniel Perdue: *Debate in Tibetan Buddhism*, Snow Lion, Ithaca, NY, 1992.

Daniel Perdue: *The Course in Buddhist Reasoning and Debate: An Asian Approach to Analytical Thinking Drawn from Indian and Tibetan Sources*, Snow Lion, Boston, 2014.

Red Pine: *The Lankavatara Sutra*, Counterpoint, Berkeley, 2012.

Sheldon Pollock: 'Mīmāṃsā and the problem of history in traditional India', *Journal of the American Oriental Society* 109: 4, 1989: 603–10.

John Powers: *Wisdom of Buddha: The Saṁdhinirmocana Sūtra*, Dharma Publications, Berkeley, 1995.

John Powers: *Hermeneutics and Tradition in the Saṃdhinirmocana-sūtra*, Motilal Banarsidass, Delhi, 2004.

Louis de la Vallée Poussin: *Mūlamadhyamakakārikās (Mādhyamikasūtras) de Nāgārjuna: avec la Prasannapadā commentaire de Candrakīrti*, Académie imperiale des sciences, St Petersburg, 1913.

Louis de la Vallée Poussin: *Vijñaptimatratasiddhi: La Siddhi de Hiuan-tsang*, Paul Geuthner, Paris, 1928–9.

Louis de la Vallée Poussin: 'Musīla et Nārada', *Mélanges chinois et boudhiques* 5, 1937: 189–222.

Louis de la Vallée Poussin and Leo M. Pruden: *Abhidharmakośabhāṣyam*, Asian Humanities Press, Berkeley, 1988–90.

Prahlad Pradhan: *Abhidharmakośabhāṣyam of Vasubandhu*, K. P. Jayaswal Research Institute, Patna, 1975.

Rajendra Prasad: *Dharmakīrti's Theory of Inference*, Oxford University Press, New Delhi, 2002.

Charles S. Prebish: *A Survey of Vinaya Literature*, Jin Luen Publishing House, Taipei, 1994.

Karin Preisendanz: *Studien zu Nyāyasūtra III.1 mit dem Nyāyatattvāloka Vācaspatimiśras II*, Steiner Verlag, Stuttgart, 1994.

Graham Priest and Jay Garfield: 'Nāgārjuna and the limits of thought', in Graham Priest: *Beyond the Limits of Thought*, Oxford University Press, Oxford, 2002: 249–70.

Graham Priest and Richard Routley: 'First historical introduction: a preliminary history of paraconsistent and dialetheic approaches', in Graham Priest, Richard Routley, and Jean Norman (eds.): *Paraconsistent Logic: Essays on the Inconsistent*, Philosophia Verlag, Munich, 1989: 3–75.

Leonard Priestley: *Pudgalavāda Buddhism: The Reality of the Indeterminate Self*, Centre for South Asian Studies, University of Toronto, Toronto, 1999.

Jean Przyluski: 'Origin and development of Buddhism', *Journal of Theological Studies* 35, 1934: 337–51.

Olle Qvarnström: *Hindu Philosophy in Buddhist Perspective: The Vedāntatattvaviniścaya Chapter of Madhyamakahṛdayakārikā*, Almqvist Wiksell International, Lund, 1989.

Olle Qvarnström: 'Haribadhra and the beginnings of doxography in India', in N. K. Wagle and Olle Qvarnström (eds.): *Approaches to Jaina Studies: Philosophy, Logic, Rituals, and Symbols*, University of Toronto Centre for South Asian Studies, Toronto, 1999: 169–210.

Sarvepalli Radhakrishnan: *The Principal Upaniṣads*, George Allen & Unwin, London 1969.

Michael Radich: 'The doctrine of **Amalavijñāna* in Paramārtha (499–569), and later authors to approximately 800 C.E.', *Zinbun* 41, 2008: 45–174.

Michael Radich: *The Mahāparinivāṇa-mahasūtra and the Emergence of Tathāgatagarbha Doctrine*, Hamburg University Press, Hamburg, 2015.

J. Rahder (ed.): *Daśabhūmikasūtra*, J.B. Istas, Paris and Louvain, 1926.

K. Kunjunni Raja: 'On the dates of Śaṃkara and Maṇḍana', *Adyar Library Bulletin* 55, 1991: 104–16.

Savarimuthu Rajamanickam: *The First Oriental Scholar*, Diocesan Press, Madras, 1972.

Chakravarthi Ram-Prasad: 'Consciousness and luminosity: on how knowledge is possible' in *Indian Philosophy and the Consequences of Knowledge: Themes in Ethics, Metaphysics and Soteriology*, Aldershot, Ashgate, 2007: 51–99.

Vijaya Rani: *The Buddhist Philosophy as Presented in the Mīmāṃsā-śloka-vārttika*, Parimal Publications, Delhi 1982.

Isabelle Ratie: *Une critique bouddhique du Soi selon la Mīmāṃsā: présentation, édition critique et traduction de la 'Mīmāṃsākaparikalpitātmaparīkṣā' de Śāntarakṣita ('Tattvasaṅgraha' 222–284 et 'Pañjikā')*, Verlag der Österreichischen Akademie der Wissenschaften, Vienna, 2014.

Noble Ross Reat: 'A Buddhist proof for the existence of God', *Journal of Indian Philosophy* 13, 1985: 265–72.

Konstanty Régamey: *Philosophy in the Samādhirājasūtra: Three Chapters from the Samādhirājasūtra*, Motilal Banarsidass, Delhi, 1990.

George N. Roerich: *The Blue Annals*, Motilal Banarsidass, Delhi, 1979.

Alexander von Rospatt: *The Buddhist Doctrine of Momentariness: A Survey of the Origins and Early Phase of this Doctrine up to Vasubandhu*, Franz Steiner, Stuttgart, 1995.

Noa Ronkin: *Early Buddhist Metaphysics: The Making of a Philosophical Tradition*, Routledge, London, 2005.

Walter Ruben: *Geschichte der Indischen Philosophie*, Deutscher Verlag der Wissenschaften, Berlin, 1954.

David Seyfort Ruegg: 'On the dGe lugs pa theory of the *tathāgatagarbha*', in J. C. Heesterman et al. (eds.): *Pratidānam: Indian, Iranian and Indo-European Studies Presented to Franciscus Bernardus Jacobus Kuiper, on his Sixtieth Birthday*, Mouton, The Hague, 1968: 500–9.

David Seyfort Ruegg: *La Théorie du Tathāgatagarbha et du Gotra. Études sur la sotériologie et la gnoséologie du Bouddhisme*, École Française d'Extrême-Orient, Paris, 1969.

David Seyfort Ruegg: 'The use of the four positions of the *catuṣkoṭi* and the problem of the description of reality in Māhāyana Buddhism', *Journal of Indian Philosophy* 5, 1977: 1–171.

David Seyfort Ruegg: *The Literature of the Madhyamaka School of Philosophy in India*, Harrassowitz, Wiesbaden, 1981 (1981a).

David Seyfort Ruegg: 'Deux problèmes d'exégèse et de pratique tantriques selon Dīpaṃkaraśrījñāna et le Paiṇḍapātika de Yavadvīpa/Suvarṇadvīpa', *Mélanges chinois et bouddhiques* 20, 1981 (1981b): 212–26.

David Seyfort Ruegg: *Buddha-nature, Mind and the Problem of Gradualism in a Comparative Perspective: On the Transmission and Reception of Buddhism in India and Tibet*, School of Oriental and African Studies, London, 1989.

David Seyfort Ruegg: *Two Prolegomena to Madhyamaka Philosophy: Candrakīrti's Prasannapadā Madhyamakavṛttiḥ on Madhyamakakārikā I.1 and Tsoṅ kha pa blo bzaṅ grags pa/Rgyal Tshab dar ma rin chen's Dka' gnad/gnas brgyad kyi zin bris*, Arbeitskreis für Tibetische und Buddhistische Studien, Universität Wien, Vienna, 2002.

David Seyfort Ruegg: 'The Indian and the Indic in Tibetan cultural history, and Tsoṅ Kha Pa's achievement as a scholar and thinker: an essay on the concepts of Buddhism in Tibet and Tibetan Buddhism', *Journal of Indian Philosophy* 32: 4, 2004: 321–43.

David Seyfort Ruegg: *The Buddhist Philosophy of the Middle*, Wisdom, Boston, 2010.

Ferenc Ruzsa and Mónika Szegedi: 'Vasubandhu's *Viṃśikā*. A critical edition', *Távol-keleti Tanulmányok* 1, 2015: 127–58.

Akira Saito: *A Study of Akṣayamati (= Śāntideva)'s Bodhisattvacaryāvatāra as Found in the Tibetan Manuscripts from Tun-huang: A Report of the Grant-in-aid for Scientific Research* (C), Miye University, 1993.

Akira Saito: 'An inquiry into the relationship between the *Śikṣāsamuccaya* and the *Bodhi(sattva)caryāvatāra*', in Upender Rao, Chodrung-ma Kunga Chodron, and Michelle Dexter (eds.): *Śāntideva and Bodhicaryāvatāra*, Eastern Book Linkers, Delhi, 2013: 1–13.

Hidenori Sakuma: 'Remarks on the lineage of the Indian masters of the Yogācāra school: Maitreya, Asaṅga, and Vasubandhu', in Ulrich Timme Kragh (ed.): *The Foundation for Yoga Practitioners: The Buddhist Yogācārabhūmi Treatise and its Adaptation in India, East Asia, and Tibet*, Harvard University Press, Cambridge, Mass., 2013: 330–66.

Geoffrey Samuel: *Civilized Shamans: Buddhism in Tibetan Societies*, Smithsonian Institution Press, Washington, DC and London, 1993.

Geoffrey Samuel: *The Origins of Yoga and Tantra: Indic Religions to the Thirteenth Century*, Cambridge University Press, Cambridge, 2008.

Rāhula Sāṅkṛtyāyana: *Dharmakīrti's Pramāṇavārttika: With a Commentary by Manorathanandin*, Bihar and Orissa Research Society, Patna, 1937.

Rāhula Sāṅkṛtyāyana: *Ācārya-Dharmakīrteḥ Pramāṇavārttikam (svārthānumānaparicchedaḥ) svopajñavṛttyā: Karṇakagomiviracitayā taṭṭīkayā ca sahitam*, Kitāb Mahal, Ilāhābād, 1943.

Shizuka Sasaki: 'The *Mahāparinirvāṇa Sūtra* and the origins of Mahāyāna Buddhism', *Japanese Journal of Religious Studies* 26:1–2, 1999: 189–97.

N. Aiyaswami Sastri (ed.): *Ālambanaparīkṣā and Vṛtti*, Adyar Library, Madras, 1942.

Stanisław Schayer: *Ausgewählte Kapitel aus der Prasannapadā* (V, XII, XIII, XIV, Nakładem Polskiej Akademji Umiejętności, Cracow, 1931.

Gregory Schopen: *Bones, Stones, and Buddhist Monks: Collected Papers on the Archaeology, Epigraphy, and Texts of Monastic Buddhism in India*, University of Hawaii Press, Honolulu, 1997: 31–2.

Gregory Schopen: 'The phrase '*sa pṛthivīpradeśaś caityabhūto bhavet*' in the *Vajracchedikā*: notes on the cult of the book in Mahāyāna', in Gregory Schopen: *Figments and Fragments of Mahāyāna Buddhism in India: More Collected Papers*, University of Hawaii Press, Honolulu, 2005: 25–62.

Gregory Schopen: 'Cross-dressing with the dead: asceticism, ambivalence, and institutional values in an Indian monastic code', in Bryan Cuevas and Jacqueline Stone (eds.): *The Buddhist Dead: Practices, Discourses, Representations*, University of Hawaii Press, Honolulu, 2007: 60–104.

Lambert Schmithausen: 'Sautrāntika-Voraussetzungen in *Viṃśatikā* und *Triṃśikā*,' *Wiener Zeitschrift für die Kunde Süd- und Ostasiens* 11, 1967: 109–36.

Lambert Schmithausen: 'Spirituelle Praxis und philosophische Theorie im Buddhismus', *Zeitschrift für Missionswissenschaft und Religionswissenschaft*, 57:3, 1973: 161–84.

Lambert Schmithausen: 'Textgeschichtliche Beobachtungen zum 1. Kapitel der *Aṣṭasāhasrikā Prajñāpāramitā*' in Lewis Lancaster (ed.): *Prajñāpāramitā and Related Systems (Studies in honor of Edward Conze)*, Berkeley Buddhist Series 1, Center for South and Southeast Asian Studies at the University of California, Berkeley, 1977: 35–80.

Lambert Schmithausen: *Ālayavijñāna: On the Origin and the Early Development of a Central Concept of Yogācāra Philosophy*, International Institute for Buddhist Studies, Tokyo, 1987.

Lambert Schmithausen: *On the Problem of the External World in the Ch'eng wei shih lun*, International Institute for Buddhist Studies, Tokyo, 2005.

Lambert Schmithausen: 'Aspects of spiritual practice in early Yogācāra', *Journal of the International College for Postgraduate Buddhist Studies* (JICPBS/Tokyo) 11, 2007: 213–44.

Lambert Schmithausen: *The Genesis of Yogācāra-Vijñānavāda: Responses and Reflections*, International Institute for Buddhist Studies, Tokyo, 2014.

Gregory Seton: 'Defining Wisdom: Ratnākaraśānti's *Sāratamā*', D.Phil. dissertation, Oxford University, 2015.

Robert Sharf: 'Buddhist modernism and the rhetoric of meditative experience', *Numen* 42, 1995: 228–83.

Parmananda Sharma: *Bhāvanākrama of Kamalaśīla*, Aditya Prakashan, New Delhi, 1997.

Richard Sherburne: *The Complete Works of Atīśa Śrī Dīpaṁkara Jñāna, Jo-bo-rje*, Aditya Prakashan, New Delhi, 2000.

Mark Siderits: *Personal Identity and Buddhist Philosophy*, Ashgate, Aldershot, 2003.

Mark Siderits: *Buddhism as Philosophy*, Ashgate, Aldershot, 2007.

Mark Siderits: 'Replacements' (review of Gombrich 2009), *Times Literary Supplement* 5596, 2 July 2010.

Mark Siderits: 'Is everything connected to everything else? What the gopīs know', in The Cowherds: *Moonshadows: Conventional Truth in Buddhist Philosophy*, Oxford University Press, New York, 2011 (2011a): 167–80.

Mark Siderits: 'Śrughna by dusk', in Mark Siderits, Tom Tillemans, and Arindam Chakrabarti (eds.): *Apoha. Buddhist Nominalism and Human Cognition*, Columbia University Press, New York, 2011 (2011b): 283–304.

Mark Siderits: Shōryū Katsura: *Nāgārjuna's Middle way: The Mūlamadhyamakākarikā*, Wisdom, Boston, 2013.

Mark Siderits: 'Deductive, inductive, both, or neither?' in Westerhoff 2016 (2016b): 120–37.

Mark Siderits: '*Apohavāda*, nominalism, and resemblance theories' in Westerhoff 2016 (2016b): 152–60.

Lilian Silburn: *Instant et cause. Le discontinue dans la pensée philosophique de l'Inde*, J. Vrin, Paris, 1955.

Jonathan Silk: 'What, if anything, is Mahāyāna Buddhism? Problems of definitions and classifications', *Numen* 49: 4, 2002: 355–405.

Amar Singh: *The Heart of Buddhist Philosophy: Diṅnaga and Dharmakīrti*, Munshiram Manoharlal, New Delhi, 1984.

Amar Singh: *The Sautrāntika Analytical Philosophy*, Dharma Cakra Publications, Delhi, 1995.

Vincent A. Smith: 'Nālandā', in James Hastings (ed.): *Encyclopedia of Religion and Ethics*, T. & T. Clark, Edinburgh, 1908–26: 9. 126–7.

David Snellgrove: *Indo-Tibetan Buddhism: Indian Buddhists and their Tibetan Successors*, Serindia, London, 1987.

David Snellgrove: *The Hevajra Tantra. A Critical Study*, Orchid Press, Bangkok, 2010.

Frits Staal: *Ritual and Mantras: Rules without Meaning*, Motilal Banarsidass, Delhi, 1996.

Theodore Stcherbatsky: *Buddhist Logic*, Motilal Banarsidass, Delhi, 1994.

Ernst Steinkellner: 'Is Dharmakīrti a Mādhyamika?', in David Seyfort Ruegg and Lambert Schmithausen (eds.): *Early Buddhism and Madhyamaka*, E. J. Brill, Leiden, 1990.

Ernst Steinkellner: *Dharmakīrti's Pramāṇaviniścaya*. Chapters 1 and 2, China Tibetology Publishing House, Austrian Academy of Sciences, Beijing and Vienna, 2007.

Daisetz Teitaro Suzuki: *Studies in the Lankavatara Sutra*, Routledge & Kegan Paul, London and Boston, 1930.

Daisetz Teitaro Suzuki: *The Lankavatara Sutra: A Mahayana Text*, G. Routledge and Sons, London, 1932.

Geshe Sonam Rinchen: *Atisha's Lamp for the Path to Enlightenment*, Snow Lion, Ithaca, NY, 1997.

Frits Staal: *Exploring Mysticism: A Methodological Essay*, Penguin, Harmondsworth, 1975.

Margaret Stutley and James Stutley: *Harper's Dictionary of Hinduism: Its Mythology, Folklore, Philosophy, Literature and History*, Harper & Row, New York, 1977.

John Taber: 'Kumārila's Interpretation of *Mīmāṃsāsūtra* 1.1.4', *Journal of Indological Studies* 18, 2006: 63–83.

John Taber: 'Dharmakīrti and the Mīmāṃsakas in conflict', in Eltschinger, Krasser, and Taber 2012: 119–66.

Junjirō Takakusu: *A Record of the Buddhist Religion as Practised in India and the Malay Archipelago (A. D. 671–695)*, Clarendon Press, Oxford, 1896.

Junjirō Takakusu: *The Essentials of Buddhist Philosophy*, Motilal Banarsidass, Delhi, 1975.

Jikidō Takazaki: *Nyoraizō shisō no keisei*, Shunjūsha, Tōkyō, 1974.

Kenneth Tanaka: 'Simultaneous relation (*Sahabhū-hetu*): a study in Buddhist theory of causation', *Journal of the International Association of Buddhist Studies* 8:1, 1985: 91–111.

N. V. Thadani: *Mīmāṃsā Sūtra of Jaimini*, Bharatiya Kala Prakashan, New Delhi, 2007.

Bhikshu Thích Thiên Châu: *The Literature of the Personalists of Early Buddhism*, Motilal Banarsidass, Delhi, 1999.

Asaṅga Tilakaratne: 'Authentication of the scripture: a study in the Theravāda hermeneutics', in Ulrich Everding and Asaṅga Tilakaratne (eds.): *Wilhelm Geiger and the Study of the History and Culture of Sri Lanka*, Goethe Institute and Postgraduate Institute of Pali and Buddhist Studies, Colombo, 2000: 1–21.

Tom Tillemans: 'The "neither one nor many" argument for *śūnyatā* and its Tibetan interpretations', in Ernst Steinkellner and Helmut Tauscher (eds.): *Contributions on Tibetan and Buddhist Religion and Philosophy*, Arbeitskreis für Tibetische und Buddhistische Studien Universität Wien, Vienna, 1983: 305–20.

Tom Tillemans: 'Two Tibetan texts on the "neither one nor many" argument for *śūnyatā*', *Journal of Indian Philosophy* 12, 1984: 357–88.

Tom Tillemans: 'Dharmakīrti, Āryadeva, and Dharmapāla on scriptural authority', in Tom Tillemans: *Scripture, Logic, and Language: Essays on Dharmakīrti and his Tibetan Successors*, Wisdom, Boston, 1999 (1999a).

Tom Tillemans: 'How much of a proof is scripturally based inference?', in Tillemans 1999a (1999b): 37–51.

Tom Tillemans: 'Metaphysics for Mādhyamikas', in Dreyfus and McClintock 2003: 93–123.

Tom Tillemans: *Materials for the study of Āryadeva, Dharmapāla and Candrakīrti*, Motilal Banarsidass, Delhi, 2008.

Tom Tillemans: 'How do Mādhyamikas think? Notes on Jay Garfield, Graham Priest, and paraconsistency', in Mario D'Amato, Jay Garfield, and Tom Tillemans (eds.), *Pointing at the Moon: Buddhism, Logic, Analytic Philosophy*, Oxford University Press, Oxford, 2009: 83–100.

Fernando Tola and Carmen Dragonetti: *Being as Consciousness: Yogācāra Philosophy of Buddhism*, Motilal Banarsidass, Delhi, 2004.

Raffaele Torella: 'Observations on *yogipratyakṣa*', in Chikafumi Watanabe, Michele Desmarais, and Yoshichika Honda (eds.): *Saṃskṛta-sādhutā. Goodness of Sanskrit: Studies in Honour of Professor Ashok N. Aklujkar*, D. K. Printworld, New Delhi, 2012: 470–87.

Losang Norbu Tsonawa: *Indian Buddhist Pandits from 'The Jewel Garland of Buddhist History'*, Library of Tibetan Works and Archives, Dharamsala, 1985.

Tsong kha pa: *The Great Treatise on the Stages of the Path to Enlightenment*, Snow Lion, Ithaca, NY, 2002.

Gary A. Tubb and Emery R. Bose: *Scholastic Sanskrit: A Manual for Students*, American Institute of Buddhist Studies, New York, 2007.

Giuseppe Tucci: *On Some Aspects of the Doctrines of Maitreya[nātha] and Asaṅga*, University of Calcutta, Calcutta, 1930.

Hakuju Ui: 'Maitreya as an historical personage', in *Indian Studies in Honor of Charles Rockwell Lanman*, Harvard University Press, Cambridge, Mass., 1929: 95–101.

Paraśurāma Lakshmaṇa Vaidya: *Aṣṭasāhasrikā Prajñāpāramitā*, Mithila Institute, Darbhanga, 1960.

Paraśurāma Lakshmaṇa Vaidya: *Saddharmalaṅkāvatārasūtram*, Mithila Institute, Darbhanga, 1963.

Paraśurāma Lakshmaṇa Vaidya: *Daśabhūmikasūtram*, Mithila Institute, Darbhanga, 1967.

Paraśurāma Lakshmaṇa Vaidya: *Bodhicaryāvatāra of Śāntideva with the Commentary Pañjika of Prajñākaramati*, Mithila Institute, Darbhanga, 1988.

Sam van Schaik: *Tibetan Zen: Discovering a Lost Tradition*, Snow Lion, Boston, 2015.

Tilmann Vetter: *Dharmakīrtis Pramāṇaviniścaya: 1. Kapitel: Pratyakṣam. Einleitung, Text der tibetischen Übersetzung, Sanskritfragmente, deutsche Übersetzung*, Österreichische Akademie der Wissenschaften, Vienna, 1966.

Giovanni Verardi: *Hardship and Downfall of Buddhism in India*, Manohar, Delhi, 2014.

Jean-Marie Verpoorten: *Mīmāṃsā Literature*, Otto Harrassowitz, Wiesbaden, 1987.

Kevin Vose: *Resurrecting Candrakīrti: Disputes in the Tibetan Creation of Prāsaṅgika*, Wisdom, Boston, 2009.

William Waldron: 'How innovative is the *ālayavijñāna*? The *ālayavijñāna* in the context of canonical and Abhidharma *vijñāna* theory', *Journal of Indian Philosophy*, 22, 1994: 199–258; 23, 1995: 9–51.

Benjamin Walker: *Hindu World: An Encyclopedic Survey of Hinduism*, Allen & Unwin, London, 1968.

Max Walleser: *The Life of Nāgārjuna from Tibetan and Chinese Sources*, Asian Educational Services, New Delhi, 1990.

Joseph Walser: *Nāgārjuna in Context: Mahāyāna Buddhism and Early Indian Culture*, Columbia University Press, New York, 2005.

Joseph Walser: 'Reading Nāgārjuna as a political philosopher', 2015 (unpublished manuscript).

A. K. Warder: 'Is Nāgārjuna a Mahāyānist?' in Mervyn Sprung (ed.): *The Problem of Two Truths in Buddhism and Vedānta*, D. Reidel, Dordrecht, 1973: 78–88.

A. K. Warder: *Indian Buddhism*, Motilal Banarsidass, Delhi, 2000.

Alex Wayman: 'The Yogācāra idealism', *Philosophy East and West* 15:1, 1965: 65–73.

Alex Wayman and Hideko Wayman: *The Lion's Roar of Queen Śrīmālā: A Buddhist Scripture on the Tathāgatagarbha Theory*, Columbia University Press, New York and London, 1974.

Claudia Weber: 'Wesen und Eigenschaften des Buddha in der Tradition des Hīnayāna-Buddhismus', Ph.D dissertation, Bonn, 1994.

Christian Wedemeyer: *Āryadeva's Lamp that Integrates the Practices (Caryāmelāpakapradīpa): The Gradual Path of Vajrayāna Buddhism According to the Esoteric Community Noble Tradition*, American Institute of Buddhist Studies, New York, 2007.

Jan Westerhoff: *Nāgārjuna's Madhyamaka: A Philosophical Introduction*, Oxford University Press, Oxford, 2009.

Jan Westerhoff: *The Dispeller of Disputes: Nāgārjuna's Vigrahyavyāvartanī*, Oxford University Press, Oxford, 2010.

Jan Westerhoff: 'On the nihilist interpretation of Madhyamaka', *Journal of Indian Philosophy* 44: 2, 2016 (2016a): 337–76.

Jan Westerhoff (ed.): Mark Siderits, *Studies in Buddhist Philosophy*, Oxford University Press, Oxford, 2016 (2016b).

Jan Westerhoff: *Crushing the Categories: Nāgārjuna's Vaidalyaprakaraṇa*, American Institute of Buddhist Studies, New York, 2018.

Annette Wilke and Oliver Moebus: *Sound and Communication: An Aesthetic Cultural History of Sanskrit Hinduism*, de Gruyter, Berlin and New York, 2011.

Charles Willemen, Bart Dessein, and Collett Cox: *Sarvāstivāda Buddhist Scholasticism*, Brill, Leiden, 1998.

Paul Williams: 'On the Abhidharma ontology', *Journal of Indian Philosophy* 9, 1981: 227–57.

Paul Williams: *The Reflexive Nature of Awareness: A Tibetan Madhyamaka Defence*, Curzon, London, 1998.

Paul Williams: *Mahāyāna Buddhism: The Doctrinal Foundations*, 2nd edn., Routledge, London, 2009.

Matthew D. Williams-Wyant: 'Nagarjuna's no-thesis view revisited: the significance of classical Indian debate culture on verse 29 of the *Vigrahavyāvartanī*', *Asian Philosophy* 3, 2017: 263–77.

Janice Willis: *On Knowing Reality: The Tattvārtha Chapter of Asaṅga's Bodhisattvabhūmi*, Columbia University Press, New York, 1979.

Moritz Winternitz: *Geschichte der Indischen Literatur*, K. F. Koehler, Stuttgart, 1968.

Unrai Wogihara: *Bodhisattvabhūmi: A Statement of the Whole Course of the Bodhisattva (Being the Fifteenth Section of the Yogācārabhūmi)*, Tokyo, 1930–6.

Unrai Wogihara: *Sphuṭārthā Abhidharmakośavyākhya*, Sankibo Buddhist Book Store, Tokyo, 1990.

Jeson Woo: 'Dharmakīrti and his commentators on *yogipratyakṣa*', *Journal of Indian Philosophy* 31, 2003: 439–48.

Ye shes mtsho rgyal: *The Lotus-Born: The Life Story of Padmasambhava*, Rangjung Yeshe Publications, Kathmandu, 1993.

Zhihua Yao: 'Dignāga and four types of perception', *Journal of Indian Philosophy* 32, 2004: 57–79.

Yoshiasu Yonezawa, 2008. '*Vigrahavyāvartanī*: Sanskrit transliteration and Tibetan translation', *Journal of Naritasan Institute of Buddhist Studies* 31, 2008: 209–333.

Alexander Yiannopoulos: 'Luminosity. Reflexive Awareness in Ratnākaraśānti's *Pith Instructions for the Ornament of the Middle Way*', unpublished MS, 2012.

Jan Yün-Hua: 'Nāgārjuna, one or more? A new interpretation of Buddhist Hagiography', *History of Religions* 10, 1970: 139–53.

Volker Zotz: *Geschichte der Buddhistischen Philosophie*, Rowohlt, Reinbek, 1996.

# Index